Innovation in Music

Innovation in Music: Cultures and Contexts is a groundbreaking collection bringing together contributions from instructors, researchers, and professionals. Split into two sections, covering creative production practices and national/international perspectives, this volume offers truly global outlooks on ever-evolving practices.

Including chapters on Dolby Atmos, the history of distortion, creativity in the pandemic, and remote music collaboration, this is recommended reading for professionals, students, and researchers looking for global insights into the fields of music production, music business, and music technology.

Jan-Olof Gullö is Professor in Music Production at the Royal College of Music, Stockholm, Sweden and Visiting Professor at Linnaeus University.

Russ Hepworth-Sawyer is a mastering engineer with MOTTOsound, an Associate Professor at York St John University, and the managing editor of the *Perspectives On Music Production* series for Routledge.

Justin Paterson is Professor of Music Production at London College of Music, University of West London, UK. He has numerous research publications as author and editor. Research interests include haptics, 3-D audio and interactive music, fields that he has investigated over a number of funded projects. He is also an active music producer and composer; his latest album (with Robert Sholl) *Les ombres du Fantôme* was released in 2023 on Metier Records.

Rob Toulson is Director of RT60 Ltd, who develop innovative music applications for mobile platforms. He was formerly Professor of Creative Industries at University of Westminster and Director of the CoDE Research Institute at Anglia Ruskin University. Rob is an author and editor of many books and articles, including *Drum Sound and Drum Tuning*, published by Routledge in 2021.

Mark Marrington is an Associate Professor in Music Production at York St John University, having previously held teaching positions at Leeds College of Music and the University of Leeds. His research interests include metal music, music technology and creativity, the contemporary classical guitar and twentieth-century British classical music, and his recently published book, *Recording the Classical Guitar* (2021), won the 2022 ARSC Award for Excellence in Historical Recorded Sound Research (Classical Music).

Perspectives on Music Production

This series collects detailed and experientially informed considerations of record production from a multitude of perspectives, by authors working in a wide array of academic, creative and professional contexts. We solicit the perspectives of scholars of every disciplinary stripe, alongside recordists and recording musicians themselves, to provide a fully comprehensive analytic point-of-view on each component stage of music production. Each volume in the series thus focuses directly on a distinct stage of music production, from pre-production through recording (audio engineering), mixing, mastering, to marketing and promotions.

Series Editors:
Russ Hepworth-Sawyer, York St John University, UK
Jay Hodgson, Western University, Ontario, Canada
Mark Marrington, York St John University, UK

Coproduction
Collaboration in Music Production
Robert Wilsmore and Christopher Johnson

Distortion in Music Production
The Soul of Sonics
Edited by Gary Bromham and Austin Moore

Reimagining Sample-based Hip Hop
Making Records within Records
Michail Exarchos

Remastering Music and Cultural Heritage
Case Studies from Iconic Original Recordings to Modern Remasters
Stephen Bruel

Innovation in Music
Technology and Creativity
Edited by Jan-Olof Gullö, Russ Hepworth-Sawyer, Justin Paterson, Rob Toulson, and Mark Marrington

Innovation in Music
Cultures and Contexts
Edited by Jan-Olof Gullö, Russ Hepworth-Sawyer, Justin Paterson, Rob Toulson, and Mark Marrington

For more information about this series, please visit: www.routledge.com/Perspectives-on-Music-Production/book-series/POMP

Innovation in Music

Cultures and Contexts

Edited by Jan-Olof Gullö,
Russ Hepworth-Sawyer, Justin Paterson,
Rob Toulson, and Mark Marrington

Routledge
Taylor & Francis Group

LONDON AND NEW YORK

Designed cover image: Jan-Olof Gullö

First published 2024
by Routledge
4 Park Square, Milton Park, Abingdon, Oxon OX14 4RN

and by Routledge
605 Third Avenue, New York, NY 10158

Routledge is an imprint of the Taylor & Francis Group, an informa business

British Library Cataloguing-in-Publication Data
A catalogue record for this book is available from the British Library

ISBN: 978-1-032-61117-4 (hbk)
ISBN: 978-1-032-61116-7 (pbk)
ISBN: 978-1-003-46210-1 (ebk)

DOI: 10.4324/9781003462101

Typeset in Times New Roman
by Apex CoVantage, LLC

Access the Support Material: www.routledge.com/9781032611167

Contents

Preface   vii

PART ONE: CREATIVE PRODUCTION PRACTICE

1 **Staging notions of space: realising compositional
   intention in 3D and stereo record production
   through Dolby Atmos**   3
   INGVILD KOKSVIK

2 **Exploring Dolby Atmos: past, present, and future**   19
   ANDY VISSER, DAN PRATT, AND ANDREW BOURBON

3 **Introducing the Dolby Atmos hyper-near field
   Tiny Studio**   35
   PAUL NOVOTNY

4 **Rap as composite auditory streams: techniques
   and approaches for chimericity through layered
   vocal production in hip-hop, and their aesthetic
   implications**   60
   KJELL ANDREAS ODDEKALV

5 **Exploring the history of distortion in drum and bass**   75
   LEIGH SHIELDS, AUSTIN MOORE, AND CHRIS DEWEY

6 **Dynamic meta-spatialization: narrative
   and recontextualization implications of
   spatial stage stacking**   90
   JO LORD AND MICHAIL EXARCHOS

7 **Vocal chops: another human/machine hybrid**   104
   RAGNHILD BRØVIG AND JON MARIUS AARESKJOLD-DRECKER

8 **"Come together, right now . . .": making remote
   multiparty in-the-box audio mixing a reality**   117
   SCOTT STICKLAND, NATHAN SCOTT, AND RUKSHAN ATHAUDA

9 A creative methodology for self-production 137
TONY DUPÉ

10 Two production strategies for music synchronisation:
as speculative entrepreneurship 151
HUSSEIN BOON

PART TWO: NATIONAL AND INTERNATIONAL PERSPECTIVES

11 Mobile classical music – recording, innovation,
networks and mediatization: three Swedish
case studies from the 1940s to 2021 169
TOIVO BURLIN

12 "Culture produces an industry": production
and promotion strategies of campus song
records by Taiwanese Synco Corporation 190
HAORAN JIANG

13 Business model innovation in the music industry 203
LIUCIJA FOSSELI

14 *Yellow music* in diaspora: re-inventing the sound
of pre-1975 record production in Sài Gòn 217
NGUYỄN THANH THỦY, STEFAN ÖSTERSJÖ, AND MATT WRIGHT

15 Innovating music experiences: creativity in
pandemic times 232
JENNY KARLSSON, JESSICA EDLOM, AND LINDA RYAN BENGTSSON

16 Connecting across borders: communication tools
and group practices of remote music collaborators 247
MARTIN K. KOSZOLKO

17 From master pieces to masterpiece: source selection
and reformatting during the republishing process
of legacy music productions 264
THOMAS BÅRDSEN

Index 279

Preface

The Innovation in Music network brings together experts in the rapidly evolving and connected disciplines of music production, audio technologies, composition, music performance, and the music industry. The Innovation in Music conference is a forum for industry experts and professionals to mix with researchers and academics to report on the latest advances and exchange ideas, crossing boundaries between music disciplines and bridging academia with industry. The conference in 2022 (InMusic22) had as its overarching theme International Perspectives. It was held on June 17–19 at the Royal College of Music, Stockholm, having been planned for 2020 but twice postponed due to the pandemic. During three days in June 2022, more than 100 music innovation experts from 22 countries gathered and presented their work in paper presentations, keynote interviews, performances, and panel discussions. A few participants were prevented from travelling to Stockholm due to pandemic travel restrictions and were therefore offered the opportunity to present papers digitally. After the conference, contributors were invited to submit articles for this publication. Due to the many high-quality and interesting contributions, we've decided to publish this volume in two books, each containing two parts. Book 1, *Innovation in Music: Technology and Creativity*, contains 20 chapters in two parts: *Composition and Performance* and *Technology and Innovation*. Book 2, *Innovation in Music: Cultures and Contexts*, contains 17 chapters in two parts: *Creative Production Practice* and *National and International Perspectives*.

The first part of the present volume opens with a contribution by Ingvild Koksvik. She presents a practice-based study of the creative process of producing a solo album as a recording artist and song-maker. The album was mixed for playback in stereo and Dolby Atmos. Based on the theoretical concepts of staging and composition design, the connection between the compositional intention, the materialisation process and the aesthetic results are examined and discussed. In addition, it is also shown how mixing in Dolby Atmos sets new premises for the staging of composition design from an artist's and songwriter's perspective. A chapter by Andy Visser, Dan Pratt and Andrew Bourbon exploring Dolby Atmos follows. Through an artistically focused lens, the possibilities of Dolby Atmos are analysed and discussed concerning both writing and experiencing music. The study results show that interaction with an audience can develop a deeper understanding of spatial sound systems' possibilities. However, many listeners still need to gain more experience with immersive music to understand or categorise it. Furthermore, this is important, as any emerging format must compete with the dominant established stereo listening paradigm. After that, in the third chapter, Paul Novotny presents a project where he, with a limited budget, has put together a Hyper Near-Field Dolby Atmos Tiny Studio. He describes the challenge for music makers to efficiently and cost-effectively implement the infrastructure required to carry out high-quality work in Dolby Atmos. Furthermore, contextual, theoretical and methodological details of room size, baffles, cabling and connectivity, speaker selection and ceilings are discussed, including assembly, choice of hardware and software, room adjustment, headphones, binaural monitoring and workflow. In Chapter 4, Kjell Andreas Oddekalv explores the production and arrangement of rap vocals and how 'chimericity', the degree to which a musical stream is experienced as being constituted by different sound sources, can create different aesthetic effects. Rap vocals contain many different types of auditory information in discrete layers of a composite compound whole and are, therefore, fruitful for analysing auditory streams. Thus, standard techniques such as backtracks – partial vocal track doublings – and back-to-back rapping exemplify how chimerism can be, more or less, opaque or transparent. In Chapter 5, Leigh Shields, Austin Moore, and Chris Dewey explore the history of distortion in drum 'n' bass. Since the mid-1990s, distorted sounds have become synonymous with the drum and bass genre, particularly with the subgenres tech-step and neurofunk. They not only explore the technology used in the beginnings of the application of distortion in drum 'n' bass but also explore the societal influences that may have been responsible for the heavy, dark and distorted themes found within. A chapter by Jo Lord and Michail Exarchos follows, in which the authors explore the creative opportunities situated in the space where sample-based musicking and spatial mixing meet, with a view to demonstrating the metamorphosis of performance into production music and how production music provides surreal staging practice, the function, and affordances of spatial sound objects within sample-based musicking and, the (re)spatialisation of recontextualised compositional results. In Chapter 7, Ragnhild Brøvig and Jon Marius Aareskjold-Drecker present a study on vocal chops, here defined as fragments of vocal samples that are processed, repitched and rearranged in rhythmic sequence to create hooks and effects. After a historical background, they give examples of vocal chops used in different recordings. Finally, they conclude that vocal chops are everywhere in current music productions, represent an integral part of many arrangements, and have become a handy tool in the producer's belt. In Chapter 8, Scott Stickland, Nathan Scott and Rukshan Athauda present a project in which they have developed a novel application and infrastructure that interfaces with an existing professional Digital Audio Workstation (DAW) platforms and addresses several critical audio mixing and music production characteristics. Their DAW Collaboration Framework provides synchronous mixing operation of multiple DAW instantiations through the transmission and reception of MIDI control data over the Internet. In Chapter 9, Tony Dupé explores the need for a more diverse conversation within music production and presents a creative methodology for self-production. The background of this project is the movement from commercial recording studios to home and locational environments, and he suggests a space within music production that feels welcoming and inspiring to music makers who identify as artistic rather than technical. In Chapter 10, Hussein Boon outlines two production strategies to develop novel music synchronisation approaches for producers when making symbolic goods. The theme of speculative entrepreneurship addresses both the volatility of a highly competitive marketplace and creating a 'sound object' capable of meeting an unspecified future audio-visual use. The presented approaches can be applied to any music style, from any location in the world, and, more importantly, by practitioners at any level of competence

The second part of the book, *National and International Perspectives*, opens with a study (Chapter 11) on mobile classical music recordings by Toivo Burlin. This examines the conditions for innovation in classical music production through mobile recording and production practices and mobility in three Swedish case studies from the 1940s to 2021. Innovation in recording and production is discussed and compared with a focus on the changed conditions for innovation in mobile classical music production, the individuals involved, the technologies, the practices and the networks used. In Chapter 12, Haoran Jiang presents a historical study of Taiwan's recording industry in the 1970s and 1980s. By using information obtained from newspaper reports, oral histories, audio files and album covers, the production and marketing strategies of the Synco Corporation are examined. Synco transformed folk songs into a new popular music genre with Chinese characteristics for student cultures. Synco also created unique marketing strategies that differed from other popular Mandarin songs by using campus tours and print media as primary marketing channels. In Chapter 13, Liucija Fosseli presents a study on business model innovation where she examines business models used by European producers and publishers who work towards the Chinese music industry. She also gives an overview of the Chinese music industry and the conditions for European songwriters to work within that market. Chapter 14 by Nguyễn Thanh Thủy, Stefan Östersjö and Matt Wright follows providing an overview of the history of the record industry in southern Vietnam before 1975 and *nhạc vàng* (yellow music), a form of popular music that became emblematic of colonial Vietnam, and so eventually also of diasporic Vietnamese culture after 1975. Furthermore, it describes how the Vietnamese/Swedish group The Six Tones has experimented with *nhạc vàng* in creating a new album with the group. In Chapter 15, Jenny Karlsson, Jessica Edlom and Linda Ryan Bengtsson present an empirical study exploring how the music industry and music practitioners in Sweden responded to the changes and how they engaged in innovation initiatives during the Covid-19 pandemic. They conclude that the restrictions during this period evoked great interest in digital experimentation despite a lack of knowledge and technological and monetary resources. Apart from the disruption the pandemic has caused, the findings imply a need for continuous development of a sustainable music industry. After that, in Chapter 16, Martin K. Koszolko presents a project on remote music collaboration software (RMCS) that offers a democratic working environment where amateurs and professionals can connect, collaborate, communicate, and learn from each other. However, to fully benefit from the innovative technologies that facilitate various music-production approaches in online collaborative creativity, he asserts that musicians need to recognise the value of and fully engage with the available communication tools, which are critical to creative crowdsourcing and enhancing outcomes of collaborative music creation. In the last chapter of the book, Thomas Bårdsen discusses the republishing process of legacy music productions. In particular, he problematises the initial steps of source selection and reformatting of productions originally produced on magnetic tape. Rather than the somewhat romantic idea of the master tape as a fixed, defined and clearly labelled object sitting in a vault with a defined reproduction method, the results indicate that the reality of music production archives is far more complex. Therefore, archivists and audio engineers must balance numerous factors to select the best source and procedure for each case. Thus, better and more critical documentation of these decisions could improve the work's past, present, and future editions.

We thank all chapter authors, conference speakers and delegates for their support, and we intend that the chapters of this book will be a lasting record of contemporary music innovations and a resource of research information for the future.

Jan-Olof Gullö
Stockholm, Sweden

Part one

Creative production practice

Staging notions of space

Realising compositional intention in 3D and stereo record production through Dolby Atmos

Ingvild Koksvik

1 INTRODUCTION

According to record producer Joel Hamilton, production is "just a transition from idea to something we can share" (The True School of Music, 2020, 15:50). This transition has always intrigued me as a recording artist and song-maker: I often enter the recording studio with the intention of what my song should feel or 'look' like when recorded. This idea is often related to notions of metaphorical or literal space while, at the same time, being both abstract and volatile. The big challenge in transitioning the idea into something worth sharing is to realise the compositional intention, to materialise what I perceive as the song's identity into recorded sound in a way that makes it feel right. In what ways might notions of space impinge upon aesthetic, performative, and compositional aspects of record production? And how might mixing in the 3D format afford new ways of realising compositional intention?

This chapter addresses a practice-based study of the production of my third solo album as a recording artist, mixed for playback in Dolby Atmos and stereo. In collaboration with recording engineer Jaran Gustavson and mixing engineer Christer-André Cederberg at Cederberg Studios in Kristiansand, Norway, I have recorded and produced eight original songs in which space influences the compositional design in various ways. In this chapter, I reveal aspects of the process, from idea to finalised recording for one of the songs. To investigate the relations between the compositional intention, the materialisation process, and the aesthetic outcome, I use the theoretical concepts of staging (Lacasse, 2000; Moylan, 1992) and compositional design (Hawkins, 2002). Moreover, I seek to demonstrate how mixing in Dolby Atmos sets new premises for staging compositional design from a recording artist and song-maker's perspective.

DOI: 10.4324/9781003462101-2

2 BACKGROUND AND THEORY

2.1 The compositional intention

A key concept in this study is the notion of *compositional intention* derived from Joel Hamilton's philosophy of record production. Hamilton claims that a production should always serve the compositional intention, which refers to the overarching compositional narrative of the song to be recorded. Thus, when Hamilton talks about record production as a transition from idea to something we can share, it is not necessarily musical ideas he refers to, but big questions like: "Why does that piece of art exist? What is the song saying at all? . . . why did you write it?" (The True School of Music, 2020, 15:25). Yet, the point is not to answer these questions but to start locating the 'identity' of the song. In practice, this means that before focusing on how the song should be performed or produced, we should start by asking ourselves what the music should feel or sound like when recorded (Mirisola, 2019).

While I recognise the complexity of intention as a concept, it is essential to emphasise that in this context, the compositional intention is not about the listener's interpretation of musical meaning. Nor does it necessarily refer to the composer's intent: In the case of the recording artist and song-maker, the compositional intention and the composer's intention would align. Yet, the way I understand Hamilton, the idea – the compositional intention – refers to the interpretation of what the song should express or feel like, as experienced by whoever is recording it.

According to Mike Howlett, the producer's task is to "make the artist believe that he, or she, has the ability to make that volatile concept, a song, into a fixed (recorded) reality" (Howlett, 2012, para. 16), and that "the song represents an individual's articulation of their unique perception of an experience, or understanding" (Howlett, 2012, para. 22). When I call the compositional intention abstract and volatile, I refer to a tacit and embodied understanding of what the song should express that, in many ways, transcends the kind of experience or understanding that Howlett addresses. Fragmented and fleeting, the ideas of what the recording should feel or sound like in the end might be challenging to concretise. Moreover, such ideas involve aesthetic and creative dimensions. As Keith Negus and Michael Pickering point out, it is

> of course a mistake to think that an artwork or cultural product is the expression of certain feelings, ideas or values which exist independently of the creative product and which simply result from the intention to communicate them . . . we do not have a fully formed, reflexively comprehended experience which we then reproduce in verbal or sonic form.
>
> (Negus and Pickering, 2002, p. 184)

Therefore, understanding the compositional intention as the overarching compositional narrative of the song to be recorded involves a conception of the 'narrative' as more than the interpretation of the lyrics: It includes aesthetic and embodied dimensions – ideas of what the song should feel, 'look' or sound like – and this may also mean notions of some kind of space.

2.2 Notions of space

In the last decades, scholars have examined the listener's perception of virtual space in recorded popular music, where literal and metaphorical interpretations of space are aligned with recording and production techniques. The large and growing body of work includes production- and reception-based approaches to space, offering concepts and strategies to understand how virtual space might be perceived (Walther-Hansen, 2020), interpreted (Brøvig-Hanssen and Danielsen, 2013), and created (Moylan, 2020).

Theoretical concepts of space can aid practitioners in understanding meaning-making and offer ways of thinking that can support creative work on different levels. For example, I particularly find Lelio Camilleri's concept of sonic space as a holistic and intuitive way of considering virtual space. Camilleri suggests understanding the recording as 'sounding matter', where

> the organization of the recording space reflects . . . the structural organization of the music itself; the sound of the record is a sort of sonicprint (sounding fingerprint) of the music of an artist in a particular period.
>
> (Camilleri, 2010, p. 199)

Realising compositional intention involves, in many ways, also creating the ideal sonicprint. Further, the concepts of proxemics applied to recorded music, which links perceived physical and social distance (Dockwray, 2017; Dockwray, Moore, and Schmidt, 2009), and acousmatic intimacy (Kraugerud, 2020) offer insights into the complex phenomenon of proximity in recorded music that may inform several aspects of the recording and production.

Yet, from recording artists' and song-makers' perspectives, notions of space exceed virtual and physical space. Just as recordings may evoke imagery in listeners' minds, imagery might also be part of the creative work. Mental imagery as part of the creative idea might be abstract in nature or more concrete and visualised. Moreover, it may be expressed either in the *production vision* – another term borrowed from Hamilton, which refers to how the song should be produced – or as part of the compositional intention, which works on a higher or more abstract level.

Notions of space in the production vision may be related to visualisation in recording and mixing:

> The use of visual imagery to describe sound occurs in many accounts by producers, which may seem to be an oxymoron, but I too have

found it helpful to form a mental image of the finished work before the
production is completed. By this process ideas for the sound character
of a particular instrument arise and can inform choices. Visualisation
is a well-known method in many areas of creative endeavour and is
clearly a common device in record production, supporting the case for
record production as an art.

(Howlett, 2012, para. 7)

Notions of space and imagery as part of the compositional intention might,
for example, involve a conception of the song's identity as belonging to
a kind of conceptual imagined space that feels a certain way. This can
be compared to the visualisation of space that a reader might experience
when reading fiction. William Moylan's linking of metaphors to the mix,
such as "sonic world", "spatial identity", and "a place of different sonic
realities" (Moylan, 2020, p. 291), may also help practitioners in the process of concretising the compositional intention and transitioning it into a
production vision.

2.3 The Dolby Atmos format

Traditional mixing in stereo allows for delivering sound signals to
two speaker channels, left and right. Thus, elements in the mix can be
placed on a horizontal axis, anywhere from the far left to the far right.
Dolby Atmos was initially designed for cinema sound. The system is
configurable for up to 64 speaker channels, including side speakers,
rear speakers, and ceiling speakers. It allows any signal to be placed
anywhere in a three-dimensional environment, on both a vertical and
horizontal axis, allowing producers to create almost boundless possibilities for immersive sound. This opens a different experience of
virtual space, with more depth, more details, and more clarity to each
sound.

Recently, new premises for dealing with space in recorded music have
emerged, as binaural listening to the 3D-format Dolby Atmos has become
available on streaming platforms like Apple Music, Tidal, and Amazon.
This means that listening to 3D recordings no longer requires a multi-channel
sound system, as a 3D experience can be simulated using regular headphones. To date, several existing recordings have been remixed in Dolby
Atmos, and more and more artists choose to offer their new releases in 3D
sound. As Dolby Atmos becomes available in more recording studios, the
technology is also within reach for more recording artists. Consequently,
the aesthetic implications of 3D sound may affect the music-making of
both major and indie artists.

2.4 Theoretical basis

The primary theoretical basis for this study includes the concepts of *staging* (Lacasse, 2000, 2005; Moylan, 1992, 2002; Zagorski-Thomas, 2010,
2014) and *compositional design* (Hawkins, 2002).

Staging as an analytical concept derives from William Moylan's term sound stage (1992, 2002), used as a metaphor for describing how the different sound elements are structured within the mix; "a platform where the positions of sources can be observed, and the spatial uniqueness of the track recognized" (Moylan, 2020, p. 322). Allan Moore's soundbox (2001, p. 121) represents a similar symbolic understanding of the mix as a kind of space. Yet, whereas Moore's concept favours the listener's interpretation, Moylan's main perspective is understanding the mix. With the 3D format, the stage changes. Zack Bresler suggests that

> when considering surround and 3D audio in particular it might be more relevant to transform the soundbox into a soundsphere, where the listener is centered on the focal point of a sphere rather than viewing a box from the outside.
>
> (Bresler, 2021, p. 41)

Derived from Moylan's work, Serge Lacasse's term phonographic staging aims to describe how the manipulation of sounds through recording technology affects how we perceive loudness, space, time, and timbre, in "a kind of acousmatic scenography", where "effects such as reverb, echo, filtering or overdubbing act as mediators of recorded sound sources" (2005, p. 1). Moreover, his work on vocal staging focuses explicitly on how technological manipulation of the vocals affects how we interpret the voice and its meaning (Lacasse, 2000).

On the one hand, staging refers to

> the perceived spatial relationship between the 'performers', and between them and us (the listeners). There are two elements to this perception of spatial relationships: the nature of the environment in which the event is happening and everybody's position in that environment.
>
> (Zagorski-Thomas, 2014, p. 73)

On the other hand, staging may also involve "the treatment of sound in ways that add meaningful context for the listener to a performance or a perceived musical 'event'" (Zagorski-Thomas, 2014, p. 78).

Compositional design is a theoretical concept borrowed from Stan Hawkins as an aid in understanding the complex inner workings of pop recordings. As an interpretative model, Hawkins outlines a range of musical codes, which he categorises as stylistic ("relatively discernible through performance, genre and musical trend") and technical (identifiable through "music-theoretical parameters" and "components of production") (2002, p. 10). The technical codes include parameters such as pitch, melody, rhythm, chord progressions, and texture. Hawkins emphasises the importance of the production-related aspects of these parameters:

> the mix, studio effects, the configurations of recording, and the polyphony of multi-tracking. Most importantly, it is through their

arrangements within the recorded audio space . . . that stylistic and technical codes are blended into the compositional design.

(Hawkins, 2002, p. 10)

According to Hawkins, "the uniqueness of any single song exists primarily through the special combinations of its codes within the framework of the compositional features" (2002, p. 12). Put another way, we could say that the song's recorded identity, including its overall sonicprint, is formed through the combination of aesthetic, performative, compositional, and technological aspects.

Admittedly, although staging and compositional design consider production-related aspects of recordings, these theoretical approaches were developed with the analysis of existing recorded music in mind. Yet, thinking in terms of staging and compositional design can aid in understanding and theorising what is going on in the transition from idea to finalised recording. This involves thinking of staging as an act, as something we do in the creative process of record-making. Further, as a practice, staging should be understood as including more sides of record production than the technical aspects of mixing: In addition to spatialisation and treatment of sounds, *what* is recorded and *how* it is being performed should also be counted as part of the staging. For example, in the production process, the "nature of the environment" (Zagorski-Thomas, 2014, p. 73) is not solely linked to the use of reverb or other technological manipulation of sound elements. Also, *which* sound elements to be chosen and what those sound elements *do* are part of the constitution of that environment. This aligns with Moore's concept of the persona-environment, where "what accompanies forms the substance of the environment for what is accompanied" (2012, p. 189). In popular music production, composition, arranging, performance, recording, and mixing are often closely linked activities – hence the choice of using the term song-making rather than songwriting in this chapter. In this way, thinking of the recording as compositionally designed takes this complexity into account. To this end, I suggest considering record production as a staging process of compositional design.

Bresler argues that in 3D audio, the "listener's experience is a staged element of the compositional design" (2021, p. 4), where the listener is placed in the centre of the soundsphere. A similar way of thinking can also apply to the creative process of working in the 3D format. When mixing in Dolby Atmos, the mixer is surrounded by loudspeakers that open for staging the compositional design from an 'on stage' perspective.

3 RECORDING AND MIXING 'VENTETID'

3.1 Case and method

'Ventetid', which translates as 'Waiting Time', is the opening track on the album *Mørketidssanger* (Dark Season Songs) (Koksvik, 2022). Initially, it was supposed to be mixed in stereo only, but at the end of the recording process, the possibility of mixing in Dolby Atmos emerged. The album was composed, produced, and performed on vocals by the author, recorded and co-produced by Jaran Gustavson, and mixed in Dolby Atmos and stereo by Christer-André Cederberg. The musicians involved were chosen based on their unique playing style and sonic fingerprint: Juhani Silvola on guitars, Lars Jakob Rudjord on keys, Erland Dahlen on drums and percussion, Lars Løberg Tofte on electric bass, and Katrine Schiøtt on cello. In several studio sessions over four months, we recorded instrument by instrument and continuously edited it, working iteratively on all the songs in each session. The creative process was based on intuition, previous experience, and exploration while, at the same time, being influenced by the awareness of the theoretical framework of staging and compositional design.

Critically self-reflective, the study used continuous dialogue as a method to gain new insights into the relations between the compositional intentions and the aesthetic considerations and decisions undertaken in the production process. I collected data by writing a log of the dialogue, the work in the recording studio, and my reflections and thinking during and between the sessions. I also made audio bounces of each song at different stages of the production process.

3.2 The compositional intention

'Ventetid' was inspired by a state of unrest related to taking in the climate crisis combined with artistic discouragement and sleep deprivation. I experienced an indefinable and composite feeling of worry and helplessness, an urge to act while feeling almost paralysed simultaneously. It was a restless feeling that 'something has to happen', but all I could do was stare into my coffee. I started to hum what would become the song's bass line, recorded it on my phone, and then forgot about it. Later, I listened through my phone recordings, picked up on the bass line, and started to sing a melody on top. At this point, a notion of space began to appear in my mind, a sense of what the song should 'look' or feel like and what its identity would be like. It was related to the initial inspiration but was also an aesthetic experience. I pictured a dark space with silhouettes of unidentified, threatening elements lurking in the corners. My aim in making this song was neither to say something specific about climate change nor my artistic struggles but rather to articulate the state of unrest I experienced, this feeling of parallel restlessness and inaction, and the feeling of being stuck in that metaphorical space. Then I wrote the lyrics, aiming to support this feeling, this state.

The starting point for the production was a rough demo recording that consisted of the lead vocals, the bass line, and an additional melodic synth figure played by Rudjord. Before we started recording, I shared the demo with Gustavson and explained the feeling and vibe I aimed to capture in the production.

- **Audio Example 1.1: Demo recording**

3.3 Recording lead vocals and synths

On the initial recording day, we kept the MIDI from the demo, transposed it down to seek a darker atmosphere, and recorded the lead vocals. Often, I prefer to do preliminary lead vocals early in the recording process and then do the final takes at a later stage to feel the virtual space and have more elements to respond to as a singer. This time, I had a strong notion of what the song should feel like right from the beginning of the recording process. And we ended up using the initial vocals takes in the end, as they had the right 'feel'.

3.4 Recording additional vocals

I attempted to explain my compositional intention to Gustavson in various ways by using metaphors and describing different types of imagery and situations. References to other recordings and sounds were also discussed. Still, finding the right way to communicate the volatile notion of the song's identity was challenging. Yet, we started to come up with ideas for the production, both literal and metaphorical. These were everything from frenetic guitars to the feeling of being stuck in a cave. Gustavson pointed out that his notion of what the song should be like when recorded was based on a combination of what he heard in the demo recording and what I told him, but to find out if we had the same understanding of the compositional intention, it would be best to explore it through sound; to continue recording to find out what direction the production should take.

To start staging the compositional design, I improvised several vocal tracks, which were edited, processed with effects, and equalised differently. I found it essential to work on the additional vocals already at this stage of the recording process to set the vibe for the other musicians and give them some indications of what kind of atmosphere I aimed for. One of the ideas for these vocal parts was to create an eerie vibe by recording high-pitched vocal lines and processing them into a bright, drone-like sound.

- **Audio Example 1.2: Lead vocals, synths, and additional vocals**

  Note: Some additional vocal elements were temporarily muted at this stage (at 00:39 and 00:48) but later included (as heard in the following audio example 1.3).

3.5 The production vision

Now, a vision for the production started to take shape. The idea was to have the lead vocals in the centre and then stage a persona-environment around the lead vocals by adding different instrumental elements, creating texture and space: Paralysis in the centre, surrounded by restlessness and anxiety. To this end, the additional vocals already recorded would also function as such an element. I aimed for a quite transparent production, portioning the different sound elements and using each sparingly.

I had some ideas for each instrument, but I also wanted to give the musicians space to try out whatever they thought could be interesting. Therefore, I decided to ask the musicians to improvise, influenced by what we already had recorded, combined with dialogue on the compositional intention and the production vision. The idea was to record a lot, remove most of it in the editing, and keep just the required fragments.

3.6 Recording guitars

On the subsequent recording day, Silvola brought various acoustic and electric guitars to the studio. As he is a performer and composer of both folk and electro-acoustic music, I was excited to see what he would do with this song.

We started recording acoustic steel string guitars. An idea for a flamenco tremolo was tried but did not feel right. Silvola then attempted to make a similar effect by playing with a small broom on the strings. Then he used a screw to create a kind of drone. He explored different textures and voicings, aiming to capture a feeling of anxiety or restlessness. To counter the steel string textures, I asked for something darker and 'uglier', and Silvola responded by adding some atmospheric electric guitars.

On the recording day, we considered the parts played with a broom the best to keep. However, we changed our minds when editing the takes afterwards. We removed a lot of the guitars and kept only some fragments; the sequence played with a screw for the instrumental part and some of the electric guitars. To further enhance the atmosphere, we used a tape echo on the latter to create a ping-pong tape delay with some saturation and automated the feedback to control the delay.

• **Audio Example 1.3: Guitars**

   Note: The electric guitar starts at 00:38, and the acoustic steel string instrumental part at 01:13.

3.7 Recording drums, percussion, and bass

For the next session, we had Dahlen on drums and percussion and Tofte on electric bass in the studio. They had been listening to the audio bounce of what we had already recorded some days prior, so they had an impression of the vibe. Nevertheless, we started by talking about the compositional intention and the production vision. We spoke of the bassline as 'the time that is passing' and 'the big ugly beast' – ideas that were saved for the mixing process later, as Tofte's contribution to this song was basically to replace some of the synth basses initially recorded.

Then the drums and percussion were recorded. Dahlen had specific ideas he wanted to try out. First, he did a couple of takes on the drum kit. Then he asked for more reverb to play on and added chimes, followed by some additional percussion. Immediately, I thought the drum kit worked very well, although it took the song in a new direction. But in the editing session the following day, I changed my mind and decided to remove the drums almost entirely and keep only some of them in addition to some of the percussion.

- **Audio Example 1.4: Drums, percussion, and bass**

3.8 Recording cello

Initially, I did not plan to include cello in this song. But we had some time left at the end of the day after Schiøtt had recorded cello on some of the other songs, so we decided to try it out. We recorded several different improvised cello parts, many of which sounded great and could have been valuable parts of the compositional design. But again, in line with the production vision, almost everything was removed in the editing afterwards, except for two short fragments.

- **Audio Example 1.5: Premix**

  Note: Cello starts at 00:49 and 01:13.

3.9 Mixing in Dolby Atmos

Cederberg explained that there are generally two main mixing approaches in Dolby Atmos. One aims towards a subtle expression, where the experience of the mix is like an expanded version of the stereo mix. The other strives towards a more expressive signature where the sound elements' locations are clarified in the soundsphere, and a more vivid space is created, for example, by letting the elements move within it.

We mixed 'Ventetid' using the latter approach. This choice was based on aspects of the compositional intention, such as the unpredictable and the sense of unrest, and the production vision of creating an environment made from different instrumental elements, which opened to utilising the Dolby Atmos tools' full potential. We worked with 12 loudspeakers, but as Dolby Atmos is stepless, we also had the opportunity to place or move sounds between them. Cederberg pointed out that 'Ventetid' is a song that could be mixed in many ways in Dolby Atmos. Yet, regarding the limited time available in the studio, we had to make some decisions. Before we started mixing, I worried that the opportunities for exact placements of the different sound elements would complicate the mixing process as there would be more to decide on. But it turned out that mixing in this format was very intuitive. When mixing in Dolby Atmos, the mixer is surrounded by loudspeakers: Instead of working with a sound stage in front, with left-right loudspeakers as in stereo, the mixer is 'on' that very stage, in the centre of the soundsphere. I experienced this listening situation in the mixing process to be closer to 'being in the world' than what I am used to from mixing in stereo. In addition, the more distinct separation of instruments and the possibilities for exact placement and movement of sound elements afforded a very hands-on approach to realising creative ideas in the mixing process, many of which would have been hard to accomplish in a stereo mix.

We started experimenting with placements in line with the idea of 'paralysis in the centre, surrounded by restlessness and anxiety'. I wanted the lead vocals to sound dryer than I usually would prefer, to enhance the contrast to the surroundings, and to make the voice feel more intimate. When mixing the backing vocals, Cederberg first spread them out in the soundsphere. I suggested letting some of the backing vocals come from behind to see if that would support the compositional intention in a better way. This idea was based on intuition, but I also had proxemics in mind and was curious how the vocals would feel when coming from behind compared to from each side. Cederberg immediately understood what I wanted to achieve and started experimenting with movements of the sound elements within the soundsphere.

The staging of the 'environment' included some of the additional vocals starting at the back of the room to being drawn forward to the front speakers in a dramatic way, elements that move in circles up in the ceiling speakers, and sounds that are sent from the front to the rear speakers via the ceiling like a wave that hits the listener. Inspired by the notion of the bass as 'the big ugly beast' from the recording session, the bass was given a distorted delay placed in the rear speakers. In addition to contrasts and clarity in the placement of many of the elements, several instruments, such as the drums and all the percussion, were placed throughout the room using room microphones in all speaker pairs: The overhead microphones were placed in the ceiling, the mono-room microphones were placed in the centre speaker, the stereo microphone that stood a few meters in front of the drum kit was placed in the side speakers, and the pair of microphones that stood several meters from the kit was placed in the rear speakers. The effect you achieve by such placements is a listening experience as if you were sitting in the very room where the song was recorded.

As a producer, I assume that my visualisation of the sonicprint of the recording and, thus, the compositional design would have been slightly different if I had initially known that the song would be mixed in 3D and what this format affords the production. For example, I could have recorded the improvised backing vocals with placements in mind, as voices coming from behind are experienced differently than voices coming from the front or the sides. I guess this could have influenced the performative and compositional aspects as well as the recording technique of both the backing vocals and some instruments.

- **Audio Example 1.6: Dolby Atmos master**

  Note: Listen for additional vocals starting at the back of the room to being drawn forward to the front speakers at 00:42 and 00:51.

After the song was mixed in Dolby Atmos, a fold-down mix to stereo was made. This mostly involved adjustment of some levels and the amount of reverb.

- **Audio Example 1.7: Stereo master**

4 DISCUSSION

4.1 Staging compositional design through recording

In the recording of 'Ventetid', the starting point was a rough demo recording consisting of a vocal line with lyrics, a bass line, and a supplemental melodic synth line. In addition, the compositional intention – the idea of the song's identity and what the recording should feel and 'look' like – involved notions of space. To transition the compositional intention into recorded sound, a production vision based on the idea of creating a persona-environment out of different instrumental elements was established. Recording one instrument at a time, the compositional design was staged step by step throughout several recording sessions. The respective musicians improvised every part beyond what was indicated in the demo. In collaboration with Gustavson, I continuously edited and processed what was recorded.

On the one hand, the staging of the compositional design was, in many ways, collaborative. On the other hand, as the producer, recording artist, and song-maker, it was significant for me to ensure that the compositional intention was realised (see, for example, Succi, 2021). To this end, continuous dialogue on creative considerations and decisions was crucial. This included explanations, metaphors, imagery, references to other recordings and sounds, and more direct ideas concerning aesthetic, performative, and technological aspects.

4.2 The compositional intention as a reference point

One of the aims of this study was to investigate the ways in which notions of space might impinge upon different aspects of record production. In the case of 'Ventetid', space as part of the compositional intention permeated the production process from idea through recording to the final mixes. This not only affected the creation of virtual space but influenced various aspects of the compositional design, like the contributions of the performers involved. Understood as the overarching idea of the song to be recorded, the compositional intention was used as a concept to identify and talk about notions of space as an implicit aspect of music-making that is often connected to intuition and gut feeling. The experience from this practice-based study is that by putting the compositional intention on top of the production process, it can also function as a reference point for creative and aesthetic decision-making in the recording and mixing process.

While letting the production serve the compositional intention might aid in the transition from an idea to an aesthetic outcome that feels right, the compositional intention is, at the same time, intrinsically a fleeting and changeable size. As Allan Moore puts it, "Sometimes, we don't know 'what we mean' until we try to express it" (2012, p. 215). Therefore, the compositional intention is not a static entity but should be understood as a flexible reference point in the creative work.

4.3 Realising compositional intention in 3D

In the case of 'Ventetid', notions of space were both parts of the compositional intention and the production vision. It significantly influenced the creation of the compositional design during the recording process, and the further staging in the 3D mix enhanced this aspect even more. While we decided to go for an expressive mixing signature for this particular song, it does not necessarily apply to every song involving space as part of the compositional intention:

> In my opinion, mixing like this is only successful when the song allows it. It is essential that the technique and tools do not get in the way of the song and the lyrics. Things should not happen in the mix that make you lose focus on the lyrics or the song's mood, which can quickly happen if you challenge too much with the use of the 3D aspect.
>
> (Cederberg, 2022, personal communication August 28)

Based on the nature of the project and the kind of production, we chose to mix 'Ventetid' in Dolby Atmos first, then do a fold-down to stereo afterwards. Paul Novotny asserts that

> a stereo to 5.1-fold-out, rather than fold-down is a preferable method because it affords each version a creatively distinct virtual acoustic environment by unique preparation. Fold-out results in two separate and unique masters that share a strong common foundation of ensemble sound.
>
> (Novotny, 2019, p. 205)

Instead of asserting which method is the best, I would suggest basing the assessment of whether to do a fold-out or fold-down on the characteristics of the music to be mixed and the intention behind using the 3D format. Cederberg pointed out that he, for instance, most likely would have chosen a fold-out approach if working on a more packed pop production. In this case, we dealt with a quite transparent recording with a lot of space that only required minor adjustments in the transition from 3D to stereo. From a pragmatic perspective, the choice of the method also has some economic implications for recording artists aiming to do 3D recordings, as doing a stereo mix first and then doing a new mix in Dolby Atmos is both time-consuming and expensive.

More important in this context, however, are the aesthetic implications of mixing in 3D before mixing in stereo. As a recording artist, it was vital for me that both versions should answer to the compositional intention, striving towards a consistent feeling. There were, for example, some reflections from the ceiling and the rear that were transferred from the 3D mix to the fold-down stereo version that would not have been present in the stereo version if we had chosen to do the stereo mix first. In this way, we ended up with a stereo version that I am convinced is closer to a realisation of the compositional intention than we would have achieved if mixed in stereo first. In my experience, using the Dolby Atmos tools in the 'main' mixing process profoundly affected not only the audio staging but also the aesthetic evaluations and the way of thinking. This affected the aesthetic outcome of the 3D version and subsequently also the stereo version, as well as my overall experience of achieving the realisation of the compositional intention. According to Bresler,

> the relative differences between traditional stereo and immersive versions of pop songs lies not in the composition, but in the mix. While aesthetic features certainly change when moving between different forms of music media, structures that define the composition remain more-or-less consistent. In other words, any aesthetic changes are attributable primarily to the media format itself and can be seen as aesthetic features of the format. Analogizing to painting, aesthetic differences between the same image painted on different surfaces is a correlate of the aesthetics of the canvas, not necessarily the image.
>
> (Bresler, 2021, p. 89)

Here, Bresler indicates that what distinguishes stereo and 3D versions of a recording is mainly the mix, which is an aesthetic, not compositional, feature. The statement that the mix is not part of the composition is, in many ways, right: 'Ventetid' in 3D and stereo is indeed the 'same' composition. Yet, at the same time, this distinction might not be as straightforward from a creative perspective. On the one hand, as shown in the case of 'Ventetid', both versions of a song may aim to answer the same compositional intention, and mixing in 3D can profoundly affect the sonicprint and aesthetic outcome of the stereo version. On the other hand, within the song-making context, aesthetic, performative, compositional, and technological aspects are often not separate entities but influence each other. This means that in the creative process of record production, performative and aesthetic elements can also be considered compositional. For example, moving the vocals steplessly within the 3D soundsphere may be used as a compositional element, affecting the vocal line being sung, how it is being performed, and its processing and staging in the compositional design.

5 CONCLUSION

In the case discussed in this chapter, Dolby Atmos was introduced at the end of the recording process. However, integrating the 3D format at an earlier stage in the song-making process opens up for thinking about the mix as a creative tool in new ways.

This chapter demonstrates how working in the 3D format affected several aspects of the staging of the compositional design of 'Ventetid'. In this practice-based study, my compositional intention was central in identifying and communicating notions of space and the song's 'identity', from the initial idea and composition through the recording process to the mixing in Dolby Atmos. Also, it functioned as a reference point for aesthetic decision-making in the recording and mixing process.

The production of this album was my first experience working in the 3D format. As a recording artist, song-maker, and producer, mixing in Dolby Atmos almost felt like 'coming home': Things I have always wanted to accomplish in my productions were suddenly possible, and it felt so natural. When the 3D mix of 'Ventetid' was folded down to stereo, the staging in the 3D version affected the stereo version and, thereby, the realisation of the compositional intention in stereo.

As a creative tool, then, Dolby Atmos offers new ways of utilising space as aesthetic and compositional elements in record production. It also affords new opportunities for realising compositional intention, but to this end, the recording process's aesthetic, performative, and compositional aspects should not be underestimated.

REFERENCES

Bresler, Z. (2021). 'Immersed in Pop! Excursions into Compositional Design', PhD thesis, University of Agder, Kristiansand.

Brøvig-Hanssen, R., and Danielsen, A. (2013). 'The Naturalised and the Surreal: Changes in the Perception of Popular Music Sound', *Organised Sound: An International Journal of Music Technology*, vol. 18, no. 1, pp. 71–80.

Camilleri, L. (2010). 'Shaping Sounds, Shaping Spaces', *Popular Music*, vol. 29, no. 2, pp. 199–211.

Dockwray, R. (2017). 'Proxemic Interaction in Popular Music Recordings', in R. Hepworth-Sawyer & J. Hodgson (eds.), *Mixing Music*, Routledge, New York, pp. 53–61.

Dockwray, R., Moore, A. F., and Schmidt, P. (2009). 'A Hermeneutics of Spatialization for Recorded Song', *Twentieth-Century Music*, vol. 6, no. 01, pp. 83–114.

Hawkins, S. (2002). *Settling the Pop Score*, Aldershot, Ashgate.

Howlett, M. (2012). 'The Record Producer As Nexus', *Journal on the Art of Record Production*, no. 06, available online at www.arpjournal.com/asarpwp/the-record-producer-as-nexus/ [accessed April 28, 2022].

Kraugerud, E. (2020). 'Come Closer: Acousmatic Intimacy in Popular Music Sound', PhD thesis, University of Oslo, Oslo.

Lacasse, S. (2000). 'Listen to My Voice – The Evocative Power of Vocal Staging in Recorded Rock Music and Other Forms of Vocal Expression', PhD thesis, University of Liverpool, Liverpool.

Lacasse, S. (2005). 'Persona, Emotions and Technology: The Phonographic Staging of the Popular Music Voice', *Proceedings of the CHARM Symposium 2: Towards a Musicology of Production (Part of the Art of Record Production Conference)*, London, available online at https://charm.cch.kcl.ac.uk/redist/pdf/s2Lacasse.pdf [accessed June 8, 2021].

Mirisola, J. (2019). '"I Need It with Fire": A Day in the Studio with Joel Hamilton', (website), available online at www.berklee.edu/news/berklee-now/visiting-producer-joel-hamilton-jumps-canyon-school-bus [accessed May 22, 2022].

Moore, A. (2001). *Rock: The Primary Text: Developing a Musicology of Rock*, 2nd ed., Aldershot, Ashgate.

Moore, A. (2012). *Song Means: Analysing and Interpreting Recorded Popular Song*, Farnham, Routledge.

Moylan, W. (1992). *The Art of Recording: The Creative Resources of Music Production and Audio*, New York, Van Nostrand Reinhold.

Moylan, W. (2002). *The Art of Recording: Understanding and Crafting the Mix*, Boston, Focal Press.

Moylan, W. (2020). *Recording Analysis: How the Record Shapes the Song*, New York, Routledge.

Negus, K., and Pickering, M. (2002). 'Creativity and Musical Experience', in D. Hesmondhalgh & K. Negus (eds.), *Popular Music Studies*, London, Arnold, pp. 178–190.

Novotny, P. (2019). 'Creating an Immersive Fold-Out – Look Ahead', in J. O. Gullö, S. Rambarran & K. Isakoff (eds.), *Proceedings of the 12th Art of Record Production Conference Mono: Stereo: Multi*, Stockholm, Royal College of Music (KMH) & Art of Record Production, pp. 205–224.

Succi, A. (2021). 'Defining and Developing a Sonic Signature in Music Mixing: A Practice-Based Approach as Modern-Day Studio Mentorship', in R. Hepworth-Sawyer, J. Paterson & R. Toulson (eds.), *Innovation in Music: Future Opportunities*, New York, Routledge, pp. 17–36.

The True School of Music. (2020). 'The Aesthetic Compass Masterclass with Joel Hamilton', (online video), Youtube, available online at https://youtu.be/mg84hNo8V2g [accessed May 5, 2022].

Walther-Hansen, M. (2020). *Making Sense of Recordings: How Cognitive Processing of Recorded Sound Works*, Oxford, Oxford University Press.

Zagorski-Thomas, S. (2010). 'The Stadium in Iour Bedroom: Functional Staging, Authenticity and the Audience-Led Aesthetic in Record Production', *Popular Music*, vol. 29, no. 2, pp. 251–266.

Zagorski-Thomas, S. (2014). *The Musicology of Record Production*, Cambridge, Cambridge University Press.

DISCOGRAPHY

Koksvik, Ingvild. (2022). [digital release] 'Ventetid', *Mørketidssanger*, Fyrlyd Records.

2

Exploring Dolby Atmos

Past, present, and future

Andy Visser, Dan Pratt, and Andrew Bourbon

1 INTRODUCTION

This chapter arose from discussions between academics and artists on the affordances of Dolby Atmos in relation to both writing and experiencing music through an artistically focused lens. During our investigations of the platforms, we noticed that the creative enquiries into Atmos need to be balanced with the more technical and affordance-based research that currently dominates the research field. As songwriters and engineers, we want to better understand how we generate novel productions when we work with immersive music technologies. To appreciate the potential of Atmos as a creative tool, we took a finished and stereo-mixed song called *Robots from Mars* and reinterpreted it as a spatial mix, primarily using the Dolby Atmos framework. This chapter investigates our experience of moving into Atmos creation as the first of many stages intended to document the creative applications of Atmos creation. The participants involved have backgrounds in academia, record production, songwriting, mix practice, electroacoustic composition, and performance. The chapter aims to bridge some of the gaps between the technical reality of implementing Dolby Atmos and the processes whereby the Atmos format is applied while attempting to understand the creative potential that makes Dolby Atmos an artistic medium rather than a technical playback system. We use Csikszentmihalyi's (1990) systems model to form a macro perspective that examines the domain and field within which new mixing approaches to Atmos sit. Using this framing, we position the mixing community as a domain of knowledge that interacts with the field of songwriters and audiences.

In 2022, it is now fair to state that Dolby Atmos has become the dominant spatialised audio format within the domain of record production. The inclusion of Atmos into the Logic Digital Audio Workstation (DAW) Apple Music, Tidal, and Amazon platforms represents a significant industry investment that has established Atmos as the largest spatial audio delivery system on the market. To better understand the format from a creative perspective, we offer an overview of how Atmos operates as a delivery system and how it currently interacts with various playback

DOI: 10.4324/9781003462101-3

systems. We also reflect on two interview sessions at Dolby headquarters in Soho with Myles Clarke. Finally, using a practice as a research method, we reconstruct a stereo mix of a song into a Dolby Atmos mix. We draw on the experience of the process and the tacit knowledge of the participants involved to gain insight into how this immersive format offers creative affordances in both music writing and music listening. The interaction of both areas offers insight into how new work can be created with spatialised audio in mind. For this creative research group, this is the first of a multi-part progressive study where we document our experiences as creative agents working with the Atmos format.

1.1 Participants

The group of participants involved in this experiment is established around our assemblage of technical, musical, and creative abilities. We engaged in practice as research to develop a bridge between past, present, and future practices in immersive music. Bruce Woolley joins the group with a wealth of historical legitimacy; his work with Trevor Horn (*Video Killed the Radio Star*) and Grace Jones (*Slave to the Rhythm*) defined an era in a time of technological and musical transition. Andy Visser arrives as an accomplished live musician and songwriter (Death in Vegas) who fulfils research, songwriting, and engineering roles in the group. Dr Dan Pratt is an established researcher and educator who brings expertise from his continuing experience as a practicing recording engineer and touring musician. Dr Andrew Bourbon, Subject Area Leader for Music Technology and Games at Huddersfield University, specialises in research and practice around immersive music technologies, specifically in Dolby Atmos.

2 THE SYSTEMS MODEL OF CREATIVITY

There is a creative aspect to recording practice that draws our participant group together, and rather than developing a technocratic approach to spatial mixing, we prefer to adopt Theberge's (2020) position that there is an "underlying musical logic that binds together both analog and digital recording technologies, and their associated practices, into something that is greater" (p. 85). Using this more musical approach of reimagining a recorded artefact into a new format, we exploit Csikszentmihalyi's (1990) systems model of creativity. The dynamic nature of the model allows us to form a framework to assist in understanding our creative interaction with the Dolby Atmos format. We take McIntyre's (2008) view that novel cultural creation is the result of an individual's interacting with the domain and field to generate new work. Such an interactive analysis of our work allows us to understand the broader history of ideas that inform our creative approach to mixing in an emerging format. Using a macro view to inform novel creation, we develop our approach to mixing in Atmos based on the assumption that creativity emerges "from a system containing the creative individual, the surrounding field of others working in the area" (Sawyer and DeZutter, 2009), and the domain, which represents established societies that have developed rules and practices around the production of new creative work (Csikszentmihalyi, 1988, 1990). When using a reflexive model such as this to assess creative work, it is important to understand that the system is not one way. It is a three-part model that interacts reflexively between different modes of creative production. Using this model as a lens into creative invention, we can see how individuals can interact with both the field and domain while also using their own history and acquired skills to influence both the culture and society that encompass their creative labor. This reflexive engagement with all parts of the systems model means that complex works can achieve cultural novelty in conversation with all aspects relating to rules and systems, invention and culture, along with individual history and tacit knowledge.

Csikszentmihalyi's systems model (1990) takes a macro view of how creation emerges out of a complex interaction of three areas that select, stimulate, transmit, and produce new creative output. The Systems Model allows us to better understand how novel material is produced through the dynamic interaction of this tripartite system. For example, a person can create music using a history of tacit knowledge collected from practices and rules that are established in the current working culture. Once the song is completed, it is then sent to the field so that the audience can evaluate and elevate the work before moving this completed work back to the domain to be absorbed into the cultural knowledge that feeds into new creations by individuals. However, the model is not restricted to circular movement; it can exchange between two areas, such as the field and domain, adjusting creative concepts and influencing the development of new practice. This investigation is useful because it examines the development of new Atmos mixing systems informed by the domain of mix practice and the societal importance of the individual practitioners. Through this form of evaluation, we can select and arrange according to Thompson's (2016) description that explains the system at work.

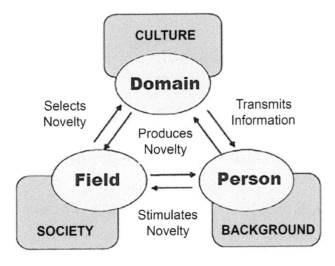

Figure 2.1 Csikszentmihalyi's 1990 systems model (McIntyre, 2011).

To select a suitable arrangement of ingredients from this body of knowledge and symbol system. This selection of ingredients is then presented
to the field, the social organization that recognises, uses and alters the
domain, to decide upon its creativity and inclusion into the domain.

(Thompson, 2016, p. 74)

2.1 Placing team members in the model

Both Woolley and Visser arrive with significant social capital from their
previous work in authoritative musical groups. They are the principal writers for the group Radio Science Orchestra, and they composed the song
Robots on Mars that we used to generate an Atmos mix. Woolley represents a nexus of change due to his influence as the first artist played on
MTV (*Video Killed the Radio Star*), as well as his genre defining work
with producer Trevor Horn, and artist Grace Jones (*Slave to the Rhythm*).
Visser brings a vast realm of experience to the table through his work as
a songwriter with Woolley and as a performer in the UK band Death in
Vegas. Bourbon and Pratt arrive with significant experience in the domain
of mixing and recording knowledge, which generates the rules and systems,
such as delivery formats and developing conventions around Atmos mixing. Once we have established a framework that defines the larger social
underpinnings of our work, we can then investigate how the interaction
of Csikszentmihalyi's tripartite system occurs using specific examples that
highlight the interactivity of domain and field that influence the creation
of new work. As such, we establish the roles of our group according to the
systems model (see Figure 2.2). This system allows us to better understand

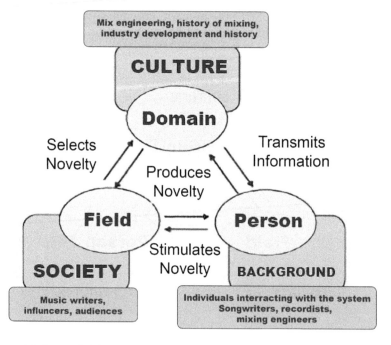

Figure 2.2 Expanded interpretation of Csikszentmihalyi's 1990 systems model.

our interactions as representatives of specific areas. For this model, we sit Woolley and Visser in the field of influencers and listeners; their role in this first part of our work is to listen and comment on the mixes that came through. Both Pratt and Bourbon operate from the emerging domain that is reinterpreting practices of recording and mixing for Atmos creation.

2.2 Specific interactivity of domain and field

After examining the broader systems model and developing classifications for the participants in this experiment, it is helpful to reduce the model and evaluate specific events. Thinking of the larger context of the systems model of creativity, it is possible to miss the significant interactions that create interesting outcomes and novel musical production. During the creative process, there are often moments that highlight the interplay between two or more sections of the systems model. Considering that the individual is always explicitly present during the creative process, it is necessary to observe the more implicit and abstract areas of the domain and the field. If we shrink our analysis down to specific events, it allows us to focus on one point and interpret how the interplay of the systems model plays out through an event. For example, when an evaluation mix is given to a songwriter, the songwriters' position in the field allows them to absorb, analyse, and give feedback to the domain with information that influences the development of new knowledge, thus creating a conversation between the field and domain. Figure 2.3 is a model that explains the focus of the domain and the field into a specific event, which then feeds back into the wider domain.

3 THE EMERGING DOMAIN OF SPATIAL AUDIO

The next section documents the systems and rules that are forming around the emerging art form of spatial audio mixing. Although spatial audio has been around for some time now, the dominance of Atmos has begun to shape the direction of spatial mixing. To better understand how Dolby has become a dominant form of spatial mixing, both Visser and Pratt conducted interviews with Myles Clarke at Dolby headquarters in Soho London. During these discussions, we were offered insight into the recruitment of mixing engineers into the Dolby platform to feed Dolby's dominance

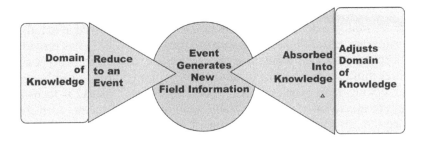

Figure 2.3 Reducing the systems model to a field event, then reabsorbing into the domain.

of the domain, and we were given demonstrations as to the effectiveness of listening to music and mixing music for Atmos systems. We frame this area of mixing engineering as an *emerging domain*, and we posit that it is populated with creatives that have a history of stereo mix engineering. This emerging domain concept was highlighted during Visser and Pratt's interview with Myles Clarke at Dolby headquarters in Soho, London, in which Clarke is still considering his approach to Atmos mixing despite having significant experience in the field as a senior music engineer at Dolby:

> There is this push of should you be mixing in Atmos first? We have got to a point where people are now mixing from the stereo stems out to Atmos. Should you be mixing, or creating, and actually, this is the thing that is slightly contrary for me is that I don't know how I feel about it.
>
> (Clarke, Dolby Interview, February 21, 2022)

To frame Atmos mixing in the domain, we think of this larger engineering pool as a sensemaking group. Weick's (1995) sensemaking properties of retrospective analysis, mapping, and plausibility are useful for understanding how rules and systems for mix practices are emerging into a new domain of Dolby Atmos mixing. Engineers use past practice to inform the future approaches using a "retrospective-oriented understanding" (Carter and Colville, 2003, p. 2) of contextual rules, symbols, and systems from the current domain of mix practice. With this understanding, we take this schema and socially decode it using a mapping process, where we develop new rules and symbols for Atmos mixing as a new process. We then use Weick's (1995) concept of plausibility to experiment with possibilities based on retrospective practice to develop emerging rules for the new domain of Dolby Atmos mixing. It is important to stress that, as an emerging practice, mix engineers are still figuring out how to retrofit stereo mixes into Dolby Atmos mixes in new and interesting ways. As a result, plausibility allows the engineering community to suggest possible ideas and experiment with putting them into practice. This experimentation is beginning to set new contextual boundaries that bracket our thinking and guide future mix decision-making.

3.1 Immersion and spatial audio

There are multiple definitions of immersion that are discussed at length in contemporary research on immersive mediums. Lee (2022) has provided a conceptual model for immersive experience in extended reality that also explores multiple dimensions of immersion. Although this research paper is not looking at an extended reality environment and instead is focussed on a pure music-based scenario, there are a number of factors identified by Lee that also are extremely pertinent in this research. Lee identifies the presence of an immersive system and an immersive experience. In this case, the immersive system is defined as the playback system through which the listener perceives the mixed experience, and the immersive experience is then a higher-level concept that requires a mental or physical involvement with a task or activity, in this case, engaging with the playback of the mix as received by the field as identified in the systems model.

In the case of *Robots from Mars* Bourbon is provided with the stems rather than the stereo mix and is then given the opportunity to create a spatial mix to be presented to the other participants based entirely on the mixer reaction to the provided stems. The playback system will feature either a 360-degree binaural environment or be reproduced by speakers that both sit around and above the listener and, as such, represent an immersive system. The spatial audio mix will then provide an immersive experience by attempting to create listener involvement in the song. The participants then engage in feedback, resulting in further revisions until a final product is authored for playback in a concert environment.

3.2 Playback systems definitions and boundaries

For our audience to receive the immersive experience intended by the team, it is important that audience members in the field can perceive sound coming from multiple positions to perceive movement and depth beyond the affordances of traditional stereo playback. Historically, single-plane multichannel speaker systems have provided this, with music encoded for the specific playback system in a channel-based format, either as discreet channels or through a system-specific encoding. For contemporary music playback, Dolby Atmos provides the system used to drive the playback system that is heard by the audience. Unlike channel-based systems where one mixed audio stream is provided for each speaker, Atmos instead provides the engineer with the ability to create objects, with sounds directly routed to those objects. These objects are then positioned in 3-dimensional space, with the Dolby renderer then reproducing the sound using the available speakers. This means that, unlike traditional surround formats, the number of speakers can vary from venue to venue, with the renderer providing optimised playback for whatever system to which it is connected. Though 7.1.4 is arguably the most common speaker arrangement for mixing Dolby Atmos, the format itself can be seen as being speaker agnostic, meaning that the renderer will create the best possible playback based on the speakers that it has access to. Such a technological change alters the mixing domain and redefines the understanding of translation and process for mix engineers.

In addition to speaker-based playback, it is also possible to render for binaural playback on headphones. The Dolby Atmos renderer can take Atmos mixes and render a binaural image that immerses the listener. Within the renderer itself, there is an ability to place a spatial distance from the listener onto each individual object, with the option to render as near, mid, far, and off. In the 'off' setting, there is no externalisation, and the sound is effectively rendered in the head of the listener as it is on traditional stereo headphone playback systems. Near, mid, and far see the sound rendered progressively further away, with the mid setting representative of a loudspeaker placed 1.5 m from the listener. There are a number of considerations in the translation of this binaural render and loudspeaker playback. Speaker systems that afford different levels of resolution at height might generate the illusion of height by bouncing audio off boundaries or may play back via a single-plane audio system. The space in which the speakers are playing also has a significant impact on the playback system. As such, it arguably requires engineers to look at the overall immersive experience rather than relying on translation accuracy to create the immersive experience. When rendered for binaural playback, there are also significant factors that influence translation. The final playback system may see the listener hearing a mix featuring the discussed distance metadata or may hear a render that does not use this data, instead creating playback based on virtual speakers in a virtual space such as that employed by Apple Spatial Audio. Different headphones, head-related transfer function variance, and the space in which headphone listening takes place can all significantly influence perception. These variants in perception in both speaker and headphone-based playback all lead to the engineer, in his case, focusing on 'bigger picture' aspects in the mix, which will be briefly highlighted in section 4.

In the playback for our demonstration mix, the audience was seated in a dome of speakers in a large performance space, which provides quite a different set of characteristics to a small studio or headphone-based system. As such, our mixing decisions were guided by translatability to the Stockholm Royal College of Music Sound Dome. The significant size of the system meant large time differences between the front and back of the system, as well as potentially large gaps between speakers, creating challenges in maintaining a coherent image, creating smooth movement, and around arrival times in transients depending on where you sat in the audience. These are always factors in considering playback of spatial music which are exacerbated in large spaces with a limited number of discreet channels into which you are rendering object-based audio.

3.3 Software 2

The Atmos renderer used to translate the immersive Atmos mix into a discreet speaker system receives audio objects from a DAW and the metadata then provides information as to where that object is to be rendered in the immersive audio field at any point in time. Beds are also provided, which, rather than being objects to be rendered, have already been mixed as a discreet 7.1.2 channel-based audio stream. In this case, the mix was undertaken using Apple Logic Pro and the built-in Atmos renderer rather than the standalone Dolby renderer. Logic provides a single 7.1.2 bed that all beds are effectively summed into, plus an additional 118 inputs as objects, resulting in 128 potential inputs into the renderer. In this case, there was a combination of objects, with some sounds provided to the renderer as objects with other objects representing virtual speakers that sounds could be bussed into. In these cases, the Atmos panner is being used more like a traditional diffusion console as found in electroacoustic music playback, offering extra control to the engineer in regard to providing dimension to the sound reproduction. This approach will also become more important in the future when the group looks to move from playback of recorded material to live performance, where latency makes using object-based audio impractical. This hybrid of channel-based and object-based audio approaches provides a unique combination of tools that afford significant control over the presentation of immersive mixes on multiple systems and provide helpful solutions in maximising translation between formats for audiences.

It is also important to note that engineers working in Atmos can remain in the DAW they are used to working in for production, recording, and mixing. A number of contemporary DAWs provide integrated Atmos mixing capable of generating an Atmos master file and can also communicate with a standalone Dolby Atmos Renderer using the Dolby Audio Bridge. This allows the renderer to receive the objects and metadata while hosted either on the same machine as the DAW or on a separate machine, which only has to focus on the rendering process. This creates increased reliability, as well as providing extended features within the software. The availability of native Atmos mixing within the DAW has allowed mixers at all levels to access the technology, removing barriers to mixing that had previously existed when working in complex surround formats. In addition to this, and perhaps even more importantly, the ability to monitor the output on headphones without the need for specialist equipment or configuration opens up this environment to creatives for exploitation and provides easy access to audiences to engage in immersive music experiences.

Once the mix is completed, the engineer must render an Audio Definition Model (ADM) master file, which contains up to 128 audio objects and all of the metadata required to define how that object is to be reproduced by the Atmos renderer in the determined speaker array performance space.

3.4 Hardware-translation

Though the playback system for this specific event was known and mix decisions made considering the properties of the space and the playback system, the mix was also provided to the band and other team members as a binaural render to be played back on headphones. It can be expected that the majority of listeners to any commercial release of the track will be listening via headphones or using a speaker playback system such as those found in sound bars, televisions, and contemporary laptops, which use an array of speakers, processing or reflecting audio from surfaces in a space to create the immersive sound field. The ability to deliver immersive music, that is to say, music that is designed to create a heightened sense of cognitive immersion by embracing the affordances of an immersive playback system into the homes of listeners, has become a driving factor in the choice of Atmos as the environment in which mixes are captured. This variety of systems means that new rules established by the emerging domain of Atmos mixing must contend with multiple systems that operate within different sonic boundaries that present the audio in vastly different ways.

4 RECONSTRUCTING A MIX

Using a constructionist approach, it is our intent to participate in the mixing, listening, remixing, and presenting of the final Dolby Atmos mix of *Robots on Mars*. We take Thompson's (2019) position that to understand processes, it is necessary to immerse in the process and experience it. However, as earlier described, we do not approach this as novice creators, and we bring to bear a wealth of knowledge in both music creation and spatial audio mixing.

> The social skills and knowledge associated with the domain of record production are acquired almost entirely informally through experience and immersion into the environment of the recording studio.
>
> (Thompson, 2019, p. 83)

Using the information gathered during interviews with Myles Clarke, we adopted the position that there is no clear way to begin a mix from either the Atmos perspective or the stereo perspective. Fortunately, both Woolley and Visser already had access to a set of multitracks that had already been mixed by Steve Dub (Chemical Brothers). To remove the question of whether we should begin with a stereo mix or an Atmos mix, we gave the multitrack files to Bourbon, but he did not receive access to the stereo mix until he completed the Atmos mix, including listening sessions where Visser and Woolley offered feedback and mix notes to Bourbon's work. The mixing sessions were mediated by Pratt, who also organised Atmos playback systems for listening sessions with Woolley and Visser, along with other members of Radio Science Orchestra.

In order to create an enhanced immersive experience, multiple processing approaches were undertaken. The main aim of the processing undertaken was to enhance characteristics of specific elements in the mix through manipulating size, static position, and movement and to undertake gestural enhancement. The nature of the change would be in response to the characteristics of particular elements in the mix. Drums, for example, provide a solid backbeat that drives the song forward, and the aim was to create a sense of engagement in the listener by creating a single wall of drums at the front of the image. To create a heightened sense of involvement, cascading reverbs were employed, creating a sense of reaction to the gesture of the drums hitting by having the reverb pass across the listener. The drums do not audibly move, but there is a sense of the energy of the drums, creating a wave of consequence through the listener. There are also multiple synth parts that have natural movement in the stereo sound field. Delay processing became increasingly important, allowing sounds to continue to have a musical impact but drift into the distance or move around the listener in response to the narrative and as a counterpoint to other elements. In a traditional stereo mix, finding space for these sounds to continue would be difficult; however, with the increased potential provided by spatial audio, it is possible to add extra layers of depth and musicality and to reinforce musical gestures in support of the song narrative and staging.

Once the mix was completed and agreed upon, we took a work in progress to present at the 2022 Innovation in Music Conference in Stockholm, Sweden.

4.1 Background discovery

The primary goal of this research was to produce and share an immersive audio mix of a music track with a large audience, listening in a multi-speaker playback environment. While the longer-term aims of the project include composing and mixing in Atmos from song inception, in this case, the track *Robots on Mars* already existed as a stereo-mixed composition. The writers, Visser and Woolley, spent some time initially with the producer, Pratt, understanding the limits and possibilities afforded in moving from a stereo to an immersive format. Work was undertaken, listening at Dolby Atmos Soho Studios in London with engineer Myles Clarke to uncover some of the idiosyncrasies of such a production process. Clarke demonstrated the techniques involved in moving the mix from stereo to Atmos. After discussion at Dolby, Visser and Wooley prepared stems for Bourbon, and the decision was taken not to let Bourbon hear the stereo mix so that he could develop an Atmos mix unencumbered by preconceptions. Immersive mixing was then undertaken by Andrew Bourbon, working remotely from the rest of the team in Huddersfield. The final Atmos mix was played back at the Innovation in Music conference in Stockholm, Sweden (2022) on an immersive audio rig, capable of being fully configured for Dolby Atmos playback to an audience of music technology experts, in the Royal College of Music Sound Dome.

5 DISCUSSION (OUTPUT/DISCOVERY)

5.1 The output

Before the presentation in Stockholm, there were several mix listening sessions at Dolby and at the University of West London's new Atmos rooms. Whilst entirely subjective at this point, some reactions were sought in relation to listening to the immersive Atmos mix of *Robots on Mars*. In the Dolby Atmos session at Soho House, London, both Visser and Woolley commented on the first iteration of the mix. Woolley's initial reaction was that he was so overwhelmed by the movement of the sounds and the spatial immersiveness the mix imparted that he didn't have time to interpret what he was hearing while the experience washed over him. At this point, we introduce the concept that the library of the mind has not yet been established for the reception of spatial mixes, and listeners need more time to adjust to hearing Atmos mixes. Another notable reaction was one of excitement by the possibilities of the format, having heard a reimagined version of the song. This form of listener reaction has been a recurrent theme in understanding the way an Atmos mix is first experienced and will be further discussed in the next section.

Reactions to the overwhelming nature of spatial audio give the mix engineers that represent the domain crucial information as to how the mix is being received by the field and feeds back into the writing after becoming absorbed into the domain of knowledge. Pratt's response to the first mix noted that the immersive experience was more emotionally driven and that it directed the music through movement and energy rather than the focussed punch of the stereo mix. However, after several listens to the Atmos mix, it was notable that the field started offering feedback that was more musical and less technical in nature. Suggestions such as louder vocals, more emotive movement, and more authoritative bass were put forward for mix revisions. As such, this knowledge informs a more musical and emotive set of motives for the domain. These driving factors should be applied when writing and creating with spatial audio as the intended medium rather than the traditional stereo format. This example reinforces the model in Figure 2.3 and concurs with McIntyre's (2008) interpretation that the interaction of field and domain generates novel creative work.

Ad hoc feedback after the Stockholm conference presentation of the Atmos rendering of *Robots on Mars* was framed in more technical terms. This was likely due to the audience for this demonstration being more familiar with spatialised audio. However, there was also a general response among polled audience members that the scale and movement of the mix on the Stockholm Sound Dome was significant in terms of both immersion and enjoyment. All this feedback from the field has allowed the research team to evaluate the audience's reaction and feed this into future projects. This information is valuable as the research group plans the next phase of writing new material while responding to the audience feedback from this first iteration of our research. This information concurs with Clarke's assertion that we need to learn how to listen to spatial audio:

Andy Visser: I noticed on all the headphone playback, on all the stuff, the Atmos stuff that I've been listening to recently, it's spatialised. You don't know where the guitar is, but you feel like everything is about.
Myles Clarke: That's what it should be. I think the idea that it's very localized is like, "Oh what's that?"
Andy Visser: That's definitely not what's going on.
Myles Clarke: I think as time goes on we'll learn how to listen.
(Clarke, Dolby Interview, February 21, 2022)

5.2 Discoveries

Two key findings arose from the early investigative sessions at Dolby Soho studios, the university playback systems, and from the subsequent playback performance to a large audience at the Innovation in Music conference in Stockholm. First, the nature of composition for an immersive format evolves for the writers because of their interaction with an audience and developing a deeper understanding of the possibilities afforded by spatial audio systems. Second, the nature of the reception of an immersively rendered composition also alters from the point of view of the audience. In terms of audience perception, regarding listening to immersive audio, the library of the mind is not yet established. In other words, most audiences have not yet had enough exposure to immersive music to make sense of or categorise it in relation to the consumption of immersive music. This is significant, as any emerging format must compete with the predominant firmly established stereo listening paradigm. It is also interesting to note that the majority of commercial popular music atmos mixes tend to focus on mixes that are best described as enhanced stereo, with the core stereo mix very much maintained with reverbs, pads, and contrapuntal elements embracing the immersive space. These are not upmixes built from the stereo but deliberate mixes that are still true to the original stereo. Limitations in binaural rendering technology also tend to lead to more consistent results from mixes that fall into this expanded stereo, and it will be interesting to see how mix practice develops as the playback formats improve and immersive music becomes more established in the public domain.

In terms of composition and production, the immersive Atmos audio format further blurs the already indistinct boundaries between composition, recording, mixing, and sound diffusion. In a traditional stereo-track writing process, the writers might start with a bass line or a guitar or keyboard riff. This instrument sound would automatically exist in a stereoscopic space, positionally represented by azimuth, but not elevation information. However, in the new immersive audio paradigm, the question of instrument placement in three-dimensional space is altered. If the instrument is positioned in a front-facing format for an immersed audience, it stands a chance of being accepted, partly out of familiarity but partly because it can still be cognitively processed as a familiar mono or stereo front-facing sound. However, if the instrument were placed behind and below the immersed audience, the audiences' established listening patterns would likely not recognise this instrument sound as positionally familiar, nor would it be processed as easily due to human head-related transfer and other psychoacoustic restrictions. In other words, composers and writers cannot continue to assume that the stereo compositional paradigm will be as useful in an immersive audio compositional process. This information was reinforced during the playback at Stockholm due to a translation system error that rotated the positioning of the mix. In the intended mix, vocals were placed front and centre with backing vocals coming from the rear left and right of the immersive image, the rotation moved the main vocals about 30 degrees to the left, and the backing vocals moved a similar amount, which tilted the attention slightly to the left. The movement of the instrumental parts was less obvious due to their unusual, synthesised timbre. But vocals were more obvious due to the historical convention that these elements come from the front and centre of a stereo mix. The nature of the immersive format meant that this rotation of image did not affect the positioning of elements as much as we would have predicted; it just changed the immersion, and since the audience was hearing this for the first time, there was no reference point for the audience, and the mix was evenly spread throughout the system. Such an interesting outcome has led us to suppose that we can be more adventurous with our immersion and

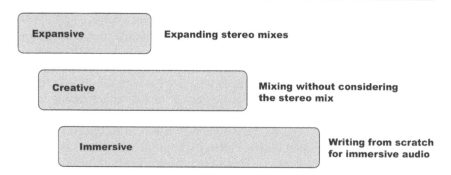

Figure 2.4 The expansion of the immersive mix (Bourbon et al., 2023).

movement through writing and creative mixing. This coincides with some of the interview data from (Clarke, Dolby Interview, 2022), who explained that mix engineers become more adventurous as they spend more time in the format. The question becomes, how do you get to a fully immersive approach, as illustrated by Clarke:

> Do you go from 0 to 100, or do you go 0 to 20, and then to 30, and settle at 50? Then you say, that is how I do Atmos, and that is what sounds good to most people.
> (Clarke, Dolby Interview, March 7, 2022)

The experiences with the initial Atmos mix of *Robots on Mars* have led us to contemplate different levels of emissivity that concur with Clarke's evaluation from our Soho interviews. The following is a model that poses different levels of immersion from expanded stereo through to new interpretations that completely discard stereoscopic imaging. This model demonstrates our absorption and members of the domain experimenting with plausible possibilities extrapolated from retrospectively driven information maps (Weick, 1995).

5.3 Next steps

In our initial step towards better understanding the creative affordances of Atmos playback, we have investigated the creative expansion of a spatialised mix. Deliberately withholding the stereo mix from Bourbon meant that he was unconstrained by the compositional and positional elements of the stereo front-facing mix. The consequent presentations to the field generated experiences that were reported back as immersive and exciting. Having explored creative approaches to expansive mixes, the next logical step is to investigate how writing from scratch alters the creative perception of our work. It will also be necessary to investigate how this method fits into the systems model of creativity.

Beyond the processes of writing and composing in an immersive audio format, there are further aspects to be considered around live performance and playback within an immersive audio context. While the technology already exists for immersive performance, there are more subtle questions to be answered concerning the live artists' performance experiences and expectations. Traditionally, stage-based monitor sound for musicians usually consists of mono or stereo speaker, or in-ear, sources that reasonably reflect the original stereo music composition both in terms of instrument placement and instrument timing. This paradigm breaks if it is applied directly to immersive 3D audio on stage. How is it possible to represent to a live performer onstage the position of a spatialised instrument (e.g., keyboard riff) that makes sense to the performer in real-time? If the decision is made to represent these 3D positioned sounds as a down-mixed stereo or mono playback, then to what extent does that affect the player's relationship to the music being played and the interactions with other members of the group on stage, and how does this function as a convincing performance?

REFERENCES

Battleson, D.A., 2013. *Sensemaking in Enterprise Resource Planning Project Deescalation: An Empirical Study*. Georgia State University.

Carter, M. and Colville, I. (2003) 'On Leading, Learning and Organizational Change: A Sensemaking Perspective', *Organizational Learning and Knowledge, 5th International Conference*, pp. 1–20.

Csikszentmihalyi, M. (1988) 'The Systems Model of Creativity', in *The Nature of Creativity*, pp. 325–339. doi: 10.1007/978-94-017-9085-7.

Csikszentmihalyi, M. (1990) *Flow: The Psychology of Optimal Experience*. 1st Ed. New York: Harper and Row.

Csikszentmihalyi, M. (2015). *The systems model of creativity: The collected works of Mihaly Csikszentmihalyi*. Springer.

Lee, H. (2020, September 13) *A Conceptual Model of Immersive Experience in Extended Reality*. https://doi.org/10.31234/osf.io/sefkh.

McIntyre, P. (2008) 'The Systems Model of Creativity: Analysing the Distribution of Power in the Studio', *Journal on the Art of Record Production*, (3), pp. 98–99.

McIntyre, P. (2011) 'Rethinking the Creative Process: The Systems Model of Creativity Applied to Popular Songwriting', *Journal of Music, Technology and Education*, 4(1), pp. 77–90.

McIntyre, P. (2015) 'Tradition and Innovation in Creative Studio Practice: The Use of Older Gear, Processes and Ideas in Conjunction with Digital Technologies', *Journal on the Art of Record Production*, 9, pp. 1–12.

Sawyer, R. K. and DeZutter, S. (2009) 'Distributed Creativity: How Collective Creations Emerge from Collaboration', *Psychology of Aesthetics, Creativity, and the Arts*, 3(2), pp. 81–92.

Theberge, P. (2020) 'Transitions: The History of Recording Technology from 1970 to the Present', in Bourbon, A. and Zagorski-Thomas, S. (eds), The Bloomsbury Handbook of Music Production. London: Bloomsbury.

Thompson, P. A. and Lashua, B. D. (2016). Producing music, producing myth? Creativity in recording studios. *Iaspm@ journal*, 6(2), pp. 70–90.

Thompson, P. (2016) 'Scalability of the Creative System in the Recording Studio', in *The Creative System in Action: Understanding Cultural Production and Practice*, pp. 74–86.

Thompson, P. (2019) *Creativity in the Recording Studio, Creativity in the Recording Studio*. doi: 10.1007/978-3-030-01650-0.

Thompson, P. and Lashua, B. (2014). 'Getting it on record: Issues and strategies for ethnographic practice in recording studios'. *Journal of Contemporary Ethnography*, 43(6), pp. 746–769.

Weick, K. E. (1995) *Sensemaking in Organizations*. Thousand Oaks: Sage Publications.

Zagorski-Thomas, S. (2014). *The musicology of record production*. Cambridge University Press..

Zagorski-Thomas, S. (2015). Developing the formal structures of artistic practice-as-research. *New Vistas*, 1(2), pp. 28–32.

3

Introducing the Dolby Atmos hyper-near field Tiny Studio

Paul Novotny

1 INTRODUCTION

If you are considering the expansion of a small stereo or 5.1 music produc-tion room to 7.1.4 Dolby Atmos, this chapter may interest you. Although this author is not a professional control room designer, in the spring of 2020 he began research that aimed to define a small Atmos studio – a single operator 7.1.4 Hyper Near-Field Tiny Studio (HN-FTS) built for the purpose of audio mixing and mastering with reliable transference to main-stream professional and consumer-level playback systems. By the spring of 2022, the creation of 3-dimensional (3D) immersive music began, and on December 9, 2022, this author released his inaugural Atmos album, *Summertime in Leith*, on which he played upright bass with Oscar Peterson protégé Robi Botos on piano. This release to digital streaming providers (DSPs) via The Orchard (distributor) stands as the first empirical evidence to indicate that successful mix/master transference from this HN-FTS to the marketplace is achievable.

In the spring of 2022, less than 200 Dolby Atmos music studios existed globally, and the HN-FTS category was undocumented. This article shares research and experience that form a novel philosophy and benchmark for the HN-FTS control room size. A HN-FTS is intended for indepen-dent professional and semi-professional music creators, institutions, and commercial studios with a constrained space and budget. It utilizes appli-cable Dolby guidelines (Dolby, 2021b) and control room design theory and reaches beyond to exemplify how socio-economic Tiny Home phi-losophies of small-scale, large-scope, and buy-local can encourage further innovation. Supporting research is gathered from diverse sources to con-vey essential understandings for a premium Atmos 7.1.4 control room that is approximately 50% smaller (24 m³) than Dolby's minimum Near-Field guideline of >50 m³. Small spaces are acoustically problematic, while paradoxically, mainstream Atmos playback in the acoustically reverb-less and high noise criterion automotive cabin is rapidly oncoming [Lucid, Mercedes Benz, Volvo]. As such, this author argues that the low reverb time (RT_{60}) of an HN-FTS is a valuable link to the hyper-small (8.5 m³ to 12 m³) electric vehicle cabin playback space.

DOI: 10.4324/9781003462101-4

This HN-FTS philosophy is distinguished by premium sound quality, thrifty economics, and a single meticulously tuned mixing position. The benchmark design utilizes Dolby's Audio Room Design Tool (DARDT) to formulate criteria for music room function, geometry, speaker layout, amplifier wattage, sound pressure level (SPL), reverb time (RT_{60}), and noise criterion (NC25). Initially, the inspiration for an HN-FTS came from the multichannel, full-range small speaker design philosophy (Fielder, 2003; Sijen, 2008) that was pioneered at Audio Design Labs Blue Sky Studio Monitors and extensively utilized at Skywalker Sound, a division of Lucasfilm. This author has over 15 years of experience working with Blue Sky speakers in three Hyper Near-Field 5.1 control rooms that provided reliable transference to broadcasters, streaming services, and Far-Field cinematic theatres. This HN-FTS philosophy presents an integrated path for small control room expansion to 7.1.4 Dolby Atmos, and the project's research methodology relies on a blending of academic texts, specialist advisement, and practical experimentation, all intended for subjective interpretation and application in the creative domain of music and audio production. Texts from Philip Newell, Dr. Floyd Toole, Alton Everest, Kenneth Pohlmann, the AES-E-Library, Sound on Sound magazine, and Dolby Professional Support contribute essential science, while hands-on knowledge is gleaned from online video interviews with the most experienced Atmos practitioners. Contemporaneous discussions located in the Metaversity of Facebook groups (Atmos Music Mixing Professionals and Atmos Post Mixing Professionals) are also referenced. The research is synthesized to form a durable philosophy that encourages the independent designing and building of a Hyper Near-Field 7.1.4 Atmos control room, which this author modestly calls Tiny Studio, a reference to the global Tiny Home movement (Carrizosa, 2021).

1.1 Tiny studio first steps

The Dolby Home Entertainment Studio Certification Guide (available from Dolby) provides foundational guidance for Atmos installations, but it generally describes larger Near-, Mid-, and Far-Field room sizes – specifically, small Atmos rooms (below 50 m³) are not described or encouraged. This author's next step was to look outside of Dolby's guidelines for Tiny Studio solutions, only to discover Philip Newell's sobering observation:

> The majority of people working in modern music recording studios have not had the necessary formal education in mathematics, acoustics, and electronics to make the standard textbooks appear as anything more than cold print, and direct contact with specialists is out of reach for most people.
>
> (Newell, 2017, p. xxviii)

This musician and author did not find Newell's book *Recording Studio Design* to be "cold print." It provided cogent information about the studio/control room system and its integration with the human hearing system.

Floyd E. Toole's book, *Sound Reproduction: The Acoustics and Psycho-acoustics of Loudspeakers and Rooms*, also yielded significant Tiny Studio determinants:

> ". . . rooms have a massive influence on what we hear at low frequencies"; ". . . there are no 'ideal' dimensions for rooms"; "Listeners have the ability to adapt to many aspects of room acoustics."
>
> (Toole, 2018, p. 43)

Innately, humans do not all hear the same because each person's pinnae (outer ears) are unique. Newel supports this fact by arguing that hard objective science and ephemeral art must co-exist in the world of sound recording (Newell, 2017).

Falling outside of the Dolby guideline, a Tiny Studio relies on the assembler's personal psychoacoustic perception to achieve its sweetest sound while utilizing science to avoid pitfalls. As will be shown, this Tiny Studio can meet many of the Dolby guidelines, but the biggest acoustic challenge is first, second, and third order, low-frequency resonances called standing waves. Guided by DARDT, the Tiny Studio makes standing waves less problematic by hyper-focusing its correlated speaker system toward a single, tuned mix-position. When seasoned audio engineers learn the characteristics of a control room, psychoacoustic assessment of translational sonic relationships is standard practice, and they often combine the use of mastering-grade reference headphones with a finely tuned speaker system to average their results for reliable playback across external speaker systems in the field. A Tiny Studio workflow also utilizes mastering-grade headphones and a tuned speaker layout but adds occasional "field trips" to listed Dolby Atmos rooms to ensure reliable crafting of translatable Atmos mixes and masters (Dolby 2023).

1.2 Why is a Tiny Studio necessary?

A Tiny Studio provides the necessary acoustic decorrelation and aural crossfeed to generate an out-of-head (external) listening experience but with direct speaker sound *hyper near* (1.2 m) to the mix-position. The economic advantages of a Tiny Studio are compelling, and they complement the affordable Atmos creator tools that are currently provided in digital audio workstations (DAWS) – Logic Pro, Pro Tools Ultimate, Nuendo, Pyramix, Ableton, and Davinci Resolve (Dolby, 2021d).

1.3 Psychoacoustics, speaker, and headphone workflows

All audio work in 360° sound benefits from the practitioner understanding human psychoacoustic perception, auditory science, and physics. For example, when recording the native sound radiation of musical instruments, "to ensure that the interaural signal differences are captured, at least one microphone [placed] every 0.15 m is necessary, which roughly corresponds to the distance of a listener's ears" (Zeimer and Bader, 2017).

Furthermore, spatial hearing relies on interaural time difference (ITD), Interaural level difference (ILD), and Head Related Transfer Function (HRTF) (Rothermich, 2021, 2022). "HRTF involves frequency dependant interaural time differentiation that is achieved with pinna filtering" (Thomas, 2020a), but headphones can facilitate a psychoacoustic perception of Atmos by synthesizing these spatial cues.

Dolby content creation specialist Margaret (Maggie) Tobin has developed the best practices for mixing in Atmos on headphones (Tobin, 2021), and her master's thesis investigates Atmos headphone-to-speaker translation. She works on a laptop with Sennheiser HD 600 s and earbuds. She argues that hybrid headphone/speaker system monitoring works, but "consumer headphones can be a bit bass heavy" and she warns, "low frequencies and the LFE channel can be difficult to judge" – because, in a 5.1 to 2.0 Dolby rendered downmix "The LFE channel is ignored" (Rothermich, pg. 95). Dolby Atmos supports autonomous headphone selection. Apple uses a proprietary playback renderer for unique binaural spatialization (with head tracking) when heard through AirPods. Some of the most experienced Atmos music mix engineers (Andrew Scheps, Greg Penny, Steve Genewick, Dave Way, and Fab Dupont) (Sheps, 2019) agree that you can only get about 85% of the way towards a satisfactory Atmos mix using headphones. In 2021 *Mix with the Masters* interview, Steve Genewick (eminent Atmos mixing engineer since July 2017, Capitol Studios) says, "it's not unusual for us to start [Atmos] mixes in binaural" (Genewick, 2021). This author's Tiny Studio praxis also utilizes mastering-grade headphones and involves a binaural translator called Virtuoso – developed by the Applied Psychoacoustics Lab (APL) team at the University of Huddersfield, UK.

1.4 Atmos economics

Building a Near-Field commercial Dolby Atmos control room is very expensive and, as reported by practitioners in the *Mix with the Masters* interview, Atmos mixing often returns minimal economic compensation because record labels are frugal, but they realize that Atmos music mixes will future-proof their catalog. The Tiny Studio philosophy and benchmark respond to this economic dilemma by providing music creators with a more affordable control room investment when compared to premium Far-, Mid-, and Near-Field Atmos rooms. See section 4, Economic Comparison, Figures 3.8 and 3.9.

1.5 Audio history, speaker location, and format evolution

Atmos stands on the shoulders of late nineteenth-century monaural sound reproduction, Blumlein patented binaural stereo sound (Fox, 1982), and 5.1 surround sound pioneered by Walter Murch in 1979 on Dolby 70 mm film for the movie *Apocalypse Now* (Ondaatje, 2002). Atmos expands the 5.1 speaker layout to add height – 5.1.2-, 7.1.4-, 9.1.6-, up to 64 speakers for cinema, and 22 speakers for music. Audio tracks can be assigned to a channel-bed or 128 audio-objects that utilize spatial location metadata which is rendered as spatial code elements/clusters to reduce data size during streaming playback (Rothermich, 2021; Nair, 2022). Objects can be monaural or stereo, and Blumlein's binaural stereo format is used for headphone playback. Atmos speaker systems are located on two planes, and the subwoofer is placed on the floor. The ear-level speakers (approximately 1.2 m above the floor) are positioned on the standard mid-plane, and the top height-plane speakers must be correctly angled and hung safely from the ceiling. The Atmos format is evolving rapidly with a community made up of pioneers who have been creating music in Atmos since 2017. In 2012, cinematic Atmos was first used in the Pixar film *Brave*, and in 2019, Amazon HD+ and Tidal introduced Atmos music on their respective streaming platforms (Dolby, 2020b).

1.6 Atmos, basic theory, and operation

7.1.4 Dolby Atmos uses 12 channels of audio. Their accumulative energy is expressed as a K-weighted, full-scale loudness measurement (LKFS). An Atmos renderer (software or hardware) does this by folding down all channels and objects into a 5.1 configuration for measurement of total loudness, targeting −18 LKFS (integrated) with a maximum peak of −1 dB to provide 17 dB of true peak dynamic range. Music mixers routinely create spatial decorrelation by cascading horizontally panned stereo reverbs. Binaural playback rendering via either Dolby Atmos or Apple Spatial Audio renderers introduces virtual binaural spatiality in positions of close, near, and far to simulate the psychoacoustic signals needed for out-of-head interaural audio immersion when listening on stereo headphones.

Atmos affords different workflows for film/TV audio post-production and music production (Dolby, 2021c). The workflow type and stage of work – pre-mix, mix, or master – to be done affects the control room design, as is exemplified by Steve Genewick's COVID-19 "guerrilla Atmos music installation" in his living room (Genewick, 2021). He used only two top-height speakers but claimed that it allowed him to create mix basics for music. In addition, he took "field trips" to other Dolby Atmos control rooms for quality assurance. Dolby strongly encourages this practice by providing a global listing of approved studios (Dolby, 2023).

1.7 A, B, and QC chains

The A and B chain and what this author calls the QC (quality control) chain make up the primary system chains for an Atmos studio. Atmos relies on a renderer, which the DAW connects to through 128 channels of input/output (i/o). The A chain involves everything used before the renderer – computer hardware and software. The B chain involves everything used after the renderer – audio interface, speaker controller, room tuning hardware/software, physical absorption, diffusion, and speakers. The QC chain is used to analyze commercially released Atmos mixes through the discrete Atmos speaker playback system or headphones. Typically, it involves an audio-visual receiver (AVR), Arvus H2–4D

Figure 3.1 Custom switch box, manufactured by Warren Beck, Toronto, Canada.

decoder, Apple TV, or a Blu-Ray player. A recent breakthrough saw macOS Monterey (12.4) provide discrete channel Atmos monitoring via 16 channels of core audio. This discovery was introduced to the Dolby Atmos Post Mix Professional Facebook group in April 2022 by David Stagle and was tested by several group practitioners. It works with Apple Music and Apple TV, and instructions are published on pro-tools-expert. com (Stagle, 2022). This thrifty Tiny Studio innovates QC chain hardware with a custom-made DB25 switch box (Figure 3.1) that toggles i/o between an ADC patch bay, Tonewinner AVR outputs, and Neve Orbit i/o. Sixteen discrete switchable two-channel i/o banks provide rapid connectivity, negate the need for additional analog to digital i/o, accommodate analog hardware insertion, enlarge the scope, reduce scale, and maintain pristine audio quality.

2 DESIGN WITH DARDT AND DO MORE WITH LESS

Available from Dolby.com, DARDT is an interactive spreadsheet tool that uses advanced macros to build the Atmos room virtually. Upon registration with Dolby, the control room design begins with the self-explanatory DARDT Quick Start Video Series. Beyond DARDT, this HN-FTS design strives to do more with less. The global Tiny Home movement inspired economical, large-scope, small-scale hardware solutions such as Anubis, Hapi MKII, the custom-made QC i/o switch box, and locally designed Canadian PSB speakers.

3 DECORRELATED SOUND FROM A CORRELATED SPEAKER LAYOUT

In the parlance of physics and philosophy, the Oxford Dictionary depicts the adjective *spatiotemporal* as a descriptor of an object that belongs to both space and time or to space-time. Discrete immersive multichannel and object-based spatial audio is perceived by the human auditory system as decorrelated sound that emanates from a speaker layout. More speaker channels present higher accuracy of auditorial location. Cinematic Far-Field Atmos theatres use speaker arrays for each audio channel with numerous speakers for audio objects, to disperse direct sound into a large room at cinematic SPL. In a 7.1.4 Tiny Studio one speaker per audio channel and phantom object images focus their direct sound to the sole mix-position to function as a well-tuned (correlated) hyper near-field speaker playback system. A highly decorrelated Atmos music mix presents very effective differences in timing, spectre, location, and volume to construct an immersive out-of-head audio experience – the opposite of "in-head localization" (Toole, 2018). A correlated mix presents the same sound from adjacent speakers to create a non-immersive paraphonic in-head sensation. When a multichannel mix is not supported with interchannel decorrelation, paraphony results, potentially leading to variant degrees of phase cancelation and comb filtering when folded down to binaural audio. This author argues that for music, custom-prepared stereo fold-downs remain superior to a static fold-down pre-set (Novotny, 2017). The Atmos renderer can create acceptable static fold-downs. When creating mixes on an untuned (uncorrelated) playback system, the result will be "unpredictable mix behaviour" when heard on a tuned (correlated) playback system. Dolby's Technical Guideline (Dolby, 2021b) provides standards for correlating speaker systems in equidistant or orthogonal layouts that vary in size from Near- to Far-field. In comparison to larger multiple mix-position Atmos rooms, a primary HN-FTS differentiation is the single mix-position limitation. This orthogonal Tiny Studio layout is highly correlated with speakers on the standard mid-plane placed away from the wall with left/center/right (LCR) aimed toward the sole operator. The front top surround speakers are placed slightly inward of the LCR field about 50° toward the mix-position and angled at 51° to aim just over the operator's shoulders. The LFE is laterally positioned on the floor between the center and right-front speakers. Direct loudspeaker sound is affected by reflections from room geometry. Low-frequency standing waves along with mid-to-high frequency diffusion influence the perception of mix decorrelation and spectral coloration. Expert Atmos mixers bake in their mix decorrelation, which should then translate reliably when heard on other correlated speaker systems that are precisely positioned, timed, and voiced for the room. This Tiny Studio speaker layout involves speaker distances that range from 102 to 126 cm (Table 3.1) to mix position, resulting in a room that looks (Figures 3.2 and 3.3), feels, and sounds like big headphones with accoustic crossfeed.

Table 3.1 Speaker Distance to Single Mix-Position

Speaker	Distance to Single Mix Position
Left	120 cm
Right	120 cm
Center	120 cm
Sub	110 cm
LS	102 cm
RS	102 cm
LRS	126 cm
RRS	126 cm
LTF	106 cm
RTF	107 cm
LTR	111 cm
RTR	111 cm

Figure 3.2 Tiny Studio.

Electronic timing adjustment in the Anubis speaker controller corrects speaker timings that are within the 24 cm range of difference.

3.1 The components of a correlated playback system

Playback system correlation can be seen as a series of components: acoustic room tuning to absorb resonances below the Schroeder frequency and diffuse soundwaves above (Brown, 2021); uniform

Figure 3.3 Tiny Studio, single mix-position.

electronic system polarization; minimal phase distortion; amplitude correction; precise system clock; speaker-delay timing; and speaker equalization with bass management that correlates frequencies below 80 Hz by sending them to a single monaural subwoofer. DARDT indicates specifications and measurements for a correlated system. Fine tuning is accomplished with real-time-analysis (RTA) and psychoacoustic perception. Playback system correlation relies on a combination of hard science and aural perception.

3.2 Small control room acoustics and the "my room principle"

Small control room dimensions invoke problematic low-frequency energy pressure zones – standing waves that must be suppressed. DARDT calculates their location and frequency. They occur in first, second, and third order. Floyd Toole describes what causes standing waves – also called eigenfrequencies, eigentones, eigenmodes, modes, or resonances:

> Sounds of all frequencies and wavelengths reflect around rooms in a somewhat chaotic manor, but when the wavelengths are of the same order as the dimensions of a room some special events occur. Between parallel surfaces that are half a wavelength apart, or multiples of half-wavelengths apart, the sound travelling in both directions add

constructively, reinforcing each other, and a standing wave develops. This is the basis of a room mode or resonance.

(Toole, 2018, p. 100)

Finding an effective method to render them innocuous in a sound field is a significant challenge because small rooms do not have enough space for low-frequency absorption material. In his AES preprint, "A controlled-reflection listening room for multichannel sound," Walker observes:

> The three main components of the sound field in the vicinity of the listener are the direct sound, the early reflections and the later reflections which merge to form the reverberant field. All these components are functions of time and frequency.
>
> (Walker, 1996, p. 1)

Walker references the *International Telecommunications Union* and *European Broadcast Union* recommendations – ITU-R BS.1116 [1] and EBU Rec.R22 (tech.Doc.3276 [3]) as "closely-controlled parameters for listening rooms for critical listening." As expected, this Tiny Studio breaks these rules, prompting this author to investigate the novel "MyRoom principle."

> Bogic Petrovic and Zorica Davidovic describe their "MyRoom principle" in a 2010 AES paper. "In general, rooms smaller than 80 m^3 are not advised to be used for a control room for stereo and surround production and reproduction . . ." (Petrovic and Davidovic, 2010, 2016). They concluded that their small-room designs (Studio 1 at 76 m^3 and Studio 2 at 33.30 m^3) could not rely on existing designs of Live-End Dead-End (LEDE), Non-Environment (N-E), Reflection Free Zone (RFZ) or Andrew Parry's design called "Early Sound Scattering" (ESS). They set out to create a new system they describe as an "acoustic treatment in which all surround speakers would be equally treated, while not compromising stereo monitoring." Every surface had to be hybrid, containing a reflective and absorptive part, providing absorption in low to mid frequency range, and diffuse reflection in mid to high range, with a crossover region in which both are present.
>
> (Petrovic and Davidovic, 2010, p. 3)

They conclude that their hybrid surface "MyRoom principle" is intended for a home studio located in an apartment/house. They propose the technical names of Non-Coherent (N-C) acoustic design or Early Reflections Delay Encryption (ERDE). Their design (Figure 3.4) is unique, and the Studio 2 room size (33.30 m^3) is comparable to this author's Tiny Studio which is (24 m^3).

Everest and Pohlmann (2022) observe that a frequency range of 20 Hz to 20 kHz spans ten octaves and represents wavelengths ranging from 57 ft to 0.6 inches. Newell (2017) tells us that absorbent material needs about "one quarter of a wavelength" to suppress the constructive effect of standing waves – approximately one meter of thickness is needed at 100 Hz.

Figure 3.4 "MyRoom principle" – Studio 1 with hybrid surfaces.

Everest and Pohlmann (2013) argue that perfect diffusion is difficult to achieve in small rooms due to less absorption, which leads to variant short reverb times. They also warn about irregular room geometry:

> modes are easy to calculate in a six-sided rectangular room with parallel surfaces. A room with different geometry, for example, splayed walls, also supports modes but the physical placement of the pressure response of the modes is distorted by the nonparallel surfaces, splaying walls does not solve mode problems; it only makes them harder to predict.
>
> (Alton Everest and Pohlmann, 2022, p. 143)

Bryan Pennington (Dolby Senior Field Applications Engineer) adds his recommendations for what he terms "a well-behaved Dolby Atmos room."

> You want to make sure it's not too big or too small . . . but I can't stress enough that bigger is not always better, you want to make sure that a room is not too big to turn out a good mix. You want to make sure that you're probably more in a rectangular room, less in a square room because you can load yourself up with acoustic problems.
>
> (Pennington, 2022, 8:35)

If the room is too dead, the mixer will over-reverberate. However, this author argues that low RT_{60} (Table 3.2) makes a Tiny Studio valuable for judging music playback in the hyper-small Atmos car cabin. Dolby says RT_{60} times are best when they are between .5 to .8 milliseconds (*Ibid*),

Table 3.2 DARTD-RT$_{60}$ Times for Tiny Studio

Measured RT60 [s]	125 Hz	250 Hz	500 Hz	1k Hz	2k Hz	4k Hz	8k Hz	Notes Average of
Measurement 1	0.07	0.07	0.09	0.05	0.07	0.06	0.14	3 samples
Measurement 2	0.07	0.16	0.14	0.17	0.07	0.21	0.27	5 samples
Measurement 3	0.07	0.08	0.07	0.07	0.09	0.11	0.06	3 samples
Measurement 4	0.11	0.12	0.16	0.11	0.16	0.15	0.22	7 samples
Measurement 5	0.07	0.09	0.08	0.08	0.08	0.08	0.03	4 samples
Measurement 6	0.12	0.08	0.07	0.44	0.41	0.06	0.14	5 samples
Measurement 7	0.10	0.10	0.09	0.09	0.09	0.09	0.07	1 sample
Measurement 8	0.17	0.09	0.08	0.06	0.07	0.07	0.08	36 samples
Measurement 9	0.12	0.13	0.10	0.12	0.12	0.07	0.08	1 sample
Measurement 10	0.10	0.11	0.10	0.10	0.08	0.11	0.13	3 samples
HN-FTS	**0.10**	**0.10**	**0.10**	**0.13**	**0.12**	**0.12**	**0.12**	
Average								

but this Tiny Studio RT_{60} is considerably less. Atmos specification for noise criteria (NC25) means the room will not have an inherent noise level that masks low-level reverb tails at −60 dB when audio is played at 85 dBC RMS. Paradoxically, mainstream Atmos playback in high-noise, low-RT_{60} automotive cabins is oncoming (Dolby, 2022). A 2016 Tesla Model XP90D has a cabin noise level ranging from 34.4 dB at idle to 67.3 dB at 140 km/h (auto-decibel-db.com, 2023). This indicates that at a cinematic playback level of 85 dB, approximately 10 dB of reverb tail will be masked at idle, and at 140 km/h, approximately 42 dB of reverb tail will be masked by cabin noise.

3.3 Hyper near-field room geometry and room volume

Room geometry and speaker layout size are two different measurements. Dolby's smallest room category is Near-Field, with a room volume of 50 cubic meters (50 m³). But Dolby's Bryan Pennington states that "there is no hard and fast minimum room size" (Pennington, 2022) (Dolby, 2021e). As such, this Hyper Near-Field benchmark precisely defines the Tiny Studio's room geometry, room volume, and speaker layout size. Table 3.3 compares the Dolby specifications (Dolby, 2021b) of a Near-Field room to this author's Hyper Near-Field Tiny Studio.

This author's Tiny Studio room geometry is rectangular. The mix-position is located at the long end. The rear wall has a 1.96 m-high, 70 mm-wide door, which functions as a bass trap when open. Room length is 4.7 m. Width is 2.57 m. The basement ceiling height is low at 1.98 m, regardless, this author perceives no appreciable compromise in dimensional separation between the standard mid-plane and the height plane speakers. After a field trip to the far-field cinematic Atmos theatre at Company 3 postproduction in Toronto, this author also realised that cinematic dimensional separation for these planes can be mildly approximated in this Tiny Studio simply by sitting about 20 cm lower. The orthogonal speaker sphere is approximately 4.2 m³, and speaker to mix-position measurements are taken from the center point of the speaker grill. In a small room with low height, orienting speakers in a tweeter-on-top vertical stance reduces side-to-side smear, improves the perception of spectral height from the

Table 3.3 Comparison of Near-Field and Hyper Near-Field

Comparison Table	Near-Field	Hyper Near-Field
Dimension	*Specification*	*Tiny Studio*
Minimum speaker layout height	2.4 m	1.75 m
Minimum speaker layout width	3 m	2.0 m
Minimum speaker layout length	3.5 m	2.4 m
Recommended room volume	>50 m³	24 m³
Speaker distance to mix-position	≤5 m (<4m recommended)	1.2 m

L/C/R speakers, and tweeters with waveguides will help to control high-frequency splay and speaker crossover. Speaker and mix-position placements should be located outside of the eigenmode peaks and valleys.

> It is very difficult to make a good quality studio, free of problematical compromises, in spaces with inadequate height. Control rooms require height because of the need to avoid acoustic problems between the parallel floor and ceiling.
>
> (Newell, 2017, p. 8)

3.4 Standing waves and the subwoofer position

DARDT calculated an optimal speaker layout with a subwoofer position that minimized standing waves in the room dimensions (Figure 3.5). The first mode was at 35 Hz, second at 69 Hz, third at 104 Hz, and fourth at 138 Hz, and axial modes were at 67 Hz, 134 Hz, 201 Hz, and 268 Hz.

3.5 Dolby room curve

The Dolby modified X curve emanates from cinematic practices that date back to the 1970s. This music-oriented Tiny Studio does not utilize the X curve or music curve, though the subwoofer is aligned to Dolby specification (pink noise plays at approx. +5 dBC above the center speaker) to balance bass-managed energy (80 Hz crossover) and low-frequency effect (LFE) with the satellite speakers. (Please see Ioan Allen's 2006 SMPTE journal paper for more information on the Dolby X curve.)

3.6 This Tiny Studio uses timbrally neutral Canadian loudspeakers

Paul Barton (Toronto, PSB founder and Chief Engineer for Lenbrook Industries Group of Companies, which includes PSB Speakers, NAD

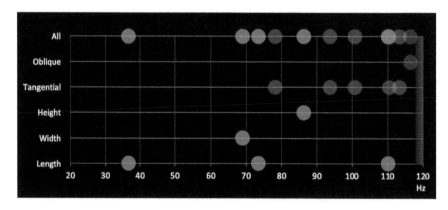

Figure 3.5 Tiny Studio, dimension of standing waves.

Electronics, and Bluesound) provided this author with generous advice and shared a compelling Canadian story involving Barton's mentor, Dr. Floyd E. Toole (Barton, 2021). Moncton, New Brunswick native Floyd Toole and Paul Barton are central figures in Canadian loudspeaker design, and their collaboration benefitted this Tiny Studio. In 1965, Floyd Toole graduated with a PhD in electrical engineering from the Imperial College of Science and Technology, University of London. His multi-disciplinary research involved binaural hearing and sound localization from signal generation. After graduation, Dr. Toole became a research scientist at the National Research Council of Canada (NRCC), where he designed an anechoic chamber. For PSB speakers, Toole did the research and Barton implemented the science. In 1991, after 26 years of research, Dr. Toole was hired as Vice President of Acoustical Engineering at Harmen International Industries, and now, in 2023, PSB is a highly respected international speaker brand possessing a long history with Dolby. Floyd Toole maintains that: "If we are to set an objective for loudspeaker performance, it should be timbral neutrality" (Toole, 2018). "The most common features of small low-cost loudspeakers are lack of bass, and an inability to play loud" (Toole, 2018).

Bryan Pennington (Dolby, 8:35) advises that: "Atmos works with all speakers and price does not denote quality," and he describes two uses of corrective speaker EQ for Atmos rooms – to make speakers sound more like each other and to help mixes translate to other environments.

For a Tiny Studio, these understandings are economically liberating since the largest expense of a larger Atmos studio is numerous high-powered speakers that are capable of meeting Dolby's SPL requirements. Paul Barton agreed with Toole and Pennington and suggested using seven passive PSB Alpha P3 bass reflex speakers with a rear-firing port that can be bunged to fully close the cabinet (like Blue Sky speakers), be partially bunged, or left fully open. These options enable flexibility when voicing the room. This orthogonal Tiny Studio speaker layout provides a 1.2 m distance from speaker to mix-position, and DARDT calculates that these PSB speakers will play at a common (RMS) level of 84 dBC with a true peak of 104.7 dB. The on-axis frequency range is 57–21,000 Hz with a low frequency cut-off of −10 dB at 43 Hz. For now, this Tiny Studio powers satellite speakers economically with multiple ART SLA 1 (2 X 100 watts) stereo amplifiers, but higher power Canadian-made Bryston power amps are preferable. Paul Barton recommended using copper 12-gauge speaker wire with the shortest lengths possible.

The 2020 TEC Award-winning PSB 10" CSIR passive subwoofer is in a slim enclosure, merely 10.2 cm deep – Paul Barton's design places the magnet in front of the speaker cone. DARDT indicated that the CSIR subwoofer should be located on the floor against the wall between the center and right speakers. The gracile enclosure afforded a position that helped to suppress standing waves. Barton's CSIR 10" and the PSB CS 500 W Architectural Subwoofer Amplifier are well suited to a Tiny Studio, and DARDT calculates that this 500-watt amp/speaker combo will peak at 103 dB, giving the subwoofer 83 dBC of common level. This Tiny Studio has 1700 watts of power in a 4.2 m³ speaker playback sphere. In theory, 2200 watts will achieve Dolby's cinematic SPL specification of 85 dBC but in practice, 85 dBC appears to play confidently with 1700 watts.

Bryan Pennington (Dolby 8:35) recommends that all Atmos studios will benefit from a single speaker manufacturer because uniform voicing crosses all models. Paul Barton agreed and suggested the PSB CS500 Universal In-Outdoor speakers for the top plane. They provide a safe, simple, and elegant mount-aim-dismount solution.

Passive speakers reduce control room heat and noise because power amps can be placed outside of the control room, and standard wiring is preferable when a repair is needed. This speaker system meets Toole's requirement for timbral neutrality and wide dynamic range while being cost-effective. Additionally, this Tiny Studio uses ATC-SCM20-ASL PRO MKII reference monitors for critical stereo listening, and when the ATCs are paired with the PSB subwoofer (2.1), the system plays to 24 Hz.

"'Small rooms' are notorious for bad bass" (Toole, 2018), and the human ear has difficulty locating sound below 80 Hz, while "below 50 Hz, localisation is all but impossible" (Newell, 2017). Based on our auditory biology, this author suggests that "eleven speakers that play to 40 Hz" (Dolby recommended) are intended for far-field cinematic rooms and perhaps not necessary for music. Frequencies below 80 Hz radiate in an omnidirectional pattern, and by directing them to a bass-managed single monaural subwoofer, system correlation is improved. Reducing satellite speaker frequencies below 80 Hz allows them to play with less distortion, more power, and wider dynamic range, while for music, single subwoofer bass management evokes the monoaural bass sound associated with vinyl. Blue Sky speaker design philosophy (Fielder, 2003; Sijen, 2008) affirms the need for bass management, and Philip Newell references Floyd E. Toole, encouraging monaural bass management when in less than "first class" acoustic conditions:

> if first class acoustic conditions are neither available nor achievable for practical reasons, then fast, flat, mono bass below 80 Hz may be greatly preferable to non-flat resonant bass in stereo.
>
> (Newell, 2018, p. 586)

3.7 Speaker isolation

ISO pucks decouple speaker energy transmission from a speaker mantle or speaker stands. They secure speaker footings during powerful compression and rarefaction cycles and mitigate external energy feedback, preventing woofer blur. Canadian acoustic design engineer Dave Morrison conceived the PSB CSIR subwoofer isolation, and as perceived by this author, Morrison's ISO pucks cleared up this Tiny Studio's L/C/R low and low-mid frequencies while improving horizontal imaging.

3.8 Measurement tools

A measuring tape or laser measuring tool and an SPL meter able to measure in A and C weights with fast and slow responses are necessary for level-matching speakers. C-weighting is used for speakers with similar spectral response down to 40 Hz, and A-weighting is used for dissimilar speakers.

3.9 SPL specifications

Based on this Tiny Studio's room geometry, an orthogonal layout was chosen in DARDT. An Atmos room must be calibrated to operate at the SPL of 79 dBC, 82 dBC, or 85 dBC. These are common root mean square (RMS) energy levels requiring an additional peak range of +20 dB. 85 dBC is used for cinematic QC, while approximately 77 dBC is common for daily music mixing.

3.10 Audio over internet protocol

Atmos control rooms often utilize the Audio Over Internet Protocol (AOIP) using ethernet (CAT 6) cabling to connect audio hardware to computers. AES67-Ravenna and DANTE are the current AOIP specifications and computer audio hardware functions within their ecosystems. 128 inputs/outputs are routinely used for Atmos.

3.11 Room tuning

The initial response measurement of this Tiny Studio was done using the free REW Room EQ Wizard (Figure 3.6) and a Soundfield Calrec microphone in the Omni pattern placed at mix-position with an SPL meter strapped on. The sweep test was calibrated to Dolby's reference test level

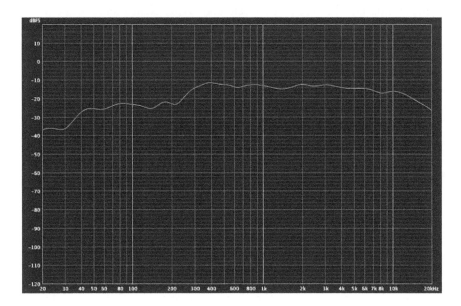

Figure 3.6 Initial Tiny Studio response, all SPL, no EQ, 1 octave smoothing.

of 75 dBC. A room's Schroeder frequency (Schroeder, 1975, 1976) guides neutralization of control room coloration by indicating the transition point between low-frequency absorption and high-frequency diffusion. This Tiny Studio's Schroeder frequency is 317 Hz. Temporarily, absorption involves 1.5" (3.7 mm) rockwool panels on the L/C/R, side walls, and ceiling, with a carpet tile floor. Uneven bass response, projected by DARDT, appears below about 400 Hz. A custom-made speaker delay calculator (Figure 3.7) indicates speaker delay timings.

This Tiny Studio now benefits from Sonarworks SoundID Reference multichannel calibration, which operates elegantly within the Anubis monitor controller. A quick and easy comparison between calibrated and uncalibrated monitoring indicates a significant improvement in room response at middle to low frequencies. A custom equalization curve is used that only tunes the frequencies below 600 Hz.

4 ECONOMIC COMPARISON

This Hyper Near-Field Tiny Studio costs about 35% of a virtually designed (DARDT) Near-Field Atmos control room. Near-Field loudspeakers use 65% of the budget, while this Hyper Near-Field loudspeaker system uses about 20%. Loudspeakers are the biggest cost advantage of a Tiny Studio because the sole mix-position is hyper near, offering affordable timbral neutrality at high SPL. Premium analogue-digital-analogue (ADA) hardware is expensive for both control rooms, but this Tiny Studio economizes by prioritizing mastering grade i/o – 16X16 Hapi MkII, 4X8 i/o Anubis, and a DB25 i/o switch-box, all costing approximately 50% less than Near-Field 32X32 i/o. The B chain is the most expensive chain in both rooms. The following bar-graphs (Tables 3.8–3.11) provide an estimation of economic comparison between Near-Field and Hyper Near-Field room types.

5 CONCLUSION

This HN-FTS philosophy establishes an Atmos small control room benchmark which is aimed toward independent professional, semi-pro, higher music education institutions, and commercial facilities. An HN-FTS control room can be approximately 50% smaller than Dolby's minimum Near-Field guideline. What follows is an eleven-point summary of attributes.

1 Meets Dolby's music SPL specification of 82 dBC +20 dB TP. 85 dBC +20 dB TP is possible, but it requires 898 watts for the sub and 126 watts per L/R front speaker.
2 Single operator, 4 m^3 speaker sphere, timbrally neutral speakers, low distortion, wide dynamic range.
3 Provides a highly correlated, tuned, and voiced playback system.
4 Compared to Near-Field, it reduces control room costs by approximately 65%.
5 Can achieve a noise compliment equal to or below Dolby guidelines of NC25.

Atmos HN-FTS Speaker Delay Calculator Novotny_09_09_23

Legend

Base Distance/Base Time ~ Speed of Sound = 1,125ft/sec ~ 1,125 ft/ms

30.5 cm = 1ms ~ 1/10th of a ms = .03 microsnds ~ 35 micro seconds = 1 centimeter.

Anubis Firmware: 1.5.11b55
Anubis Buffer: 64 ms

Speaker	ATC 2.0	PSB 7.1.4-64KB Anubis Buffer=1.33 ms	Distance to mix in cm	Difference in cm	Difference in Microseconds	Speaker Delay	Delay Setting
LS	No correction required	Room Timing Correction	122	4	0.013114754	0.013114754	1.428
RS	"	Room Timing Correction	122	4	0.013114754	0.013114754	1.428
C	"	Room Timing Correction	122	4	0.013114754	0.013114754	1.428
LFE	"	Room Timing Correction	110	16	0.052459016	0.052459016	1.441
SL	"	Room Timing Correction	102	24	0.078688525	0.078688525	1.487
SR	"	Room Timing Correction	102	24	0.078688525	0.078688525	1.487
Left Side-Rear	"	Base Distance	126	0	0	0	1.33
Right Side-Rear	"	Base Distance	126	0	0	0	1.33
TL	"	Room Timing Correction	106	20	0.06557377	0.06557377	1.487
TR	"	Room Timing Correction	107	19	0.062295082	0.062295082	1.48
TRL	"	Room Timing Correction	113	13	0.042622951	0.042622951	1.457
TRR	"	Room Timing Correction	111	15	0.049180328	0.049180328	1.457

Figure 3.7 Tiny Studio, speaker delay calculations.

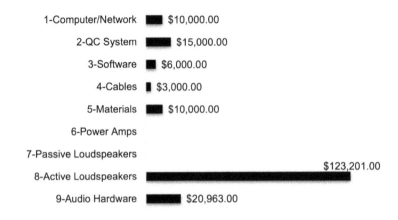

Figure 3.8 Hardware, software, materials, near-field and hyper near-field comparison.

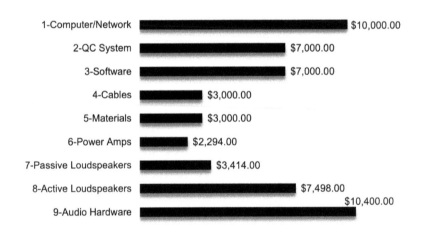

Figure 3.9 A chain, B chain, QC chain, near-field and hyper near-field comparison.

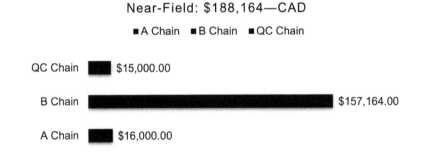

Figure 3.10 Near Field economic breakdown by chain

Figure 3.11 Hyper Near Field economic breakdown by chain

6 Provides essential room decorrelation and crossfeed for out-of-head control room monitoring. Subjectivly, this Tiny Studio sounds like a big set of headphones.
7 Has a low RT_{60} time, which is valuable for judging playback in an Atmos automotive cabin and makes electronic room tuning highly effective.
8 With careful subwoofer selection, placement, electronic tuning, and a rear door bass trap in a rectangular room, this HN-FTS can render standing waves suitably innocuous at the sole mix-position.
9 Workflow utilizes headphones, discrete speaker playback, and comparative field trips.
10 Offers low-energy consumption, quiet and cool studio operation.
11 Encourages individual solutions for large-scope, small-scale, affordability, and sustainability.

A Tiny Studio will not meet "first class acoustics" (Newell, 2018), and it won't be listed in the Dolby.com database of approved Atmos studios, but this control room works very well, and it is likely one of the smallest Atmos control rooms imaginable. It provides a scientifically tuned playback system which then relies on psychoacoustic perception and refinement to create a sweet sound that translates to outside playback environments. In an onboarding email with Dolby, Ceri Thomas responded.

> We do have rooms which are, as you describe, Hyper Near-Field, as they do not meet our best practices, they would not be eligible for listing on Dolby.com. That doesn't mean you can't still personally create in them.
>
> (Dolby, Thomas, Brooks, Kanau, 2022)

In conclusion, this author advocates for further research and development of the HN-FTS philosophy and benchmark, inviting Pro Audio manufacturers to recognize the Atmos Hyper Near-Field Tiny Studio as a viable category for specific development. This author argues that independent music creators can confidently assemble their own 3D Atmos audio HN-FTS which is distinguished by premium sound quality, thrifty economics, and a well-tuned mixing position. This HN-FTS benchmark introduces sturdy and adaptive solutions that consider essential music business and socio-economic context, which routinely require the independent music creator to do more with less.

REFERENCES

Allen, I., (2006). *The X-Curve: Its Origins and History*, (Website), available online from, www.associationdesmixeurs.fr/wp-content/uploads/2015/10/Dolby_The-X-Curve__SMPTE-Journal.pdf [Accessed 24 Jul. 2022].

Alton Everest, F., and Pohlmann, C. K., (2013). *Handbook of Sound Studio Construction, Rooms for Recording and Listening*, McGraw-Hill, Kindle-iPad edition. Pg. 20, 27, 111, 56, 143.

Alton Everest, F., and Pohlmann, C. K., (2022). *Master Handbook of Acoustics, Seventh Edition*, McGraw-Hill, Kindle-iPad edition. Pg.489.

Auto-decibel-db, *The Car Interior Noise Level Comparison site – Auto innengeräusch vergleigch*, (Website), available online from, www.auto-decibel-db.com/index_kmh.html [Accessed 06 Apr. 2023].

Barton, P., (2021). *PSB Speakers, Designer, Engineer, Business Owner at Lenbrook Industries, I Had Numerous Telephone Discussions with Paul between September and December 2021*, (Website store), available online from, www.psbspeakers.com/product-category/series/alpha/.

Brown, P., (2021). *Divide and Conquer – The Schroeder Frequency*, (Website), available online from, www.prosoundtraining.com/2021/10/14/divide-and-conquer-the-schroeder-frequency/ [Accessed 24 Jul. 2022].

Carrizosa, P., (2021). *Could Tiny Homes Be the Adorable, Affordable and Sustainable Housing That Our Planet Needs?*, (Website), available online from, https://ideas.ted.com/impact-of-tiny-homes-on-the-environment-and-affordable-housing/.

Dolby, (2019). *Dolby Atmos Home Entertainment Studio Certification, Guide*, 08.07.19, professional.dolby.com, (link is no longer available, Dolby no longer certifies rooms) [Accessed 25 Jun. 2021].

Dolby, (2020a). *Dolby Atmos Music Via Headphones, Webinar 3: How to Create Dolby Atmos Music on Headphones, Ceri Thomas*, (Website), available online from, https://professional.dolby.com/events/dolby-atmos-music-via-headphones/ [Accessed 28 Jul. 2022].

Dolby, (2020b). *Why Dolby Atmos, DLB_Atms_WP_v04_200807*, (Website), available online from, https://professional.dolby.com/siteassets/content-creation/dolby-atmos/why-dolby-atmos-white-paper.pdf [Accessed 15 Jun. 2022].

Dolby, (2021a). *The DARDT Quick Start Video Series*, (Website), available online from, https://professionalsupport.dolby.com/s/article/HE-DARDT-Quick-Start-Video-Series?language=en_US, [Accessed 7 Jul. 2021].

Dolby, (2021b). *Dolby Atmos Home Entertainment Studio, Technical Guidelines*, 06.05.21, professional.dolby.com, (Website), available online from, https://dolby.my.salesforce.com/sfc/p/#700000009YuG/a/4u0000000lFHc/UYA0IZeD-632SUXVmEPmUcr.wIuhpHp6Q7bVSl4LrbUQ [Accessed 12 Sept. 2021].

Dolby, (2021c). *Dolby Atmos Post Production Learning*, (Website), available online from, https://learning.dolby.com/hc/en-us/sections/360010367372-Dolby-Atmos-Post-and-Music-Production-Learning [Accessed 12 Jan. 2022].

Dolby, (2021d). *Dolby Professional Support, What DAWs Support Dolby Atmos*, (Website), available online from, https://professionalsupport.dolby.com/s/article/What-DAWs-support-Dolby-Atmos?language=en_US [Accessed 20 Sept. 2022].

Dolby, (2021e). *What Room Dimensions Are Needed to Mix Content in Dolby Atmos for Home Entertainment?*, (Website), available online from, https://professionalsupport.dolby.com/s/article/What-room-dimensions-are-needed-to-mix-content-in-Dolby-Atmos-for-Home-Entertainment?language=en_US [Accessed 6 Jul. 2022].

Dolby, (2022). *Experience the Future of in-Car Entertainment with Dolby at the AES 2022 Conference*, (Website), available online from, https://professional.dolby.com/music/dolby-atmos-for-cars/#gref [Accessed 15 Jun. 2022].

Dolby, (2023). *Dolby Atmos for Cars: Volvo Cars*, (Website), available online from, https://professional.dolby.com/music/dolby-atmos-for-cars/volvo/ [Accessed 06, Jan. 2023].

Dolby Thomas, C., Brooks, E., and Kunau, M., (2022). *Dolby Atmos Onboarding Email* [Accessed 5 Feb.].

Dolby, Developer, (2022). *Dolby Atmos Is an Immersive Audio Format That Can Be Delivered Via Multiple Audio Codecs . . .* (Website), available online from, https://developer.dolby.com/technology/dolby-atmos/overview/#:~:text=Dolby%20Atmos%C2%AE%20is%20an,(but%20NOT%20Dolby%20Digital) [Accessed, 25 Aug. 2022].

Fazenda, B., Angus, J., and Cox, T., (2015). *The SOS Guide to Control Room Design, Making Space, Mixing/Production*, (Website), available online from, www.soundonsound.com/techniques/sos-guide-control room-design [Accessed 12 July 2022].

Fielder, L., (2003). *Dolby Labs, Analysis of Traditional and Reverberation-Reducing Methods of Room Equalization*, JAES-2249, Vol.51, No. ½, January/February.

Fox, B., (1982). *Early Stereo Recording (Alan Blumlein)*, Studio Sound and Broadcast Engineering, Great Britain, May, 1982.

Genewick, S., (2021). *White Lightning, Staci Greisbach*, (Website), available online from, https://mixwiththemasters.com/videos/mixing-in-atmos-2-staci-griesbach-white-lightning/part/1 [Accessed 04 Jul. 2022].

Kunst, A., (2019). *Purposes Headphones Are Used for in the United Sates 2017 (What Do You Use Your Headphones for?), STATISTA*, (website), available online from, www.statista.com/statistics/696862/uses-of-headphones-in-the-us/ [accessed 15 May 2022].

Lucidmotors, (2021). *Lucid Air Is the World's First Vehicle to Integrate Dolby Atmos*, (website). available online from, www.lucidmotors.com/media-room/lucid-air-is-first-vehicle-to-integrate-dolby-atmos [accessed 27 Aug. 2022].

Murch, W., (2012). *Walter Murch on the Digital Revolution*, (Website), available online from, www.filmdetail.com/2012/03/16/walter-murch-on-the-digital-revolution/ [accessed 6 Jul. 2022].

Nair, S., (2022). *Clustering, an Expanded Version of My Avid Blog Post, Atmos Post Mixing Professionals, Facebook Private Group*, (website), available online from, http://facebook.com [accessed 10 Aug. 2022].

Newell, P., (2017). *Recording Studio Design*, Fourth Edition, (9781138936072), Audio Engineering Society Presents, (AES), Routledge, Taylor Francis Group, Kindle-iPad edition.

Newell, P., (2018). *Philip Newell Acoustic Design*, (Website), available online from, http://philipnewell.net/index9.html [accessed 20 Jul. 2022].

Novotny, P., (2017). *Creating an Immersive Fold-Out – Look Ahead*, Proceedings of the 12th Art of Record Production Conference, Mono: Stereo: Multi – Stockholm 2017, KMH.

Ondaatje, M., (2002). *The Conversations, Walter Murch and the Art of Editing Film*, Humble Sounds, Vintage Canada Edition, Randomhouse.ca., iBooks version, Pg. 23.

Pennington, B., (2022). *Dolby Atmos Music Creation 101: Studio Setup and Tuning*, (website), available online from, www.youtube.com/watch?v=pPDY6mXBmgs The interview starts at 8:35 in the transcript [accessed 15 Apr. 2022].

Petrovic, B., and Davidovic, Z., (2010). *Acoustical Design of Control Room for Stereo and Multichannel Production and Reproduction, a Novel Approach, MyRoom Principle*, AES paper #8295.

Petrovic, B., and Davidovic, Z., (2016). *A Novel Approach of Multichannel and Stereo Control Room Acoustic Treatment, Second Edition*, AES paper #9526.

Rothermich, E., (2021). *Mixing in Dolby Atmos, #1 How It Works*, Kindle e-book, www.dingdingmusic.com.

Rothermich, E., (2022). *Logic Pro 10.7.3, Monitor Dolby Atmos through Apple's Spatial Audio Engine, Music Tech Explained, the Visual Approach*, (website), available online from, www.youtube.com/results?search_query=music+tech+explained [accessed 28 Jul. 2022].

Scheps, A., (2019). *Andrew Scheps Talks to Awesome People, YouTube – PureMix*, (website), available online from, www.youtube.com/watch?v=cnX4pVrxqq0 [accessed 12 Apr. 2022].

Schroeder, R. M., (1975). *Diffuse Sound Reflected by Maximum Length Sequences*, Journal of the Acoustical Society of America, 57, Pg. 149–150.

Schroeder, R. M., and Gerlach, R., (1976). *Response to "Comments on 'Diffuse Sound Reflection by Maximum Length Sequences'"*, Journal of the Acoustical Society of America, Vol. 60, Pg. 268.

Stagle, D., (2022). *How to Listen to Dolby Atmos without Costly Hardware*, (Website), Available online from, www.pro-tools-expert.com/production-expert-1/how-to-listen-to-dolby-atmos-without-costly-hardware?fbclid=IwAR0Qr32l9UPcmJpXQxf-KJr7cEyDcCRFrXrGQX-2DP1FtCuIZRjegQos-BxA [accessed 25 Aug. 2022].

Sijen, P., (2008). *Design Philosophy: Blue Sky Studio Monitors, AudioDesignLabs*, (website) available from, http://audiodesignlabs.com [accessed 28 Aug. 2021].

Tobin, M., (2021). *Mixing for Headphones, Dolby Atmos Creation 101*, (Website), available online from, www.youtube.com/watch?v=qs1tffnAjPE [accessed 28 Jul. 2022].

Toole, E. F., (2018). *Sound Reproduction: The Acoustics and Psychoacoustics of Loudspeakers and Rooms*, Third Edition, Audio Engineering Society Presents (AES), Routledge, Taylor & Francis Group, Pg. 16 Kindle-iPad version. Pg. xvii, xix, 321.

Walker, R., (1996). *Optimum Dimension Ratios for Small Rooms, 100th Convention of the Audio Engineering Society*, Preprint 4191 (H-4).

Zeimer, T., and Bader, R., (2017). *Psychoacoustic Sound Field Synthesis for Musical Instrument Radiation Characteristics*, JAES, Vol. 65, No. 6.

DISCOGRAPHY

Novotny, P., (2022) Featuring Robi Botos, [Apple Music] *Summertime in Leith, in Concert at the Historic Leith Church*, TR10026, Triplet Records, Toronto, Canada.

4

Rap as composite auditory streams

Techniques and approaches for chimericity through layered vocal production in hip-hop, and their aesthetic implications

Kjell Andreas Oddekalv

1 COMPOSITE AUDITORY STREAMS, CHIMERAS AND OTHER BEASTS

Human listening is fundamentally attuned to retrieving information about the listener's surroundings. Where is a sound source located? What is the sound source? And in the cacophony of everyday soundscapes – which sounds originate from the *same* sound source and which belong to a *different* auditory stream altogether? Musical listening uses the same listening apparatus and cognitive processing system as any other type of listening, meaning that discerning sound sources, dividing musical wholes into parallel constituent parts and attending to these different interacting and interdependent streams is a fundamental part of the very act of listening to music.

This 'stream separation' is an intuitive part of discourses and workflows for people working with music. Just consider a symphonic score dividing the musical whole into not only individual instrumental streams but also instrument groups (woodwinds, brass, percussion, strings, et cetera). This showcases how these streams are *composite* – the layers can be pried apart, but they are tied together, and one can attend with resolutions of varying granularity. The whole can be subdivided into groups, and each group can be subdivided into smaller groups, individual instruments, individual *voices* within instrument streams and even the constituent parts of voices, motifs or other musical lines or narratives. Similarly, and perhaps even more intuitively, this is evident in the workflows and listening when working with multitrack recordings – particularly in digital audio workstations (DAWs) where the music is represented visually with a horizontal time dimension and a vertical division into tracks. In addition to individual instrument tracks (and often multiple tracks for each instrumental stream), someone working with a DAW interface will often work with track groups, busses – which might be used specifically for effects processing, yielding separate 'effects streams' – and other types of summing or dividing tracks into compound or individual streams.

DOI: 10.4324/9781003462101-5

In this article, the interaction between auditory stream separation as a cognitive listening phenomenon and as a music production technique will be explored using a specific musical framework – the vocal streams and tracks of rap music. In particular, Albert S. Bregman's concept of "chimericity" (Bregman, 1990) will be applied in the analysis of various vocal production techniques, showing how different types and degrees of chimericity can have different aesthetic effects. This relates to Ragnhild Brøvig-Hanssen's concept of *opaque and transparent mediation* (Brøvig-Hanssen, 2018). There will be a brief discussion of these aesthetic effects' relationship with the cultural politics of hip-hop and a presentation of examples of particularly creative and impactful applications of *chimericity techniques*.

2 STREAMS, SCHEMATA AND LINES – FLOW, LAYERING AND RUPTURE

Listening is an exercise in sorting information. We constantly, both consciously and subconsciously, filter auditory information to make sense of what it is and particularly what its origins are. This is the central foundation of Bregman's *Auditory Scene Analysis* (1990). We can easily distinguish between different sound sources, and we can determine where those sound sources are situated in relation to us – how far away they are, in which direction, whether they are stationary or moving and so on. In short, Bregman shows how the temporal organisation and different constituents of sound events inform our perceptual system concerning how to best organise our sounding environment. An important consequence of this theory is that our perceptual grouping of sound must be flexible. For *musical listening*, this entails that in some situations, we might sort a track of music as one single auditory stream, while in other situations when we can listen to that track closely, we might sort a snare drum, piano and voice(s) into different streams, attending more closely to a single one or specific interaction(s) between them as we parse the musical information.

Rap vocals are particularly fruitful for the analysis of auditory streams because they contain many different types of auditory information, which can be separated into discrete layers of a composite compound whole. We have already picked out a stream – the vocal – from the musical whole, and this stream contains both linguistic information (semantic, phonological, syntactical, et cetera) and musical information (musical rhythm, melody, phrasing and other parallelisms). This vocal stream is also both part of compound auditory streams and part of creating other perceptual streams – musical schemata or reference structures. Take *metre*, for example. As listeners, we experience metre as a salient organising schema for our musical experience, even though it is not explicitly part of the sound hitting our ears. Or, in the words of Justin London: "Meter is a perceptually emergent property of a musical sound, that is, an aspect of our engagement with the production and perception of tones in time" (2012, p. 4). In composite auditory streams, such cognitive reference structures can be considered as distinct layers just as much as sounding instrument streams. We can and do selectively (and/or subconsciously) attend to metre or other non-sounding schemata when listening to music.

Since it first became a topic of musicological attention in the early nineties (with Cheryl Keyes' 1991 dissertation *Rappin' to the beat: Rap music as street culture among African Americans* and later Robert Walser's 1995 article "Rhythm, rhyme, and rhetoric in the music of Public Enemy"), rap flow analysis has honed in on how rappers' *lines* – lyrical phrases whose endpoints are typically demarcated by rhyme – are structured in relation to the musical framework of the instrumental track (colloquially referred to as "the beat"). Scholars from the field of music theory, such as Adam Krims (2000), Felicia Miyakawa (2005), Kyle Adams (2008, 2009, 2015, 2020), Oliver Kautny (2009, 2015), Ben Duinker (2020, 2021) and Robert Komaniecki (2017, 2019) have all homed in on the structural relationship between the musical and (music-)metrical framework of the musical background and the phrase boundaries and segmentation of the rappers' lyrical lines. That this relationship is most commonly a 1:1 ratio of musical bar to lyrical line and that this standard is also varied – sometimes to a significant degree – has also been shown in corpus studies by Nathaniel Condit-Schultz (2016) and linguist Jonah Katz (2008). This 1:1 relationship is not nearly as common in other types of vocal music, owing to the high syllable density of rap music. The nature and significance of the difference between structures where lines and bars coincide and where this convergence is suspended have been the topic of articles by, among others, John J. Mattessich (2019) and Kjell Andreas Oddekalv (2022a). In a composite auditory stream, the boundaries of the music metrical layer (a cognitive reference structure/schema) and the rapper's lines are two distinct layers that might be glued together when lines and bars coincide or might be more easily pried apart when the two diverge from one another.

Thus, the rap stream and its segmentation – the division into lyrical lines – can be considered one singular stream in Bregman's "stream segregation" framework. However, there are complications. First, there is a question of what constitutes a 'line'. This is a central question that has been tackled in different ways in the rap analysis field. Both Condit-Schultz (2016) and Ohriner (2016) track different criteria that might indicate 'line endings', like the position of stressed rhymed syllables, breathing pauses and linguistic (syntactical and phonological) clues. It seems clear that 'lines' are not easily quantifiable – the position of their boundaries can be ambiguous and depend on several different interacting parameters. This is supported by literary linguist Nigel Fabb, who claims that "lineation, the division of text into lines, is a kind of implied form, not an inherent fact of the text" (Fabb, 2002, p. 136). Lineation depends on the triangulation of many different types of "evidence" and is thus – much like metre and other cognitive reference structures – something that is derived from a listener's emergent interpretation of the music as it unfolds.

According to Tricia Rose (in concordance with artist Arthur Jafa), the aesthetics of hip hop and other Black art forms can be viewed as "center[ed] around three concepts: *flow, layering* and *ruptures in line*" (Rose, 1994, p. 38). Rap, like graffiti and breakdance, is characterised by fluid, forward movement that is "broken abruptly with sharp angular breaks" and contains multiple types of layering. Rose exemplifies layering in rap with "layer[ing] meaning by using the same word to signify a variety of actions and objects" (p. 39), but – like flow and rupture – layering "can be found in the vast majority of rap's lyrical and musical construction" (p. 59). The layering of rhyme, parallel rhythmic figures on the boundaries of musical metre – the stacking of what Fabb calls "evidence for lineation" – is one obvious interpretation of 'layering in rap', which intimately interacts with flow and rupture in line. When lines and bars do not line up, this relationship becomes even more subtle and nuanced, emphasising the layering inherent in composite auditory streams. However, the layering (and rupture) that this article circles in on is the layering of multiple vocal tracks in the production of rap music – the rap stream might be 'one stream' of the composite whole, but it is rarely truly just *one stream*.

3 THE RAPPING CHIMERA

In recorded rap music, the 'rap stream' – the musical stream consisting of the 'rapped performance' – will most often consist of multiple recorded tracks. For one, there might be 'comping' (short for "compiling", meaning the splicing-together of multiple recordings to one single track), or the musical line (not to be confused with the flow's division into *lyrical* lines) might be split between different rappers or clearly separated recordings of a single rapper's voice. Additionally, tracks are usually layered in some way to create emphasis on certain words or syllables. Like Bregman, I liken this merging of multiple voices or sound sources into a single stream to the mythological chimera – a beast with one body and multiple heads – illustrated in Figure 4.1.

Figure 4.1 'The Rapping Chimera'.

Source: Illustration by Sebastian Bruknapp Sjem

3.1 Chimericity, transparency and opacity in vocal production

Bregman connects the concept of chimericity to a "failure" of the scene analysis process in ecological listening: "Normally, in perception, emergent properties are accurate portrayals of the properties of the objects in our environment. However, if scene analysis processes fail, the emergent perceived shapes will not correspond to any environmental shapes. They will be entirely chimerical" (Bregman, 1990, p. 4). In music, on the other hand, artists will exploit the nature of our listening apparatus to purposefully create chimericity:

> Natural hearing tries to avoid chimeric percepts, but music often tries to create them. It may want the listener to accept the simultaneous roll of the drum, clash of the cymbal, and brief pulse of noise from the woodwinds as a single coherent event with its own striking emergent properties. The sound is chimeric in the sense that it does not belong to any single environmental object.
>
> (Bregman, 1990, pp. 459–460)

This is exactly what happens in the layering of multiple vocal tracks on a rap recording, and depending on how easy it is to identify the different sources that come together as 'one sound' – the multiple heads of the chimera – a musical event or passage can be more or less chimeric. The sound is simultaneously 'one' *and* 'multiple'.

It is clear that a recorded vocal performance is in no way a 'naturalistic' reproduction of a live performance, and scholars have pointed this out and discussed the impact technology and the recording process has on the finished product. Jonathan Sterne (2003), for example, argues in great depth for the importance of the technological medium in the relationship between listener and music: "The medium does not mediate the relation between singer and listener, original and copy. It *is* the nature of their connection" (Sterne, 2003, p. 226). Many other scholars have explored how technology and the recording studio environment impact the communication of vocals specifically. Serge Lacasse (2000) introduced the concept of "vocal staging" – how technological manipulation of the voice, both in physical space and on recorded media, is central to the listener's reception of a song. Peter Doyle (2005) puts the analytical lens on the communication of *space*, both in how a recorded space is transmitted onto a recording and how the experience of space is manipulated by recording techniques and technological manipulation of recordings. Particularly relevant to this article is his analysis of *voice doublings* in the work of Mary Ford and Les Paul. The precise doublings of the same person's voice singing the exact same phrases create an effect that is virtually impossible to recreate outside of a recording context. Emil Kraugerud (2021) argues that doublings can be used to portray and communicate intimacy, while Freya Jarman-Ivens (2011a, 2011b) notes that the overdubbing and doubling of vocal tracks in the music of The Carpenters creates an effect of "vocal gloss".

The effects that sound recording has on the music that reaches the ears of someone listening to a recording – what Mark Katz (2010) calls "phonograph effects" – are evident. However, it is not always the case that these effects are obvious or even noticeable to the listener. Ragnhild Brøvig-Hanssen (2010, 2018) coined the terms "opaque and transparent mediation" to differentiate between instances where the listener is being made aware (or rather, is *likely* to take notice) of the technology's impact on the sound and when they are not:

> Transparent mediation implies that the listener's focus is directed towards what is mediated and not the technological media-tion itself, whereas opaque mediation implies that the listener is attracted to the act of mediation itself, *in tandem with* that which is mediated.
>
> (Brøvig-Hanssen, 2018, p. 1)

This concept of transparency and opacity is applicable to the experience of chimericity as well. When it is obvious to the listener that a musical phrase is the result of the combination of several parallel or subsequent auditory streams – or, in the words of Bregman, "an image derived as a composi-tion of other images" (1990, p. 459) – the chimericity is more opaque than when this combination of different sound sources is less noticeable. In other words, something is *more chimeric* when the different heads of the creature are easily identifiable and *less chimeric* when they are not, and the compound creature – the single body the heads sprout from – is what the listener hears. For something to be chimeric, however, both the multiple heads and the single originating body must be present. Another important point differentiating chimericity from Brøvig-Hanssen's opaque and transparent mediation is that chimericity is not necessarily communicated through technological means. While most of the examples used in this article are reliant on the affordances of the recording studio and/or post-production technology (and could thus be analysed as more or less opaque or transparent mediation), there are some that are fully transferrable to a live performance. Something *can* be opaquely chimeric and simultane-ously completely transparently mediated.

3.2 Types, modes and voices – categorising chimericities

In analysing the rapping chimera, there are certain dimensions that will influence if and to which degree something is experienced as chimeric. The first is identified and presented by Bregman, who differentiates between *sequential* and *simultaneous* organisations of larger objects. Sequential (or horizontal) organisation occurs when sounds from different sources are grouped together into a single coherent stream. A sequentially organ-ised object can be considered chimeric if it is simultaneously experienced as 'one' and identified as constructed from multiple sources. An example of this type of chimericity is presented in Figure 4.2, where the 'back-to-back' rapping of West Coast rap crew Jurassic 5 from the chorus of

Chali 2na

Now I'mma say this one time, boy, and that's my word

Zaakir

We' rockin' shots and not fire through the Hindenburg

Marc7   *Akil*

The contribution is clear, you add water to bone

ALL 4

And get the Jurassic 5 on the microphone

Figure 4.2 'Back-to-back' rapping in Jurassic 5's "Concrete Schoolyard" (from 0:25).

"Concrete Schoolyard" (first released in 1997) creates a coherent flowing stream even as the different lines are rapped by different rappers.

The four rappers divide the lines between them, with Chali 2na and Zaakir rapping lines one and two, respectively, Marc7 and Akil splitting the third line in the middle, and all four rapping the final line together. This consistent change of sound source is perfectly clear to the listener, so the first three lines are not chimeric in the sense of there being any doubt as to where the sound(s) originate. However, it is just as clear that there is a coherent musical stream that connects the entire passage. The lines are connected through rhyme, meaning that Zaakir's line is experienced as a continuation of the flow from Chali 2na's. The listener is also primed – both by the context, the semantic content and genre convention – to hear the third line as 'one line', even if it is split between Marc7 and Akil. It is opaquely chimeric, as each head of the rapping chimera is clearly identifiable, yet the heads are all connected to one singular body – the musical construct of the four-bar section (or lyrical *quatrain*). This exemplifies the aesthetic dimensions of Rose's flow and ruptures in line, as the continuous forward-flowing movement is being challenged by potential ruptures. The coinciding boundaries of musical metre and line are reinforced as a point of rupture by the changing of rappers, yet the ruptures cannot quite manage to break the flow completely, as rhyme and structural expectation urge us to experience the entire section as one compound musical narrative.

The final line and Akil's part of the penultimate line exemplify the other type of chimericity derived from Bregman – the simultaneous (or *vertical*) organisation – which also evokes the third of Rose's dimensions, *layering*. The final line, where all four Jurassic 5 emcees rap together, does not "belong to a single environmental object" but is a musical stream "with its own striking emergent properties". Like an orchestral unison *tutti* section or a 'stack' of doubled instrument tracks spread across the stereo field in a rock recording, it is a chimeric musical utterance where the compound body of the chimera is the originator, even as we are keenly aware of its many heads. The layering of the four *different voices* contrasts with the preceding half-line part rapped by Akil, which also showcases layered chimericity. Akil's part consists of two equally loud tracks – a 'doubling' or 'dub' of the *same voice*. When the heads of the rapping chimera are perfect twins (or triplets or more) like this, the chimericity is usually more transparent than when they consist of different voices. Whether a listener interprets and experiences the passage as originating from two (or more) sources or whether the doubling is heard as an 'effect' modulating a single source depends on several parameters. If the doubled tracks are approaching perfect replication of one another, they might be harder to pry apart. Similarly, depending on how they are mixed – their placement in the stereo field, if they are 'glued together' using equalization, compression, reverb, et cetera – the doubling might create a *chorus* effect or what Jarman-Ivens calls "vocal gloss". The listener's interpretation will inevitably be influenced by their predispositions, previous experience and expertise, as some listeners are more familiar with and/or drawn to the aspects of sounds that stem from their production or how they are manipulated, while others mostly disregard these factors in their listening (and our focus as listeners is very rarely consistent – each listening is different). This type of *same voice* chimericity can thus be experienced as transparent or opaque depending on the listener, or it might be heard as transparently chimeric but opaquely mediated – the creature is heard as one rather than as many-headed, but the presence of some sort of technological manipulation is felt. Note that the recording/arrangement technique used in Akil's passage above, with two equally loud tracks doubled in their entirety and mixed together, is somewhat uncommon (although some rappers, like Jadakiss, make extensive use of the technique), and there are other more common same voice doubling-techniques to which I will return shortly.

In addition to the different *types* of chimericity (sequential/horizontal and layered/vertical) and the difference in *voice* (same voice versus other voice), another dimension is significant in influencing how chimeric a passage is – namely, the *mode* of performance. Whether it is the same voice that is overdubbed multiple times or different voices doubling or going back-to-back, the tracks will blend together more and be more transparently chimeric if the tracks have the same or similar performance modes. "Performance mode" refers to whether it is, for example, 'rapped', 'sung', spoken, whispered, et cetera. Note the scare quotes on the terms "rapped" and "sung". Rap's identity as a vocal performance style has been discussed widely (Adams, 2015; Ohriner, 2019a, 2019b; Komaniecki, 2019; Hognestad, 2023; Oddekalv, 2022b), and while it is noted by many that it has been referred to as "rhythmic speech", it is a type of musical expression much closer to song – both rhythmically *and* melodically – than speech. Rap's speech-likeness exists on a continuous scale – specific rapped passages can be characterised as 'more speech-like' or 'more sung'. A type of mode difference, then, is when rapped tracks are 'sung' to different degrees. This can be very clearly audible (and opaque), like in Ms. Lauryn Hill's "Doo Wop (That Thing)" (1998), where the doubled 'backtracks' – doublings of key words and syllables, typically rhymes and/or line endings – are sung with different tones than the (quite sung) rap, harmonising the rapped melody.

3.3 Backtracks, dubs, ad-libs – transparent and opaque

The 'backtrack' technique is perhaps the most common way of recording and producing rap vocals. I choose to introduce the term to differentiate it from other types of vocal layering or doublings, as backtracks are typically reserved for doubling only some words/syllables of the main track (rather than full lines), and they also (typically) perform a 'background' role. Note, however, that they are also dissimilar to most types of 'backing vocals' in the sense that they are not (typically) a fully separate musical 'part' but rather an enhancement of the main vocal track. The choice of the term 'backtrack' is in one part because it communicates this background role well, but it is mostly because it is the term that I was introduced to in my own practice as a rapper. In recording, every verse was always followed by overdubbing 'backtracks'. Thus, 'backtracks' are a specific type of vocal layering, or 'dubs' (short for 'overdubs' and/or 'doublings', and the common colloquial term used by rappers, hip-hop 'heads' and the popular music field as such). Backtracks as a phenomenon are not exclusive to rap music, of course, but it is in rap music where this type of vocal doubling is present more often than not.

In the example from Ms. Lauryn Hill, the backtracks are very audible and opaque due to the use of 'different mode' between the tracks. In contrast, the majority of rap recordings will utilise much more transparent backtrack doublings, where same voice mode doublings are mixed more quietly and performed as similarly as possible to the main track. In Out-Kast's "Skew It on the Bar-B" (1998) featuring Raekwon, for example, all three verses (by André 3000, Raekwon and Big Boi, respectively) feature very transparent backtracks where the doublings are used to create emphasis rather than drawing attention to the separate sound source(s). It sounds much more like 'one' than 'multiple' unless the listener actively attends to the vocal arrangement/production. Note also that the choruses are doubled in their entirety, like the previous examples from Jurassic 5 (and Jadakiss), but still mixed in quite a transparent manner.

There are multiple different approaches to backtracks. Anecdotally, in my own experience with working with different rappers and producers, I have encountered some that 'comp' out backtracks from different 'takes' of the main track, some that record a single backtrack placed centrally in the stereo field alongside the main track, while yet others (including myself) typically record two backtracks panned left and right. Depending on the mix and the precision (including time stretching or moving syllables in post-production) of the doubling, the latter is potentially more opaquely chimeric than the former, but there are huge variations from track to track and artist to artist.

Note also that in addition to backtracks, it is common to include 'ad-lib tracks' in a rap recording. This technique comes across quite clearly in Big Boi's verse on "Skew It on the Bar-B". Ad-libs are the interjections of words or vocables (see Wallmark, 2022) that are not doublings of the main track. Most often, ad-libs are clearly part of a separate stream from the main vocal, but there are examples where they are arguably part of an opaquely chimeric compound stream. Listening to Lil Pump's "Gucci Gang" (2017), for example, the 'crew ad-libs' (different voices) placed on the first beat of the bars and in between the main vocal's lines are consistent enough both in frequency and placement that they can be perceived as part of the compound (and composite) rap stream. This type of different voice sequential chimericity is so opaque that many listeners will probably not experience it as chimeric at all.

Variations of same voice and different voice, same mode and different mode can be used to create quite different degrees of chimericity within a single track. One example of an artist using a combination of these techniques to great aesthetic effect is American rapper Chika and the track "SONGS ABOUT YOU" (2020). The first verse begins without backtracks before an interesting mode shift occurs in the line beginning at 0:29. Here, the introduction of a same voice backtrack in (harmonised) sung mode prompts the main track to be heard as 'sung' rather than rapped. As the backtrack homes in on distinct musical pitches, the listener is pushed into organising the rap's melody in the same 'pitch quantised' framework (note that this is a perceptual process, not a technical tuning of the audio track), and as Chika continues in an undeniably fully sung mode utilising a wider range of tones, we hear the main track and backtrack as a harmonising two-headed chimera, even as the backtracks only double two short passages. Even as Chika returns to the narrower range of the 'more rapped' mode, listeners are likely to keep hearing the mode as 'sung'.

In the second verse (from 1:35), the common type of same voice/ same mode backtracks is introduced. This is quite transparent, mainly functioning as an added emphasis on the doubled words. It is clearly somewhat more opaquely chimeric than the previous example from OutKast; however, the doublings are (probably completely deliberately) less 'tight' (that is, they differ more from the main track in terms of exact timing). At 1:46, the backtrack is pitched down, drawing attention to the backtrack in a clear act of opaque mediation – using technological processing to create an 'other voice' out of a recording of the 'same voice'. This, in turn, makes the chimericity more opaque. Similarly, but using a different type of other voice, the passage starting at the two-minute mark makes use of the backup singers that have previously been part of the chorus and as (wordless) background harmony. The second and fourth lines are doubled by a perfectly rhythmically tight sung harmony – utilising both different voice and different mode chimericity. Note that as Chika again switches mode from rapped to sung in the following four-bar section, the sung backtracks are no longer from her backup singers, but rather going back to the same technique as was used in verse one – same voice, same mode, but doubling in opaque harmony rather than transparent unison. And as Chika returns to the rapped mode at 2:18, the pitched down 'ogre voice' is layered with the main track – first quite low in the mix, before erupting loudly on the final word of the passage, the chimericity (and mediation) going from somewhat transparent to fully opaque.

3.4 What Is 'natural'? – cultural politics and opacity

Questions of transparency and opacity, whether regarding technological effects or chimericity, inevitably touch upon cultural politics. Listeners and artists assign certain values to music that is perceived as 'authentic' or 'natural', romanticising recordings that 'sound like a live performance'. This is at the crux of Brøvig-Hanssen's opaque and transparent mediation. Recorded music is obviously never unmediated by technology – it is never truly 'authentically' a naturalistic reproduction of a live performance, and listeners do not really expect it to be either. Nevertheless, transparent mediation, where the role of technology is not immediately apparent to the average listener, can be said to create an illusion of non-mediation. As certain recording techniques have become ubiquitous within a genre, they can paradoxically *become* 'transparent' to the encultured listener. This is particularly the case when they in some way represent or symbolise the 'natural' or unmediated – or as Brøvig-Hanssen puts it, "opaque mediation is experienced as both unnatural *and* natural, depending on various factors" (Brøvig-Hanssen, 2018, p. 2).

Same voice/same mode backtracks, for example, are clearly 'unnatural' in the sense that a rapper cannot perform two parts simultaneously in a live context. Yet, they are a standard feature of recorded rap music. One reason is their subtle nature and transparent chimericity. While they are less 'natural' than, say, a different voice/same mode backtrack, they also blend more into the mix. In this manner, they are unintrusive and transparent, while they at the same time resemble and represent the live hip-hop staple of a 'hypeman' or 'crew' doubling rhymes and line endings.

As both amateur performers and listeners have become familiar with the sonic possibilities afforded by the modern digital (home) recording studio, however – preferences for 'authentic representation' in recorded music seem to have diminished greatly. Listeners not only accept and expect opaque technological mediation and chimericity – many are also drawn to their aesthetic effects.

3.5 Opaquely mediated opaque chimericity – Kendrick Lamar

One hip-hop artist who has experimented widely with fully opaque mediation and chimericity in his vocal production is Kendrick Lamar. His 2011 album *Section.80,* in particular, features some creative and uncommon techniques. On the track "F*ck Your Ethnicity", the first verse begins without any backtracks at all, and the symmetrical line/bar structure – "convergent metrical structure" (Oddekalv, 2022a, 2022b) – establishes a certain 'standard verse structure' familiar for most listeners. Then, as he 'flips the flow', increasing the syllable density and introducing asymmetry in the line/bar relationship, backtracks are gradually faded to the point that they take over as 'lead' (at around 1:32) before fading back down as the breakneck pace of the flow subsides. Here, the chimericity works together

Figure 4.3 Layered and sequential chimericity in Kendrick Lamar's "A.D.H.D".

with other musical parameters to build up and release the tension of the flow and the narrative of the verse.

On "A.D.H.D.", this shifting relationship between main and backtracks is taken even further, underpinning the track's title and topic. The backtracks fade in from 0:30, and as the verse unfolds, the backtracks quickly evolve from being background to the lead to being first fully equal and then dominant, culminating in a passage approaching sequential chimericity as the main track is nearly inaudible when doubled. This creates an effect where the backtracks and main track seem to go back-to-back from word to word in the final line of the passage illustrated in Figure 4.3, particularly since the backtracks double less common words (not rhymes/line endings).

Here, the arrangement of the chimericity clearly references the 'scattered mind' of the titular condition and how it is augmented by cannabis and codeine. The opaque chimericity and mediation serve a narrative function as well as an aesthetic one.

4 CONCLUSIONS

As Kendrick Lamar shows with his creative use of opaque chimericity and opaque mediation, there is great aesthetic potential in how one layers and sequences vocal tracks in rap. Exploiting the listeners' auditory perceptual apparatus and what Bregman calls "stream segregation", the 'rapping chimera' creates various aesthetic effects by presenting compound and composite musical streams that are constituted by a combination of different sound sources. These techniques can be both layered and sequential, and they can be made up of different 'same voice' sources or 'different voices' (or even 'same voice *as* different voice') as well as different 'modes' (primarily 'rapped' and 'sung' to different degrees). This resulting *chimericity* – the degree to which the musical stream is experienced as *one* and *multiple* simultaneously – can be more or less opaque to the listener. This is similar to but different from how Brøvig-Hanssen shows how the presence of technological mediation can be opaque or transparent. Both rely on the listener's perceptual interpretation and organisation of the music, and the combinations of opaque and transparent chimericity and technological mediation respectively are powerful tools in the musician's or producer's arsenal.

REFERENCES

Adams, K. (2008). 'Aspects of the Music/Text Relationship in Rap', *Music Theory Online*, 14.

Adams, K. (2009). 'On the Metrical Techniques of Flow in Rap Music', *Music Theory Online*, 15(5).

Adams, K. (2015). 'The Musical Analysis of Hip-Hop', in Williams, J. A. (ed.) *The Cambridge Companion to Hip-Hop*. Cambridge: Cambridge University Press, pp. 118–134.

Adams, K. (2020). 'Harmonic, Syntactic, and Motivic Parameters of Phrase in Hip-Hop', *Music Theory Online*, 26(2).

Bregman, A. S. (1990). *Auditory Scene Analysis: The Perceptual Organization of Sound*. Cambridge, MA: The MIT Press.

Brøvig-Hanssen, R. (2010). 'Opaque Mediation: The Cut-and-Paste Groove in DJ Food's "Break"', in Danielsen, A. (ed.) *Musical Rhythm in the Age of Digital Reproduction*. Farnham: Ashgate, pp. 1–16.

Brøvig-Hanssen, R. (2018). 'Listening to or Through Technology: Opaque and Transparent Mediation', in Bennett, S. and Bates, E. (eds.) *Critical Approaches to the Production of Music and Sound*. New York: Bloomsbury Academic, pp. 195–210.

Condit-Schultz, N. (2016). 'MCFlow: A Digital Corpus of Rap Transcriptions', *Empirical Musicology Review*, 11(2), pp. 124–147.

Doyle, P. (2005). *Echo and Reverb: Fabricating Space in Popular Music Recording, 1900–1960: Music/Popular Culture*. 1st ed. Middletown, CT: Wesleyan University Press.

Duinker, B. (2020). *Diversification and Post-Regionalism in North American Hip-Hop Flow*. PhD, McGill University, Montréal.

Duinker, B. (2021). 'Segmentation, Phrase, and Meter in Hip-Hop Music', *Music Theory Spectrum*, 43(2), pp. 221–245.

Fabb, N. (2002). *Language and Literary Structure: The Linguistic Analysis of Form in Verse and Narrative*. Cambridge: Cambridge University Press.

Hognestad, J. K. (2023). 'Rap a cappella: Prosodiske strukturer i en norsk rapstemme', in Diesen, E. I., Markussen, B. and Oddekalv, K. A. (eds.) *Flytsoner: Studiar i flow og rap-lyrikk*. Oslo: Scandinavian Academic Press, pp. 177–204.

Jarman-Ivens, F. (2011a). 'Karen Carpenter: America's Most Defiant Square', in *Palgrave Macmillan's Critical Studies in Gender, Sexuality, and Culture*. New York: Palgrave Macmillan US, pp. 59–93.

Jarman-Ivens, F. (2011b). *Queer Voices: Technologies, Vocalities, and the Musical Flaw. Palgrave Macmillan's Critical Studies in Gender, Sexuality, and Culture*. New York: Palgrave Macmillan US.

Katz, J. (2008). 'Towards a Generative Theory of Hip-Hop', in *Music, Language, and the Mind*. Medford, MA: Tufts.

Katz, M. (2010). *Capturing Sound: How Technology Has Changed Music, Revised Edition*. 1st ed. Berkeley, CA: University of California Press.

Kautny, O. (2009). 'Ridin the Beat: Annahärungen an das Phänomen Flow'. in Hörner, F. and Kautny, O. (eds.) *Die Stimme im HipHop Untersuchungen eines intermedialen Phänomens*. Bielefeld: Transcript Verlag.

Kautny, O. (2015). 'Lyrics and Flow in Rap Music', in Williams, J. A. (ed.) *The Cambridge Companion to Hip-Hop*. Cambridge: Cambridge University Press, pp. 101–117.

Keyes, C. L. (1991). *Rappin' to the Beat: Rap Music as Street Culture Among African Americans*. PhD, University of Michigan Press, Ann Arbor, MI.

Komaniecki, R. (2017). 'Analyzing Collaborative Flow in Rap Music', *Music Theory Online*, 23(4).

Komaniecki, R. (2019). *Analyzing the Parameters of Flow in Rap Music*. PhD, Indiana University, Bloomington, IN.

Kraugerud, E. (2021). *Come Closer: Acousmatic Intimacy in Popular Music Sound*. PhD, University of Oslo, Oslo.

Krims, A. (2000). *Rap Music and the Poetics of Identity: New Perspectives in Music History and Criticism*. Cambridge, NY: Cambridge University Press.

Lacasse, S. (2000). *'Listen to My Voice': The Evocative Power of Vocal Staging in Recorded Rock Music and Other Forms of Vocal Expression*. PhD, University of Liverpool, Liverpool.

London, J. (2012). *Hearing in Time: Psychological Aspects of Musical Meter*. Oxford: Oxford University Press.

Mattessich, J. J. (2019). 'This Flow Ain't Free: Generative Elements in Kendrick Lamar's To Pimp a Butterfly', *Music Theory Online*, 25(1).

Miyakawa, F. M. (2005). *Five Percenter Rap: God Hop's Music, Message, and Black Muslim Mission: Profiles in Popular Music*. Bloomington, IN: Indiana University Press.

Oddekalv, K. A. (2022a). 'Surrender to the Flow: Metre on Metre or Verse in Verses? – Lineation Through Rhyme in Rap Flows', in Sykäri, V. and Fabb, N. (eds.) *Rhyme and Rhyming in Verbal Art, Language and Song*. Helsinki: Finnish Literature Society/SKS, pp. 229–245.

Oddekalv, K. A. (2022b). *What Makes the Shit Dope? The Techniques and Analysis of Rap Flows*. PhD, University of Oslo, Oslo.

Ohriner, M. (2016). 'Metric Ambiguity and Flow in Rap Music: A Corpus-Assisted Study of Outkast's 'Mainstream' (1996)', *Empirical Musicology Review*, 11(2), pp. 153–179. doi: 10.18061/emr.v11i2.4896.

Ohriner, M. (2019a). 'Analysing the Pitch Content of the Rapping Voice', *Journal of New Music Research*, pp. 1–21.

Ohriner, M. (2019b). *Flow: The Rhythmic Voice in Rap Music: Oxford Studies in Music Theory*. New York: Oxford University Press.

Rose, T. (1994). *Black Noise: Rap Music and Black Culture in Contemporary America: Music/Culture*. Hanover, NH: University Press of New England.

Sterne, J. (2003). *The Audible Past: Cultural Origins of Sound Reproduction*. Durham, DC: Duke University Press.

Wallmark, Z. (2022). 'Analyzing Vocables in Rap: A Case Study of Megan Thee Stallion', *Music Theory Online*, 28(2).

Walser, R. (1995). 'Rhythm, Rhyme, and Rhetoric in the Music of Public Enemy', *Ethnomusicology*, 39(2), pp. 193–218.

DISCOGRAPHY

Chika. (2020). [digital release] "Songs About You", on *Songs About You*. CHIKA/ Warner.

Jurassic 5. (1997). [digital release] "Concrete Schoolyard", on *Jurassic 5 EP*. Rumble Records/Interscope.

Kendrick Lamar. (2011a). [digital release] "A.D.H.D.", on *Section.80*, Top Dawg Entertainment/Section.80.

Kendrick Lamar. (2011b). [digital release] "F*ck Your Ethnicity", on *Section.80*, Top Dawg Entertainment/Section.80.

Lil Pump. (2017). [digital release] "Gucci Gang", on *Lil Pump*, Tha Lights Global/ Warner Records Inc.

Ms. Lauryn, H. (1998). [digital release] "Doo Wop (That Thing)", on *The Miseducation of Lauryn Hill*. Ruffhouse Records LP.

OutKast. (1998). [digital release] "Skew It on the Bar-B", on *Aquemini*, Arista Records LLC.

5

Exploring the history of distortion in drum and bass

Leigh Shields, Austin Moore, and Chris Dewey

1 INTRODUCTION

As a music that features such a strong, diverse, and faithful following, it is no wonder that drum and bass has a rich cultural history. Its impact has been significant, particularly in black culture, and its roots can be traced back to the children of the Windrush era, Caribbean carnivals, and UK sound system culture (Murphy and Loben, 2021). Aside from strong underground roots, drum and bass has seen mainstream and chart success with groups including Chase and Status and Pendulum, with DJ Fresh becoming the first drum and bass act to hold a No. 1 UK chart position (Kreisler, 2012). The music now reaches and unites fans across the globe, and as its popularity has steadily grown, so too has the interest in the production techniques.

Despite it being such a popular and influential style of music, guidance that currently exists on the early production techniques of drum and bass is mostly anecdotal and informal. Thus, this chapter acts as a transfer of discourse and provides an academic discussion on the early use of distortion.

Whilst researching drum and bass, one will find many articles that concern themselves with the socio-cultural influences responsible for the conception of the genre and its impact on the electronic music community – key contributors are discussed in the following section, and topics include detailing the history of the music, its genre predecessors and how it evolved from those earlier forms of jungle and proto-drum and bass. One will also find many discussions regarding the culture and how geographical location, class systems, and other societal factors helped shape what we refer to as the 'scene'. As well as this, one will also find research that details the compositional elements, which mostly involve analysis of the rhythmic and percussive elements and how they come to define the genre conventions. This research contributes to the limited amount of academic output that has been conducted into what is arguably one of the most important musical movements in the UK's rich electronic music history. We will build on the history already laid out for us by Quinn, Rathbone, Reynolds et al., and explore the technology, production methods, and the attitudes and motivations responsible for developing the harsher

DOI: 10.4324/9781003462101-6

and more aggressive sonic characteristics found in this music. Drum and bass is made of many subgenres (intelligent, liquid, darkcore, etc.), but the focus of this article is on the tech step sound that developed from 1995 onwards.

Since the mid-1990s, distorted sounds have become synonymous with drum and bass, particularly with two notable subgenres known as tech-step and neurofunk (Reynolds, 2000). Despite the existence of articles and forum discussions that have briefly highlighted the types of distortion used and speculation as to what technology was responsible, no analysis appears to have taken place that explores why it was used, why it became such an important tool, or why audiences responded to it so readily that it became a staple of the production aesthetic.

The main body of research that explores distortion in music production is linked to electric guitar distortion. There exists a plethora of investigation into rock and metal, and good examples of such work have been done by Herbst (2017), who explores the historical development and production techniques of distorted electric guitar as well as discusses some more of the defining sonic characteristics of distortion and the equipment responsible.

Therefore, this chapter, with its focus on a pioneering subgenre of drum and bass provides a unique insight into how distortion has been utilised from both a creative and technical perspective and fills a gap in the academic literature.

1.1 Drum and bass/jungle literature

In this section, we provide a short review of some of the key contributors to scholarship on drum and bass, how their works relate to this study, and highlight various themes that have been the subject of discussion. Quinn (2002) investigates the history and subculture of the genre and explores drum and bass' emergence from acid house in the early 1990s, the geographical space in which it occupied, and the importance of the black culture it came from, all the while referencing pop culture moments such as brit pop and how it may have polarised audiences and pushed the genre further into the underground. To further discuss the origins of jungle and highlight influential jungle and drum and bass record labels (even showing location, owner, and date of establishment), Rathbone (2014) investigates, among other themes, the landscapes that were important in providing a platform for jungle and drum and bass to develop (namely pirate radio and record shops). These journal publications, documentaries, and online articles related to the history and influence of the jungle/drum and bass scene are useful in providing a social and cultural context to this work.

Whilst discussing tech step, we invariably discuss subgenres and their inception in this chapter, and some interesting research has already been done by Mcleod (2001), whose work specifically deals with subgenre naming conventions as examples of consumer culture and cultural appropriation. This helps when furthering the understanding of how listeners interpret the use of distortion in music. Ferrigno (2011) discusses the influence of science fiction in drum and bass and analyses how producers began using samples from sci-fi films and how the sci-fi genre was able to emphasise how drum and bass were expressing the feelings of socio-economic and racial alienation felt by the youth of the time. Other perspectives on this exist, however, as during my conversation with an artist responsible for producing music at the time referred to during this chapter, this notion was dismissed in favour of a more experimental ideology being employed.

2 DISTORTION AS A PRODUCTION TOOL

As a key aspect of this chapter, it may be useful to provide a brief overview of what happens when a signal is subject to distortion.

An electronic circuit features a point at which it will overload; this clip point is a point at which the voltage cannot rise any higher and the resulting signal becomes distorted. This distortion is non-linear; that is, the input signal and output signal feature a relationship where the amplitude levels are not linearly related (Pirkle, 2019).

There are many devices that feature non-linear processing as a part of their intended effect, such as solid-state distortion and overdrive units, vacuum tubes, and analogue filters such as those found on Moog low pass units (Pirkle, 2019), but often producing distortion on a recording device such as on an analogue mixing console is generally avoided, particularly when the intention is for the pre-amp to provide clean amplification without adding any character (Owsinski, 2017).

Distortion introduces harmonic content to the frequency spectrum and can be used to add depth, character, and aggression. Moore (2020) identified 'aggressive' as a popular descriptor for distortion and a particularly distinctive timbral characteristic of Drum and Bass production. As a rule, it is generally avoided when monitoring and playing back audio, but it is extensively used in a creative and artistic way to add texture and character to elements of a production, notably applied to bass and drum elements. Bourbon (2019) explores how distortion can have a perceived impact on the sound of a record and explores the different harmonic structures that can be created by using interfaces such as desk input channel strips, compression, and digital plug-ins. He concludes that low-level harmonic distortion adds "a sense of size and weight to delivery through to heavy distortion creating a sense of aggression or destruction" and that "distortion plays an important role in manipulating the performance gesture and emotion" (p. 35).

This has been commonplace in rock music production for decades, and the earliest use of distortion as a guitar effect can be traced as far back as the 50s before becoming more widespread through the 1970s when metal and rock music emerged. At this time, companies like Marshall gave early metal guitarists access to amplifiers designed to produce distortion (Herbst, 2017). It can be suggested that much of Herbst's work is in a similar commentary to ours but with a change of focus on the genre. Whereas it is well documented how distortion became an important feature in metal production and the methods used to achieve it, there is a gap in this narrative when it comes to drum and bass production. Initial research suggests that this was created by driving the input gain on analogue desks and creating clip distortion before moving on to using guitar pedals (Grid et al., 2021). In personal communication with Graham Sutton (artist name Boymerang) in 2021, he attributes his use of distortion in productions such as *Soul Beat Runna* to the guitar pedals he used when he was playing in punk bands:

> It seemed like a good idea at the time, tracks were becoming more aggressive and it was a good way to make bass cut through without eating up too much headroom.

This created a new sound and texture, which was the catalyst for diverging drum and bass into new subgenres such as tech step. This change happened around 1995 and dictated in no small way to the specific time frame for the research as it denotes a change in direction and audience. The end time bracket for this study is around 1997–98, which is the time at which the popularity of the DAW began to increase, particularly after Cubase released the VST format in 1996. For more on the consequences of the interfaces and new generation digital music production, one may look to Reuter (2021) as he discusses the new generation of the DAW and how digital practices have been overlooked due to an analogue recording studio perspective. An important difference found here is in the continued use of distortion effects across these genres; for example, guitar pedals and amplification are still widely used in metal music production, whereas, in contemporary drum and bass production, distortion is now more often created using digital processes employed by using VST instruments and effect plug-ins. One can argue that there is a similarity in the production aesthetics of metal and the more aggressive forms of drum and bass. The same can also be said for dubstep, and its American variants, bro-step and riddim.

Zagorski-Thomas (2014) observes that signature sounds found in music can be, in some cases, related to the sound of a type of technology. These deliberate exaggerations are referred to in his book, *The Musicology of Record Production*, as 'Sonic Cartoons' and are deemed a sort of caricature of sound, that is, sounds that aren't created naturally but instead by means of processing with technology and by layering and combining sounds, or some other form of manipulation, in the recording process. Distortion is a signature sound of drum and bass and creates a sonic cartoon of sorts which allows musicians and producers to express themselves differently and to embrace the technologies that have been used in other genres of music (rock and metal, for example) to be able to create new soundscapes and sonic textures that appeal to underground music listeners. Zagorski-Thomas (2014) argues that signature sounds can relate to a group as well as an individual. Throughout this research, we will highlight the groups or producers and labels who were the most influential in creating and pushing the signature sounds that we now associate so readily with drum and bass music.

3 THE INTRODUCTION OF DISTORTION TO DRUM AND BASS

Drum and bass is the result of an evolution and development of jungle and breakbeat hardcore. The drum and bass genre subsequently spawned a multitude of subgenres, each defined by their instrumentation and musical focus. The first tracks that came to define the drum and bass genre as we know it today were relatively minimal and clean in their production. The now standard 2-step style that is prevalent originated with Alex Reece's *Pulp Fiction.* Alex Reece was signed with Goldie's Metalheadz label when it started in 1995 (Terzulli, 2021) and is considered a game changer for the genre. The track has a distinct lack of layered breaks and samples found in the jungle records of the time, and Pulp Fiction was the first of a wave of tracks that featured a more minimal production. "There's nothing to that tune, no big breakdown. It's drums and a bass" (Fabio, 2021). The bassline itself is sampled from Devotion by MC Solaar and is warm, clean, and compliments the jazzy horn samples featured throughout. LTJ Bukem and Bailey then paved the way for what was coined 'intelligent drum and bass', which featured a more sophisticated and technical approach to production, with atmospheric pads and more jazz based influences. A good example of this is found in LTJ Bukem's *Horizons,* released on Looking Good Records in 1995. The response to this more popular and musical style of drum and bass was tech step. Nathan Vinell (Skynet), during an email conversation in January 2022, explains that for him, distortion was an effect already being utilised in his production of other genres:

> I started using distortion early in my productions of drum and bass. I was coming from a techno background, which is heavily reliant on distortion, which I loved and started using more and more in DnB. This was the first early development of Tech Step for me.

This suggests that the use of distortion was already prevalent in other genres of electronic music but had not yet found its footing in drum and bass.

3.1 Tech step

Although sharing the same basic rhythmic pattern and structure of drum and bass, this new style stripped it of its multiple layers of Amen breaks and reggae samples (Murphy and Loben, 202) and instead featured harder, more aggressive drum programming and more electronic and tense atmospheres coupled with oppressive reece basslines. The name comes from the style being a combination of its similarity in style to Detroit techno of the time and the 2-step drum pattern established by *Pulp Fiction.* There are a few key proponents of Tech Step, including Ed Rush, DJ Trace, and Nico from *No U Turn Records*, and Hockman (2014) has documented much of the origin story in his ethnographic study into breakbeats. What happened at *No U Turn* was a collaboration between the engineer (Nico) and artists

(Dom & Roland, Ed Rush, etc.) to create a sound that was a response, in part, to the commercial drum and bass that featured more pop music elements as created by the likes of Goldie, Bukem and Roni Size.

In Hockman's interview with Nico, Nico suggests that there was no doubt in his mind that it was the DJs who were most passionate and excited about their music and that the combination of engineer and DJ led to some great collaborations (Hockman, 2014). One of these collaborations spawned a very rare production that was the result of five producers in one evening in the *No U Turn* studio entitled EDTRAFIENICAL and was a collaboration between Ed Rush, DJ Trace, Fierce, Nico, and Optical. The track has been posted on the No U Turn YouTube channel with accompanying text and images of the studio at the time. The track was released by Sublogic Recordings as an ultra-limited edition pressing and was a hand-numbered run of 150 copies remastered from the original DAT (Reaper, 2009). This track epitomises the key characteristic of distortion in Tech Step as a result of Nico and *No U Turn's* influences.

Christodoulou (2020) tells us that the defining feature of tech step is the distorted bass sound. This was achieved by sending the recorded basslines into analogue equipment effects such as distortion and overdrive, and this was the most common method of introducing distortion until Nico introduced the use of the distortion pedal into the production process in order to make the basslines more prominent in the mix. In his interview with Hockman (2014), Nico discusses the development of this method:

> I wanted to hear what the sub bass was doing . . . in the track I'd just been up all night making, whilst driving my car home early in the morning. The tiny speakers in my old car revealed nothing of the powerful bass that I knew was there. A dash of distortion made every note clear. Once I'd done this a few times, Trace, Ed Rush and everyone else didn't want the bass without the distortion.
>
> (Sykes as cited in Hockman, 2014)

The distortion added here by Nico provided additional harmonic content that made the sub-bass appear in the upper-frequency range and thus audible in smaller speaker systems. This technique is used in modern production practice so that the listener can perceive low-frequency content while listening on mobile phone and laptop speaker systems.

3.2 Interview approach and methodology

It is important that contributions to this chapter were made by the producers and artists responsible for shaping the early sound of drum and bass and for developing the use of distortion firsthand, contributions that can only be made by those who have a certain level of understanding and knowledge as a result. The artists who agreed to participate are considered pioneers of the sound and bring a degree of credibility to this research.

Interviews took place over a period of 12 months (May 2021–May 2022) with seminal producers whose early body of work contributed to the development and inclusion of distortion as a production method. These include Dom & Roland, a producer who has been releasing drum and bass records for over 25 years on Moving Shadow, 31 Records, Prototype, and Renegade Hardware; Cris Stevens, the producer and engineer who collaborated with T Power with releases on SOUR and DJ Only Records; Sappo, former BBC Radio 1 DJ and pioneer of the drum and bass scene; Optical, producer and owner of highly regarded drum and bass label Virus Recordings; TC, Bristol based DJ and producer who has worked with Pendulum, Sub Focus and has released music with RAM records and OWSLA; and Skynet, a producer responsible for launching Audio Blueprint, a record label that influenced the growth of the neurofunk subgenre.

The interviews were a combination of semi-structured video conference calls and email conversations. Key themes and topics for discussion were identified beforehand through the authors' knowledge as drum and bass practitioners and through analysis of online discussions and pre-existing interviews.

Themes, as the starting points for discussion, were:

- When distortion was first used as an effect
- Which of their tracks were the first to use distortion
- What methods were used to achieve it
- What the response was from other producers

Once these key themes were established, the conversations became more open to allow for the inclusion of other related topics. The use of qualitative interviews as a research method has been used by a number of researchers in the field of music, including Moore (2019), Murphy and Loben (2021), and Belle-Fortune (2005), offering increased validity to the research as it allowed for the interviewees to occasionally steer the direction of the interview and to converse using their own words and language.

3.3 Introducing distortion

Dominic Angas, as Dom & Roland, is one of tech step's most revered names and whose sound has been described as heavily engineered, precise, and industrial in nature. Dom was heavily involved with *No U Turn* records, and even though *No U Turn's* aesthetic was already something of a gritty one, Dom's Tech Step was even more so, particularly during his time spent signed to Moving Shadow (a record label founded by Rob Playford in 1990).

He notes:

> I suppose I was definitely the most distorted person on there (Moving Shadow). I wouldn't say I was the instigator of distortion or anything, but yeah, it was just trying to find that sort of angle that other people didn't have.
>
> (Angas, personal communication, 2021)

Much of his early approaches to producing music were experimental in nature, and through this experimentation, he discovered that distortion could be used as a tool to help mix and improve loudness as well as provide aesthetic properties to his music.

> I would still say that my first few records I didn't really have a clue what I was doing I was just going 'Oh, I like that sound, but like I didn't really know how to EQ anything; It wasn't until later I discovered all of that. It was much later when I realised that distortion could be used as a tool to help mix and there are so many aspects of mixing that distortion can help with.
>
> (Angas, personal communication, 2021)

Dom enjoyed the nature of analogue equipment creating sounds that were not necessarily the intended result:

> Another thing I've always loved about making music is that the use of distortion can cause ghost sounds, like sounds that aren't actually there, but they're sort of created by the molding of two other sounds, so like for instance, when you put a kick and a bass through the distortion and, especially back when we were using MIDI, things wouldn't trigger at exactly the same time. So, because of the different layering happening in slightly different places, over time it would create a different (effect) because it's going through the distortion. It would create a different tone each time you get a hit.
>
> (Angas, personal communication, 2021)

This approach introduced sonic artefacts into his music that would not have appeared if not for the experimental nature of the production process and the unexpected results of using a variety of different equipment.

At the same time as Dom & Roland was experimenting with distortion, DJ Trace was also contributing to this new, more gritty direction. Stevens (2022) suggests that distortion used in drum and bass was in an embryonic state and, due to the inherent flaws and limitations in the gear around that time, most producers were trying to find out how to make their music loud and clean. The inclusion of distortion ran counter to that and was looked at with some disdain.

> For me, that all changed when we received The Mutant (Rollers Instinct) back from DJ Trace with its dirty distorted basses. I think everyone took notice of that and quested to make the most deranged bass they could.
>
> (Stevens, personal communication, 2022)

The original track sent to DJ Trace to remix was *Mutant Jazz*, produced by Stevens' collaborator T Power and producer MK-Ultra. Mutant Jazz is regarded as a pioneering drum and bass track featuring horn melodies, piano and ambient synth elements, and jungle breakbeats. The DJ Trace remix of T Power's Mutant Jazz provided a significant change in atmosphere from the original and features reversed piano effects, horn stabs, and a Reese bassline made famous by producer Terrorist with his track 'Renegade' the year before. This style of production went on to become extremely popular throughout 1996–1997, with *No U Turn* and Metalheadz pushing the boundaries.

Although drum and bass had established itself as a popular new direction for electronic music, having seen a number of iterations in a short space of time (jungle, intelligent, breakcore, ragga), it took artists such as Dom & Roland and DJ Trace to continue pushing their more aggressive creations before it was accepted as a new direction for the genre, with audiences eventually being receptive to the harsh and gritty character that was emerging.

3.4 Lacking equipment and resources

A recurring theme that has presented itself through the outcomes of the interviews is that the limited access to resources meant that they had to stretch the capabilities of the equipment they had in order to get as many outcomes as possible from it. There wasn't as much access to the myriad of tools that are available today to augment our music, and artists like Dom & Roland and Optical had to "buy cheap shit and abuse it" (Angas, personal communication, 2021). Angas elaborates: "I remember going to Maplin's in Hammersmith with Matt Optical when we were making a lot of music together and we just we just look for shit that would be like oh, that's £20, let's get that". A prominent example of equipment that was available and owned by most of the contributors to this discussion was the analogue mixing desk.

Angas recalls a time when, owing to a distinct lack of knowledge of audio production when he started out, there would inevitably be times when he would purposefully drive the gain up on his analogue mixing console and use the sound that came out of it.

> I did have a desk made by Studer, who are quite well known for making tape machines, and I had this really old desk which was made in 1969, it was like a broadcast console and I'd never found anything that distorted quite like that and I kept that for a long time and from at least the mid 1990's to about 2010, a lot of distortion came from that.
> (Angas, personal communication, 2021)

This was an approach shared by producer Cris Stevens. Cris joined forces with T Power on an album under the name Chocolate Weasel (T Power is well known for releasing on SOUR and for collaborating with Shy FX). He used distortion on a number of tracks on their first album in 1995, but in 1996, it became much more prevalent.

> I was the in-house engineer at SOUR records around this time, and it was almost a set and dedicated channel on the console for an over-

driven sine wave for bass (AKAI S1000). I recall a doing a session with Shy FX and UK Apache (Take heed and take check, 1994) where Apache blew the mic diaphragm out. We recorded using the damaged mic (plus recorded with a fresh mic). I really liked the damaged mic and convinced Andre (Shy FX) to go with it.

> (Stevens, personal communication, 2022)

Like a lot of producers at this time, Cris and Marc Royal (T Power) were driving console pre-amps and overloading outboard inputs.

> We did the second album at Marc's home, and it allowed us the time to experiment with audio, plus, we were actively trying to dirty everything so we would do a lot of reamping, or record to tape (too hard), pull the tape out, mash it around, record the playback from a small speaker. We also did some parallel stuff with guitar pedals, and had some old, not perfectly functioning outboard (Watkins Copy Cat, and Eventide H910). Also, for that album Marc had a Korg Trinity keyboard that had a digital distortion, and you could map it to the modulation ribbon. We also had an Ensoniq DP4+ which had some distortions that were very 'digital' but suited the material.
>
> (Stevens, personal communication, 2022)

The approach to creating new and interesting drum and bass music by artists such as T Power and Dom & Roland was an experimental one. Abusing the limited hardware available generally yielded sonic outputs that were distorted or broken, and the resulting sounds were not always of the hardware's original intended design. There also seemed to be no make or model of equipment preferred when it came to creating distorted effects in this way. Unlike equipment used for drum programming or sampling, such as the ubiquitous Akai S950 samplers and Roland TR-808 drum machines, the equipment identified previously is a diverse range of technology that meant that even though records followed a common formula in terms of arrangement and structure, they contained their own individual sonic texture and character.

Another proponent of the use of driving input gain to create distortion is Andrew Sappleton, otherwise known as Sappo, a Steinberg Product Specialist across the UK who has worked at BBC Radio 1 and 1XTRA for five years, along with mainstream jungle/DNB labels such as V Records, Frontline records, Emotif, World dance, Intalex Flex, Rinse out, Formation, and many more. Sappo tells us that it was the combination of a number of pieces of hardware that were responsible for the distorted sounds he was creating in 1995–1996, evident in tracks such as Dark & Dirty, Like Dis, and Go on Bad which were released on Rinse Out and Flex Records. Among the equipment Sappo used (including an AKAIS950 and a Yamaha TG), he used a Studiomaster Diamond 8–2 Mixer mixing desk "driven hard on the pots, all of my early flex and rinse out stuff 1995–1998 have so much of this sound in there" (Sappleton, 2021).

Matt Quinn 'Optical', an artist who is well renowned and responsible for creating (with Ed Rush) what is considered to be one of the most important drum and bass albums of all time (Wormhole), was also abusing gain inputs to achieve saturation and distortion.

> I have always used some kind of gain driving from subtle saturation all the way to full crushed distortion since my first release in 1992 (Little Matt & Uprock "Calm Down" – Fat Chuna) I was 19 at the time and we had been experimenting with driving up gains.
> (Quinn, personal communication, 2022)

In an AMA Reddit thread, *No U Turn* artist and future Virus records owner Optical (2013) substantiated this abuse of desk input gain as he would "try every bit of gear I could find and try to push the input or output to see what it did". He used "pretty much anything with a gain" before settling on using Focusrite Green EQ's and a Mackie desk gain as staples for saturating drums and bass. On discussing what made much of the Virus sound, he suggests that the Mackie 32/8 desk was a part of the aesthetic for the label and that despite having owned many desks, some very high-end, something about that desk worked well with the samplers and other equipment they had.

The Mackie 32/8 often comes up as being the desk that had some of the most pleasing distortion created as a product of driving the inputs, so much that it has been sought after by producers looking to recreate the sound in more recent times. Bristol-based producer TC began releasing music in the early 2000s and was inspired by the mid-90s distorted sound. In an interview with TC, he tells us that for him, distortion was used to achieve level control without using compression, and "you feel like you can trust saturation to never let peaks go over 0 and cause clipping, I was always after the channel distortion sound of the Mackie desk" (Caswell, personal communication, 2021).

It is difficult to suggest why the Mackie 32/8 is well referenced, or at least has achieved cult status as achieving the best tone, but it may be down to accessibility and cost. Mackie tells us on their website that with so much home recording happening in the 90s, musicians began looking for a high-quality, yet affordable, mixer. Mackie unveiled its 8-bus mixing console just as the ADAT and other multitrack digital tape formats were flourishing ("Legendary 8-Bus Console Receives Electronic Musician Editors' Choice Legacy Award", 2021). Johnson (2021) has created an Audio Unit plug-in called the MackEQ and provides a Mackie distortion with treble and bass controls included. In the description, Johnson references drum and bass production:

> I got something else. I think it might be useful: certainly, it can get the correct type of tone, but I don't believe I have the true 100% 90's drum and bass madness exactly down. There's a texture in there, especially when you start aggressively distorting highs, that just defies being captured in a plugin.

In that last comment may lie an answer to the question of why we want to recapture the old 90s sound, what many producers seek to reproduce, created by analogue gear that can't yet be replicated with digital technologies. Although perhaps not all people can spot the difference, Dom & Roland discuss using a digital desk to achieve a similar sound:

> I had a Yamaha digital mixer, one of the first ones, and that was digital, and I know everyone goes on about how digital distortion is nasty and you need a good bit of analog to get distortion. But I used to clip that thing all the time and I mean a lot of the things that are now considered classics, like you know, The Tramen break, were all really distorted through this digital desk. And, you know, it's quite amusing to hear people say 'oh god, have you heard the Tramen? Have you heard that amazing analog distortion on it? and actually, yeah, it was a digital desk.'
>
> (Angas, personal communication, 2021)

The contributors all weave a common thread through their discussions, and by constructing our ideas through the collection and analysis of the data, we can synthesise the interview responses and use comparative methods to identify the most prevalent themes:

- Distortion was achieved by overloading input gain on analogue desks and guitar pedals
- Producers have a preference for analogue over digital and were using cheap, often damaged, or malfunctioning analogue equipment. They were also often combining a variety of hardware gear
- Distortion was used to help with mixdowns (e.g., achieving optimal loudness)
- Distortion was used to develop new sounds and new approaches and to push the boundaries of drum and bass
- The resulting sonic character was used as a response to the more popular and mainstream forms of drum and bass, a character that was described as deranged, aggressive, abused, and gritty
- Much of the understanding and learning was achieved by experimentation and was explored early in the production journey

4 CONCLUSION

Distortion is the changing of the appearance or sound of something in a way that makes it seem strange or unclear (Collins Dictionary, 2022). In 1995, the sound of distortion ran counter to the aesthetic featured in jungle and the early forms of drum and bass at the time and, at first (as suggested by Stevens), was met with some derision, until a number of producers began to experiment with the few pieces of equipment they had access to and started to push it to its limits. This abuse of the hardware, occasionally due to a lack of knowledge and understanding of what was occurring on a technical level, created a new and exciting direction for drum and bass music. The audience responded to this new direction with vigour and enthusiasm, which was evidenced in the growing fanbase both in the UK and overseas, and perpetuated the need for a more aggressive timbre, an aggression that could only be achieved by employing the use of distortion.

The aim of this study was to explore the motivations behind using distortion in drum and bass production and to identify some of the equipment used. The salient themes emerging as a result of the input from the interviewees are the use and abuse of cheap technology due to a lack of resources and an experimental approach to production, which created a gritty and more aggressive aesthetic that ran counter to the more popular forms of drum and bass of the time. The distortion we have identified as being created mostly by overloading analogue desk inputs, but also using guitar pedals and other audio equipment that featured a gain control.

By using the interview method, we were able to retrieve information from the source and uncover new and interesting commentary, although there are some limitations with this approach, one being that we rely on the interviewee's memory of events that happened some 28 years ago and who may experience some filtered versions of the events. Future work will continue to include interviews with key practitioners and investigate the move from hardware to software distortion and how it has influenced today's production methods.

> Over the years after digital took off distortion has changed – producing good distortion has not really been possible with digital plug ins. I feel today's music is way too clean and polished, giving it a lot less attitude as during the early days of Techstep and Neurofunk. I prefer to have grit, edge, and attitude in my sonics, which comes from hardware distortion.
>
> (Vinell, personal communication, 2022)

We can then further explore why we are often fixated on trying to recapture the sonics of the past and if Skynet's statement perhaps sums up the feelings of many other producers – that despite developments made in digital plug-in technology and the myriad of software emulations of vintage equipment available, whether we are able to break new ground and create drum and bass with the same "grit, edge and attitude" as that which originated back in 1995.

REFERENCES

Belle-Fortune, B. (2005). *All Crews: Journeys Through Jungle/Drum and Bass Culture*. London, UK: Vision Publishing.

Bourbon, A. (2019). Hit hard or go home – Exploration of distortion on the perceived impact of sound on a mix. In *Proceedings of the 12th Art of Record Production Conference*, pp. 19–36. Stockholm: Royal College of Music (KMH) & Art of Record Production.

Christodoulou, C. (2020). Bring the break-beat back!: Authenticity and the politics of rhythm in drum 'n' bass. *Journal of Electronic Dance Music Culture*, *12*(1), 3–21.

Collins Dictionary. (2022). *Distortion*. Collins English Dictionary, Retrieved from: https://www.collinsdictionary.com/dictionary/english/distortion

Fabio. (2021). *Comment on Terzulli, P. (2021). Who Say Reload*. [S.l.]. London, UK: Velocity Press, p. 42.

Ferrigno, E. D. (2011). The dark side: Representing science fiction in drum "n" bass. *New Review of Film and Television Studies*, *9*(1), 95–104. https://doi.org/10.1080/17400309.2011.521722

Grid, T. et al. (2021). *Kit Lists of Dnb Hardware Studios Past and Present*. Retrieved 17 March 2021, from www.dogsonacid.com/threads/kit-lists-of-dnb-hardware-studios-past-and-present.794515/

Herbst, J. P. (2017). Historical development, sound aesthetics and production techniques of the distorted electric guitar in metal music. *Metal Music Studies*, *3*(1), 23–46. https://doi.org/10.1386/mms.3.1.23_1

Hockman, J. (2014). *An Ethnographic and Technological Study of Breakbeats in Hardcore, Jungle and Drum & Bass*. Retrieved August, from http://oatd.org/oatd/record?record=oai%5C:digitool.library.mcgill.ca%5C:121313%5Cnpapers2://publication/uuid/8ADF3E0E-EE11-4836-AB15-E91A314B2FE6

Johnson, C. (2021). *Airwindows Mackity: Mac/Windows/Linux AU/VST – Gearspace.com*. [online] Gearspace.com. https://gearspace.com/board/product-alerts-older-than-2-months/1348411-airwindows-mackity-mac-windows-linux-au-vst.html [Accessed 17 August 2022].

Kreisler, L. (2012). *DJ Fresh and Rita Ora Become UK's First Drum & Bass Official Singles Chart Number 1*. [online] Officialcharts.com.

McLeod, K. (2001). Genres, subgenres, sub-subgenres and more: Musical and social differentiation within electronic/dance music communities. *Journal of Popular Music Studies*, *13*(1), 59–75. https://doi.org/10.1111/j.1533-1598.2001.tb00013.x

Moore, A. (2020). Dynamic range compression and the semantic descriptor aggressive. *Applied Sciences (Switzerland)*, *10*(7). https://doi.org/10.3390/app10072350

Murphy, B. & Loben, C. (2021). *Renegade Snares*. London: Jawbone Press.

Owsinski, B. (2017). *The Recording Engineer's Handbook*. Burbank, CA: BOMG Publishing.

Optical. (2013). *I am Optical AMA (Virus Recordings)*. Reddit. Retrieved 15 January, from https://www.reddit.com/r/edmproduction/comments/1vagak/i_am_optical_ama_virus_recordings/.

Pirkle, W. (2019). *Designing Audio Effect Plugins in C++: For AAX, AU, and VST3 with DSP Theory* (2nd ed.). Abingdon, UK and New York, USA: Routledge.

Quinn, S. (2002). Rumble in the jungle: The invisible history of drum'n'bass. *Transformations*, *3*(3), 1–12.

Rathbone, S. (2014). *Exploring the Jungle: Contemporary Archaeology Gets a Little bit Darker*. Oxfordshire, UK: Taylor & Francis.

Reaper, T. (2009). *'Edtrafienical is Getting a Release!', DogsOnAcid.com*. Retrieved 30 October, from https://www.dogsonacid.com/threads/edtrafienical-is-getting-a-release.652699/

Reuter, A. (2021). Who let the DAWs out? The digital in a new generation of the digital audio workstation. In *Popular Music and Society*, pp. 1–16. Oxfordshire, UK: Taylor & Francis.

Reynolds, S. (2013). *Generation ecstasy: Into the world of techno and rave culture*. Florence: Taylor and Francis.

Stevens, C. (2022). *Interviewed by Leigh Shields*.

Terzulli, P. (2021). *Who Say Reload*. [S.l.]. London, UK: Velocity Press.

Zagorski-Thomas, S. (2014). Sonic cartoons. In *The Musicology of Record Production*, pp. 49–69. Cambridge: Cambridge University Press. doi:10.1017/CBO9781139871846.005

DISCOGRAPHY

Bukem, L. (1995). *Horizons*. Watford, UK: Looking Good Records.

Burke, D., Hutchison, D., Settle, B. & Sykes, N. (2010). *Edtrafienical*. London, UK: Sublogic Recordings.

Quinn, personal communication, M. (1992). *Calm Down*. London, UK: Fat Chuna.

Reece, A. (1995). *Pulp Fiction*. London, UK: Metalheadz.

Royal, M. (1995). *The Mutant Remix*. London, UK: Sour.

Sappleton, A (1996a). *Like Dis*. Huddersfield, UK: Flex Records.

Sappleton, A. (1996b). *Go on Bad*. Huddersfield, UK: Flex Records.

Sappleton, A. (1996c). *Dark & Dirty*. Huddersfield, UK: Flex Rinse Out.

Sutton, G. (1997). *Soul Beat Runna*. UK: Regal.

6

Dynamic meta-spatialization

Narrative and recontextualization implications of spatial stage stacking

Jo Lord and Michail Exarchos

1 INTRODUCTION

This chapter explores the creative opportunities situated in the space where sample-based musicking and spatial mixing meet. Previous work by Exarchos (2019a; 2019b; 2020; 2021a; 2021b) has demonstrated the relationship between the sample-based aesthetic and the effect of the exponential juxtaposition of textural and spatial *staging*, particularly in self-sampling practice. In the context of music production, sound staging can be defined as the organization of sound sources within the boundaries outlining a schematized sonic environment (Moylan, 2012; 2014, 2020; Lacasse, 2000; Moore and Dockwray, 2008). Further scholars (for example, Zagorski-Thomas, 2009, 2010; Liu-Rosenbaum, 2012; Holland, 2013) have theorized on the placement of musical elements within the space of a popular music mix, and the concept of staging has emerged as a useful theoretical notion: in essence, it suggests conceptualizing a music mix as a 'stage' where the placement – but also the dynamic movement and manipulation – of musical elements (their mediation) has thematic and narrative implications (meaning) for both listeners and producers. Lord (2022a, 2022b) has examined the creative potential in spatial mixing, arguing for the benefit of non-proprietary formats and practices in contemporary music production. This collaborative study imagines a multi-step, iterative, practice-based framework offering developmental opportunities for spatial recontextualization. The research investigates the implications of staging as a conscious narrative and contextual strategy across multiple steps of a creative trajectory, including composition, recording, performance, beat-making, remixing, and stereo and spatial mixing. The journey is relayed via autoethnographic retelling of significant events in workflow and praxis, and phenomenological descriptions of sonic events and developmental constructs. Background texts and research are interweaved throughout the discussion of practice in the main body of the text, which recounts five creative phases: the construction of a sample-*creating*-based foundational beat; the progression to a full, mixed song production, incorporating live performances in stereo; its spatial mixing; the (re)sampling of phonographic "ephemera" (Zak III, 2001) from the latter, to create a

DOI: 10.4324/9781003462101-7

new sample-based remix; and a spatial mix of the remix production. These phases are reflected in the musical outputs of five tracks/mixes available via the companion website (Gutter Turtle Records, 2022). The aim of the study is to illustrate the narrative and recontextualization implications of staging juxtaposition; the function and affordances of spatial sonic objects as they are deployed in performance, production, and sample-based music; the conscious construction of sonic signatures as contextual signifiers throughout the developmental process; and their recontextualization as part of the dynamic metamorphosis of phonographic stages texturally and spatially.

2 PHASE 1 – 'FREIGHT TRAIN' STEREO DEMO: MAKING THE BEAT

The first part of the creative process in this stud entailed the creation of an original *beat* made out of self-created and then manipulated source samples. The term 'beat' is used here interchangeably with 'sample-based hip-hop production' referring to a complete instrumental music production or backing, not just the organization of percussive/drum elements. This highlights the genre's rhythmic priorities: Williams (2010, p. 19) extends Schloss's (2014, p. 2) definition of 'beat' as a sample-based instrumental collage "composed of brief segments of recorded sound" to also include non-sample-based elements in the instrumental production. The rationale behind the creation and manipulation of the source material lies in the premise that sample-based Hip Hop owes its sonic aesthetic to the recontextualization of sonic characteristics (signatures) derived from – and embedded within – phonographic ephemera, a premise that expands on the notion of sample-based Hip Hop's reliance on "musical borrowing" (Williams, 2010) toward the significance of a 'mechanical borrowing'. "These characteristics include signal flow colorations and staging phenomena" (Exarchos, 2021a, p. 52), referring to Zagorski-Thomas' (2009, 2010) "media-based" and spatial or "functional" staging techniques expressed materially on records. For a self-sampling beat-maker, the added onus lies in the creation of convincing phonographic 'others', which not only maximize textural and spatial signatures within the source material but, further, 'distance' one's own work. Looking at beat-making practice as "meta-music" (Mudede, 2003), the following words echo the driving manifesto behind the creative concept:

> if otherness equates perspective rather than just difference, the *meta* process (sample-based composition/production) has to sonically manifest 'perspective-ness': the sound of discursive workflow, manipulation, a meta-phonographic process interacting with manifestations of – past/other – phonographic processes. In other words, for recontextualization to function, it has to assume an initial context and, therefore, source samples need to carry markers of having first belonged to a sonic 'else-when' and 'elsewhere' (original emphasis).
>
> (Exarchos, 2021a, pp. 52–53)

Pickering (2012, pp. 25–26) coins the term "elsewhen" to highlight "the temporal distance brought about by recorded music", noting that: "Musical repeatability means that we are able to hear music from various previous periods and identify them, even on a decade-by-decade basis, by their characteristic musical sounds". Practically speaking, at the beginning of the creative practice here, a lengthy cassette recording of free-jazz improvisation on electric guitar and electric piano becomes the subject of severe, performative media- and effects-based manipulation. The source recording is played back via a Foldy Makes Sidecar – a modified Walkman with a playback speed control dial – enabling real-time 'varispeed' (simultaneous pitch and time) manipulation of the recorded audio content. Not only does this process result in striking performative 'warping' and detuning artefacts over the source audio, but it also infuses it with lo-fi tape media characteristics that further distance the source – the intention here being to imbue yet another layer of alterity upon past/own content. The output of this manipulation is routed, in series, through a chain of hardware (Boss '63 Fender Reverb) spring reverb/amp emulator, (Red Panda Tensor) tape effects emulator, and (Black Cat) super fuzz pedals, which are simultaneously 'performed' in response to the cassette player manipulations. The resulting artefacts range from glitched, lo-fi revenants of electric piano and guitar – retaining some remnants of their harmonic and melodic figures – through to synthesizer-like textures and completely recontextualized, distorted noise. These become the foundational sample-based layers behind 'Freight Train', sampled directly into and chopped live on an MPC X sampling drum machine and juxtaposed against additional drum programming, and 808 sub-bass, created and/or captured within the MPC environment.

The elements of the beat are output into a (Dangerous 2-Bus+) summing mixer, with parallel limiting and harmonic processing, via a transformer stage. Inserted into the final stage of the summing mixer's signal flow is a (Dramastik Audio Obsidian) VCA-style stereo analogue compressor (combining SSL Bus and Neve 33609 compressor characteristics) with further transformers. The beat-making process, balancing, and processing on the MPC have taken place whilst monitoring through this analogue mixing chain, and stems from 'Freight Train' are exported to facilitate the following song-production phase.

3 PHASE 2 – 'NEON AEON' STEREO MIX: ADDING PERFORMANCES

The second phase of the creative process focuses on progressing from the beat construction to the recording, mixing, and production of a full 'song', featuring additional vocal, electric bass, and electric guitar performances. These have been captured with adherence to specific era-informed signal flows and recording practices (albeit via emulation where original hardware has been unavailable). As a collaboration between the two authors, 'Neon Aeon' uses the 'Freight Train' beat as a foundation but restructures it to support a more linear iteration of verse-chorus-middle eighth sections defined by the lyrical content. The resulting electronica/rock crossover is referential to mid-1990s post-grunge work, such as Garbage's (1995) self-titled debut album, which has inspired the choice of instrumentation, recording, and mixing techniques for the production of the live performances. Furthermore, the lyrical/narrative content has driven experimentation with the sonics of both vocals and guitar textures, which have been additionally exploited in the mixing process (and feature clearly in the introduction and coda sections).

The recording strategy attempts to imbue the new vocal and guitar/bass performances with timbral and spatial signifiers that tie them both to the referenced era/style, as well as a(n) actual unified space and location. At the same time, complementary timbrality to the textures featured in the foundational beat is pursued, responsively and consciously matching the fuzzy, warped samples in 'Freight Train', with driven, distorted, and/or harmonically enhanced signatures on the newly captured vocal and instrumental layers for 'Neon Aeon'. The performed sources are captured live and overdubbed using both close/contact and room/farther microphones within the same space. This aims at repeating imprints of the room ambience over each overdub, adding to an inferred shared space, which 'glues' the performances into a unified footprint (this is further exploited and enhanced in the mixing process). In a study that focuses primarily on compression in mastering, Moore (2021, p. 58) provides a useful, if narrow, definition of 'glue' as a characteristic that "creates a cohesiveness to program material" and which "may impart subtle distortion, colouration and rhythmic movement". Citing Cousins and Hepworth-Sawyer (2013, p. 74), he also preempts it with a wider understanding as "a by-product of gain control, making the track sound like a whole entity rather than its individual parts". The two (left- and right-side) guitar parts that can be heard in the 'Neon Aeon' stereo mix are performed with a Telecaster-style guitar via a (Cry Baby) wah-wah pedal and into a tube amplifier with onboard spring reverb. The amp is recorded with a dynamic microphone positioned very close to the guitar cabinet and a phase-matched farther condenser microphone capturing the amp with some degree of recording room ambience. Both microphone inputs are routed into hardware preamplifiers, with the closer microphone driven quite hard into a tube preamp. The tube preamp is also used for the lead vocal microphone – the same condenser used in the room position for the guitar performances. A handheld bullet microphone (a Shure 520DX typically used for harmonica) captures a secondary layer of the lead vocal performances in close proximity (double-tracked and spread in stereo for the choruses in the 'Neon 'Aeon' stereo mix), routed through the (Red Panda Tensor) tape effects emulator pedal, and the respective signal path of spring reverb and fuzz deployed for the source samples' manipulation. These, plus additional backing/effect vocal layers and whispers, are manipulated live using the pedal chain in real-time to the vocal performances (but only on this secondary microphone). The layering, processing, and double-tracking strategies here fulfil a dual role: providing timbral and spatial depth opportunities for the more traditional stereo mix and also furnishing the creators with multiple layers that can be exploited in the forthcoming spatial mix. Finally, the bass guitar is recorded both amplified and through direct input, taking advantage of the hardware preamplifiers previously used for the electric guitar.

The mixing process emulates a typically mid-1990s rock workflow/ setup within a Digital Audio Workstation (DAW). In pursuit of textural 'glue' between both beat and new instrumental layers, every element of 'Freight Train' has been output individually, contributing to a multi-track that features separate drum parts, sub-bass, layers of manipulated samples, guitars, bass, and vocal performances. Emulated channels and processors of era-specific mixing setups (Neve console channels, compressors, and equalizers; multi-track and master tape emulations; and reverb/spatial effect emulations of hardware processors) are closely observed in the constructed DAW mixing environment, contributing to the end 'Neon Aeon' stereo mix.

Although the song functions as an independent entity (and will be released by the authors in both stereo and spatial formats in its current form), as part of this study, it also represents an intermediate step in the wider trajectory: furnishing the authors/producers with a dynamic phonographic statement, which provides a plethora of opportunities for sampling moments of crystallized stages (Moylan, 2020) – or phonographic ephemera – and recontextualization. As the authors remarked at the InMusic paper presentation: "This is not the song – this is the song we made to make the song". The mixed song elements have been output with all their timbral, processing, and (with and without) effect/spatial colorations as stems and elements, providing textural and spatial options for the following spatial mixing phase.

4 PHASE 3 – 'NEON AEON' SPATIAL MIX: EXPLORING PARALLEL SPACE

Lord has previously established a basic framework comprising several specific elements for appraisal when approaching spatial staging practice (Lord, 2022a, 2022b). This framework considers both the sonic content and sonic context of the musical work; the stylistic qualities and limitations of performance music and production music; instrumentation; spectromorphology of sonic elements; and the lyrical and musical narratives as guide influence in determining the spatial sound stage and in further informing how binaural phenomena may be exploited as a tool to enhance production for headphone-based delivery. Spectromorphology is a term coined by Smalley (1986), which refers to characteristics of sound as 'spectra' and how these change over time ('morphology'). This phase of investigation draws upon this framework to produce the spatial 'Neon Aeon' mix. Using this framework, the characteristics of 'Neon Aeon' can be noted as follows: performed and produced mono and stereo sonic content providing a mixed context; a lyrical narrative that explores themes of parallel worlds and universal disruption; comprising a combination of produced electronic and recorded acoustic instrumentation (drum-set samples and sampled instrumentation ('Freight Train'), recorded bass and guitars, and both clean and manipulated vocal layers). Methods drawing from practice as research, experimental phenomenology, and spectromorphological analysis have been employed in the synthesis of spatial placement (Smalley, 1986; Ihde, 2012; Zagorski-Thomas, 2015). The multi-tracked instrumentation featured in the stereo demo has been 'destacked' with comprising elements used as individual sound sources in the spatial domain rather than as a textural/timbral blend as initially seen in the stereo demo version. Further, particular attention is paid to the spectro-timbral qualities of sources for informing pitch-height placements (Cabrera and Tilley, 2003; Lord, 2022a, 2022b). This can readily be seen across elements of the vocal stage, particularly in the verses where they present an opposed quad placement. The clean voices were panned high and close rear-left, and high and mid-field front-right, and the pitch/time manipulated vocals (using the Shure 520DX microphone through the Red Panda Tensor pedal) were placed in opposition equidistant from the listener and ear-level rear-right and front-left. To create enhanced width among this quad placement, vocal ad-libs are positioned slightly rear-left on level with the ear, and slightly higher but in line with the ear 90° to the right of the listener.

The piece purposefully retains some stereo and mono sound field components, providing a conceptually blended sound stage that retains mono-bass presence and presents combined percepts of internalization and externalization when heard on headphones (Lord, 2022b). This combination of perceptions is used to enhance and further the creative interpretation of the narrative and provide difference and complexity within the sonic space. The lyrical content and spectromorphology of recurring musical motifs are used to inform repeating spatial signatures and sonic cartoons that reinforce and enhance the surrealism of the thematic narrative (Zagorski-Thomas, 2018). For example, this can be seen in the dynamic staging of the wah-wah guitars, whereby the pitch-bends afford low-high automated movements. This can also be observed in the static right-left configuration of the aforementioned vocal ad-lib placements, which imply movement and interaction through a suggestive call-and-response cartoon.

Further to the spatial staging exploration, this phase of the study also investigates parallel processing in the spatial domain. Past phenomenological research data has shown that listeners may often perceive a lack of definition in spatialized productions, particularly when compared to stereophonic versions of the same piece (Lord, 2022b). This lack of definition may be due to the inherent nature of a spatial sound field allowing for more separation through image spread and depth, particularly when Head Related Transfer Function (HRTF) filtering is applied to format the content for headphone-based listening. However, as is typically seen in stereophonic approaches to production, often greater impact and definition of sources may be achieved through parallel processing applications. Due to a general lack of creative spatial music production research, this practice is not much explored within the spatial domain. Therefore, this phase of the study attempts to navigate this gap in research knowledge and explore the issue of definition retention through applied practical approaches to spatial parallel processing. Could parallel processing aid definition retention without impacting the functionality of the spatial processing and affect the overall spatial quality? Using the Dear VR plugin spatialization tool as a channel insert affords the ability to return the spatialized signal to parallel processing busses using post-insert or post-fade auxiliary sends. In this study, a hybrid approach to parallel processing is adopted where both spatialized and non-spatialized signals are paralleled using analogue-modelled processor plugins. The overarching goal of this practice is to create definition, timbral enhancement, harmonic texture, and 'glue' through blended parallel dynamic control and saturation. The lead voices have been spatialized individually and sent to a parallel stereo bus where light 'peak-catching' compression and gentle equalization are applied to the combined signals using an API Vision channel strip, the output subtly blended into the original signals. Care has been taken not to be too heavy with compression as this may result in the content losing the spatialized character and unwanted artefacts being enhanced. Likewise, high frequencies are either subtly boosted or left flat so as not to impact height perception.

The parallel drum bus contains both mono and spatialized sources (kick and snare and hats, respectively), which are fed into an API Vision channel strip for saturation and blended dynamic control. The predominantly mono nature of the source audio and the characteristics of the sampled drums afford the channel parameters to be a little bolder than those on the lead vocal, with boosts to high, high-mid, and low frequencies following a modest amount of compression. The parallel guitar bus also contains a combination of spatialized and non-spatialized signals (amped wah-wah and clean DI captures, respectively). Although, not all of the guitar channels have been routed to it so as to create variation in the color, texture, and dynamics of the combined guitar mix. The intention of the guitar bus processing is to increase 'grit' and edginess, and this is achieved through the saturation and harmonic enhancement afforded by a Friedman Buxom Betty amp simulator. All bass channels remain in mono, determined by the less directional lower frequency content, and are subsequently paralleled to an 1176 emulation.

This hybrid approach to parallel processing affords increased creative agency in production without a perceivable negative impact on the spatial qualities of the sound field. Further, the spatial perception is retained not only through judicious consideration of routing and mix blending but also through the exclusion of specific spatialized elements from the parallel busses (e.g., backing voices). Although increased definition, harmonic, and textural enhancement are achieved through post-spatialized processing approaches, the inherent difference in the characteristics of the spatial sound field does impact the resultant output. As such, the hybrid approach works particularly well by processing a combination of sound fields, either blended or individually, which affords the potential for varying levels of creative experimentation. This is a simple, practical experiment with only one parallel bus for each group of instrument sources. Future experimentation could investigate more complex routing and a multi-bus approach.

This phase attempts to contextualize the lyrical and sonic narratives using a hybrid combination of spatial and non-spatial staging and processing approaches. Although this has been achieved to an extent, there are limitations in the sonic content (the style of vocal delivery, particularly) and the sonic context (the blend of performed and produced music) that require a negotiation between creative practice and interpretation of narrative.

5 PHASE 4 – 'FLIPPED' STEREO RE/MIX: FLIPPING THE SPATIAL SAMPLES

One of the opportunities situated in the space between 'mechanical borrowing' and spatial mixing, particularly in the binaural domain/format, lies in the potential for exploiting (sampling/playing with) expanded stages. Phase 3 has provided reimagined stages of the 'Neon Aeon' mix, which have inspired the selection of samples, as well as the ensuing composition for the 'Flipped' remix/beat. Both lyrical content/vocal motifs *and* their expansive staging have affected the choice of material for sampling in this phase (for example, the spatial gesture of the 'sinking to the top' phrase), whilst the sample-based 'play' with these multi-dimensional objects has driven the beat-making toward the end structure in the final 'Flipped' beat. The spatial source material has been provided in stems form, enabling a hybrid approach between more traditional record sampling (typically in stereo) and remixing, which relies on access to separate elements comprising a master. The beauty of a non-proprietary format is that spatial staging is not only retained within the exported individual elements (or groups of elements) but also available to a maker (sample-based musician, mixer) deploying classic tools. As Lord (2022b) attests:

> To take a democratic approach to spatial audio . . . requires a low-cost or open source spatial system that can reflect and accommodate the current social behaviour of headphone-based listening whilst also being flexible enough to work within any DAW. . . . It must also provide an accommodation for legacy audio formats for both the source and output delivery (mono/stereo wav files etc.). . . . *To achieve a democratic approach to spatial music production and consumption both the means of creation and delivery need to be accessible to everybody* (original emphasis).
>
> (Lord, 2022b, p. 113)

In this scenario, it has been a case of recording and (rhythmically) chopping the stereo playback of vocal, guitar, bass, and sub-bass spatial stems from a computer straight back into the MPC environment. The 'chops' are then triggered percussively (using the drum pads of the MPC) into reimagined, juxtaposed sequences. This has led to the more repetitive (and sometimes stuttered) vocal motifs of the 'Flipped' composition, with guitar, bass, and (distorted) sub-bass contrapuntally accentuating the lyrical sequences. Particular drivers for these choices have been the enhanced harmonic processing of the guitars, made more aggressive by the textural choices in the 'Neon Aeon' spatial mix, which, in turn, inspired some of the industrial synth additions in the 'Flipped' composition. These include the new Moog, Korg, and Roli performances, which have been recorded directly into the MPC but via similar preamp and spatial effect emulations as those deployed for the live instrumentation in the 'Neon Aeon' stereo mix (for reasons of textural and spatial glue). The portamento figures in many of the synth performances (leads and pads) are part of a conscious strategy to create gestures that are both musically emotive but also fruitful to automation (spatial movement) in the forthcoming spatial mix phase.

As part of the 'flipping' process, the samples have been tuned down, partly to variate the remix further from the initial composition ('Neon Aeon') but also as a response to the darker timbral staging ephemera resulting from the 'Neon Aeon' spatial mix. 'Flipping' in hip-hop parlance refers to first exposing and then manipulating, truncating, reordering, and generally recontextualizing a phonographic source within a sample-based production (see Exarchos, 2019b, p. 37). The new structure, in turn, with its non-linear and simpler/repetitive vocal structure, has accentuated aspects of the linear narrative, turning them into focal points. The expanded spatial stages in the reimagined motifs have turned verse elements into main sections, and the remix structure has 'flipped' the song progression into an A-B structure more representative of dance music arrangements. Key changes and dynamic variations are suggested by the additional synth parts, arpeggiations, and pads, while latter verse elements (vocal sonic objects) are turned into source content for 'C' sections (the equivalent of middle eighths for dance structures). The power of these sonic objects – with their expanded width, depth, and height dimensions – enable the beat-maker/remixer with the potential to reimagine their placement in the new composition despite their original song-writing function. One of the striking features that can be observed as a result of the chopping process upon elements carrying variating spatial stages is the effect of "staging rhythms . . . rhythmical shifts between momentary, or at least short, staging architectures 'frozen in time' on the micro-structural level" (Exarchos, 2021b, p. 145).

The mixing process here follows a similar paradigm to the 'Freight Train' beat, outputting the MPC elements into the analogue summing mixer – with parallel dynamic and harmonic processing via multiple transformer stages – before gentle peak-control courtesy of the hardware VCA compressor. All balancing and harmonic/spatial processing on the MPC has taken place through this analogue summing and compression chain to ensure that the "mixing (sonic) mechanics . . . carefully negotiate the dynamics of *contrast* and *integration* through the materiality of textural and spatial manipulation" (Exarchos, 2021a, p. 53, original emphasis). Stems out of this phase have been provided for the following re-spatialized mix process.

6 PHASE 5 – 'FLUXED' RESPATIALIZED MIX: STAGE STACKING ARCHI-TEXTURES

This phase explores the re-spatialization and recontextualization of the phase 4 'Flipped' remix and observes how the consequent spatial and non-spatial staging rhythms (Exarchos, 2021b), additional instrumentation, and remix processes affect the sonic and musical narratives informing new staging architectures. Again, using the aforementioned framework established by Lord (2022a, 2022b), the characteristics of the phase 4 mix are noted as follows: produced and sampled mono and stereo content providing a production music context; a combination of sampled and recorded instrumentation in both spatial and non-spatial formats; MPC and genre-based stylistic processing providing a darker and more aggressive quality to the remixed sonic content; and a simplified lyrical motif that focuses in on one of the original themes (universal disruption).

The phase 4 spatial sample-based reference mix is retained in the first introductory minute of the piece before expanding into the re-spatialized phase 5 content. The intention is to provide perceptual contrast, which creatively works with and has been informed by the lyrical content and the context of the narrative progression. The flipping from one hybrid spatial stage to another is intended to generate an audible feel of flux when the lyrics present the cue 'flipped the flux and I tripped the system'. In the phase 3 spatial mix, the lyrical narrative informs the spatial staging through close whispering vocals and the dynamic panning of samples, wah-wah guitars, and vocal chops. However, the phrasing and delivery of the lead voices meant that most lead spatialization is static and simple. The sample-based nature of the flipped remix has afforded the ability to chop and flip between these static micro stages, making them appear more dynamic and complex. The lead voices that were originally panned high and close rear-left and high and mid-field front-right in the phase 3 spatial mix were pitched-shifted down in the phase 4 remix. This now presents them as lower in the spatial sound field, in a horseshoe configuration around the rear and sides of the listener's head. On first listen direct from the MPC, Lord noted this configuration as metaphorically representative of The Simpsons character Mr. Burns' hair. This experience in itself reinforces the notion that pitch correlates to elevation perception in the binaural domain. A benefit of this phenomenon in the phase 5 practice is that it frees the height layer for further placements, which, combined with the 'flipped' micro-staging architectures, affords more complex spatial stage stacking.

The glitch-pan style edits (spatially panned chops), the focused lyrical narrative, and shorter vocal phrasing afforded further development of the call and response vocal motif initially established in phase 3. This phase also sees the recontextualization of previous staging practices, such as the low-high pitch-height panning – applied to the wah-wah guitars in phase 3 – now similarly applied to the synths. Again, in this phase, a hybrid approach to spatialization has been implemented using both non-spatialized and spatialized sources in the final mix. Although in this phase, a more surrealist approach is employed than in phase 3. This is due to the new sonic context providing a higher level of creative agency in constructing sonic cartoons and staging influenced by the spectromorphology of the content and narrative (Smalley, 1986; Zagorski-Thomas, 2018; Lord 2022a, 2022b). The kick, snare, and cymbals were all spatialized in this phase; the kick has been placed inside of the listener's head, the snare placed atop of the head and the cymbals equidistant behind the listener left and right. MPC samples are spatialized in a wide-pseudo stereo configuration front left and right. The synths and voices are spatialized using automation to dynamically pan them throughout the height and lower layers. Toms, subs, and guitars remain non-spatialized in the stereo sound field.

In this phase, parallel processing is not a necessary consideration, as the additional instrumentation (808 subs, synths, and beats) and MPC processing through phase 4 have provided the 'glue', texture, saturation, and sonic fatness expected of such a production music context. The combination of vintage and stylistic recording signatures, phase 3 parallel processing, the phase 4 MPC processing, and the EQ filtering applied as a function of spatial panning in phase 5 (Lord 2022a, 2022b) further enhance the grit and upper harmonic content of certain sound sources (e.g., the vocal distortion of the lyrically cued 'top' vocal). This, in turn, benefits the darker and more aggressive qualities of the remix instrumentation and, consequently, the recontextualization of the sonic narrative. The upper harmonic enhancement is not only beneficial creatively but also serves functionally to enhance height perception through the generation of higher frequency content.

7 CONCLUSIONS

The primary spatial mix (phase 3) attempted to contextualize the lyrical narrative through conceptual blending and changing sonic space. However, this aim was better achieved in the fluxed re-spatialization mix (phase 5), where the chopped vocal samples created a more specific narrative theme focused on the 'flipped the flux' and 'shell of a ghost' lyrical lines. The simplified arrangement afforded 'glitch-edit' style spatial panning of both beat and vocal chops, which enhanced the sonic concept and reinforced the narrative without fundamentally altering it. Further, this allowed for lyrically informed positioning of sonic sources, such as the 'top' sample overhead, whilst the characteristics of the phase 4 processing (e.g., pitched down vocals) reopened the higher level sound field for a new set of spatialized sources. This further evidences the relationship between pitch-height and examples of how pitch-modulation of sources can affect the perception of height placement in the spatial domain. It also reinforces the understanding that higher frequency content is fundamental for enhanced height perception, and pitch-height placement should be considered when determining higher-level source positions.

One of the issues explored in the phase 3 investigation is the lack of definition as a consequence of the binaural spatial filtering process. This study attempted to counter this issue through the exploration of spatial parallel processing and through blending mono and stereo sources alongside the spatial sound field. Although parallel processing using analogue-modelled plugins did help to retain definition and add texture, saturation, and 'glue' following phase 3, these characteristics were further reinforced through the addition of synths, subs, beats, and MPC processing in the phase 4 remix stage. This helped to provide fatness and 'glue' regardless of the further spatialization applied in phase 5. In fact, the HRTF used in the spatialization process in phase 5 further enhanced the distortion and processing applied through the MPC remix process in phase 4.

Interestingly, the hardware-based stemming process impacted the fidelity of the spatialization pertaining to the individual stems. This resulted in a perceived lack of resolution in the spatial sample output from phase 4 compared to when the same samples were experienced through direct playback from the MPC. However, the primary spatial enhancement has not been lost, and the original, albeit manipulated, spatial staging can be heard throughout the staging rhythms in both the 'Flipped' (phase 4) and 'Fluxed' (phase 5) mixes, specifically exampled through the vocal ad-libs in the 'Fluxed' mix.

REFERENCES

Cabrera, D. and Tilley, S. (2003, July) Parameters for auditory display of height and size, *Proceedings of the 9th International Conference on Auditory Display*, Boston, MA, USA.

Cousins, M. and Hepworth-Sawyer, R. (2013) *Practical mastering: A guide to mastering in the modern studio*. New York, NY: Focal Press.

Exarchos, M. (2019a) '(Re)engineering the cultural object: Sonic pasts in hip-hop's future', in Hepworth-Sawyer, R. et al. (eds.) *Performance, production, technology, and business*. New York, NY: Routledge (Innovation in Music), pp. 437–454.

Exarchos, M. (2019b) 'Sample magic: (Conjuring) phonographic ghosts and meta-illusions in contemporary hip-hop production', *Popular Music*, 38(01), pp. 33–53. doi: 10.1017/S0261143018000685.

Exarchos, M. (2020) 'Sonic necessity and compositional invention in #BluesHop: Composing the blues for sample-based hip hop', *Journal of Popular Music Studies*, 32(03), pp. 99–119.

Exarchos, M. (2021a) 'Making records within records: Manufacturing phonographic "otherness" in sample-based hip hop production,' in Hepworth-Sawyer, R., Paterson, J., and Toulson, R. (eds.) *Future opportunities*. Oxon: Focal Press (Innovation in Music), pp. 37–55.

Exarchos, M. (2021b) '"Past" masters, present beats: Exponential sound staging as sample-based (re) mastering in contemporary hip hop practice', in Braddock, J.-P. et al. (eds.) *Mastering in music*. Oxon: Focal Press (Perspectives on Music Production), pp. 136–154.

Holland, M. (2013) 'Rock production and staging in non-studio spaces: Presentations of space in left or right's "buzzy"', *Journal on the Art of Record Production*, 8.

Ihde, D. (2012) *Experimental phenomenology: Multistabilities.* 2nd edn. Albany, NY: State University of New York.

Lacasse, S. (2000) *'Listen to my voice': The evocative power of vocal staging in recorded rock music and other forms of vocal expression.* Unpublished PhD thesis. University of Liverpool.

Liu-Rosenbaum, A. (2012) 'The meaning in the mix: Tracing a sonic narrative in "when the levee breaks"', *Journal on the Art of Record Production*, 7.

Lord, J. (2022a) 'Redefining the spatial stage: Non-front-orientated approaches to periphonic sound staging for binaural reproduction', in Paterson, J. and Hyunkook, L. (eds.) *3D audio.* London: Routledge (Perspectives on Music Production), pp. 256–273.

Lord, J. (2022b) *The phenomenal rise of periphonic record production: A practice-based musicological investigation of periphonic recomposition for binaural reproduction.* Unpublished PhD thesis. University of West London.

Moore, A. (2021) 'Towards a definition of compression glue in mastering', in Braddock, J.-P. et al. (eds.) *Mastering in music.* London: Routledge (Perspectives on Music Production), pp. 44–59.

Moore, A. F. and Dockwray, R. (2008) 'The establishment of the virtual performance space in rock', *Twentieth-Century Music*, 5(2), pp. 219–241.

Moylan, W. (2012) 'Considering space in recorded music', in Frith, S. and Zagorski-Thomas, S. (eds.) *The art of record production: An introductory reader for a new academic field.* Surrey: Ashgate, pp. 163–188.

Moylan, W. (2014) *Understanding and crafting the mix: The art of recording.* 3rd edn. Oxon: CRC Press.

Moylan, W. (2020) *Recording analysis: How the record shapes the song.* New York, NY: Focal Press.

Mudede, C. (2003) *The turntable, C Theory.* Available at: https://journals.uvic.ca/index.php/ctheory/article/view/14561/5407 (Accessed: 2 December 2020).

Pickering, M. (2012) 'Sonic horizons: Phonograph aesthetics and the experience of time', in Keightley, E. (ed.) *Time, media and modernity.* Basingstoke: Palgrave Macmillan, pp. 25–44.

Schloss, J. G. (2014) *Making beats: The art of sample-based hip-hop.* Middletown, CT: Wesleyan University Press (Music/Culture).

Smalley, D. (1986) 'Spectromorphology and structuring processes', in S. Emmerson (ed.) *The language of electro-acoustic music.* Basingstoke: Macmillan, pp. 61–93.

Williams, J. A. (2010) *Musical borrowing in hip-hop music: Theoretical frameworks and case studies.* Unpublished PhD thesis. University of Nottingham.

Zagorski-Thomas, S. (2009) 'The medium in the message: Phonographic staging techniques that utilize the sonic characteristics of reproduction media', *Journal on the Art of Record Production*, 4.

Zagorski-Thomas, S. (2010) 'The stadium in your bedroom: Functional staging, authenticity and the audience-led aesthetic in record production', *Popular Music*, 29(2), pp. 251–266.

Zagorski-Thomas, S. (2015) 'Developing the formal structures of artistic practice-as-research', *New Vistas*, 1(2), pp. 28–32. https://doi/uwl.18.

Zagorski-Thomas, S. (2018) 'The spectromorphology of recorded popular music: The shaping of sonic cartoons through record production', in Fink, R., Latour,

M., and Wallmark, Z. (eds.) *The relentless pursuit of tone: Timbre in popular music*. New York, NY: Oxford University Press, pp. 345–365.

Zak III, A. J. (2001) *The poetics of rock: Cutting tracks, making records*. Berkeley, CA: University of California Press.

DISCOGRAPHY

Garbage. (1995) [digital release] *Garbage*. US: Mushroom.

Gutter Turtle Records. (2022) 'Spatial stage stacking'. *SoundCloud*. Available at: https://soundcloud.com/user-411406192/sets/spatial-stage-stacking (accessed: 28 October 2022).

7

Vocal chops

Another human/machine hybrid

Ragnhild Brøvig and Jon Marius Aareskjold-Drecker

1 INTRODUCTION

Over the past decade, vocal chops have become an important part of the popular music scene and dominated the hit charts. In 2016, about twenty percent of all the songs on the Billboard Hot 100 contained vocal chops (Billboard 2016). Scrutiny of recent charts suggests that this figure is increasing, despite claims (starting already in 2015 or 2016) that the use of vocal chops will have a limited lifetime. Why are so many producers and listeners attracted to such exaggerated use of the vocal? There is a body of literature discussing the musical manipulation of the voice, particularly the use of the vocoder and autotune (Brøvig-Hanssen and Danielsen 2016; Marshall 2018; Prior 2009, 2017, 2018; Provenzano 2018, 2019). Vocal chops have received less attention, save for "how-to" musical production tutorials (see, for example, Levine 2021) and insider industry observations. This paper will delve into this particular way of manipulating the vocal that can be heard on numerous tracks of the 2010s and 2020s. We will first draw attention to some of the predecessors of vocal chops, framing this effect as the most recent incarnation of producers' and listeners' enduring fascination with vocal manipulation. Drawing on ecological affordance theory, we will further speculate on what it is that people find so fascinating about this effect. We will also demonstrate various approaches to creating vocal chops and the various effects that these approaches produce, arguing that the intense exploration of this technique in recent years has led to its normalization and to its progressively subtler integration into music productions.

But first, what is a "vocal chop"? "Vocal chops" are defined for this paper/article as *fragments of vocal samples that are processed, repitched, and rearranged in rhythmic succession to create hooks and effects*. In his study of sample-based hip-hop, Joseph Schloss similarly defines "chopping" as the alteration of a sampled phrase "by dividing it into smaller segments and reconfiguring them in a different order" (2004, p. 206). As well as manipulated in terms of their order, the chops are transposed and their formants shifted, often into an unnatural range (that transforms the sound of the voice) and sometimes as much as an octave higher than the

DOI: 10.4324/9781003462101-8

average speech pitch range. Each chop (or sample) is usually quite short, consisting of a brief lyrical and melodic phrase, a single word and tone, or a single vowel. The ways in which the vocal chops are manipulated and juxtaposed contribute a peculiar non-human element to the sound while introducing rather abrupt, unexpected melodies. In songs within the electronic dance music (EDM) genre, the vocal chop melody is usually incorporated into the section following the pre-chorus or the section following the song's buildup (sometimes referred to as the "pop-drop" section). In pop productions, vocal chops are frequently used to create hooks in the intro, re-intro, or bridge and as "ear candy" in other sections of the song. Famous examples that use vocal chops include "Where Are Ü Now" (2015) by Diplo and Skrillex featuring Justin Bieber and "This Is What You Came For" (2016) by Calvin Harris featuring Rihanna.

2 THE RISE OF VOCAL CHOPS

Although vocal chops clearly represent a fresh addition to the popular music palette, composers and performers have always been fascinated with the playful and exaggerated manipulation of the voice. We will first present a brief sampling of the ways vocal manipulation has been used in music recordings from the 1950s to the 1990s, then discuss how it developed into the musical feature that we now recognize as vocal chops. We will only mention a few of the many examples, but they will clearly demonstrate a longtime cultural investment in vocal manipulation as a powerful musical asset.

As is commonly done when discussing inspirational sources of technological experimentation, we will start with some examples from the avant-garde movements of the 1950s. Pierre Schaeffer, for one, is known as a pioneer in sound experimentation for his work manipulating sounds' tempo and pitch levels, playing them backward, fragmenting them by cutting off their beginnings or ends and juxtaposing and rearranging the fragments. His experimentation with vocals can be heard in "Etude Pathétique" from 1948. His contemporary, Karlheinz Stockhausen, not only transformed the vocal track but also combined it with electronic sounds; in the electro-acoustic mass "Gesang der Junglige" from 1955–56, the vocals are combined with sine tones, clicks, and filtered white noise. Other examples of avant-garde vocal manipulation include John Cage's "Fontana Mix with Aria" (1958) and Nam Jun Paik's "Etude for Pianoforte" (1959–60). Using vocals in such ways during the 1950s and 1960s was, however, most common within the electro-acoustic experimental scene associated with a select group of composers who had access to the specific studios with the custom-built technological equipment that facilitated these processes.

In the early 1970s, the use of turntables in hip-hop music to supply a backing track for MCs soon evolved into the quite advanced live manipulation of sounds via the juggling of records. The sound sequences of the vinyl records were transformed into short loops, backspinned, played at various speeds, or disrupted by a stutter or other abrupt transition between the sounds. Fragmented vocal sounds resulted from the abrupt transitions between the played records, which either cut them off before they finished or started them abruptly (that is, in the middle of their temporal duration). It was also common to isolate a human vocal sound (typically, an interjection of some sort) from one record and add it to another that was spinning, thus using it more like an instrument than a narrative voice.

The onset of early hard-disk recording systems and samplers in the late 1970s – such as the Synclavier and Fairlight systems – also facilitated vocal manipulation, as can be heard in Kate Bush's "The Dreaming" (1982), which relies heavily on the Fairlight CMI. The Fairlight was very expensive and only allowed for a second or two of sound. It was thus not until the explosion of lower-priced samplers with larger memories (allowing for several seconds of sampled sound) starting in the early 1980s – including EMU's Emulator (1981), SP-12 (1987), Akai's S900 (1986), MPC60, and S1000 (both 1988) – that vocal manipulation via sampling began to appear on a large array of tracks. For example, Paul Hardcastle scored a big synth-pop hit in 1985 with "19," which featured a prominent vocal chop as its main hook, and Black Box's house hit "Ride on Time" from 1989 is entirely formed out of vocal chops and samples taken from Loleatta Holloway's 1980 disco hit "Love Sensation." In the 1990s, with the development of sequencer programs as well as increased computer power and disk speed, more complex vocal edits became commonplace. Vocal samples and chops were an important part of the aesthetics in much house music, for example, including Todd Terry's "House Is a Feeling" from 1991 (which features a sample from the classic "My House" by Rhythm Control [1987]), Underworld's "Cowgirl" (1994), and much of Todd Edwards's music, including "Guide My Soul" (1993), "Saved My Life" (1996), and his mix of Sound of One's "As I Am" (1998). Other subgenres of EDM also contributed significantly to introducing heavily warped vocals to a larger audience, including Aphex Twin's "Window-licker" (1999), Squarepusher's "My Red Hot Car" (2001), and BT's "Somnambulist" (2003), which famously holds the Guinness world record for most vocal edits in a song (6,178 in all!). Vocal edits also became more common in underground hip-hop music at that time, with tracks such as Danger Mouse's "Dirt Off Your Shoulder" (2004), Three 6 Mafia's "Stay Fly" (2005), and J Dilla's "One for Ghost" (2006) and "Bye." (2006). At the same time, the "chipmunk soul" sound, introduced by RZA and popularized by a young Kanye West, became prominent in hip hop. This style uses samples from vintage soul records and pitches them up to an unnatural-sounding level that also happens to suit a hip-hop tempo, in turn evoking the sound of the turntablism of the 1970s. An example of this particular manipulation can be found in Kanye's debut single, "Through the Wire" (2004), with its sample of the David Foster-produced Chaka Khan song "Through the Fire" (1984).

By 2010, vocal edits had entirely overtaken mainstream music, and in the years to follow, the means of manipulation now commonly referred to as vocal chops began its ascent to a "golden age" between 2014 and 2018 when several chart-topping songs had vocal chops as a main feature in the chorus. Scrutiny of recent charts suggests that this musical feature remains very present today as well, but it also has transformed into a subtler version of itself; we will return to this development at the end of this paper. An important predecessor of vocal chops is the 2009 hit "Pon De Floor" by the electronic trio Major Lazer featuring Vibz Kartel. This vocal chop drop received major attention when it was included in Beyoncé's megahit "Run the World (Girls)" in 2011. Vocal chops also gained mainstream attention in 2015, with DJ Snake and Major Lazer's hit "Lean On" featuring Mø. Other popular hits from the same time that featured vocal chops include "The Chainsmokers" (2014) by Kanye featuring sirenXX, "Say My Name" (2014) by Odesza, "The Only Way Is Up" (2015) by Martin Garrix and Tiësto, and "Roses" (2015) by the Chainsmokers featuring Rozes. Skrillex, with his dubstep-influenced sound, also played an important role in popularizing vocal chops. While he had already used this technique in "Scary Monsters and Nice Sprites" (2010), his collaboration with Jack Ü, Diplo, and Justin Bieber in "Where Are Ü Now" brought the effect major attention with its violin-like vocal chop. Skrillex continued his success with both Bieber and vocal chops in "Sorry" (2015). As mentioned earlier, about twenty percent of all the songs on the Billboard Hot 100 in 2016 contained vocal chops. Some of the hits from 2016 to 2018 that featured vocal chops include "I Took a Pill in Ibiza (Seeb Remix)" (2016) by Mike Posner and Seeb, "This Is What You Came For" (2016) by Calvin Harris featuring Rihanna, "Cold Water" (2016) by Major Lazer featuring Justin Bieber and Mø, "Let Me Love You" (2016) by DJ Snake featuring Justin Bieber, "Gold" (2016) by Kiiara, "It Ain't Me" (2017) by Kygo and Selena Gomez, "Scared to be Lonely" (2017) by Martin Garrix and Dua Lipa, and "Jealous" (2018) by TRXD feat Harper. In more recent years, vocal chops have become a staple of the biggest hits and an integral part of mainstream popular music production as well as several subgenres of EDM. What is it, then, that so many producers and listeners find fascinating about vocal chops and vocal manipulation more generally?

3 THE CHARACTERISTIC HUMAN/MACHINE HYBRID

One reason for our fascination with vocal chops is that they at once affirm and subvert our abiding familiarity with vocal sounds. Drawing upon James Gibson's theory of ecological perception, Eric Clarke notes that sounds afford meanings to the listener via that listener's prior experiences with similar sounds (2005, 2018). Dennis Smalley likewise notes that the listener has a "natural tendency to relate sounds to supposed sources and causes" (1997, 110). The sound of the voice represents something utterly human to us, and it is thus in a category of its own in terms of our sensitivity to its manipulation. Since the womb, that is, we have been exposed to the sound of the human voice every day, which makes it a strong indexical sign of the human body and a correspondingly clear throughline from its source to its musical performance to a recording of that performance (or a manipulated version of it). Moreover, the voice is our primary tool for communicating with others and expressing ourselves; it represents a ready bridge between people and a ready vehicle for our inner thoughts and feelings. We, therefore, maintain a very intimate relation to vocal sounds despite our awareness of their many mediated, commodified, and depersonalized manifestations.

Moreover, our intimate familiarity with vocal chops makes us particularly capable of detecting what Gibson (1986) refers to as an "invariant," that is, the characteristic unchanging and recognizable features of varying perceptual stimuli. While the vocal sound may, when manipulated, manifest perceptually in a variety of ways, its invariant features remain constant and assures that the listener identifies the sound as a vocal sound.

Whereas some musical manipulations exploit and hyperbolize the intimate and expressive capacities of the voice, vocal chops play with the voice's ambiguous status as both an index of the human and a sign of the mechanical – that is, a commodity detached from the human. Vocal chops thus introduce two parallel frames of reference as we experience them: (1) the sound as it appears in an everyday "unmediated" real-world context, which follows strict acoustic laws, and (2) the context of the music recording, wherein the voice is often highly manipulated, and anything goes in that regard. These respective frames of reference do not merge but instead commingle or mix without dissolving, like a vinaigrette. The psychological negotiation between them generates an experiential tension that piques our interest.

Producers cultivate this human-machine hybrid. They may, of course, be more or less conscious of the vocal chops' *inherent* ambiguity, created by the vocal's unique way of keeping its invariants intact when manipulated. Yet, the very nature of vocal chops suggests that neither the producers nor the listener experience this characteristic sound as completely acousmatic (which it has no identifiable source). While vocal chops sometimes tilt toward the human and other times toward the synthetic, producers seem vigilant that their manipulations might preserve the unique qualities of the vocal and fortify the listener's acknowledgment of these sounds as originating with the human voice.

Not all sounds have the capacity to establish two parallel frames of reference: their original versions may not be so well established as a comparative background, perhaps, or their mediated versions become promptly normalized to the extent that we cease to think of them as mediated. This may, of course, happen to the voice as well, especially when it is processed through subtle reverb and compression, for example. But when the vocal sound is audibly disrupted and roughly juxtaposed with other vocal sounds, its differentiation from how we are used to hearing it in an everyday context is pronounced, so we thus experience it as something familiar made slightly unfamiliar. The manipulated vocal might still come to be normalized in turn, but never to the extent that it erases the everyday voice as a frame of reference – at least, not as long as it is recognizable *as a voice*. This signature ability of vocal chops to activate a tension between two parallel frames of reference that are working together instead of canceling each other out ultimately spurs our active and enduring interest in these sounds (for a discussion of the experience of sounds with parallel frames of reference, see also Brøvig 2023).

Moreover, it adds to the compositional palette a type of sound that is very different from both vocal sounds and synthetic sounds thanks to its robust invariants – or, more precisely, thanks to the listener's robust ability to identify a vocal's invariants despite aggressive manipulation. It acquires some of the qualities of each of them and transcends their limitations without being experienced as an amalgamation of the two. For example, the absolute elasticity of the synthetic, which transcends the acoustic constraints of a voice, is here transferred to the vocal, as is evident from its pitched sound, its cut-off beginning and ending points, and the abrupt transitions between its tones. Yet, the complex texture of vocal sounds (including the rich vocal vocabulary and the alternation between different vowels and consonants), their profound implicational and associative potential, and the uniqueness of every one of them distinguishes vocal chops from any synthetic sound. The vocal chops thus belong somewhere between – the condition that explains their uniqueness and cultural durability.

4 VARIOUS TAKES ON VOCAL CHOPS

Even though vocal manipulations, and vocal chops in particular, display general features that help to explain our fascination with them, their specific applications are both various and creative. In what follows, we will delve into four recent tracks in which vocal chops are central but used in quite different ways. All the tracks are from what we have identified as the golden age of vocal chops, between 2014 and 2018: "I Took a Pill in Ibiza (Seeb Remix)" (2016) by Mike Posner and Seeb, "Sorry" (2015), produced by Skrillex and performed by Justin Bieber, "Jealous" (2018) by TRXD featuring Harper, and "Scared to Be Lonely" (2017) by Martin Garrix and Dua Lipa.

4.1 Seeb's remix of "I Took a Pill in Ibiza" by Mike Posner

The Seeb remix of "I Took a Pill in Ibiza" (2016) took vocal chops to new heights in mainstream music in the very year that the use of vocal chops peaked on the charts. In a personal interview, Espen Berg from Seeb, a tropical house-inspired Norwegian duo, explains that while they were working on the remix, vocal chops were still quite exotic (Berg 2017). A few songs had included the technique, including "Lean On" by Major Lazer and DJ Snake featuring Mø, but Berg did not see it as a common feature of chart-toppers at that time. He explains how Seeb, when working on a Kiesza remix, dropped a short sample of vocal into Simpler, a sampler plug-in in Ableton Live. Then they experimented with moving the loop points, which determine which part of the sample is played back and repeated, and adjusting the amount of portamento, which changes how the sample moves between pitches. For "I Took a Pill in Ibiza," the duo brought a part of Posner's vocal performance into Ableton Live and gave it a similar treatment, creating a new melody from a single sample. To process the sound further, they created a rack (that is, a collection of processing plug-ins working as one unit) with distortion and sidechain-compressed reverb keyed by the bass drum sound. The vocal chop phrase in "I Took a Pill in Ibiza" appears after the two choruses and lasts for 16 bars (0.58–1.35 and 2.32–3.09). Here, the vocal chops are the center of attention and supply arguably the most memorable hook in the whole track. The melody line initially sounds like a lead synthesizer before exposing itself as a manipulated vocal; it then transitions into Posner's normal singing voice at the conclusion of each round of the chorus. As such, the vocal chop melody retains the feeling of a vocal performance while at the same time adhering to the sound and genre-specific arrangement typical of an instrumental drop. Berg adds that he frequently uses his non-dominant hand to perform his vocal chop parts. According to him, left-hand playing for a right-handed person introduces both a different choice of melodies and an intentionally flawed (or humanized) timing.

4.2 "Sorry" by Skrillex featuring Justin Bieber

"Sorry" (2015), which features a vocal performance by Justin Bieber, represents a very different approach to vocal chops. Whereas Seeb manipulated and repeated a single sample to create an entire phrase, the vocal chop part in "Sorry" repitches and repeats its single sample without shaping or deploying it as a phrase. Correspondingly, whereas the vocal chop part in the Seeb example lasts for 16 bars, it only lasts for one bar in "Sorry," cropping up four times in the chorus in response to Bieber's vocal, as well as twice in the intro. The song's producer and co-writer, Skrillex, released a video on Twitter showing how he created the part (Skrillex 2016). In this video, Skrillex explains that the demo of the song featured the vocals of topliner Julia Michaels. This demo track was replaced with Bieber's vocal in the production version of the song, which was in a different key, presumably to better suit Bieber's vocal range. However, Skrillex kept a phrase from Michaels's performance (which includes a short adlib) as a foundation for the vocal chops. With Ableton Live's pitch tool, he then pitch-shifted the sampled melody down a fourth (to the new key) and then up an octave, then used the result as a repeating hook (1.08–1.21). The high pitch and altered transients transform the voice into a machinic or hypernatural vocal sound, even as its natural gliding transitions between notes and its complex portamento differentiate it from a synthesizer, adding an organic layer to the hook that would not be achievable with a purely instrumental sound.

4.3 "Jealous" by TRXD featuring Harper

The use of vocal chops can also be more elaborate and rely upon complex audio editing and processing, as is apparent in "Jealous" (2018) by TRXD featuring Harper. The Norwegian producers David Atarodiyan and Truls Dyrstad explain in a personal interview that they often base their productions on already finished and recorded vocal toplines or acappellas. These toplines usually have all the parts one would find in a pop production – that is, verses, prechoruses, choruses, and a "mid 8" part – but they seldom use all of them in their songs (Atarodiyan and Dyrstad 2017). Instead, the leftover vocal parts are often transformed into vocal chops. While they began working with vocal chops using a sampler (recall Seeb's process for "I Took a Pill in Ibiza"), they transitioned to the exclusive use of editing and pitching in a DAW because it is far less restrictive than the sampler. In "Jealous," the vocal chops supply three different motives: motive 1 is present in the intro (0.00–0.06), "mid 8," and outro of the song; motive 2 is very subtle and low in the mix and serves as a background in the verses (for example, 0.11–0.14); and motive 3 constitutes the lead part of the choruses (0.49–1.00). Motive 1 is heavily filtered and repitched, which results in a sound reminiscent of a lead synthesizer but with a distinctive vocal identity thanks to its particular phrasing and timbre. Motive 2, which is quite distant and reverberated, sounds almost like a normal sung voice except that it has some abrupt transitions between its clips. Motive 3 takes the relatively unmanipulated vocal line of the chorus's opening as its point of departure, then filters it to various extents, cuts it up, and repeats different sections of it, all without obscuring the source. Motive 3, in particular, comes across as less instrumental and more human than Seeb's vocal chops but more manipulated than the pitching approach used by Skrillex in "Sorry," thanks to its cut-ups and constant filtering adjustments.

4.4 "Scared to Be Lonely" by Martin Garrix and Dua Lipa

While the vocal chops in the three previous examples maintain, in one way or another, a connection to the vocal performance in the same song, the Dutch DJ and producer Martin Garrix used a vocal from the sample library Splice to create his vocal chops for the track "Scared to Be Lonely" (2017). During a workshop at the Amsterdam Dance Event (ADE) in 2017 (Garrix 2017), Garrix showed how he created the vocal chop part. Having selected the vocal sample, he then used FL Studio's Splicer to cut it up and wrote a melody based on various pitches from the same sample. Garrix came up with several ideas the first day then shelved them all. Later on, he came back to them and chose one around which to create a production inspired by future bass (a subgenre of electronic music). With his team, he wrote a topline and later recruited Dua Lipa to perform the song, though he made no attempt to replace the vocal chop with her singing. To generate a driving, pumping effect on the vocal chops, he used sidechaining compression keyed by a ghost kick drum – that is, a kick drum that is not audible in the music and is only used for keying a sidechain compressor. The sound of the vocal chops (1.03–1.17) evokes a lead synthesizer and fits well into a future-bass drop. Yet, it still suggests associations with a vocal sound thanks to its harmonics, glissando, and peculiar character stemming from its processing and formant shift. Moreover, the vocal chops constitute the lead part in the chorus, as in the Seeb example above, which is traditionally performed by a vocalist, and its catchy melody sustains the overall pop vibe of the song.

The examples above demonstrate that vocal chops can be realized in quite different ways and to quite different effects and ends. Notably, they all derived from different sources: Seeb used a phrase from the lead singer's vocal performance, TRXD used leftovers from the song's topline, Skrillex used the vocal from the track's demo (which featured a vocalist other than the final lead one), and Garrix used a vocal from a sample library. Moreover, the duration of these samples varies too, from a full-phrase sample, as in Skrillex's "Sorry," to short bursts, as in the tracks by Seeb and TRXD. In terms of methods, Seeb used the sampler plug-in Simpler, Skrillex used Ableton Live's pitch tool, TRXD edited them manually in a DAW, and Garrix used FL Studio's Splicer. Each producer also treated the samples differently by cutting them up and using pitching, filtering, and different processing effects, such as sidechain compression, reverb, and distortion. The extent to which the vocal samples were manipulated differs: some of the vocal chop parts (including that in the Garrix example) sound almost like synthesizer leads but retain hints that the source was a vocal, whereas others (including the TRXD example) tilt more toward the human sound and leave no doubt about the source whatsoever. Lastly, the placement and function of the vocal chops in the arrangement of the tracks vary, too. In the Seeb and Garrix examples, the vocal chop parts supply the main hooks of the songs, whereas the vocal chop phrase in the Skrillex example functions more as a response to the main vocal in the choruses. In the TRXD example, three different vocal chop parts have unique functions. As a technique, then, vocal chops contain a plethora of possibilities, uses, and effects.

5 THE FUTURE EVOLUTION OF VOCAL CHOPS

This brief discussion of a few songs has revealed some common techniques for making vocal chops. While, as we have shown, the exaggerated voice has been used in music production for several decades, the last ten years have witnessed an explosion of vocal chops in mainstream popular music productions. This trend has been so substantial that an analysis of the most popular songs on Spotify in 2020 and 2021 shows that vocal chops are everywhere in current music productions and now represent an integral part of many arrangements. (Notable exceptions are songs with a 1980s or 1990s vibe, such as the Weeknd's "Blinding Lights" [2020] or Olivia Rodrigo's "Good 4 U" [2021].) We have speculated that one of the main reasons for the attraction to vocal chops by producers and listeners is their ambiguous status as both human and mechanical. This creates an experiential tension that piques our interest while also offering a very unique sound to experiment with when creating music. Although vocal chops have indeed become normalized at this moment of writing, at least within certain groups of listeners and producers, we have argued that listeners maintain a very intimate relation to the vocal sound thanks to its unique exposure to us through life. As such, despite repeated aggressive manipulation of it, the listener has a robust ability to identify a vocal's invariants, and this, in turn, has prevented it from becoming a purely acousmatic sound.

As well as being used in an exaggerated way in a drop or melodic climax, there appears to have been a development during the last couple of years wherein vocal chop techniques are also used more subtly – such as appearing throughout a song as more uniform and integrated contributions to the sound. An example of this shift is Justin Bieber's "Peaches (ft. Daniel Caesar, Giveon)" (2021), which features a call-and-response effect between normal and processed vocals (0.09–0.30) and several processed vocal fragments that brings depth to the track (1.47–1.49). Another example can be found in Dua Lipa's "Don't Start Now" (2020), which, despite its tight and dry 1970s disco sound, accommodates both barely discernible vocal chop effects (for example, 1.07–1.09) as well as a very modern vocal chop drop in the "mid 8" (1.59–2.09) and outro (2.46–3.00). Perhaps the opaque and exaggerated days of vocal chops are about to give way to a more transparent or introverted presence that recalls changes in the use of vocoders and autotune as well. Still, vocal chops, like the vocoded and autotuned voice, continue to traffic in the productive and attractive tension between the human and the synthetic, even as the technique has made the familiar journey from innovative and exciting through cliché to simply useful and effective – one more handy tool in the producer's belt.

REFERENCES

Atarodiyan, D., and T. Dyrstad. (2017). Personal interview with the authors.

Berg, E. (2017). Personal interview with the authors.

Billboard. (2016, 19 December). How the Pop-Drop Became the Sound of 2016, *Billboard* (website), available online from www.billboard.com/articles/columns/pop/7625628/pop-drop-sound-of-2016-chainsmokers-justin-bieber-switched-on-pop [Accessed August 2022].

Brøvig, R. (2023). *Parody in the Age of Remix: Mashup Creativity vs. the Takedown*. Cambridge, MA: MIT Press.

Brøvig-Hanssen, R., and A. Danielsen. (2016). *Digital Signatures: The Impact of Digitization on Popular Music Sound*. Cambridge, MA: MIT Press.

Clarke, E. (2005). *Ways of Listening: An Ecological Approach to the Perception of Musical Meaning*. New York: Oxford University Press.

Clarke, E., A. E. Williams, and D. Reynolds. (2018). Musical Events and Perceptual Ecologies. *The Senses and Society*, 13(3): 264–281, DOI: 10.1080/17458927.2018.1516023

Garrix, M. (2017, 24 October). Martin Garrix Masterclass [Full] ADE Sound Lab XL 18.10.17 @ DeLaMar Theater. *Video posted on YouTube by Dave Rook*, available online from www.youtube.com/watch?v=6k-Gs8BeQc8

Gibson, J. J. (1986). *The Ecological Approach to Visual Perception*. Hillsdale, NJ: Lawrence Erlbaum Associates.

Levine, M. (2021, 12 December). Creating Vocal Chops and Other Sampler Tricks, part 1, *Yamaha Music USA* (website), available online from https://hub.yamaha.com/proaudio/recording/creating-vocal-chops-and-other-sampler-tricks-part-1/ [Accessed August 2022].

Marshall, O. (2018). Auto-Tune in Situ: Digital Correction and Conversational Repair. In *Critical Approaches to the Production of Music and Sound*, eds. S. Bennett and E. Bates, pp. 175–206. New York: Bloomsbury Academic.

Prior, N. (2009). Software Sequencers and Cyborg Singers: Popular Music in the Digital Hypermodern. *New Formations*, 66(Spring): 81–99, DOI: 10.3898/newf.66.06.2009

Prior, N. (2017). On Vocal Assemblages: From Edison to Miku. *Contemporary Music Review*, 36: 1–19.

Prior, N. (2018). *Popular Music, Digital Technology and Society*. Los Angeles: Sage.

Provenzano, C. (2018). Auto-Tune, Labor, and the Pop-Music Voice. In *The Relentless Pursuit of Tone in Popular Music*, eds. R. Fink, M. Latour, and X. Wallmark. Oxford Scholarship Online. DOI: 10.1093/oso/9780199985227.001.0001

Provenzano, C. (2019). Making Voices: The Gendering of Pitch Correction and the Auto-Tune Effect in Contemporary Pop Music. *Journal of Popular Music Studies*, 31(2): 63–84.

Schloss, J. G. (2004). *Making Beats: The Art if Sample-Based Music*. Middletown, CT: Wesleyan University Press.

Skrillex (2016, May 28). Sorry But We Didn't Steal This. *Twitter Tweet*, available online from https://twitter.com/skrillex/status/736328422901714944

Smalley, D. (1997). Spectromorphology: Explaining Sound-Shapes. *Organised Sound*, 12(1): 35–58.

DISCOGRAPHY

Aphex Twin. (1999). 'Windowlicker'. Available at: Spotify (Accessed 31 July 2022).

Beyoncé. (2011). 'Run the World (Girls)'. Available at: Spotify (Accessed 31 July 2022).

Bieber, Justin. (2015). 'Sorry'. Available at: Spotify (Accessed 31 July 2022).

Bieber, Justin, Ceasar, Daniel and Giveon. (2021). 'Peaches'. Available at: Spotify (Accessed 31 July 2022).

Black Box. (1989). 'Ride on Time'. Available at: Spotify (Accessed 31 July 2022).

BT. (2003). 'Somnambulist'. Available at: Spotify (Accessed 31 July 2022).

Bush, Kate. (1982). 'The Dreaming'. Available at: Spotify (Accessed 31 July 2022).

Cage, John. (1958). 'Fontana Mix with Aria'. Available at: Spotify (Accessed 31 July 2022).

The Chainsmokers featuring Rozes. (2015). 'Roses'. Available at: Spotify (Accessed 31 July 2022).

Danger Mouse. (2004). [Vinyl LP] 'Dirt Off Your Shoulder'. *From: The Grey Album*. Not on label.

Diplo and Skrillex featuring Bieber, Justin. (2015). 'Where are Ü Now'. Available at: Spotify (Accessed 31 July 2022).

DJ Snake featuring Bieber, Justin. (2016). 'Let Me Love You'. Available at: Spotify (Accessed 31 July 2022).

DJ Snake, and Major Lazer featuring Mø. (2015). 'Lean On'. Available at: Spotify (Accessed 31 July 2022).

Dua Lipa. (2020). 'Don't Start Now'. Available at: Spotify (Accessed 31 July 2022).

Edwards, Todd. (1996). 'Saved My Life'. Available at: Spotify (Accessed 31 July 2022).

Edwards, Todd, and The Messenger. (1993). 'Guide My Soul'. Available at: Spotify (Accessed 31 July 2022).

Garrix, Martin, and Dua Lipa. (2017). 'Scared to be Lonely' Available at: Spotify (Accessed 31 July 2022).

Garrix, Martin, and Tiësto. (2015). 'The Only Way is Up'. Available at: Spotify (Accessed 31 July 2022).

Hardcastle, Paul. (1985). '19'. Available at: Spotify (Accessed 31 July 2022).

Harris, Calvin featuring Rihanna. (2016). 'This is What You Came For'. Available at: Spotify (Accessed 31 July 2022).

Holloway, Loleatta. (1980). 'Love Sensation'. Available at: Spotify (Accessed 31 July 2022).

Jack Ü, Skrillex, Diplo, and Bieber, Justin. (2015). 'Where are Ü Now'. Available at: Spotify (Accessed 31 July 2022).

J Dilla. (2006a). 'One for Ghost'. Available at: Spotify (Accessed 31 July 2022).

J Dilla. (2006b). 'Bye'. Available at: Spotify (Accessed 31 July 2022).

Khan, Chaka. (1984). 'Through the Fire'. Available at: Spotify (Accessed 31 July 2022).

Kiiara. (2016). 'Gold'. Available at: Spotify (Accessed 31 July 2022).

Kygo, and Gomez, Selena. (2017). 'It Ain't Me (with Selena Gomez)'. Available at: Spotify (Accessed 31 July 2022).

Major Lazer, Afrojack, and Vibz Kartel. (2009). 'Pon De Floor'. Available at: Spotify (Accessed 31 July 2022).

Major Lazer, Bieber, Justin, and Mø. (2016). 'Cold Water (featuring Justin Bieber and Mø)'. Available at: Spotify (Accessed 31 July 2022).

Nam Jun Paik. (1959–1960). 'Etude for Pianoforte'. Available at: Spotify (Accessed 31 July 2022).

Odesza. (2014). 'Say My Name (Feat. Zyra)'. Available at: Spotify (Accessed 31 July 2022).

Posner, Mike, and Seeb. (2016). 'I Took a Pill in Ibiza (Seeb Remix)'. Available at: Spotify (Accessed 31 July 2022).

Rhythm Control. (1987). 'My House – Acapella'. Available at: Spotify (Accessed 31 July 2022).

Rodrigo, Olivia. (2021). 'Good 4 U'. Available at: Spotify (Accessed 31 July 2022).

Schaeffer, Pierre. (1948). 'Etude Pathétique'. Available at: Spotify (Accessed 31 July 2022).

Skrillex. (2010). 'Scary Monsters and Nice Sprites'. Available at: Spotify (Accessed 31 July 2022).

Sound of One and Edwards, Todd. (1998). 'As I Am – Todd Edwards Mix'. Available at: Spotify (Accessed 31 July 2022).

Squarepusher. (2001). 'My Red Hot Car'. Available at: Spotify (Accessed 31 July 2022).

Stockhausen, Karlheinz. (1955–1956). 'Gesang der Junglige'. Available at: Spotify (Accessed 31 July 2022).

Terry, Todd. (1991). 'House is a Feeling'. Available at: Spotify (Accessed 31 July 2022).

Three 6 Mafia. (2005). 'Stay Fly'. Available at: Spotify (Accessed 31 July 2022).

TRXD featuring Harper. (2018). 'Jealous'. Available at: Spotify (Accessed 31 July 2022).

Underworld. (1994). 'Cowgirl'. Available at: Spotify (Accessed 31 July 2022).

The Weeknd. (2020). 'Blinding Lights'. Available at: Spotify (Accessed 31 July 2022).

West, Kanye. (2004). 'Through the Wire'. Available at: Spotify (Accessed 31 July 2022).

West, Kanye. (2014). 'The Chainsmokers'. Available at: Spotify (Accessed 31 July 2022).

8

"Come together, right now ..."

Making remote multiparty in-the-box audio mixing a reality

Scott Stickland, Nathan Scott, and Rukshan Athauda

1 INTRODUCTION: BACKGROUND AND RELATED WORK

With a nod to the Beatles album *Abbey Road*, this chapter documents the evolution of a new online audio mixing and music production collaboration platform, implementing a design philosophy that:

- Eschews bandwidth-intensive high-quality or high-resolution audio streaming in favour of low-bandwidth data transfer;
- Requires access to only typical residential Internet bandwidths;
- Co-opts an existing Digital Audio Workstation (DAW) platform favoured by professional audio mixing engineers and music producers; and
- Enhances collaborative interactions by providing effective real-time communication.

Online music collaboration is not a new phenomenon, though it is fair to say that the COVID-19 pandemic brought a renewed focus on musical interactions facilitated by the Internet. Launched in 1998, the Rocket Network represented the first foray into online audio- and MIDI-file sharing amongst remote collaborators by accessing the network's cloud storage server over the Internet (Price, 2001; Thornton, 2006). In the ensuing years, major DAW/sequencer platforms, including Steinberg's Cubase VST, Emagic's Logic, and Avid's Pro Tools, integrated the Rocket Network's RocketControl middleware to provide direct synchronisation and distribution of DAW-based audio and MIDI assets by way of the central storage server (Eyers, 2004). In addition to being the first collaborative solution for music producers and musicians, the Rocket Network was the first example of asynchronous collaboration, where participants work offline and then upload their contributions post-factum.

Since 2003, which saw the demise of the Rocket Network after its acquisition by Avid, a capacity to interact synchronously or asynchronously largely delineates how developers approached online music

DOI: 10.4324/9781003462101-9

collaboration. A real-time audio-streaming approach generally typifies synchronous platforms and encompasses collaborations in direct-to-DAW remote recording (Pejrolo, 2014), telematic performance (Chafe, 2009; Bouillot and Cooperstock, 2009), long-distance instrumental music tuition (Dammers, 2009) and remote auditioning of audio material (Production Expert, 2017). Some notable pioneering approaches to synchronous audio streaming include Source Elements' Source Connect (Source Elements, 2020), JACK and JackTrip (Cáceres and Chafe, 2010), Steinberg's VST Connect (Steinberg Media Technologies GmbH, 2020b), Audiomovers' Listento (Audiomovers LLC, 2021), Soundwhale (Soundwhale, 2020), Sessionwire Communications' Sessionwire Studio (Sessionwire Communications Inc., 2020), ConnectionOpen (ConnectionOpen, 2021) and Ferguson and Hook's real-time online music production case study and presentation at Innovation in Music 2019 (Ferguson and Hook, 2021; Focusrite Audio Engineering Ltd., n.d.). Asynchronous platforms can facilitate DAW-specific and DAW-agnostic music production and composition collaboration, often with no restrictions on audio quality nor, in most cases, the number of participants, while maintaining the architectural concepts established by the Rocket Network: a centralised cloud-based audio and project file archive, and asynchronous contributions and communication. Innovative platforms include Avid's Cloud Collaboration (Avid Technology Inc., 2020), Steinberg's VST Transit (Steinberg Media Technologies GmbH, 2021), Splice's Splice Studio (Splice.com, 2022) and Spotify's Soundtrap (Spotify USA Inc./ Spotify AB, 2022).

Despite the revolutionary impact the mentioned platforms have made on how the music industry collaborates online, they were found wanting when we examined their ability to provide a collaborative real-time audio mixing environment. The synchronous audio streaming platforms cannot synchronise the audio mixing functions of multiple remote DAW instantiations working on an audio mix. We interviewed several Australian professional audio mixing engineers to determine the conditions under which they would consider a potential online collaborative mixing environment ideal (Stickland, Athauda and Scott, 2022b). Their responses allowed us to generate a short list of conditions, which included:

- Using the same DAW platform and version with which they undertake their typical in-studio audio mixing;
- Mixing and monitoring audio material at the exact resolution they experience in-studio, typically ≥48 kHz sample rate and ≥24-bit bit depth, or high-resolution audio (Melchior, 2019);
- Real-time monitoring of the remote collaborator(s) audio mixing operations; and
- Communicating with the collaborators using a dedicated but separate audio-visual stream. Figure 8.1 identifies this gap in online music collaboration approaches.

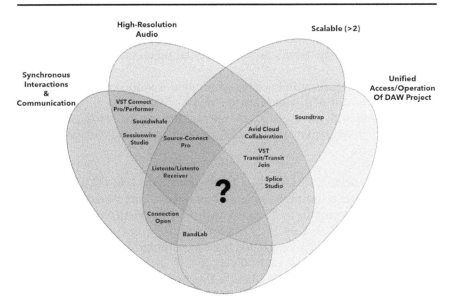

Figure 8.1 The examined collaboration platforms and their ability to render the conditions for collaborative and democratised online audio mixing, noting that not one existing platform provides all four conditions.

Source: Stickland, Athauda and Scott (2022a)

2 THE DAW COLLABORATION FRAMEWORK

To address the gap and provide all four critical conditions articulated by the mixing engineers we interviewed, we conceptualised, designed, developed, tested and evaluated a novel web application and networking infrastructure, collectively referred to as the DAW Collaboration Framework (DCF). A summary of that effort follows and points to essential articles and conference papers chronicling the developmental journey.

2.1 The DCF's architecture and operation

The DCF adopts a hybrid asynchronous/synchronous approach from an operational perspective. The collaborative DAW project and high-resolution audio assets, stored on a cloud server, are distributed and locally instantiated before a collaboration session. This process reflects industry-standard pre-mixing preparation practices insofar as an audio mixing engineer imports a recording session's high-resolution multitrack audio stems into a DAW before commencing the mix (Paterson, 2017). However, once instantiated, the DAW audio mixing project synchronously streams DAW-generated control data for synchronised multiparty operation across the collaboration framework.

The DCF's user interface and communication means are encapsulated in the web application, termed the DAW Collaboration Interface Application (DCIA). The DCIA performs two fundamental functions:

- Creating a closed online group to provide a videoconferencing and text-chat means of communication; and
- Interfacing with the users' DAW application instances to receive and transmit DAW-generated control data from and to the collaboration's participants.

Therefore, we needed to identify a professional-standard DAW platform that can generate, transmit, receive and instantiate control data for transport over the Internet in as close to real-time as possible. This search, conducted in 2018, led us to Steinberg's Cubase Pro and its Generic Remote feature that allows users to create a customised mapping of MIDI continuous controller (CC) and note events in the form of a distributed and importable XML file to Cubase's functions, commands and operation (Stickland, Scott and Athauda, 2018). Figure 8.2 illustrates the DCF's high-level architecture based on the ability to transport MIDI control data.

The DCF's collaborators begin with a distributed DAW project and high-resolution multitrack audio assets, downloaded from cloud storage

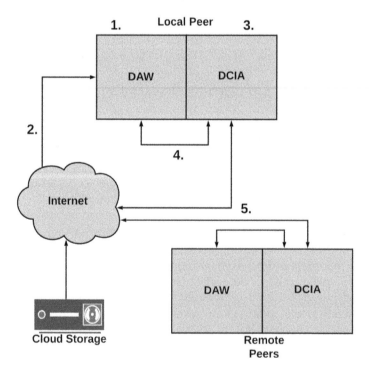

Figure 8.2 The DCF's high-level architecture, showing: 1. A local DAW instantiation; 2. Downloading DAW project and multitrack audio files from cloud storage; 3. Navigating to the DCIA via the web browser; 4. Interfacing the DCIA with the DAW via virtual MIDI ports; and 5. The DCIA receives and transmits DAW-generated MIDI events over the Internet.

and instantiated on their local production computer. Then, opening a Chromium-based web browser (Google LLC, n.d.), all collaborators navigate to the DCIA's URL and join a collaboration room where they can communicate and interact in real-time using the DCIA's videoconference and text chat features, fulfilling the first fundamental function previously mentioned. To interface the DCIA with each collaborator's DAW instantiation and subsequently link all DAW instantiations, the collaborators select and assign the DCIA's virtual MIDI ports as described in Section 2.2.

2.2 Implementing WebRTC and Web MIDI APIs and cloud media servers

Central to the DCIA's secure communication streams and DAW control data transfers are the WebRTC and Web MIDI application programming interfaces (APIs) (World Wide Web Consortium, 2018, 2015). WebRTC establishes secure real-time P2P and limited multi-P2P audio-visual streaming channel connections, providing the DCF's videoconferencing capability. Importantly, WebRTC can also create multiple data channels that run concurrently with, but separate from, the media channels and can transport arbitrary binary data by co-opting the semi-reliable Stream Control Transmission Protocol (SCTP) (Stewart, 2007). Creating several data channels provides the necessary infrastructure for the DCF's text-chat facility and, crucially, the reception and transmission of DAW-generated MIDI event data (Stickland, Athauda and Scott, 2019). Interfacing the DCF with Cubase Pro's Generic Remote is achieved by employing virtual MIDI input and output ports that the DCIA's Web MIDI implementation can access and direct the flow of MIDI information to and from the established WebRTC data channels. Furthermore, the virtual MIDI ports facilitate DAW transport functions and navigation synchronisation by streaming MIDI Timecode (MTC) quarter frames and MIDI Machine Control (MMC) messages generated by a *master timekeeper* and transmitted to all other online participants. Figure 8.3 shows the interplay between the DCF-DAW virtual MIDI ports and respective WebRTC data channels.

With the collaborators' DAW projects instantiated and online group communication established, the final step is to navigate to the DCIA's MIDI port selection boxes and choose the appropriate virtual MIDI input and output ports. Figure 8.4 illustrates this procedure. Once established, each local DCIA instantiation will begin receiving MIDI CC and Note events from Cubase Pro's Generic Remote and transmitting them as strings that include the collaborator's username, MIDI status and data bytes and a timestamp, then on to all other participants. Similarly, the group's master timekeeper selects the DCIA's virtual MTC and MMC MIDI ports, while all other collaborators assign the virtual ports and activate external synchronisation for playback (see Figure 8.4). The MIDI port configuration allows the DCF to replicate in-the-box audio mixing operations and playhead navigation performed on any local DAW instantiation on all other remote instantiations in the group.

Furthermore, the master timekeeper's playback and transport control operations will trigger identical operations on the remaining DAWs set to external

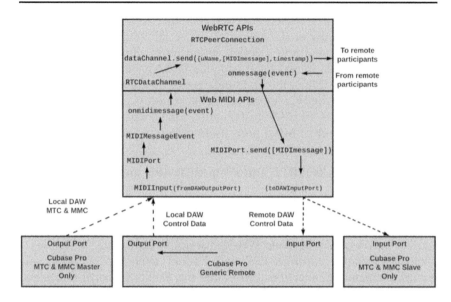

Figure 8.3 The DCF's Web MIDI and WebRTC implementations for interfacing with the Cubase Pro DAW.

synchronisation. Since the DCF only streams low-bandwidth control data and not bandwidth-intensive high-quality or high-resolution audio, all collaborators monitor their DAW's audio playback in the exact resolution as the project's audio assets. All the while, the collaborators can discuss and critique the audio mixing decisions using the DCIA's videoconference or text chat.

In order to scale the DCF to accommodate a multiparty collaboration model, it was necessary to incorporate a media server into the networking infrastructure (Stickland, Athauda and Scott, 2021). We settled on LiveSwitch Inc.'s LiveSwitch Cloud server facility (LiveSwitch Inc., 2023), which allowed us to test various connection architectures, including P2P mesh, mixing via a multipoint connection unit (MCU), and hybrid mixing/routing via an MCU dedicated to the DCF's audio-visual media streams, and a selective forwarding unit (SFU) to distribute the DCF's data streams. Remote registration with, and access to, the LiveSwitch Cloud Gateway server requires an authorisation token implementation as a security measure. As such, we established a NodeJS web server that serves the DCF's various files and generates a JSON Web Token (JWT) for each participant by accessing and correlating several client-side and server-side objects (see Figure 8.5).

The testing showed that the most efficient and reliable architecture encompassed three LiveSwitch Cloud MCU servers:

1. A Media server to perform essential transcoding, mixing and distribution of the collaborators' audio-visual streams;
2. A Data server to receive and distribute the DCF's text-chat messages and DAW-generated MIDI CC and note event data; and
3. A Timecode server to receive and distribute the DCF's MTC and MMC event data.

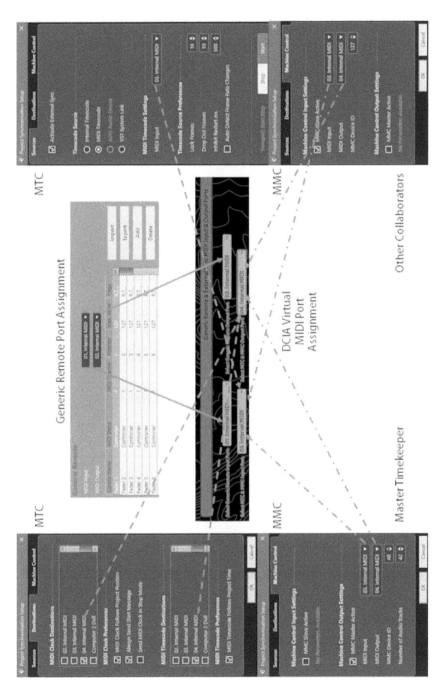

Figure 8.4 The DCIA's virtual MIDI port and Cubase Pro's Generic Remote, MTC, and MMC MIDI port assignments (Steinberg Media Technologies GmbH, 2023).

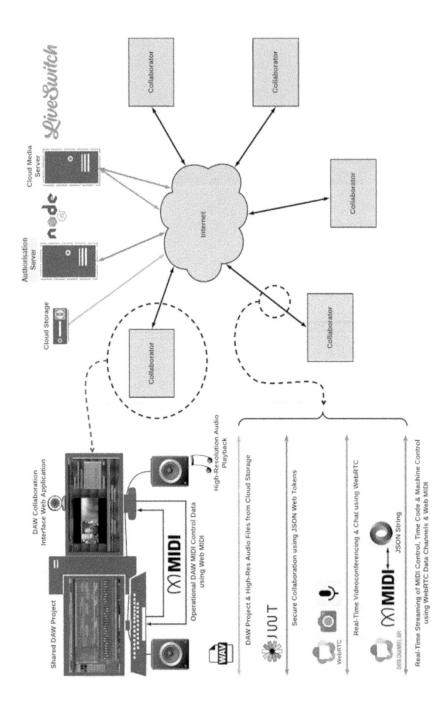

Figure 8.5 The DCF's assets and signal flow to and from the DCIA and DAW (LiveSwitch Inc., 2023; Steinberg Media Technologies GmbH, 2023).

Our tests culminated in a DCF prototype that could synchronise multiple instantiations of a Cubase Pro project, particularly in-the-box mixing operations, including level, panning and plug-ins common to all DAW instantiations. The prototype also accommodated synchronised DAW playback, navigation and other transport functions by assigning one Cubase Pro instantiation as the master timekeeper, with all remaining instantiations set to an external synchronisation playback mode. At the time, the test environment included 50-Mbps and 100-Mbps limits as typical client and server Internet connection speeds in Australia, respectively (Gregory, 2019). Consequently, the DCF prototype demonstrated a capacity to scale to 30 online participants without exceeding the imposed bandwidth limits (Stickland, Athauda and Scott, 2021).

2.3 Real-world deployment and testing evaluations

We deployed the DCF prototype with two audio mixing engineers we had previously interviewed, asking them to complete a series of five mixing projects as outlined in Table 8.1 (Stickland, Athauda and Scott, 2022a). Mix Projects 1 and 4 adopted an approach employed by the mixing engineers when working with their clients. The engineers share a completed version of the mix with the clients by uploading the mix audio file to cloud share folders, in these cases, using Dropbox. The client(s) assess the mix and provide the engineers with written feedback, requesting various changes. The engineers attend to the requests, and then the process starts again. As the mixing engineers admitted, this asynchronous and iterative approach is far from ideal but is not uncommon in the industry. Conversely, Mix Projects 2, 3 and 5, conducted synchronously, used the DCF to provide a collaborative and democratic audio mixing process and instantaneous feedback.

The evaluations used several quantitative and qualitative Inductive Phenomenological Analysis (IPA) (Smith, 2004) methods; the metrics applied include:

Quantitative Metrics

- Mixing session and total active mixing times;
- The number of required mix iterations;
- Time spent working on the various mixing elements; and
- The number of insert and effect send plug-ins utilised in the mix; and

Qualitative Metrics

- Comparisons between asynchronous and DCF-enabled synchronous collaborative online audio mixing paradigms;
- The benefits, disadvantages and merits of engaging in the DCF-enabled mixing environment;
- Comparisons between peer-to-peer and multiparty collaborative mixing; and
- Improvements and potential additions to the DCF environment.

Table 8.1 The Five Mix Projects Undertaken by Two Audio Mixing Engineers, Eleven Recording Musicians and the Author (Stickland)

Mix Project	Participants	Audio Mixing Paradigm/ Approach Employed	Data Collected	Mix Project Details
1	Audio Mixing Engineers Author (Stickland)	Asynchronous Mixing using cloud storage (Dropbox) and written feedback from the client	Audio Mix Journal entries	No. of tracks: 39 Style: Pop/ Rock Duration: 4:02
2	Audio Mixing Engineers Author (Stickland)	Online Real-Time Collaborative Audio Mixing using the DCF	Screen recordings Semi-structured interview responses	No. of tracks: 42 Style: Pop/ Rock Duration: 4:22
3	Audio Mixing Engineers Third-Party Clients (One per engineer) Author as Observer (Stickland)	Online Real-Time Collaborative Audio Mixing using the DCF	Screen recordings Semi-structured interview responses	No. of tracks: 41 Style: Pop/ Rock Duration: 4:18
4	Audio Mixing Engineers Members of a band/ensemble (Five members in one, six members in the other)	Asynchronous Mixing using cloud storage (Dropbox) and written feedback from the client	Audio Mix Journal entries	No. of tracks: 38 Style: Pop/Soul Duration: 4:07
5	Audio Mixing Engineers Members of a band/ensemble Researcher as Observer	Online Real-Time Collaborative Audio Mixing using the DCF	Screen recordings Semi-structured interview responses	No. of tracks: 42 Style: Pop/ Rock Duration: 4:28

The findings of our IPA process identified several beneficial facets of the DCF's performance and mixing outcomes compared to the engineers' existing asynchronous method for developing a mix with clients outside of the studio environment. These included:

- Time savings owing to reduced active mixing times, demonstrated by an average time reduction of 40.0% when mixing one-on-one and 11.8% when engaged in multiparty mixing;

- The ability for the engineers to receive critical and constructive feedback from the clients as the mix progressed rather than once the mix version was complete;
- The potential to eliminate ambiguities in the feedback given to the engineers, especially when clients can execute or advise on mixing operations to achieve the desired result;
- The opportunity to expand one's knowledge of audio mixing through real-time observation and high-resolution audio monitoring of new or different mixing techniques;
- The ability to build rapport and familiarity between the mixing engineers and clients, assisting with understanding the ultimate results the client(s) is/are after;
- The opportunity to collaborate in person with musicians and other audio engineers, irrespective of their location; and
- The overarching sense of teamwork and ownership of the final mix results for all collaborators.

Nevertheless, the participants provided views on the operational aspects of the DCF's workflow that detracted from the audio mixing experience, such as:

- The engineers' perceived loss of autonomy and awareness of the scrutiny, real or perceived, over every mixing decision as it happened;
- The restrictions placed on the participants, including the choice of DAW, selection and number of plug-ins, and maximum number of tracks;
- The workflow limitations, including a loss of on-screen DAW "real-estate" to accommodate the DCF's videoconference, idiosyncrasies such as selecting a track before editing the track's plug-ins, and some mixing techniques do not currently generate control data, including group tracks/auxiliary buses creation, input/output routing options, adding insert and send plug-ins as the mix progresses, automation events, and cycle markers;
- Repeated muting/unmuting of the DCF's videoconference microphone source to eliminate delayed echoes if the DAW playback was through studio monitors; and
- Only the engineers control the DAW playback, necessitating playback requests from the other collaborators.

2.4 A novel audio mixing paradigm

Our research's *felix exitus* was to discover how audio mixing engineers and other stakeholders, such as musicians, can collaborate on a mixing project over the Internet when attended mixing and in-studio interactions are not possible or convenient. We unearthed a novel audio mixing paradigm in developing and deploying the DCF in real-world scenarios. For every one of the research participants, experiencing the DCF-facilitated online milieu provided their first opportunity to work on an audio mixing project remotely, but with the benefit of real-time interactions and communication, high-resolution audio mixing material and monitoring and the ability to practically contribute to the evolution of a mix as it happens, irrespective of location. Given the benefits borne out of our real-world deployment and testing articulated in Section 2.3, we believe the DCF has the potential to render the mixing engineers' asynchronous operational mode of iterative mix file cloud storage/sharing and post-factum client feedback a less desirable option for the audio mixing industry. Nonetheless, we also believe that the DCF requires further development and refinement before the DCF can manifest such potential.

3 FUTURE DEVELOPMENT

Our research participants provided valuable feedback, especially highlighting restrictions to their customary mixing workflow, for us to consider when devising a future development strategy. Resolving their concerns is crucial if the DCF is to be embraced by the audio mixing and music production industry.

3.1 Integrating heterogenous DAW platforms

One of the strongest criticisms of the DCF provided by the research participants was its limitation to only interface with the Cubase Pro DAW platform. Presently, several DAW platforms include control surface integration and, crucially for extending the DAW interfacing capability of the DCF, also include user-defined MIDI/DAW function mapping capabilities. Table 8.2 summarises the DAW platforms best positioned for exploring

Table 8.2 DAW Platforms With User-Defined Control Surface Mapping/Scripting

DAW Platform	Control Surface Compatible	User-Defined Mapping/Scripting
Pro Tools	✓	✓ (EUCON SDK)
Ableton Live	✓	✓ (TXT file format)
Logic Pro	✓	✓ (Lua scripting)
FL Studio	✓	✓ (Python scripting)
Studio One	✓	✓ (Control Link feature)
Reason	✓	✓ (Remote Developer licensing)
REAPER	✓	✓ (Web browser interface)
Bitwig Studio	✓	✓ (Open Controller API)

potential DCF integration. Such exploration can lead to developing cross-DAW translation templates or wrappers, which the DCF could implement to link like-functions across a range of DAW platforms.

3.2 Extending DAW mixing functionality

The DCF's interfacing with remote and local DAW instantiations allows for the transmission and reception of MIDI control data generated by the specific DAW platform. The DCF currently interfaces with the Cubase Pro DAW platform, and the DCF's functionality is restricted purely by the number of operations and functions that generate user-defined MIDI messages when executed. This restriction does not lie with the DCF's design but rather the limited selection of DAW features that generate MIDI control data messages through Cubase Pro's Generic Remote feature. With the release of Cubase Pro 12 in early 2022, Steinberg introduced a new MIDI remote integration via script (JavaScript/JSON) and mapping capabilities that will eventually replace the long-standing Generic Remote feature (Steinberg Media Technologies GmbH, 2022). This upgrade aligns Cubase Pro with the DAWs in Table 8.2. At the time of writing, Steinberg's nascent MIDI Remote implementation does not include all "in-the-box" functions; however, future upgrades should expand its scripting capabilities. Early experimentation has shown that the existing implementation can address some of the DCF's limitations, such as the synchronised addition of new audio and group tracks.

3.3 Resolving concurrency issues

The in-studio testing regime uncovered a concurrency issue; participants could execute simultaneous conflicting mixing actions. Therefore, future work can investigate implementing two discrete approaches to address the issue of collaborators performing opposing mix changes simultaneously:

1. **Centralised approach:** A centralised solution assigns a "host" of the collaboration session who controls the collaborators' control data transmission. The host can enable/disable each collaborator to transmit control data by implementing permissions in a centralised connection architecture at the Data Server. This feature can only disseminate "'enabled' collaborators" control data while filtering all other data. The LiveSwitch Cloud client software development kit includes assigning "roles", which caters to this centralised model. Furthermore, since the message originator's username prepends every control data message transmitted and received by the DCIA, identifying a participant's username and data is readily accessible.
2. **Decentralised approach:** A decentralised solution allows each collaborator to filter other collaborators' actions by determining which control data streams will transmit to their local DAW instantiation.

Typical of these approaches is the possibility of conflicting actions remaining if more than one collaborator is "allowed" to transmit control data. Therefore, the third approach for investigation is a process that identifies potential opposing actions and resolves them, such as buffering recent control data and filtering out such actions generated by different collaborators.

3.4 Improving control data message resolution

Utilising MIDI 1.0 messages as DAW control data provides some limitations in functionality. Binary DAW functions, such as mute and solo buttons/switches, either on or off, can be readily mapped to MIDI Note On and Note Off events. Similarly, DAW functions with values on a continuum, such as level faders, pan-pots and plug-in parameters, can be mapped to MIDI Continuous Controllers (CCs), with values restricted to 128 gradations owing to the MIDI 1.0 specification determining that CC values range between 0 and 127 (MMA Inc., 2019). To illustrate this limitation, the operation of a level fader, capable of significant positional variations, can only generate a maximum of 128 different fader-position control data messages.

Accommodating the MIDI 2.0 Universal MIDI Packet and Capability Inquiry protocols (The MIDI Association, 2021) will improve the current resolution restrictions once implemented in various DAW platforms. Work is underway to realise this implementation; for example, Steinberg has updated their VST 3 software development kit to support the MIDI 2.0 standard (Steinberg Media Technologies GmbH, 2020a). MIDI 2.0 provides a 32-bit resolution, compared with the 7-bit resolution MIDI 1.0 currently delivers (The MIDI Association, 2021). Furthermore, MIDI 2.0 presents an opportunity to investigate and experiment with its Profile Configuration and Property Exchange capabilities, potentially enhancing the DCF's cross-DAW platform compatibility.

3.5 Online pay-per-use/subscription offering

Several existing collaboration platforms on the market charge their customers subscription or licence fees. Given their success in the remote music collaboration industry, it appears that customers are prepared to pay for these useful collaboration features, and as such, we plan to offer the DCF as a Software-as-a-Service (SaaS) model. We plan to launch the DCF by initially targeting the Cubase Pro community of users and adopting a SaaS pay-per-use or low-cost subscription model to establish a base of early adopters for critical feedback and feature suggestions. As the DCF's DAW platform compatibility increases, we can pursue new markets and investigate extending the DCF's DAW-specific wrappers to include translation tables that homogenously link in-the-box mixing operations and functions for cross-DAW collaboration.

3.6 Online audio/music production education

One of the more intriguing findings presented in Section 2.3 was the opportunity the DCF's environment provides to expand one's knowledge of audio mixing and music production practices by observing and aurally identifying changes executed by a professional mixing engineer in real-time. Crucially, one can interact with an expert practitioner in the moment and clarify one's understanding of the concepts and techniques of in-the-box mixing. Recognising the didactic potential of the DCF, we intend to explore opportunities the DCF could present for enhanced delivery of online audio and music production education.

For instance, industry leaders in the online audio education domain offer undergraduate and postgraduate music production degrees, combining cutting-edge music production techniques with DAW-based music technology tools (Berklee Online, 2022b; Berklee Online, 2022a; dBs Institute of Sound & Digital Technologies, 2022; Point Blank, 2022). Williams (2021) notes that online delivery of distance learning techniques typically employs "an 'in-house' *Virtual Learning Environment* (VLE) that facilitates browser-based display of reference and interactive material" (p. 207). Such VLEs include text-based information, downloadable high-resolution audio files, embedded procedural videos, interactive quizzes, asynchronous message-based "discussion" sections, videoconferencing and assignment-submission portals.

Interestingly, several audio frequency analyses of videos included in some institutions' VLEs reveal sub-high-resolution, lossy audio, antithetical to critical listening discernment, a crucial asset for professional audio engineering (see Figure 8.6). Moreover, a video presentation cannot address students' questions that could arise during the presentation. This

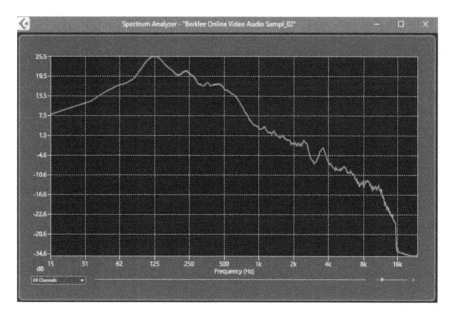

Figure 8.6 A frequency analysis of an embedded video's audio track from an industry-standard VLE, showing a drastic reduction of frequency content above 16 kHz.

Source: Steinberg Media Technologies GmbH (2023)

lack of synchronous interactions during the introduction of new music production concepts highlights how incorporating the DCF as a complement to embedded video allows for hands-on real-time tutorials, thereby providing students with high-resolution audio examples, a means to interact with the instructor during the presentation of information and an opportunity to demonstrate practical knowledge and skill acquisition in real-time.

4 CONCLUSION

We have presented a unique online music production collaboration framework that recognises the ground-breaking work of the pioneers in the domain and, through an analysis of the various collaboration solutions they provide, identified a facet of music production, the audio mixing phase, that required a different approach. Specifically, we conceptualised, designed, developed and tested our framework, the DCF, to satisfy four crucial criteria that provide:

1. Synchronous interactions and communication with other collaborators;
2. Mixing and monitoring of high-resolution multitrack audio;
3. Scalability beyond a single P2P connection; and
4. Equal and unified access to a professional-grade DAW platform.

The DCF can now take its place in the spectrum of online music collaboration platforms, occupying the space first depicted in Figure 8.1 and now presented in Figure 8.7.

The DCF allows us to capture and transmit customised MIDI CC and Note messages mapped to specific DAW operations through the DAW's

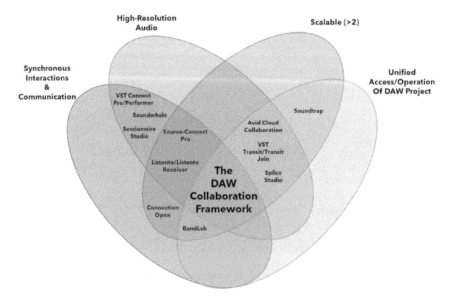

Figure 8.7 The DCF delivers on all four criteria for online audio mixing collaboration.

capacity to integrate an external control surface. While we have demonstrated the DCF's capability by interfacing with the Cubase Pro DAW platform, we have also identified similar mapping and control-data generation methodologies for several of the most popular professional-grade DAW platforms. The next phase in the DCF's evolution is investigating these various approaches to determine how we can encapsulate their control data within WebRTC data channel messaging protocols. Success in this endeavour will ideally render the DCF as a DAW-agnostic collaboration framework and, possibly, provide cross-DAW compatibility.

Furthermore, we intend to pursue deployment opportunities for the DCF, including a commercial pay-per-use or subscription service for Cubase Pro users, then branch out to other DAW communities as the DCF's DAW compatibility evolves. We believe the DCF can be a cost-effective solution for professional remote audio mixing with global reach. We also propose to conduct quantitative and qualitative research into the DCF's efficacy within the online audio and music production education realm by establishing partnerships with industry-leading educational institutions.

REFERENCES

Audiomovers LLC (2021). Audiomovers Listento, *Audiomovers LLC* (website), available online from https://audiomovers.com/wp/ [accessed August 2021]

Avid Technology Inc. (2020). Producing Software for Music – Cloud Collaboration – Pro Tools, *Avid Technology Inc.* (website), available online from www.avid.com/pro-tools/cloud-collaboration [accessed March 2020]

Berklee Online (2022a). Music Production Bachelor's Degree – Berklee Online, *Berklee Online* (website), available online from https://online.berklee.edu/music-degrees/undergraduate/music-production [accessed August 2022]

Berklee Online (2022b). Music Production Master's Degree – Berklee Online, *Berklee Online* (website), available online from https://online.berklee.edu/music-degrees/graduate/music-production [accessed August 2022]

Bouillot, N. and Cooperstock, J. R. (2009). Challenges and Performance of High-Fidelity Audio Streaming for Interactive Performances, *Proceedings of the International Conference on New Interfaces for Musical Expression*, Pittsburgh.

Cáceres, J.-P. and Chafe, C. (2010). JackTrip: Under the Hood of an Engine for Network Audio, *Journal of New Music Research*, Vol 39, No 3, pp. 183–187.

Chafe, C. (2009). Tapping Into the Internet as an Acoustical/Musical Medium, *Contemporary Music Review*, Vol 28, No 4–5, pp. 413–420.

ConnectionOpen (2021). Low Latency, Uncompressed Audio, Online Collaboration Software, *ConnectionOpen* (website), available online from www.connectionopen.com/ [accessed August 2021]

Dammers, R. J. (2009). Utilizing Internet-Based Videoconferencing for Instrumental Music Lessons, *Update: Applications of Research in Music Education*, Vol 28, No 1, pp. 17–24.

dBs Institute of Sound & Digital Technologies (2022). Online Masters in Music Technology & Sound Engineering, *DBS Music Holdings Ltd.* (website), available online from www.dbsinstitute.ac.uk/ma-music-production-sound-engineering-online [accessed December 2022]

Eyers, D. (2004). 'Ambiguous Live'– Exploring Collaborative, Dynamic Control of MIDI Sequencers, in Wiil, U.K. (ed.) *Computer Music Modeling and Retrieval: International Symposium, CMMR 2003, Montpellier, France, May 26–27, 2003, Revised Papers*, Heidelberg, Springer Berlin, pp. 54–63.

Ferguson, P. and Hook, D. (2021). Ground Control and Cloud Booths: Using Dante to Break Geographical Barriers to Music Production, in Hepworth-Sawyer, R., Paterson, J. and Toulson, R. (eds.) *Innovation in Music: Future Opportunities*, 1st edition, Oxon, Routledge, pp. 89–105.

Focusrite Audio Engineering Ltd. (n.d.). Focusrite Enables 'World-First' Cross-Border Interactive Performance, *Focusrite Audio Engineering Ltd: Case Studies* (website), available online from https://pro.focusrite.com/case-studies/live-sound/rednet-enables-%E2%80%98worldfirst%E2%80%99-cross-border-interactive-performance [accessed October 2020]

Google LLC (n.d.) Chromium OS – The Chromium Projects, *Google LLC* (website), available online from www.chromium.org/chromium-os [accessed October 2020]

Gregory, M. A. (2019). How to Transition the National Broadband Network to Fibre To The Premises, *Journal of Telecommunications and the Digital Economy*, Vol 7, No 1, pp. 57–67.

LiveSwitch Inc. (2023). WebRTC Experts, Build Interactive Video Today | Try Live Switch! *LiveSwitch Inc.* (website), available online from www.liveswitch.io/ [accessed March 2023]

Melchior, V. (2019). High-Resolution Audio: A History and Perspective, *Journal of the Audio Engineering Society*, Vol 67, No 5, pp. 246–257.

The MIDI Association (2021). Details about MIDI 2.0, MIDI-CI, Profiles and Property Exchange, *The MIDI Association* (website), available online from www.midi.org/midi-articles/details-about-midi-2-0-midi-ci-profiles-and-property-exchange [accessed May 2021]

MMA Inc. (2019). The Complete MIDI 1.0 Detailed Specification, *MMA Inc.* (website), available online from www.midi.org/specifications-old/item/the-midi-1-0-specification [accessed February 2020]

Paterson, J. (2017). Mixing in the Box, in Hepworth-Sawyer, R. and Hodgson, J. (eds.) *Mixing Music*, 1st edition, New York, Routledge, pp. 77–93.

Pejrolo, A. (2014). Remote Collaboration: Long-Distance Recording Projects, *Sound on Sound March 2014*, pp. 138–147.

Point Blank (2022). Music Production (Logic) – Sample Course | Point Blank Music School, *Point Blank* (website), available online from https://vle.pointblankmusicschool.com/notes/online/0/itp-logic-course-sample/lesson0.php [accessed December 2022]

Price, S. (2001). Rocket Network Compatability, *Sound on Sound October 2001* (website), available online from www.soundonsound.com/techniques/rocket-network-compatability [accessed December 2020]

Production Expert (2017). Streaming Mixes from DAW to Web Browsers Using LISTENTO Plug-in by Audiomovers, *Production Expert* (online video), available online from www.youtube.com/watch?v=jlgYNOQnGnE [accessed August 2021]

Sessionwire Communications Inc. (2020). Sessionwire, *Sessionwire Communications Inc.* (website), available online from www.sessionwire.com/ [accessed July 2020]

Smith, J. A. (2004). Reflecting on the Development of Interpretative Phenomenological Analysis and its Contribution to Qualitative Research in Psychology,
Qualitative Research in Psychology, Vol 1, No 1, pp. 39–54.

Soundwhale (2020). Soundwhale: Audio Post and Music Collaboration Software, *Soundwhale* (website), available online from https://soundwhale.com/
[accessed July 2020]

Source Elements (2020). Source Elements – Source-Connect, *Source Elements*
(website), available online from http://source-elements.com/products/source-
connect [accessed March 2020]

Splice.com (2022). Collaborate with Splice Studio | Splice, *Splice.com* (website),
available online from https://splice.com/features/studio [accessed February
2022]

Spotify USA Inc./Spotify AB (2022). Soundtrap – Make Music Online, *Spotify
USA Inc.* (website), available online from www.soundtrap.com/ [accessed
August 2022]

Steinberg Media Technologies GmbH (2020a). About MIDI in VST 3 – VST,
Steinberg Developer Help (website), available online from https://developer.
steinberg.help/display/VST/About+MIDI+in+VST+3 [accessed October
2020]

Steinberg Media Technologies GmbH (2020b). VST Connect Pro | Steinberg,
Steinberg Media Technologies GmbH (website), available online from www.
steinberg.net/en/products/vst/vst_connect/vst_connect_pro.html [accessed
March 2020]

Steinberg Media Technologies GmbH (2021). VST Transit: Music cloud collabo-
ration | Steinberg, *Steinberg Media Technologies GmbH* (website), available
online from https://new.steinberg.net/vst-transit/?et_cid=15&et_lid=22&et_
sub=VST%2520Transit [accessed August 2021]

Steinberg Media Technologies GmbH (2022). New in Cubase 12: Time to Embrace
a New Era | Steinberg, *Steinberg Media Technologies GmbH* (website), avail-
able online from www.steinberg.net/cubase/new-features/ [accessed June
2022]

Steinberg Media Technologies GmbH (2023). *Cubase Pro 12.0.60* (software),
available online from www.steinberg.net/cubase/ [accessed March 2023]

Stewart, R. (2007). RFC 4960: Stream Control Transmission Protocol, *The IEFT
Trust* (website), available online from https://tools.ietf.org/pdf/rfc4960.pdf
[accessed May 2019]

Stickland, S., Athauda, R. and Scott, N. (2019). Design of a Real-Time Multiparty
DAW Collaboration Application using Web MIDI and WebRTC APIs, *Proceedings of the International Web Audio Conference 2019*, Trondheim.

Stickland, S., Athauda, R. and Scott, N. (2021). Design and Evaluation of a Scal-
able Real-Time Digital Audio Workstation Collaboration Framework, *Journal of the Audio Engineering Society*, Vol 69, No 6, pp. 410–431.

Stickland, S., Athauda, R. and Scott, N. (2022a). A New Audio Mixing Paradigm:
Evaluation from Professional Practitioners' Perspectives, *Creative Industries
Journal*, available online from https://doi.org/10.1080/17510694.2022.2088
164 [accessed June 2022]

Stickland, S., Athauda, R. and Scott, N. (2022b). Professional Views of Digital
Audio Workstations and Collaborative Audio Mixing, *Chroma: Journal of
the Australasian Computer Music Association*, Vol 38, No 1.

Stickland, S., Scott, N. and Athauda, R. (2018). A Framework for Real-Time Online Collaboration in Music Production, *Proceedings of the Australasian Computer Music Conference*, Perth.

Thornton, M. (2006). Source Elements Source-Connect: Remote Recording Plug-in for Pro Tools, *Sound on Sound May 2006*, pp. 126–129.

Williams, D. (2021). Designing Vocational Training for Audio Engineers at a Distance, in Daniel Walzer, M. L. (ed.) *Audio Education: Theory, Culture, and Practice*, 1st edition, New York, Routledge, pp. 207–220.

World Wide Web Consortium (2015). Web MIDI API, *World Wide Web Consortium* (website), available online from www.w3.org/TR/webmidi/ [accessed July 2021]

World Wide Web Consortium (2018). WebRTC 1.0: Real-Time Communication Between Browsers, *World Wide Web Consortium* (website), available online from www.w3.org/TR/webrtc/ [accessed December 2020].

9

A creative methodology for self-production

Tony Dupé

INTRODUCTION

This chapter explores the need for a more diverse conversation within music production. This aligns with an evolution of both sound scholarship and affordable technology. The what, where and who of music production has shifted sufficiently to embrace a generation of self-producers working from home or project studios.

The rationale set out here underpins a larger project in the making of a creative manual for self-producers. The idea that the intended reader of such a manual (songwriter or composer) might benefit from an entirely different language and perspective to existing production or home recording books is important to the project. There is, therefore, an intention within the manual to use a different tone and perspective towards the development of a lived music practice, which includes production.

It is hoped that the discussion here might also translate into a more useful and inclusive approach within music production education, which reflects the experience of students as they work on their music in their spaces. My understanding of music production comes primarily from my lived experience as a music producer, self-producing music artist and, more recently, an academic and lecturer in music production. Autoethnography is employed as a central framework for this chapter alongside artistic research, music production scholarship and sound studies.

My practice-based research accepts what Kathleen Coessens (2021, p. 7) refers to in music practice as "an appreciation of the value of sensorial experience and of qualities in the interaction between human beings and their environment". Coessens (ibid.) recognises the value of embodied knowledge and sensorial experience as an alternative to a "cognitivist, conceptual and systematic approach". Perspectives such as Coessens have the potential to enrich music production practice, education and scholarship and to extend the conversation from techniques and the technical, which dominate music production discourse.

The autoethnographic thread within this chapter is employed to convey an embodied and located approach to music production. In *Music Auto-ethnographies* (2009), Brydie-Leigh Bartleet and Carolyn Ellis make the

DOI: 10.4324/9781003462101-10

point that autoethnography is an open conversation between researcher and reader rather than a statement of fact. Bartleet and Ellis assert that autoethnographic writing invites the reader into an evocative tale of musical and personal entanglement, from which the reader can reflect on and consider incorporating into their own practice. This nonhierarchic, personal and lived perspective is effective in diversifying the conversation and participation in music production.

Autoethnography, sensorial studies and artistic research are in full flourish in music scholarship; however, music research is typically delineated from music production practices and scholarship. This is reflected in the research frameworks and focus where music production scholarship is comparatively less creative and experiential.

Today, self-producers find themselves on both sides of the (mostly metaphoric) glass window – as both artist and producer. This chapter explores the foundations and hallmarks of an exclusionary perspective within music production literature that connects to outmoded divisions of labour and environment in practice. By updating music production discourse to acknowledge the recent paradigm shift in music production practices and valuing individual perspectives and approaches, we can encourage diverse participation and conversations.

GLOSSARY

This research uses the term music artists, which I define as people such as myself who create original contemporary music. They are essentially composers and songwriters and, at times, it feels more correct or clear to use those terms instead. I also use the term musicians for those who are primarily performers, and sometimes put everyone in a basket called music makers. There is even one instance of using the term artist-producer as that is how Paula Wolfe (who is cited here) self-identifies. I am using these terms broadly and inclusively, and I would ask that the reader allow some licence and overlap.

SOUND STUDIES AND MUSIC PRODUCTION

At its core, music production is a human experience of sound. Exploring the breadth and complexity of sound in our lives is central to research in sound studies. According to Jonathan Sterne (2012, p. 2), it "redefines what sound does in the human world and what humans do in the sonic world". Mark Grimshaw-Aagaard (2019, p. 22) writes that "sound is a perception... is formed not only from the sound waves... but also from the memory, knowledge, reason, experience of physical spaces, expectation, emotion, mood, imagination and so on".

Moving from a focus on the sound wave to the personal experience of it is a framing that is an encouraging idea for the songwriter, composer and aspiring self-producers who might possess artistic or sensorial capabilities rather than technical confidence. Sound studies research in everyday listening explores the complexity and subjectivity that we bring to listening in music and music production.

MUSICKING AND MUSIC PRODUCTION

Music production practice connects well with Christopher Small's concept of music making as an imperfect, embodied, affirming and community-forming activity. Small (1998) invented the verb *musicking* to describe such a practice that works against the many and varied hierarchies, prejudices and myths around music and musical abilities. Small's reclamation of musical practice to the makers is powerful in encouraging engagement and a redefinition of what it is to be a musician, songwriter, composer or producer.

These ideas extend to what I regard as a necessary framing of music production as a *musical* practice that is a form of making that exists in all kinds of environments for all kinds of outcomes.

SELF-PRODUCTION AS A DISTINCT FORM OF MUSIC PRODUCTION

Self-production is not a new concept, but it is now arguably the dominant form of music production. This shift has been foreseen by many music production scholars (Moorefield 2005; Leyshon 2009; Cole 2011; Théberge 2012). Simplified, low-cost, high-quality music technology has never been more abundant or easy to use, and there are experts across many platforms to assist with tutorials, podcasts and forums. The impact of this, according to Pat O'Grady (2020, p. 212), "has disrupted ideas about who can record music and where they can record it". This shift and disruption of the who and where in music recording brings opportunities for new perspectives and processes in education, scholarship and practice.

As a music artist, producer and lecturer, I encounter so many songwriters, composers and musicians who have not yet embraced self-production as they do not identify as being technical. I believe a contemporary, reframed and creative path to self-production would facilitate a more inclusive, diverse participation within the field. I consider myself an instinctively *artistic* (rather than technical) music-maker whose recording practice focuses on an ongoing conversation between the musical work and meanings, the location (outside and inside) and the participants. I believe in the importance of play, experimentation, positivity, limitations, regime and how the making of a record can be a rich and fulfilling personal experience. I have produced around a hundred albums, including my own, many of which have found acclaim on an international level. In the past ten years, this experience has opened up a path for me into lecturing and academia. Entering the education setting, I was surprised that the value system and perspectives I had developed in my practice were largely absent. Instead, there was a focus on equipment and technical processes, with musicality, environment and community barely represented in curriculum. I registered a dissonance between my experience and understanding of music production and the dominant discourse. When I started teaching production for a songwriting degree, I realised (at least in part) why so many have not embraced self-production, since the conversation is almost entirely technical, amusical and comprehensively gendered. In contrast, my own lived experience of making records with songwriters and for myself was the exact opposite.

TECHNOLOGY, CANONS AND CONSEQUENCES

The exclusionary and mythologised nature of the general discourse in music production informs some of the prohibitive factors in its evolution as an embodied creative practice for the everyday person.

Repeated Takes (1995) is an examination of the history of music recording from its inception through to the end of the twentieth century. Author Michael Chanan charts the development of technology and the record industry and its impact on music. He identifies the "dearth of serious writing about the record industry (as opposed to a mass of anecdotal stuff about recording artists)" (1995, p. 7). This begins the industry frame of reference for music production scholarship, which positions technology centrally whilst also examining the commercial and cultural domain that surrounds the product of the recording. It is worth noting, however, that in Chanan's opinion, the record industry merits serious writing, whereas the subject of the recording artist is derided. Virgil Moorefield (2005, p. 5) identifies the cult of personality that grew up around Phil Spector and created "the first 'star' brand-name producer". According to Alan Williams (2018, p. 159), "this is how the stage was set for creative recordists to weave narratives of studio wizardry into their own marketing mythologies". Williams (2010, p. 10) cites Mark Lewisohn's book *The Beatles Recording Session* (1988) as a turning point in the clear establishment of interest (and an industry) of process over product. The canonisation of producers, studios and technology is as problematic in music production as the great works, composers and songwriters are in music.

The perspective of the genius producer in the mythologised recording studio still dominates the popular discourse around music production. Robert Wilsmore (2019, p. 246), in *Coproduction: Towards a Collaborative Practice in Production,* identifies that "the record producer has long been represented by the image of the lone figure of a man sat at a large mixing desk bestrewn with knobs and faders". Whilst acknowledging the problematic gendering, he also contentiously claims it to be "a romantic and seductive image" (ibid.) and casts the producer as someone who "saves the artists from their failings" (ibid.). In surveying music production literature, he cites *Behind the Glass* (2000) in reference to interviews that bring out the human, yet, Willsmore still feels the need to remind us that "there is probably enough evidence to suggest that they are literally the god from, or with, the machine" (ibid., p. 247).

This outmoded casting of producer and technology as the saviour of the fallible artist perpetuates a disempowerment to the aspiring, creatively focused self-producer.

The cover image of *Behind the Glass* (Massey 2000) conveys a range of issues pertaining to music production and gender. The male gaze shot over the producer's shoulder as he operates the complex technology (which fills the page) to suggest his knowledge and control. The woman, recessed and framed by this technology, appears to inform the title Behind the Glass. This perspective is interpretable as defining her as a painting or object exhibited for the benefit of the viewer. The singer is situated in a large empty space where, judging by their relative attire, the air conditioning seems to be very different from the aptly titled Control Room. She is not returning the gaze but seemingly more striking a pose. *Behind the Glass* is a very well-respected and circulated title as it interviews the most well-known producers, and it sits in many university libraries. There must have been no reflection on how the image reads as it was used again for *Behind the Glass Volume II* (2009). It's not hard to see how music production reproduces gendered stereotypes and how the music artist might feel intimidated by the identity and technology leap required to self-produce.

Women in the Studio (2019) examines how the gendering of music production impacts female practitioners and how new technologies and environments are key to the empowerment of female artist-producers. The opportunity to work away from perceived male territory is identified and explored by feminist scholar and artist-producer Paula Wolfe. She articulates the benefits of artistic development, creative control, getting to know your specific equipment and space and the flexibility of managing everyday responsibilities (p. 109).

The idea that the commercial recording studio is inherently problematic in terms of power dynamics and creative atmosphere is also respectively explored by Alan Williams and Damon Minchella. Williams argues in *Divide and Conquer: Power, Role Formation and Control in Recording Studio Architecture*,

> The physical properties of recording studio design impose social order designations – technician/observer/guard – musician/observed/inmate and naturalize this order as musicians unconsciously internalize their subordinate position.
>
> (2007, p. 3)

This language is in stark contrast to Willsmore's and yet describes the above image accurately. The discrepancy in perspective reflects how music production scholarship is predominantly invested in the vantage of the producer and their technology. In contrast, Williams is insightful in expressing a commonly experienced perspective of the musician, one which resonates with my experience of being recorded in such environments.

Music artist and academic Damon Minchella explores the impact of place on performance and creativity through his own experience and interviews with musicians and producers. He highlights how "a space and its atmosphere can engender or inhibit the creative process" (2018, p. 50) and describes music-making environments as "embodied emotional spaces" (ibid., p49). The research reveals that "due to the quality of relatively inexpensive recording equipment . . . the need for clinical and sterile environment has been obviated: atmosphere and perceptual input take precedence" (ibid., p. 56).

These perspectives suggest to me that the ideal of contemporary music production should not be a large mixing console and an acoustically treated and isolated environment but rather a creatively focused, non-hierarchic, emotionally responsive space. In such a paradigm, production would diversify participation to become a more attractive proposition to artists who might identify as creative rather than technical. These principles underpin my proposed creative self-production methodology, where the (reimagined) field becomes more attentive to the experience and atmosphere of the practitioners. This would be enacted through a tone and language that embraces the artful, personal and embodied elements of self-production. The framework is practice-based and aligns with the premise that contemporary composition and songwriting are so enmeshed in production that a direct and ongoing conversation is possible. The motivation of expression and creating new music is powerful for songwriters and composers, and if production becomes imbued with creative, located and personal notions, then a productive and documented musical life is created. This is an appealing outcome for a self-producer that would be framed through creative exercises in listening, composing, art-making and reflection.

I have successfully explored a creative pedagogy when working with undergraduate songwriters and composers in music production and composition. The approach is well supported by the ideas of philosopher and educator Maxine Greene. According to Greene (2000, p. 21), there is a prospect of discovery and hope in the connection of art and imagination to the learning compared to the reification that can occur with the issuing of facts.

I believe that this approach is a side door into self-production where a creative environment houses knowledge, and access is easier for those that have an appetite and curiosity for making.

MUSIC PRODUCTION AS AUTOETHNOGRAPHY

My own path into music production was informed by recording outside of the commercial studio in a way that is commonplace now but was less common in the late 1990s. Post-band, post-city living, post-long-term relationship, I moved to an oversized house on a headland in a small coastal town south of Sydney, Australia. I established a tranquil yet productive environment where other music artists would visit and immerse themselves in creative activity as I translated the proceedings. Given the capacity of the house and its proximity to the ocean, small parties of musicians and friends would visit to record, swim and create memories, Figure 9.1.

My own experiences in music and music production (the good, the bad and the ugly) directed me to create a positive and non-judgmental environment where the artist's experience is prioritised. My focus was on the music, the people and the place, and this allowed the creation of many wonderful records, communities and collective memories, which are, in my mind, the most desirable of outcomes. I explored self-production on days off from producing others, resulting in my first solo album, *Everything's a Love Letter* (2004/2022).

Figure 9.1 Music recording, Gerroa, NSW Australia.

I started learning Pro Tools when it was initially released, which allowed me to make rhythmic loops, arrange my performances, and layer beyond the eight tracks of an analogue tape machine. In this sunlight-filled environment next to the ocean, and with editing on my side to easily erase mistakes, I could experiment with learning other instruments, including piano, pump organ and clarinet. There was also a constant flow of inspiring people coming to play, and I was able to record a variety of instruments and observe, document and reflect on performance, technique, timbre and different songwriting and compositional styles. I also had the opportunity to work closely with music-makers and understand them personally and professionally. This, to me, is music production, and every person contributing is engaged in a multitude of ways. It is embodied, professional, community-making music practice that is focused and productive. Author Eva-Maria Houben, in *Musical Practice as a Form of Life,* asks, "When does a musical situation come to an end?" (2019, p. 10). It seems to me that when you are making a recording, it never really does.

Everything's a Love Letter as a listening experience takes me back to a time and place more than any visual representation could ever do. The microphone, as an open-eared listener, captures this engagement between the emotional and musical complexities of the artist with the shape, contents and atmosphere of the room. As a self-producer and within that process of production, I heard my album exhaustively in its evolution and in great detail. Working in that space, I heard every take, every mistake, every workaround, every invention, and I heard them more times than anyone ever will. The recordings imprinted on my mind as I looked out my window to a seven-mile beach. Listening back now, I can hear the rooms (and beyond), the people, the hurdles and, perhaps most importantly, I sense myself and others in that place and at that time. Photos such as Figure 9.2 represent an external perspective of myself at that time and place, whereas the recordings connect more directly and clearly with my internal understanding of that world.

From the music artist's perspective, a recorded work can be considered an autoethnographic document and a sensory love letter to oneself, a sound postcard from a time past. This perspective on recording and production attends to the artist's relationship to their work and recognises how a creative life is actually a lived experience involving a place, a cast of characters and prevailing matters of the heart and head. *The Sound of a Room, Memory and the Auditory Presence of Place* (Street 2020) is a personal, poetic, and philosophical account of the relationship between sound and place through recording, listening back and reflection.

If we whisper, or sing or shout, however, the room responds and offers us information about its size, shape and even contents. This sense of relationship between us and where we are at any given moment is both extremely moving and at the heart of this study (p. 13).

Figure 9.2 Author, Gerroa NSW Australia.

Street's tone and language is an example of what I consider a creative and artistically appealing perspective on the experience of sound. It inspires me to make sound, record and listen back, which is the endgame for developing a self-production practice. This embrace of the potential and life within place and space contrasts with the general discussion within music production discourse around workspaces that are typically seen as a problem to overcome. In this comparison, we see the language shift from the positive in Street's work to the negative, where typically, we are encouraged to address sound in a room by absorption, isolation, seeking to minimise and eradicate this invisible artefact. Yet in practice, as suggested by Minchella's research, "there is a unique impact on sound and the creative process in every space" (2018, p. 56), and the relationship that the participants have with that space is an important characteristic of the process and outcome. The perspective of a self-produced work as a creative container of a lived world opens the door to new ways of considering music production as an art-making practice open to domestic, creative and experimental approaches.

LISTENING AS A COMPLEX, CULTURAL AND EMBODIED ACTIVITY

Central to my proposal is the opportunity for a more diverse conversation and participation in music production if we set aside the technical focus and instead examine the human, artistic, experiential, embodied, located and musical. I believe this conversation will allow non-technical identifying music makers to explore and expand their relevant existing skills, such as understanding modes of listening and musicality. As music makers and consumers, we are deeply invested in both. Whilst writing this, I can tune in to the soundscape around me and identify its elements in musical or compositional terms. I can hear the durational conversation between the low register drone of the passing plane up against the ticking clock, a neighbour's dog, the space around me and the swirl of subtle abstracted tones in my mild tinnitus. I can identify timbre, feel, metaphor and much more that connect to composition and intersect with the lived experience. Pauline Oliveros explored the practice of *Deep Listening* (2005) as connected to mindfulness and composition, but there is a synchronicity with the self-producer as they connect and disconnect the interior and the exterior in the processes of listening while performing, recording and mixing in lived environments.

Listening to the interconnectedness (or musicality) of sound clearly extends to the cultural dimension and can be experienced in any environment. For example, when I voted in my country's general election at my child's primary school this year, there was dub music loudly permeating the scene of food and voting queues and children playing. There is, of course, a whole cultural and political dimension to this music, which registers and floats somewhere in my brain together with the physical weight of its low-end ebb. I process the experience through these critical and embodied perspectives and witness how the music creates energy and positivity. At one moment, I changed my listening mode and traced the bassline, considering how it fell against the pulse. This shift is a natural consequence of being musically curious and demonstrates an instinctive toggling of listening modes that music artists can easily identify or adopt as part of a self-production methodology. Clearly, recognising and choosing listening modes and identifying relationships is particularly helpful in a music production skillset. Understanding how the final work will be heard is also an important part of a producer's role; this is typically well-understood by songwriters, composers and musicians. Those who work with lyrics understand the interconnected and interpersonal relationship through the words and musical accompaniment in the writing. In general, they have a historied music listening practice where they connect to their favourite records through a range of abstract, emotional, situational and personal forms of understanding. On paper, it's complex, but to the person, it is intuitive and deeply managed. The ability to zoom in and out of elements and perspectives is an important skill in music production, as is understanding the interconnectedness of the elements and how they might shift the amorphous and personal experience of music. The capacity to switch modes of listening also allows subjectivity and freshness, which facilitates the necessary ability to listen repeatedly and differently to the work being made.

My point here is that music artists understand so much through their complex and intimate relationship with the experience of music and listening. If we can recognise and explore these elements within music production, then the field shifts to an achievable and appealing place for self-producers. Alternatively, if music production is cast centrally as an operation of technical equipment and sonic processing, there is so much left aside.

PERFORMANCE AWAY FROM IMMEDIATE APPRAISAL

One of the potential freedoms of self-production is that there is nobody listening when you are performing. One day, I had the good fortune to record US artist Cat Power in a series of straight-to-analog 2 track recordings for touring artists. It was a smallish room that we were in together, and I sensed her need for privacy, so I enquired if it would be better if I left her alone in the recording stage. She agreed, and I pressed record on a tape spool and left the room. When I listened back later to the recording, I felt a sense of a person playing mostly to herself in a room (as is natural for most songwriters). I also sensed her inclining her song slightly to a formless listener, an understanding ear in the open microphone rather than someone like myself whose presence is immediate, unfamiliar and necessarily critical.

For me, as an improvising musician in the digital realm with the capacity to edit and compile takes, I have the freedom to make mistakes and experiment widely in private. I can stay in artist and performance mode and review later. Personally, I enjoy the freedom of playing without anyone present. I know I play better when no one is watching or listening, and in this way, self-production is central to my practice. Of course, I also know artists who delight in having a producer for the external perspective so they can focus on the artistic and not have to consider the technical. However, I believe it is possible to manage some of these often distinct roles and perspectives by narrowing the parameters of the technical knowledge required and clearly delineating the roles or modes.

LIMITATIONS AND ROLE SWITCHING

In self-production, we become experts on our set of conditions. When working within the same software program in a narrow capacity with the same hardware equipment, instruments, spaces and style of music, we have the perfect opportunity to learn by repetition of elements. In this mode, we can more comfortably switch between operational and creative mindsets. As described earlier, we already switch between listening modes in everyday life, as music listeners and as musicians, and therefore, it is easily understood that the artist and producer roles could also be toggled when that is helpful.

When working in home or project studio environments, the hurdles we have are usually known; we can adapt and solve them and hopefully move through a project with a focus on the music. Self-production in this mode can be somewhat on your own terms, but I also believe the opportunity to record in new environments can be managed by embodying distinct roles in the process.

A few years ago, I made a recording in an isolated church in the Australian desert using about a dozen microphones, including outside in the open air, stereo pairs in the room, inside the pipe organ cabinet and on the church walls. The outside microphones were then transmitted into the inside of the church and played out through transducers on the internal structure of the church (*Assembly* 2017).

It was a large technical undertaking, and because of the location's remoteness and conditions, it required a lot of planning. I spent the first day setting it up, testing signal flow, solving problems and making improvements where I could. I was a producer and project manager leading up to and during the first day of the experience. I listened at night to my test recordings to make sure they were technically acceptable. On the second day, I awoke in the disused vicarage adjacent to the church, switched on the recording setup, made some tea and walked into the church as an artist. Once in this mode, I only needed to press record and move to the instrument to start playing. Figure 9.3 shows the movement from recording engineer to recording artist as a relocation and a shift of focus.

I was blind to the recording process but attuned to the reverberant birdsong inside the church, the organ under my fingers and in the space and the strangeness of this European cultural monolith in the Australian desert. I am invested in the responsive nature of composition and songwriting; therefore, to be immersed in a different environment when creating is to connect with culture, history, narratives and sonic and spatial complexity.

Figure 9.3 Author, Pella Church, Victoria, Australia.

As a music artist, I want production to give me more possibilities to make music and to be creative. I don't want it to diminish performance or the overall experience as a result of the necessary pragmatism, and sometimes frustration, of the technical in the process. These ideas recognise the value of a separate recording person whilst suggesting how the issues might be mitigated in self-production to enable the freedom of performance. The ability to clearly switch roles of artist and recorder is key to being able to perform both to a high level. This is easier performed in a permanently installed studio such as a home or a project studio but is achievable in a mobile studio to enable an interaction with new acoustic and cultural locations.

CONCLUSION

Music production is increasingly in the hands of the music-makers, and the implications and opportunities of this should be reflected in music education, scholarship and a definition of musical practice. In the shift from recording studios to domestic and community spaces, there is an intersection with the lived experience. With the flourishing scholarship and perspectives in embodiment and sound studies together with a more creative pedagogy, there is the possibility of a divergence in music production language, tone and focus.

From the point of view of the music artist, there is a sea of embodied experience, reflection and exploration in the process and outcomes of self-production. They possess many important skills, which are just not highlighted as music production skills because of the prevailing dominant perspectives of technology. If we value identity, environment, performance, artistry and the complexity of listening, working in an ongoing dialogue with the musical material, then there is much to discuss where ideas and opinions would come from a range of voices. These discussions will facilitate a more diverse engagement with production that will enrich the experience and outcomes for songwriters and composers.

REFERENCES

Bartleet, B.-L. and Ellis, C. (2010). *Music Autoethnographies Making Autoethnography Sing: Making Music Personal*. Bowen Hills, Qld: Australian Academic Press.

Chanan, M. (1995). *Repeated Takes: A Short History of Recording and its Effects on Music*. London: Verso.

Coessens, K. (2021). *Sensorial Aesthetics in Music Practice*, 133–150. Leuven: Leuven University Press.

Cole, S. (2011). The Prosumer and the Project Studio: The Battle for Distinction in the Field of Music Recording. *Sociology*, 45(3), 447–463.

Greene, M. (2000). *Releasing the Imagination: Essays on Education, the Arts, and Social Change*. San Francisco: Jossey-Bass.

Grimshaw-Aagaard, M. (2019). What is Sound Studies? In: M. Bull ed., *The Routledge Guide to Sound Studies*. London: Routledge.

Houben, E.-M. (2019). *Musical Practice as a Form of Life*. Bielefeld: Transcript Verlag.

Leyshon, A. (2009). The Software Slump? Digital Music, the Democratization of Technology and the Decline of the Recording Studio Sector within the Musical Economy. *Environment and Planning*, 41(6), 1209–1331.

Massey, H. (2000). *Behind the Glass: Top Record Producers Tell How They Craft the Hits*. San Francisco: Miller Freeman Books.

Minchella, D. (2018). The Poetics of Space: The Role and Co-Performance of the Spatial Environment in Popular Music Production. In: E. Bates and S. Bennett eds., *Critical Approaches to the Production of Music and Sound*. New York: Bloomsbury.

Moorefield, V. (2005). *The Producer as Composer: Shaping the Sounds of Popular Music*. London: MIT Press.

O'Grady, P. (2020). Sound City and Music from the Outskirts: The De-Democratisation of Pop Music Production. *Creative Industries Journal*, 14(3), 211–225.

Oliveros, P. (2005). *Deep Listening: A Composer's Sound Practice*. New York: Universe.

Small, C. (1998). *Musicking: The Meanings of Performing and Listening*. Hanover: University Press of New England.

Sterne, J. (2012). Sonic Imaginations. In: J Sterne ed., *The Sound Studies Reader*. London: Routledge.

Street, S. (2020). *The Sound of a Room: Memory and the Auditory Presence of Place*. London: Routledge.

Théberge, P. (2012). It's the End of The World as We Know It: The Changing Role of Studio in Age of the Internet. In: S. Firth and S. Zagorski-Thomas eds.,

The Art of Record Production: An Introductory Reader for a New Academic Field. Surrey: Ashgate.

Williams, A. (2007). Divide and Conquer: Power, Role Formation, and Conflict in Recording Studio Architecture. *Journal on the Art of Record Production*, 1.

Williams, A. (2010). Pay Some Attention to the Man Behind the Curtain-Unsung Heroes and the Canonization of Process in the Classic Albums Documentary Series. *Journal of Popular Music Studies*, 22(2), 166–179.

Williams, A. (2018). Weapons of Mass Deception: The Invention and Reinvention of Recording Studio Mythology. In: E. Bates and S. Bennett eds., *Critical Approaches to the Production of Music and Sound*. New York: Bloomsbury.

Wolfe, P. (2020). *Women in the Studio: Creativity, Control and Gender in Popular Music Sound Production*. London: Routledge.

DISCOGRAPHY

Cat Power (2001). "To be a Good Woman" and "Troubled Waters" on *Live & Direct* Spunk Records.

Saddleback (2004/2022). [CD/Vinyl] *Everything's a Love Letter*, Preservation/ Oscarson.

Dupé, T. (2018). *Assembly: Organ and Birds at Pella Desert Church*. https://tony-dupe.bandcamp.com/

10

Two production strategies for music synchronisation

As speculative entrepreneurship

Hussein Boon

1 INTRODUCTION

The focus of this chapter is Music Synchronization (hereafter referred to as music sync or sync), documenting two approaches that can be adopted by music production creatives. For this discussion, I define a music production creative as any one of the forms of music producer, including those who are self-producing artists (see Burgess, 2013, pp. 9–19 for a discussion of six functional typologies). This chapter locates these activities under the general theme of speculative entrepreneurship. This umbrella term addresses both the volatility of a highly competitive marketplace coupled with the creation of a 'sound object' (as defined in the following section) capable of meeting an unspecified future audio-visual use. For individual creators, this speculative activity is amplified due to its being a self-initiated activity, with potentially limited access to insider knowledge, and therefore falls into creative cultural work which Hesmondhalgh (2018, p. 31) describes as "risky business" with no guarantees that their work will be successful. The risk of conducting creative work within these competitive marketplaces, especially those of hyper-competition and "survival-of-the-fittest situation" (Canham, 2021, p. 6), places creatives in conditions of job precarity and/or lack of security as an ongoing condition, especially post-COVID-19.

This chapter positions music-sync activities as not just an area of practice but also as meeting the essential needs and requirements of music supervisors who act as 'gatekeepers' with whom music-production creatives will deal when creating and submitting work for consideration. A music supervisor's role is broadly defined as overseeing "all music related aspects of film, television, advertising, video games and any other existing or emerging visual-media platforms as required" (Guild of Music Supervisors, 2022).

The requirements of music supervisors may appear to be those that concern sound and/or song quality relating to "musical vision, tone and style that best suits the project" (Guild of Music Supervisors, 2022); also see Tangcay (2022) for other discussions. However, evidence also points to other crucial aspects that can affect decision-making, including obtaining

DOI: 10.4324/9781003462101-11

audio-sample clearance (see Blistein, 2023 for a discussion of De La Soul's long-standing issues in this area). This requires producers to exercise strict control of sample use, which includes samples sourced via subscription services such as Splice or libraries offered as royalty-free due to additional licensing or usage restrictions regarding broadcast rights. Sample use, and therefore (sample) clearance, can lead to quite perilous negotiation situations when clearing rights for film or TV use:

> None of us thought to think about the samples and the sample issue and, of course, as soon as it got into the, well, the guy, basically, who I sampled . . . They said he's basically calling up Warner Brothers in America and saying he's going to sue them for millions of dollars.
>
> (Behr et al., 2017, p. 235)

In this example, the song had already been released but had not sold enough to attract the copyright holder's attention. This is a quite frequent situation with underground music styles, especially those with limited white-label releases. However, the song was later identified as suitable for use in a movie, bringing it to the attention of the original writer of the sampled recording.

Equally important are those tracks or styles that rely upon incorporating drum breaks, such as the ubiquitous *Amen Break* used in Drum and Bass (aka Drum'n'Bass, DnB, and D&B), or even those styles of music that sample audio from films as part of their aesthetic. Styles emanating from mashup cultures, even if some consider these as having an "ambiguous legal status" (Brøvig-Hanssen and Jones, 2021, p. 2), will also find that this status ambiguity evaporates when music is under consideration for visual-media use. All of these will create licensing issues, for which producers will need to consider workarounds when confronted with these sorts of situations. Identifying these issues early in the production process and resolving them makes the music supervisor's task more straightforward.

This area is important to music creators as music sync offers "exposure to new audiences" (Klein et al., 2017, p. 225) as "the last unimpeded pathway to our ears" (Klein et al., 2017, p. 224). This also includes the positioning of catalog works in series such as *Stranger Things* ('Dear Billy', 2022), which fuels renewed interest in the music and artist for a newer generation of music listeners (Savage, 2022). The use of popular music songs in TV can be traced to what Thompson (1996) refers to as Television's Second Golden Age and has its inception with *Miami Vice* ('Brother's Keeper', 1984). The series was created "when an NBC executive sent executive producer Anthony Yerkovich a memo that read simply 'MTV cops'" (Bignell, 2007, p. 167). Since the success of this show, the use of popular music songs to soundtrack emotional elements has been adopted by ever-increasing numbers of shows such as *Grey's Anatomy* ('Thunderstruck', 2022), using 2,034 songs over its currently 400 episodes. Kaye (2007, p. 223) highlights that the deliberate use of popular music songs is to arouse emotions. Whilst popular music songs can aid feeling within drama and dramatic scenes, Frith (2002, p. 282) also counters that pop song usage can also "make historically important or dramatically intense scenes mundane".

1.1 Two methods overview

There are a number of points to keep in mind with the production strategies outlined in this chapter. Firstly, this type of work can be conducted from any location in the world. Secondly, this work can also be conducted by practitioners with various levels of experience. Lastly, these methods are applicable to any style of music, which does not imply a strictly Western-only focus. In fact, applying these methods to atypical popular music may carry some novel production advantages.

The first production method is concerned with aspects of creative vision in what I term the re-cover, discussed in detail later in this chapter. The second method is a more familiar production approach similar to creating stems (see Bullen, 2022, for a number of standalone applications). This leads to the producer acting much like a music library and taking advantage of new revenue opportunities afforded not only by traditional libraries or production music houses but also those afforded by online production music services such as YouTube, TikTok Sound, and Epidemic Sound (see Ivors Academy, 2019, for campaigns against composer buyouts). The point to appreciate when considering either method is that music supervisors or agents for online production libraries "value distinctiveness and evocativeness . . . whether sparse or lush, authentic or synthetic" (Lambert, 2016, p. 211) and that the approaches outlined here aim to foreground this distinctiveness in production work. This is because music, especially in a crowded marketplace, may need to create a more distinctive separability from other similar types of music.

The idea of a sound or music object, as described for the purpose of this chapter, can be understood from a number of positions. Butler refers to "an object of belief" (1988, p. 520), which, within Butler's own theory of performativity, is established through a "stylized repetition of acts" (Butler, 1988, p. 520). Put simply, the association of certain styles of music with particular film genres (Dowling and Harwood, 1986, p. 204), such as police procedurals or spy movies, through this repetition establishes a type of musical style (sound object) deemed suitable for genre-based films. An analogue of this idea in popular music can be found where some songs or albums are described as being 'cinematic' in the manner in which they evoke qualities of a soundtrack in the listener's ear/mind. This type of occurrence both demonstrates how a soundtrack is understood and appreciated culturally and how a standalone sound object can be appreciated as work that possesses these qualities albeit in a decontextualized context, that is, without visual accompaniment where any 'visuals' are imagined by the listener, acting as a stimulus-response to the audio.

Creators must also consider their music as having a use-value, especially in visual settings, especially to communicate "a message-relevant executional cue" (MacInnis and Park, 1991, p. 162). In other words, the music serves some communication purpose built up over time through association, especially with certain film genres or deliberately designed to grab attention. A good example of this is Holst's *Mars, the Bringer of War* (Holst, 1916), and its ongoing cinematic association with ideas of conflict, particularly the interval sequences of root > 5th > ♭5th, or directly root > ♭5th. The former can be heard in the James Bond cue *007 Takes The Lektor* (Barry, 2020), and both interval sequences are a central underpinning for the Stargate television series SG-1 ('In the Line of Duty', 1998). Cook observes that composition work, especially one based on style or genre (arguably equally applicable when using descriptive labels such as tension music), reveals what they refer to as a postmodernist approach that displays a "discernible musical logic" (Cook, 1994, p. 35). This approach is one where work is informed by and conducted under conditions of constraint by the medium. These constraints can be time-based, where only a few seconds of music might be required to establish a link, or they can be audience-specific, where "One or two notes in a distinct musical style are sufficient to target a specific social and demographic group" (Cook, 1994, p. 35). This type of working process implies a deconstruction of musical elements to a set of features where these features have an associative corollary. This association may, especially when successful, become the accepted musical expressive accompaniment for visuals through repeated use, thus referring back to Butler's object of belief.

1.2 Speculative entrepreneurship

There are two ideas underpinning speculative entrepreneurship. The first is best summarized as creating works for a future, as yet, undefined audio/visual use, and the second is working in conditions of precarity. For the individual producer these activities also reveal the blurring of boundaries of "cultural production, the line between paid and unpaid work, between 'professionals' and 'amateurs'" (Hesmondhalgh and Baker, 2010, p. 13) where this division, especially unpaid work, can tend to be accepted by those starting out as an aspect of career progression. This unpaid work is also a feature of platforms (Brown and Quan-Haase, 2016, p. 447) that profit from creatives using these same platforms to promote their own work.

Most library music is created with a speculative use value in mind. To this end, the music must resemble an existing style or format (sound object) yet not be so specific as to restrict other potential applications. In terms of speculative working, creative labour, and marketplaces, individuals are not only competing with other creators and companies but also with the gradual emergence of AI either assisting or creating music for visual media use (Aiva, 2015; Wonder, 2021; Xhail, 2022). The competition of markets and, therefore, the risk in producing creative products becomes one that is layered and complex. Anecdotal advice provided by music supervisors for those starting out in sync work (defined in what follows) but do not yet have an established track record in this area is to cut their music to visuals rather than just submit audio. The argument here is that music supervisors tend to think more visually; therefore, a visual accompaniment may assist in demonstrating music suitability. Sources for visuals to cut music to have traditionally been unreleased student films as well as replacing existing scores of already released films or TV shows. Whilst the latter cause copyright issues, especially if used on a public platform to showcase work, the emergence of online platforms like The Cue Tube (2022) means that high-quality footage and resources are available to assist in developing skills in this area (see Rose, 2009, for more general information on cue spotting).

Finally, researching music supervisors by using resources such as IMDB and reviewing their areas of interest can be useful in refining whom to send work to. Interviews with music supervisors are also useful sources of information on individual supervisor's music style preferences, such as Patsavas's favouring of Indie (Leas, 2015), which could also be advantageous in directing music-sync production activities.

1.3 Music synchronization background

Music sync is "the ability to synchronize music in a timed relation to a visual component" (Gammons, 2011, p. 103) and covers a wide range of media applications of licensed music. This covers TV, Radio, Films, Adverts, and Games, as well as other more recent formats such as podcasts and influencer videos on platforms such as Instagram, TikTok, and YouTube. The global market is healthy, with TV and Radio (Figure 10.1) accounting for the largest publishing royalty "supplying 38.8% of total global publishing revenue, the equivalent of EUR 3.29 billion in 2018" (IMPF, 2020, p. 13).

There are four broad areas of sync to consider. The first is the use of songs, originals, or covers. In any piece of recorded music, there are two rights, "one for the use of the song and another for use of the master

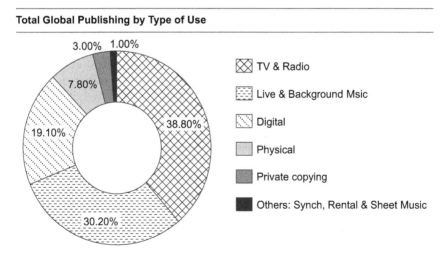

Figure 10.1 Total global publishing by type of use.

Source: IMPF (2020)

recording" (Anderson, 2013, p. 371). The publisher will deal with the song or composition right, with the master right "usually controlled by the record company" (Rose, 2009, p. 199). However, separate negotiations between co-licensors to clear all rights can present issues, especially when the various parties do not communicate with each other, with the master right as the main impediment in most negotiations. Kassabian (2001, pp. 2–3) refers to film scores that make extensive use of pre-recorded songs, either using original recordings or as covers, as "compiled scores" which rely upon establishing "*affiliating identifications*". This, in turn, relies upon an audience's familiarity with the song; this familiarity is acquired prior to and external to the film.

A second use is to obtain music from music libraries (sometimes referred to as production music), usually for smaller fees, with all rights secured as a combined license. Music libraries range from long-established labels in the UK, such as De Wolfe or KPM, to film-studio libraries, such as CBS and Universal. More recently, music libraries also take advantage of online distribution, and these include companies such as Audio Network and Epidemic Sound. Further to this, large platforms such as YouTube also offer library music for content creators who are subscribed to their service, as does TikTok, which struck a deal with Anthem Production Music and Entertainment and 5Alarm Music (TikTok, 2021). The advantage to users is that music sourced from these libraries is guaranteed to not be subject to takedowns or copyright strikes that can result in accounts being suspended and de-monetized.

Library music also operates as a non-exclusive right, meaning the music can be used by other media production companies. Therefore, the same music could be used many times for different types of production (Rose, 2009, p. 204). This highlights the challenge of using library music for any TV or film production, especially if there is a requirement to create a particular thematic universe. For example, the British police procedural TV show *The Sweeney* ('The Ringer', 1975), in addition to its bespoke theme tune, used over 350 pieces sourced from a variety of UK library music houses (Boon, 2022). Whilst library music can present something of an issue, it is also the case that securing a song from a record label for sync does not guarantee exclusivity either. Imogen Heap's *Hide and Seek* is a good example, having been synced on at least 15 TV shows (Leach, 2020), reinforcing its value to the visual medium (Lambert, 2016, p. 199).

The third form is for the production company to commission a soundtrack (see Kassabian, 2001, p. 2, for discussion on bespoke scores, which she refers to as "assimilating identifications"). In this instance, the production company should "specify all the rights the musicians are giving . . . in your letter of agreement" (Rose, 2009, p. 199). It is important to ensure that rights being granted to production companies only extend to the stated or particular use of the film or TV show. Doing this allows the composer additional exploitation opportunities "in another movie or game, as you wish" (Gammons, 2011, p. 110). The production company must not be provided with a blanket right that allows them to use the music or adapt it for future productions. This is an important point that should be considered in all music-sync situations.

The final broad use of music sync is one where a mechanical license can be obtained, allowing the company to record a cover version of the song. This can be quite a lucrative sector, with global mechanical license revenue accounting "for 16.5% of collections, equivalent to €1.4 billion" (IMPF, 2020). More recently, there has been a growing trend for songs to be re-orchestrated in film and TV series. Among these include the film *Rogue Agent* (2022), which features a music box interpretation of The Cure's *Friday I'm In Love* by composer Hannah Peel. This builds on her earlier music box covers EP called Rebox (Peel, 2010) and *Tainted Love* (McParland, 2011) used on *American Horror Story* ('Return to Murder House', 2018). TV shows such as *Bridgerton* also follow this developmental approach using Ariana Grande's *thank u, next* ('Diamond of the First Water', 2020), which is given a type of period authenticity performed by a string quartet. It is worth noting that this process not only creates new master (recording) rights for further exploitation – especially third-party commercial licensing – but also represents a means of realizing the latent potential in the use of pre-existing songs to develop the visual narrative, hence why a novel version of a pre-existing song, discussed later, has a utility beyond that of a cover version.

1.4 Method 1 – creative vision and re-cover approaches

This first method approach can be described as a combination of creative vision and the practice of the 're-cover'. In essence, this involves transcending the compositional framework (Brett, 2021, p. 119) to frame the song in an intriguing and novel fashion. A number of approaches can be identified as crucial to this approach, including:

- re-harmonization,
- re-interpretation,
- re-contextualization,
- re-arrangement
- re-orchestration.

An early example of re-interpretation is Vanilla Fudge's version of The Supremes' *You Keep Me Hanging On* (Vanilla Fudge, 2016). This is a good indicator of a dramatic re-interpretation, so much so that it could pass as an original. Examples of re-contextualization include Johnny Cash's series of *American Recordings*, where human frailties, vulnerabilities, and end-of-life circumstances reveal new meanings within the songs (Johnny Cash, 2002). Examples of re-arrangement/re-orchestration have already been mentioned for shows such as *Bridgerton*. Yet this activity can also be executed in a quite simplistic fashion, such as the player piano versions of Radiohead songs in the TV series *Westworld* ('Chestnut', 2016) and the aforementioned use of Hannah Peel's music box.

Ki:Theory's *Stand By Me* (Ki:Theory, 2014) demonstrates what can be described as a novel approach to Ben E. King's (1961) classic that combines all of the identified requirements for the re-cover. This version has been used in a number of settings, including *Fear the Walking Dead* ('Children of Wrath', 2017) and *The Following* ('Trust Me', 2014). There are some specific transformations applied to the arrangement and harmonic context that enable it to present as novel instance of the re-cover approach.

The first is the change of emphasis for the harmonic sequence from the major key to the minor, emphasizing vi, IV, and V (see Table 10.1). Avoiding the major I chord and the attendant dominant tonic cadence of King's original (bars 6–7) has the generally profound effect of re-siting the melody to the Aeolian mode (natural minor), resulting in the progression i, ♭VI, ♭VII (Biamonte, 2010, pp. 101–103).

Coupled with the harmonic shift from major to minor, the song also displays careful dynamics management from its opening use of muted guitar through to its fulsome conclusion as a means of driving the song forward. As part of its transformations, the song features three changes of vocal register for the melody, which can be simply categorized as low, mid, and high. The low version is achieved by pitch-shifting the recorded voice down an octave. This helps to give a more grainy and sinister character to the song, which suggests that the audio file has been transposed down an octave rather than using a pitch-shifting plugin. The mid can be thought of as the voice of the singer within their usual vocal register. The high version is performed in what can be referred to as the emphasis register, with a more prominent use of distortion and saturation. This register delivers on the intensity of the performance and remains at this level for the remainder of the song. The melody is also doubled at specific points by a pitch-shifted guitar to add additional texture.

The track also makes use of a number of instrument entry points, typically on the eighth bar of each section, which introduce dynamic changes in the song. This is an interesting approach and shifts attention away from the first bar of each verse as the locus of change. Therefore, change is signaled less by the lyrical content and more by these dynamic arrangement cues. Examples of these include the introduction of the bass at bar eight of the first verse and the 808 kick-drum entry at bar eight of the second verse. For the third verse, the voice shifts to the higher, shouty register is also where the drums are introduced.

Table 10.1 Comparing Harmonic Differences Between Two Versions of Stand By Me

Bar Number	1	2	3	4	5	6	7	8
Ben E. King	C (I)	C	Am (vi)	Am (vi)	F (IV)	G (V)	C (I)	C
Ki:Theory	Am (i)	Am	Am	Am	F(♭VI)	G(♭VII)	Am (i)	Am

Whilst the track generally follows Ben E. King's original arrangement, it also introduces a novel five-bar middle section to provide some additional variety and to build tension. This section introduces new accompaniment material that was not present in the original 1961 recording, mainly focused on a two-bar piano figure that outlines a 3:3:2 rhythm pattern. This piano figure utilizes a melodic sequence introduced in the fifth bar of the third verse played by the guitar, using notes a third apart.

Throughout the recording, it should be noted that many smaller sections that can be described as 'ear candy' are distributed around the stereo field. Some of these examples include the use of intermittent guitar parts with pitch-shifting effects similar to Digitech's Whammy Pedal in verse three, and the use of distorted vocal samples at the end of verse one that pan from right to left. All of the parts introduced in each verse are then brought together for the closing verse with an additional part, which is a sequence of stuttering guitar power chords. These types of adaptation, especially when using or repurposing internally generated material, are indicative of what can be described as content-based transformations (Ramirez and Reiss, 2017, p. 1).

Overall, Ki:Theory's recording is a good example of where the new recording changes the meaning of the song in such a way that it increases the number of potential visual applications. Therefore Ki:Theory's production exhibits qualities that ensure continued engagement with a classic song, whilst the recording and performance are also able to stand as creative work on their own merit.

1.5 Method 2 – a mechanical decomposition

The second method is essentially a decomposition of the two-track master or recording project into more discrete but musically meaningful elements capable of being used as an underscore, which has some similarities with remixing and preparing track stems for mixing and/or mastering. Whilst this can appear to break the unity of the recorded work, in visual-usage contexts, music has always been edited in such a way as to fit the scene.

Dodge (2020) outlines an approach to ensure that an audio track is treated in such a way as to allow its inclusion in a variety of formats suitable for synchronization opportunities. In addition to the track mix, a number of stems or parts are also extracted to form the library. Table 10.2 outlines Dodge's suggestions for a typical approach for a song-based production.

The instrumental groupings should be revised to take into account variations in production style. The number of track outputs can also increase depending upon the complexity of the recorded song and the number of available parts, but it should not be less than already outlined in Table 10.2. The aim here is that groups or collections of parts should work together coherently to tell something of a story and present as many distinctive motifs (Bang, 2020, p. 6) or combinations as possible. Producers can build upon these suggestions by also providing a variety of loop

Table 10.2 18-stem suggestions (Dodge, 2020)

3 min. 30 sec. Full Track With Vocals	3 min. 30 sec. Instrumental	30-seconds Full Track With Vocals	30-seconds Instrumental	60-seconds Full Track With Vocals	60-seconds Instrumental
Drums & Bass	Alt Mix	Guitar 1 Stem	Guitar 2 Stem	Vocal Stem	Background Vocal Stem
Bass Stem	1-minute Loop 1	30-second Loop 2	30-second Loop 3	5-second Sting 1	5-second Sting 2

lengths that work with the shorter video format utilized by platforms such as TikTok. Therefore, five-second stings can be augmented with loopable five-, 10- and 15-second versions of the track, with or without vocals. Dodge views this work as a necessary part of the overall recording and production process rather than an add-on procedure. Some composers utilizing this approach describe their work as "always looking for ways to stretch a song's income" (Dodge, 2020). Music producers undertaking this approach may also find that, over time, they have built a number of consistent library music examples that can be deployed quite quickly for demos and mockups (Burlingame, 2014).

This stem-based approach can also be applied to other library formats within the field of artificial intelligence (AI). Two AI production applications, Dynascore (Wonder, 2021) and Xhail (2022), utilize this approach. In essence, audio files are tagged for various parameters such as key, tempo, and emotion and added to a large library of audio files. Based on user input, the AI recombines these files into unique pieces to be incorporated into the visual or musical context. This procedure resembles the practice of combinatorics, which has been fashionable in music for several centuries (such as Mozart's Dice Game, for example; see Nolan, 2000, for a short but detailed history). Creators supplying audio files to Xhail are paid if their stem files are used. Dynascore offers an additional layer of control where the user can further shape the dynamics of the track by specifying where dynamic changes occur in sync with visuals. Xhail also has a number of safeguards in place against unwanted repetition stems that "are coded by the AI to ensure they will never meet again in the same configuration" (Clancy, 2021, p. 308). Individual stems have "a limited commercial life span" and are removed from the database (Clancy, 2021, p. 308). It is notable that this approach is very different from the more traditional library music house, where the same production or stock music track might be used many times over (Boon, 2022).

The argument against this stem-based approach is that it runs counter to the idea of the unified musical and artistic work. Yet, the music supervisor's biggest task might well be "'Finding a consistency and focus in the choice of pre-existing music'" (Lewandowski, 2010, p. 871) to which a set of audio files derived from the decomposed master will be consistent, due to being drawn from the same source, and therefore fulfilling some of these requirements. It then follows that the deconstruction of recorded parts into constituent elements or sonic groups *is* to offer as much flexibility as possible within the system of possible uses (Gammons, 2011, p. 104) whilst still allowing the music to sound complete. If every production were utilized to generate a number of useful artifacts, then what is being pitched is a collection rather than just a single song. In effect, a "'breakdown package that editors can tailor for visual, right down to the singular elements'" (Dodge, 2020). This is particularly important because editing might well be "performed by non-trained musicians (or even 'non-musicians')" (Donnelly, 2005, p. 128), which also includes user-generated content on social media and podcast producers. In this context, the music producer acts more like a library, considering how to maximize each track and part as fully as possible. Finally, the same collection can be pitched for lots of sync opportunities, thereby extending the utility of the recording beyond the song.

1.7 Conclusions

The work outlined in this chapter describes a creative working context that offers some freedom for the creative audio producer with a specific aim in mind. These methods also assist less experienced and younger producers to develop their craft within a reasonably stable, structured, and organized approach. Both methods facilitate a number of transferrable skills and knowledge building, including those of:

- combining creative ideas and contextual information;
- adapting well to different styles of music and production;
- operating a digital audio workstation and being location non-specific;
- bringing areas of future employability and servicing a market into closer relationship with the craft of making derived products from a singular work;
- developing areas of entrepreneurship, such as understanding the configuration of markets.

The methods also do not necessarily dictate that there is a particular type of composition, recording, or mix that can be considered as 'better' than another when evaluating the use of music to support a visual story-telling narrative. What they do offer music-production creatives are further opportunities to present their work in situations capable of generating income, thereby addressing entrepreneurship as much as the creative-making activities and building career identities (Bridgstock, 2013, p. 131).

The main concluding points are for these approaches to be encouraged as a means of developing not just technical and creative skills but also practitioner identities. In attempting to meet the demands of supervisors, producers need to consider creating quite radical revisions of the original source material. The five identified points of the re-cover can act as a starting point to develop these activities. Radical revisioning of well-known songs is an activity that could prove worthwhile to manage the idea of undertaking risky business. Whether producers elect to use either one or both methods, they must see the work they do as entrepreneurial, as solving a problem in the marketplace, and that this problem is the use of music to support a visual storytelling narrative.

REFERENCES

Aiva (2015). 'Created with AIVA', *YouTube* (website), available online from www.youtube.com/playlist?list=PLv7BOfa4CxsHAMHQj0ScPXSbgBlLglRPo [accessed January 2023].

Anderson, T. (2013). 'From Background Music to Above-the-Line Actor: The Rise of the Music Supervisor in Converging Televisual Environments', *Journal for Cultural Research*, Vol. 21, No. 3, pp. 223–240.

Bang, D. (2020). *Crime and Spy Jazz on Screen, 1950–1970: A History and Discography*, Jefferson, North Carolina, McFarland & Company.

Barry, J. (2020). '007 Takes the Lektor', *YouTube* (website), available online from https://youtu.be/nh899s-3whE [accessed January 2023].

Behr, A., Negus, K. and Street, J. (2017). 'The Sampling Continuum: Musical Aesthetics and Ethics in the Age of Digital Production', *Journal for Cultural Research*, Vol. 21, No. 3, pp. 223–240.

Ben E. King (1961). 'Stand By Me', *American Edition 66*. Available at: YouTube Music [accessed January 2023].

Biamonte, N. (2010). 'Triadic Modal and Pentatonic Patterns in Rock Music', *Music Theory Spectrum* (website), Vol. 32, No. 2, available online from www.jstor.org/stable/10.1525/mts.2010.32.2.95 [accessed January 2023].

Bignell, J. (2007). 'Seeing and Knowing: Reflexivity and Quality', in McCabe, J. and Akiss, K. (eds.) *Quality TV: Contemporary American Television and Beyond*, London, I.B. Tauris, pp. 158–170.

Blistein, J. (2023). 'De La Soul's Music Is Coming to Streaming Services – For Real This Time', *Rolling Stone* (website), available online from www.rollingstone.com/music/music-news/de-la-soul-music-streaming-services-1234655234/ [accessed January 2023].

Boon, H. (2022). 'Cyborg Composers: AI as Collaborative Assistant, as Creator and as Competitor', *Library Music in Audiovisual Media – RMA*. University of Leeds, 15–16 September 2022, available online from https://youtu.be/23D20mgotQ0 [accessed January 2023].

Brett, T. (2021). *The Creative Electronic Producer*, Abingdon, Oxon, Routledge.

Bridgstock, R. (2013). 'Not a Dirty Word: Arts Entrepreneurship and Higher Education', *Arts and Humanities in Higher Education*, Vol. 12, No. 2–3, pp. 122–137.

'Brother's Keeper' (1984). *Miami Vice*, Series 1, episode 1. NBC. 16 September, 22:00.

Brøvig-Hanssen., R. and Jones., E. (2021). 'Remix's Retreat? Content Moderation, Copyright Law and Mashup Music', *New Media & Society*, Vol. 21, No. 3, pp. 1–19.

Brown, B. A. and Quan-Haase, A. (2016). '"A Workers' Inquiry 2.0": An Ethnographic Method for the Study of Produsage in Social Media Contexts', in Fuchs, C. and Mosco, V. (eds.) *Marx in the Age of Digital Capitalism*, Leiden, Brill, pp. 447–481.

Bullen, T. (2022). 'Stems in Music Production – Everything You Need to Know', *Pro Tools Expert* (website), available online from www.pro-tools-expert.com/production-expert-1/2020/7/6/stems-in-music-production [accessed January 2023].

Burgess, R. J. (2013). *The Art of Music Production: The Theory and Practice*, 4th edition, New York, Oxford University Press.

Burlingame, J. (2014). 'Remote Control Prods: Hans Zimmer's Music Factory as a Breeding Ground', *Variety* (website), available online from https://variety.com/2014/music/news/remote-control-prods-music-factory-as-breeding-ground-1201173763/ [accessed January 2023].

Butler, J. (1988). 'Performative Acts and Gender Constitution: An Essay in Phenomenology and Feminist Theory', *Theatre Journal*, Vol. 40, No. 4, pp. 519–531, The Johns Hopkins University Press. https://doi.org/10.2307/3207893 [accessed January 2023].

Canham, N. (2021). *Preparing Musicians for Precarious Work*, Abingdon, Oxon, Routledge.

'Chestnut' (2016). *Westworld*, season 1, episode 4. HBO Entertainment. Available at: HBO [accessed January 2023].

'Children of Wrath' (2017). *Fear the Walking Dead*, season 3, episode 8. Valhalla Entertainment. Available at: Amazon Prime Video [accessed January 2023].

Clancy, M. (2021). 'Reflections on the Financial and Ethical Implications of Music Generated by Artificial Intelligence', *PhD thesis*. Trinity College Dublin, available online from http://www.tara.tcd.ie/handle/2262/94880 [accessed January 2023].

Cook, N. (1994). 'Music and Meaning in the Commercials', *Popular Music*, Vol. 13, No.1, pp. 27–40.

The Cue Tube (2022). 'The Cue Tube Where Music Meets Film', *The Cue Tube* (website), available online from https://thecuetube.com/ [accessed January 2023].

'Dear Billy' (2022). *Stranger Things*, season 4, episode 4. 21 Laps Entertainment. Available at: Netflix [accessed January 2023].

'Diamond of the First Water' (2020). *Bridgerton*, season 1, episode 1. Shondaland. Available at: Netflix [accessed January 2023].

Dodge, C. (2020). 'How to Make the Most Money from a Song: Split It into 20 Pieces', *Rolling Stone* (website), available online from www.rollingstone.com/pro/features/artists-money-split-music-revenue-streams-1086415/ [accessed January 2023].

Donnelly, K. J. (2005). 'Music on Television 1: Music for Television Drama', in *The Spectre of Sound: Music in Film and Television*, London, BFI Publishing, pp. 110–133.

Dowling, W. H. and Harwood, D. L. (1986). *Music Cognition*, New York, Academic Press.

Frith, S. (2002). 'Look! Hear! The Uneasy Relationship of Music and Television', *Popular Music*, Vol. 21, No. 3, pp. 277–290.

Gammons, H. (2011). *The Art of Music Publishing: An Entrepreneurial Guide to Publishing and Copyright for the Music, Film, and Media Industries*, Abingdon, Oxon, Focal Press.

Guild of Music Supervisors (2022). 'What Is a Music Supervisor', *Guild of Music Supervisors* (website), available online from www.guildofmusicsupervisors.com/what-is-a-music-supervisor [accessed January 2023].

Hesmondhalgh, D. (2018). *The Cultural Industries*, 4th edition, Los Angeles, SAGE Publications.

Hesmondhalgh, D. and Baker, S. (2010). *Creative Labour: Media Work in Three Cultural Industries*, Abingdon, Oxon, Routledge.

Holst, G. (1916). *The Planets*. [Orchestral suite]. London, Curwen.

IMPF (2020). *Independent Music Publishing Global Market View 2020*, IMPF, available online from www.impforum.org/wp-content/uploads/2020/10/Global-Market-View-2020-Independent-Music-Publishing.pdf [accessed January 2023].

'In the Line of Duty' (1998). *Stargate SG-1*, Series 2, episode 2. Showtime. 3 July.

Ivors Academy (2019). 'The Ivors Academy Calls for Solidarity against Buyouts', *Ivors Academy* (website), available online from https://ivorsacademy.com/news/the-ivors-academy-calls-for-solidarity-against-buyouts/ [accessed January 2023].

Johnny Cash (2002). 'Hurt', *American IV: The Man Comes Around*. Available at: YouTube Music [Accessed 6 January 2023].

Kassabian, A. (2001). *Hearing Music*, Abingdon, Oxon, Routledge.

Kaye, P. (2007). 'Writing Music for Quality TV an Interview with W.G. "Snuffy" Walden', in McCabe, J. and Akiss, K. (eds.) *Quality TV: Contemporary American Television and Beyond*, London, I.B. Tauris, pp. 221–227.

Ki:Theory (2014). 'Ki:Theory – Stand By Me ("Fear The Walking Dead" Soundtrack S03E08) – Official Video', *YouTube* (website), available online from https://youtu.be/rS5Eb2q27OU [accessed January 2023].

Klein, B., Meier, L M. and Powers, D. (2017). 'Selling Out: Musicians, Autonomy, and Compromise in the Digital Age', *Popular Music and Society*, Vol. 40, No. 2, pp. 222–238.

Lambert, S. (2016). 'Music Synchronisation and Non-Music Brand Relationships', in Rutter, P. (ed.) *The Music Industry Handbook*, Abingdon, Oxon, Routledge, pp. 198–214.

Leach, S. (2020). 'Imogen Heap's "Hide and Seek" Is Still the Go-To Song for Teen Dramas, 15 Years Later', *Bustle* (website), available online from www.bustle.com/p/imogen-heaps-hide-seek-is-still-the-go-to-song-for-teen-dramas-15-years-later-22915684 [accessed January 2023].

Leas, R. (2015). 'IQ & A: TV & Film Music Supervisor Alex Patsavas on Soundtracking the O. C., Mad Men, the Twilight Series, the Astronaut Wives Club, and More', *Stereogum* (website), available online from www.stereogum.com/1808743/qa-tv-film-music-supervisor-alex-patsavas-on-soundtracking-the-o-c-mad-men-the-twilight-series-the-astronaut-wives-club-and-more/interviews/ [accessed January 2023].

Lewandowski, N. (2010). 'Understanding Creative Roles in Entertainment: The Music Supervisor as Case Study', *Continuum: Journal of Media & Cultural Studies*, Vol. 24, No. 6, pp. 865–875.

MacInnis, D. J. and Park, C. W. (1991). 'The Differential Role of Characteristics of Music on High- and Low-Involvement Consumers Processing of Ads.', *Journal of Consumer Research*, Vol. 18, No.2, pp. 161–173.

McParland, P. (2011). 'Hannah Peel – Tainted Love', *YouTube* (website), available online from https://youtu.be/hEAwOgsCVZk [accessed July 2022].

Nolan, C. (2000). 'On Musical Space and Combinatorics: Historical and Conceptual Perspectives in Music Theory', *Bridges: Mathematical Connections in Art, Music, and Science – Bridges Conference*, pp. 201–208, available online from http://archive.bridgesmathart.org/2000/bridges2000-201.html [accessed January 2023].

Peel, H. (2010). 'Rebox', *Bandcamp* (website), available online from https://hannahpeelmusic.bandcamp.com/album/rebox [accessed January 2023].

Ramirez, M. A. M. and Reiss, J. D. (2017). 'Stem Audio Mixing as a Content-Based Transformation of Audio Features', *2017 IEEE 19th International Workshop on Multimedia Signal Processing (MMSP)*, pp. 1–6, doi: 10.1109/MMSP.2017.8122275 [accessed January 2023].

'Return to Murder House' (2018). *American Horror Story*, Series 8, episode 4. FX. 17 October.

'The Ringer' (1975). *The Sweeney*, Series 1, episode 1. ITV. 2 January, 21:00.

Rogue Agent (2022) *Rabbit Track Pictures*. Available at: Netflix [accessed January 2023].

Rose, J. (2009). *Audio Postproduction for Film and Video*, Burlington, MA, Elsevier/Focal Press.

Savage, M. (2022). 'Kate Bush Is Number One, Thanks to Stranger Things', *BBC* (website), available online from www.bbc.co.uk/news/entertainment-arts-61843442 [accessed July 2022].

Tangcay, J. (2022). 'How "Stranger Things" Landed Metallica's "Master of Puppets" for Epic Finale (EXCLUSIVE)", *Variety* (website), available online from https://variety.com/2022/artisans/news/stranger-things-metallica-master-of-puppets-1235307853/ [accessed January 2023].

'Thunderstruck' (2022). *Grey's Anatomy*, season 19, episode 6. Shondaland. Available at: Disney+ [accessed January 2023].

Thompson, R. J. (1996). 'Television's Second Golden Age: The Quality Shows', *Television Quarterly*, Vol. 28, No. 3, pp. 75–81.

TikTok (2021). 'Explore Royalty-Free Music in Our New Audio Library', *TikTok* (website), available online from www.tiktok.com/business/en-GB/blog/audio-library-royalty-free-music [accessed January 2023].

'Trust Me' (2014). *The Following*, season 2, episode 3. Outerbanks Entertainment. Available at: Amazon Prime Video [accessed January 2023].

Vanilla Fudge (2016). 'You Keep Me Hangin On', *The Complete Atco Singles*. Available at: YouTube Music [accessed January 2023].

Wonder (2021). '1,000 Dynamic Compositions; Infinite Unique Soundtracks!',
    Medium (website), available online from https://news.wonder.inc/1-000-dy-
    namic-compositions-infinite-unique-soundtracks-1bb10b2a56fe   [accessed
    January 2023].
Xhail (2022). 'About Us', *Xhail* (website), available online from https://xhail.
    com/about/ [accessed January 2023].

Part two

National and international perspectives

11

Mobile classical music – recording, innovation, networks and mediatization

Three Swedish case studies from the 1940s to 2021

Toivo Burlin

1 INTRODUCTION

Mobile recordings of "classical" music have been produced under various conditions using acoustic and electric, analog and digital equipment alike. Indeed, mobile recordings of all music, not just classical, and the changing methods for producing them are as old as recording technology and practice itself. The American-born brothers Fred and Will Gaisberg pioneered the commercial mobile recording of music from 1898 onwards. In the years around the turn of the twentieth century, they spread the technology and the prototype for commercially recorded music first in Europe, then the rest of the world. They recorded Enrico Caruso in 1902, but they also made recordings of very local music cultures globally (Tschmuck, 2012, p. 25; Roy & Rodríguez, 2022). The mobile recording expeditions undertaken by the record industry in the early twentieth century were responsible for creating the first music recordings in many countries (Roy & Rodríguez, 2022). Later, radio stations developed a practice of recording in mobile studio buses, which could be equipped in various ways. The expeditions – for example, in Sweden – recorded local folk music from the 1940s onwards (Ramsten, 1992). In the 1970s, influential rock bands used mobile equipment to produce LPs. The mobile-produced recordings were made in many disparate locations – very different from the definitive location of the fixed music studio, and thus challenging the practice that emerged in such locations.

Both mobile and stationary studios have received a logical technological continuation in recent decades in the form of the network studio in the 1990s and, more recently, the Digital Audio Workstation (Théberge, 2004, 2012). In the twenty-first century, increased Internet capacity has led to the continued development of methods to share files and even play together in real-time over large distances – even more so with the outbreak of the Covid-19 global pandemic in 2020, music creators were forced to refine their methods to play and record together remotely.

DOI: 10.4324/9781003462101-13

In this study, this author investigates and compares *mobile recording and production practices in networks as a key to innovation in classical music production and mediatization of the recordings*. I will examine three case studies of the mobile recording of "classical music" – interpreting classical in its broadest sense – ranging from tape recordings for 78 rpm discs in the 1940s and 1950s (Discofil) to reel-to-reel tape recordings for LP production in the 1970s (BIS Records) to co-produced compositions and recordings in digital networks in 2020–2021 (Antennae Media). Further, I consider the cases in the specific historical and geographic context of Sweden as a relevant area for studying music production in the Western industrial world. It is therefore asked: How has innovation in recording and production occurred, and in what forms has it appeared? How are the mobile recordings primarily situated, in a "place" – as a specified church or concert hall – or a "non-place", as a kind of network-distance-co-production? How are the recordings mediatized – and how is the music shaped in that process?

1.1 "Going mobile": background and related work

This study draws on and is influenced by academic research into the music industry in a variety of areas, especially the fields of music and innovation, mobile music production and classical music record production.

"Innovation" is the first crucial field of inquiry. What does innovation mean in relation to "invention"? The close connection between invention, innovation and creativity has been thoroughly discussed and contextualized by, for example, Peter Tschmuck in his broad study on creativity and innovation in the music industry (Tschmuck, 2012). In his study, Tschmuck makes some essential points about how innovation and invention differ and what this means in a music industry context. In short, Tschmuck's conclusion, which is closely connected to views advanced by Schumpeter (1934, 2021) and Brooks (1982), is that compared to invention, innovation is a more complex process. It involves putting an invention on the market; it requires entrepreneurs to shape a product or service so that it can be sold. Without such a process, the invention will not be of relevance as an innovation. Innovations, however, can be of different kinds. Tschmuck argues, developing the earlier ideas of Schumpeter and Brooks, that there are three principal types of innovation: technological, social and aesthetic innovations (Tschmuck, 2012, p. 197).

Mobile music production and mobile recordings of classical music have been investigated from various perspectives, both historically, ethnographically and in the context of different countries, including New Zealand, the Netherlands and Spain, and industries (Thomas, 2002; Van de Staey, 2013; Thulin, 2017; Gopinath & Stanyek, 2014; Dromey & Haferkorn, 2018). Studies have even covered the mobile aspects of early phonography on a global level, from South America to Russia, China and Australia, and Norway (Roy & Rodríguez, 2022; Bårdsen, 2019). In much recent research, however, "mobility", when linked to music recording or listening, seems to be primarily associated with digital technology and media, more so than analogue technology or recording buses. In this article, I work with "mobility" as a broader phenomenon, ranging from driving the recording bus to recording local orchestras to connecting instrumentalists in studios or via computers through a network. The latter has been discussed from various perspectives by Paul Théberge, and I draw on his work here (Théberge, 2004, 2012). In particular, I want to mention Théberge's theory of the evolution of the studio from a concrete "place", a specific room for recording with a particular sound, to a "non-place", a standardization of the studio as a global environment, which is reinforced with digital technology, where the digital "space" is completely detached from the real place and the Internet has made it possible for this non-place to be everywhere, anywhere, anytime (Théberge, 2004). "Networks" means both social and technological connections – from small social communities to broadcasting, musical distribution and social media networks (Tschmuck, 2012).

In some previous work, this author has touched on two of the three cases discussed in what follows, although not from an innovation perspective. The study – on classical music production in Sweden (Burlin, 2008a) – was both an overview and a detailed investigation of the changing conditions for the production of classical music phonograms during a period spanning from the early electrical recordings to the breakthrough for digital recording, the first CDs released by BIS in 1983. Among other record companies, it presented Swedish Society Discofil (SSD), pioneers of state-of-the-art classical music production in the 1950s and 1960s. Much of the early history of SSD, however, when they were producing lacquer discs and small editions of 78 rpm records in their mobile recording studio, was left out. It will be presented here in more detail. I interviewed Mark Blomberg (b. 1929), who was the music engineer at SSD in the 1950s, and BIS founder Robert von Bahr (b. 1943), both of whom in that way have contributed to this article.

My third case is much more recent, "Lars Bröndum and Antennae Media." It comes from 2020–2021 and is about music composition and the production of classical or art music in the twenty-first century, where the processes of combining notated scores, improvisation, aleatorics, computerization and advanced production – all in computer networks – worked together in an innovative direction. For the sake of transparency, I should say that this author was peripherally involved in the project as a musician on a few tracks. However, the project is solely the composer and producer Lars Bröndum's, and this author's position as a relative outsider has given the opportunity for some distance and, hopefully, objectivity. Like SSD in the 1950s and BIS in the 1970s, Bröndum's label Antennae Media is a one-person company, but in contrast to them, Antennae Media is the primary distributor of Bröndum's own music. Bröndum has offered information and invaluable perspectives, but the analysis here is this author's own.

To summarize: In this article, I will present and develop some perspectives on innovation and mobility in classical music production. I will compare three historical cases to show the changing ways that innovation in the technological and compositional domains has affected classical music recording over the last 80 years.

2 CASE STUDIES

2.1 Discofil in the 1940s and 1950s: from swedish proto hi-fi to international hi-fi record production

The first case study is of the Swedish record label Recorda/Discofil and its recording tours in the early 1950s. The company was founded in 1945 by Hans Peter Kempe (1920–1994), a young musician, poet, musicologist and recording enthusiast and a member of the wealthy Kempe family, owners of the Swedish forestry company Mo & Domsjö, the largest of its kind in Europe for a period. Hans Peter Kempe grew up in a cultured, well-educated environment. His father's family was a mining family from Ångermanland and Stockholm and owned the Mo & Domsjö pulp factories. Through his mother, he was connected to the Hammarbergs, a Gothenburg merchant family. He thus came from a wealthy background and had considerable financial, social and cultural capital. A knowledge of music as well as a large network of contacts became important personal resources. Of his upbringing, Kempe himself said:

> I grew up in a really upper middle class family with all the traditions that class had at the time, and it was especially evident at the big weekends and in connection with the special etiquette that you had to have, both in your clothing and your way of speaking and way of behaving, that's what I grew up with.
>
> (Nävermyr, 1993; Burlin, 2008a, p. 300)

Kempe's childhood environment was clearly and deeply marked by music and by a social proximity to the Swedish cultural elite of his day. His mother, like all his siblings, played musical instruments. In line with bourgeois tradition, his mother also held a literary salon attended by many artists, such as the painter Nils Dardel. Classical music, which at this time was simply *music* to the upper classes, was the natural reference point for the Kempe family (Nävermyr, 1993; Burlin, 2008a, p. 301). The family attitude found expression in the patronage of musical amateurs among both friends and employees. In 1926, Hans Peter's father, Carl Kempe, the manager for Mo & Domsjö, founded a choir called Kempekören, made up of 150 workers (and singers) from the industrial plants in provinces Västerbotten and Ångermanland, a choir that still exists today. The combination of industry, music patronage and other cultural activities seems to have been characteristic of the Kempe family. Hans Peter Kempe would implement this heritage in his own way, but first, he broke with the family's business tradition. He devoted himself to music at his boarding school (Humanistiska läroverket, Sigtuna) and went on to study musicology at Uppsala University in the 1940s. He developed extensive interests and talents in music and the arts: he played the piano, directed his own choir, wrote poetry and composed music in a Swedish romance tradition and developed an interest in pedagogy (Burlin, 2008a, p. 301).

From an early age, Kempe also took an interest in music recordings and became a great collector of records. As an enthusiastic discophile, he had visionary ideas for the future of phonogram production. He objected to the way 78-rpm records lacked information about the time and place of the recording and the equipment used, and he wanted to make improvements in this regard. As a humanist and an aesthete, he also wanted to emphasize aspects of phonogram production that until then had been completely neglected, including beautiful cover illustrations. With plenty of capital to invest and an extensive network of contacts, he was in an excellent position to independently develop a phonogram company along these lines, and in 1945–1962, he did just that (Burlin, 2008a, p. 302).

The first step, in 1945, was founding the small company Recorda in Stockholm. Kempe started out making recordings with high-quality ribbon microphones and engraving lacquer discs for friends and relatives who wanted to immortalize their performances for the future. During the period 1945–1948, he changed the company name to Discofil and moved his recording activities to Sigtuna. Here he built a quite advanced music studio in his home, complete with an engraving machine. He hired his brother-in-law, the engineer Mark Blomberg, as a music engineer. At this stage, they were cutting small editions of records, anywhere from five copies to a few dozen. Soon, they began cooperating with record company Cupol and movie company AB Europa Film, who pressed small editions of discs for Discofil. In 1950, they moved the recording studio to Cinema Tranan at Fredhäll in Stockholm. In 1951–1952, they added more equipment to the studio, including a Lyrec TR-2 mono tape recorder (for tape recording instead of engraving lacquer discs). Later, they also added Neumann U47 and U49 microphones. By now, they were one of the most advanced music studios in Sweden, matched only by Radiotjänst (the Swedish Broadcasting Corporation) with whom they frequently collaborated (for example, by hiring their music engineers Tage Olhagen and Kjell Stensson); AB Europa Film; and the jazz-oriented Metronome, who also produced the first complete recordings of Sibelius' symphonies (Burlin, 2008a, pp. 182–186, 302–303).

During the period 1952–1954, Discofil left the stationary studio for a while and conducted its external recording activities using a bus and car and the Lyrec TR-2 tape recorder. They recorded musicians and artists from upper Norrland to southern Sweden: amateur choirs, orchestral associations and solo artists performing music in different styles and repertoires (Burlin, 2008c). Any choir or orchestra that wanted to make a record contacted Discofil. If possible, Discofil would arrange recordings with more artists in the same geographical area during the desired time period, and then the team of Kempe and Blomberg would go out and produce the recording. The more ensembles that could be recorded at the same time, the lower the price for each individual group (Burlin, 2008a, pp. 303–305). Discofil produced 78-rpm lacquer discs from the tape recordings, and other companies made matrices and performed the pressing (Burlin, 2022a). None of these recordings were released in large numbers on 78-rpm records; rather, they were produced in small editions, with one exception, a six-record box set in 1950 (Burlin, 2008a, p. 304). Kempe and Blomberg's largest project was a recording of a Gothenburg choir consisting of 3,000 singers. According to Blomberg, it was the most complicated recording – both technologically and musically innovative – they ever made:

> It was outdoors, it was an arena somewhere. As we were going to record these 3,000 people, there were, I think four or five sub-conductors, and then a main conductor who took care of it all, and then we had to place several microphones to make it sound sensible . . . It was such a long time lag.
>
> (Burlin, 2008a, p. 305)

Contemporaries of Discofil, as the music critic Bengt Pleijel, connected their business concept with the new opportunities for musical study and development of ensemble playing through recordings that the gramophone record seemed to have revealed in the years after 1950 (Pleijel, 1953, p. 120). For Discofil, it was driven by a desire to discover and document the music that actually existed in Sweden and, of course, to use technology: Discofil was active in a time when tape recorders, and thus recording opportunities, were not yet generally available, and consequently, there was something truly solemn and extraordinary about being documented on a recording. Recordings stemmed out of a genuine interest in the music that was recorded, and in a kind of pioneering spirit, it was amateurs who were documented. Recording the music was the primary thing; financial concerns were secondary. Mark Blomberg says:

> You got a fantastic insight into Swedish music life, which was of a fantastic power that you did not think existed. . . . It was unique in that way, because the people we came in contact with had never had the opportunity to hear themselves before, because tape recorders were not really out there in every man's cabin at the time. And definitely not anything of quality, and copying tapes could not be done just like that without further ado . . . then it was only ¼ inch tapes that mattered.
>
> (Burlin, 2008a, p. 304)

Let us turn now to some of the 78-rpm recordings and present tentative analyses in relation to the research questions. For this study, 78 digitized files in all were listened to (of about 100 recordings in total) – a few will be discussed in more detail. They have been made available by the National Library of Sweden in Stockholm. The musicians on the recordings are mostly amateurs and not professional players and exhibit varying levels of musicianship. Thus, some recordings are excellent, while others have errors in intonation, rhythm and overall playing quality. Initially, the records produced under the Recorda and Discofil trademarks were saved on lacquer discs and thus recorded without too many – if any – repeated takes and, because of the direct engraving technology, without edits (Chanan, 1995, p. 142). This changed in about 1952 when Discofil started to record on reel-to-reel tape recorder instead, leading to clear improvements in recording quality, as Hans Peter Kempe related on a marketing record (Kempe, Hans Peter, Discofil, 1952). It is not likely that any tape editing was done at the time (Nävermyr, 1993).

Early in 1952, Kempe felt the time was right to contact the big players on the Swedish music scene. Hugo Alfvén – the oldest and most successful of the Swedish composers of the time and a conductor as well – was the first. Kempe's likely first contact with Alfvén came in a letter in 1952. In this, he referred to his father "Dr. Carl Kempe", in connection with a request to record Alfvén directing the Kempekören for a pair of 78-rpm records, "in a small, limited edition" where "Mo & Domsjö companies cover all costs". Kempe also pointed out that "the recording could most conveniently take place in connection with the rehearsal" because "a large audience significantly worsens the acoustic conditions" (Kempe, 1952).

The recording came to fruition later that year. Hugo Alfvén's patriotic song "Sveriges flagga" (The Flag of Sweden) was recorded with at least three other songs in a performance by Kempekören with Alfvén conducting, to mark the choir's twenty-fifth anniversary, October 18–19, 1952. The song for the men's choir, with text by K.G Ossiannilsson, was composed for Sweden's Flag Day in 1916. The resulting recordings of pieces such as "Sveriges Flagga", "Härlig är jorden", "Olav Trygvason" and "Champagnevinet" were described in 1953 as "reputable" and possessing "a vocal brilliance that is reflected in an excellent way in the recording" (Alfvén, Hugo/Kempekörerna, *Sveriges flagga, Olav Trygvason*, Discofil, 1952). "Sveriges flagga" and the other songs were recorded with the Lyrec TR 2 mono tape recorder and probably with two microphones on October 17, 1952, in the Samlingslokalen – which had excellent acoustics – in Husum, near the city of Örnsköldsvik. There was no audience. The song is short at approximately two minutes. The performance is well balanced, with all four parts clearly audible and sonorous, because of both the quality of the performance and the recording. Hugo Alfvén was very aware that the recordings he made of his own music this late in life would become normative for future performances, and thus he gave them a special authenticity with his interpretations and comments. The recording was one of the first truly professional ones by Discofil; first, it was recorded on tape, and second, it engaged one of the most experienced composers and conductors in Sweden. At the same time, it was also a family affair, made with the help of the family network and resources: the choir of industrial workers recorded by the son of the family patriarch.

By helping establish a personal and friendly connection between Kempe and Alfvén, it paved the way for Kempe's next project. With Alfvén conducting the release of Alfvén's rhapsody *Midsommarvaka* at Christmas in 1954, Kempe (Figure 11.1) and Blomberg (Figure 11.2) produced their first LP – even recording it in stereo (Nävermyr, 1994; Burlin, 2008a, pp. 199–215, 299–338). With this release, Discofil changed its name to Swedish Society Discofil in order to compete in the international record market as a hi-fi record label recording with a two-microphone "AB" setup, and it marked the end of the mobile recording era (Alfvén, Hugo/Kungliga hovkapellet, *Midsommarvaka*, Discofil, 1994). Later, in 1957, Swedish Society Discofil also recorded Alfvén's late works

Dalarapsodi and *Svit ur Den förlorade sonen* – music partly composed
for the LP medium (Alfvén, Hugo/Kungliga hovkapellet, *Dalarapsodi,*
Discofil, 1957). During the years 1954–1961, SSD produced and released
an impressive catalogue of LPs: seven 25-cm mono LPs, 23 editions of
30-cm mono LP's, seven boxes of two to six LPs each, three EPs and nine
stereo LPs. Swedish Society Discofil's beautifully crafted LPs marked the
beginning of a more self-aware and confident Swedish music industry,
with less German and British dominance (Burlin, 2008a, pp. 199–210,
309–338) (Figures 11.1 and 11.2).

Let us connect back to the purpose of *mobile recording and production
practices, in networks, as a key to innovation in classical music production and mediatization of the* recordings, and ask: how has innovation in
recording and production occurred, and in what forms has it appeared in
this case? Was the mobile recording primarily situated in a "place" or a
"non-place"? Regarding innovation, the Discofil recordings overall, and
especially in the "Sveriges flagga" example, represent a combination
of technological, social and aesthetical innovations (Tschmuck, 2012,
p. 197). In this case, the recording "Sveriges flagga" and the other songs

Figure 11.1 Music producer Hans Peter Kempe (1920–1994), founder of Swedish
Society Discofil, in the early 1950s.

Source: Photograph: Sallstedts Bildbyrå

Figure 11.2 Music engineer Mark Blomberg (b. 1929) during the stereo recording of *Midsommarvaka*, October 6 or 7, 1954. Blomberg used one Lyrec TR-2 mono tape recorder modified for stereo and two amplifiers, one for each channel, with two Neumann U47 microphones in one AB setting.

Source: Photograph: Beata Bergström

were produced with Kempe's and Blomberg's mobile recording bus using a tape recorder and a mono set of microphones. In Husum, it is thus definitely recorded in a specific "place." The recording was mediatized, but only moderately, in that it was reproduced in about 200 copies but also was played on Radiotjänst broadcasts. The recording fixed the structure and national message of the musical composition – thus shaping the nationalist choir composition for the modern time.

2.2 Summary

During its period of operation, Hans Peter Kempe's Recorda/Discofil/SSD developed from a hobby endeavor to a highly professional company that invested in advanced technology, took an innovative attitude to production and, over time, achieved better and more advanced productions. The company was highly mobile, traveling by car and bus to record different types of classical music in locations around Sweden, always situated its recordings in distinct places. It used and expanded personal networks of musicians and engineers. Its recordings were mediatized, first moderately, with small editions of 78s. Overall, its work was innovative and trendsetting in many ways: musically, technologically, aesthetically and socially. The recordings influenced Swedish record production and awareness of Swedish classical music for many decades to come.

2.3 BIS records in the 1970s and 80s: from low-budget Swedish hi-fi to global hi-fi record company

My second case study is of BIS Records, which today is one of the world's foremost record companies specializing in classical music recordings of exceptional quality and even still producing the rare audiophile format SACD in the 2020s. Although still headquartered in Stockholm, BIS produces its recordings all over the world: in Japan, for example (BIS www.bis.se). In 2023, it was announced that BIS was acquired by Apple and its Platoon platform (BIS https://www.bis. se "history"). However, this international connection has not always existed. BIS was founded by Robert von Bahr in Stockholm in 1973 (Burlin, 2008b). Like Hans Peter Kempe, Robert von Bahr is self-taught as a music engineer and producer. BIS began in the early 1970s as a one-person company producing advanced low-budget recordings using a mobile recording studio and continued as such throughout the decade (Burlin, 2008a, pp. 238–239).

Again, somewhat like Kempe, von Bahr started his recording business on a semi-professional level while studying at university and conservatory. He originally founded BIS as a kind of protest against the difficulty of releasing an LP with his wife, Gunilla von Bahr, having been offered a very disadvantageous contract with AB Europa Film for the release of a self-produced recording. After the record became a minor success, he decided to start his own company. For ten years, it remained a one-person business, with von Bahr acting as producer, music engineer and managing director. Initially, BIS released LPs that focused on a particular type of musician. They were featuring young, unestablished musician friends of von Bahr's, playing an international repertoire. The musicians would set the programs, which generally resulted in LP productions with very varied styles. In the mid-1970s, however, von Bahr realized that this kind of LP, except when it featured the very biggest stars, was not very profitable. More and more, the records began to focus on the repertoire. At the same time, BIS gained international representation in several countries. Its international breakthrough came in 1975 with the release of an LP featuring opera singer Birgit Nilsson. During its first decade, BIS produced and released 200 LPs, or about 20 records a year. Later, in 1983, BIS became one of the first record labels in the world to release CDs, completely abandoning the LP medium in the mid-1980s. (Burlin, 2008a, p. 276). This ten-year period of development, both production-wise and technologically, as well as on the business side, laid the foundation for BIS to become one of only a few globally successful record companies specializing in classical music.

From the start and during the 1970s, BIS' repertoire consisted of previously unrecorded classical music from all subgenres, eras and styles of Western music as well as a complete series of works by various composers. The repertoire recorded during this period (and the decades after) generally exhibits a breadth of styles and a range of participating musicians, and it represented composers that no Swedish company had before BIS. BIS thus paved the way for a Swedish classical music phonogram production that could assert itself internationally. The focus, therefore, was not solely on Swedish music; rather, with BIS, Robert von Bahr directed both the company's activity and the phonogram products towards a broader international market. This also proved to be a recipe for success. During the 1970s, recordings included Renaissance music, organ music and works by composers such as Modest Mussorgsky, Igor Stravinsky, Alban Berg and Olivier Messiaen. Nordic music was nonetheless abundantly represented in the BIS repertoire. In addition, BIS released previously unrecorded music by Nordic composers such as Sibelius, Grieg, Stenhammar and Nielsen. Because of this latter investment, the company came to be regarded as representative of a "practical Nordicism" (Hedwall, 1979) – a contrast to the dominance of Swedish compositions released on SSD. But from the beginning, von Bahr's purpose with BIS was twofold: to allow skilled but unknown musicians and composers to become better known, as well as to place Sweden on the musical world map (Burlin, 2008a, pp. 238–239).

BIS production practice during the 1970s involved a Revox A77 stereo reel-to-reel tape recorder and two microphones that were "directly mixed" via a mixing desk. During the entire period of 1973–1983, BIS worked with only two microphones – like SSD – but not according to any particular method. Robert von Bahr had no technical training at all but relied entirely on practical experimentation and his background as a musician to learn how to place the microphones for a good sound (Burlin, 2008a, p. 293).

When recording musicians, von Bahr used to edit the tape immediately after the recording session, perhaps in a church or a concert hall. During the night, while the performers were sleeping, von Bahr cut together the current day's takes so that they were ready the next morning for a first hearing. The musicians had to listen and approve or reject the result right up until a fully edited master tape had been created. When the producer and the musicians left the recording room after three or four days of work, the tape was already complete. By following this working schedule, recordings could be completed in a reasonable time. The recordings were always produced in a mobile manner: first in different Swedish locales, such as churches and castles, and later moving around the world to find the best local venue for the music (Burlin, 2008a, p. 299).

In terms of recording technology and aesthetics, BIS worked with no dynamic range compression – not reducing the dynamic range of the sound – but tried to reproduce the music as it was considered to sound naturally, e.g., in a specific concert hall or church, with varying results but always with some connection to an ideal of auditory truth connected with both the music and recording place cherished in hi-fi circles since the 1960s (Björnberg, 2020, pp. 230–236; Rumsey & McCormick, 2014, pp. 394–395). An example of such a typical BIS recording is the medieval and Renaissance music ensemble Joculatores Upsalienses' LP, *Antik musik på Wik* from 1974, which was recorded at the medieval castle, Wiks Slott, outside Uppsala (Joculatores Upsalienses, *Antik music på Wik*, BIS 1974). However, BIS later sometimes used "spots" on instruments and vocals. The company's practice of extreme auditory close-ups of solo instruments sometimes drew criticism (Burlin, 2008a, pp. 238, 239, 250, 251, 293), but this is contested by von Bahr (Burlin, 2023).

Now, returning again to the larger questions of the article – how and in what forms did innovation in recording and production occur? Were the mobile recordings primarily situated in a "place" or a "non-place"? Robert von Bahr made – as Kempe – mobile recordings and was also both the company engineer and the producer. He started out recording musicians in his own network and moved later to recording more established musicians. BIS recordings clearly developed over time, both technologically and artistically/aesthetically, and von Bahr's concept or "invention" – artist-led and musician-selected repertoires on low budget but hi-fi quality recordings – changed as it became an "innovation", that is, a saleable product for the market. Under the influence of commercial wisdom, BIS gradually shifted its attitude toward music production and music aesthetics and moved toward producing highly mediatized recordings centered more around a repertoire than an individual musician. The LPs made by BIS in the 1970s are clearly situated at places such as churches and castles – as Wiks Slott – but the places changed from local ones in Sweden to local places around the world.

2.4 Summary

Robert von Bahr's BIS found its way to success through trial and error, via low-budget but innovative recordings, a strong emphasis on mobility when recording, and the exploitation and expansion of networks, beginning with unknown Swedish musicians and eventually moving to working with musicians on a global level. BIS has worked hard at staying technologically up-to-date and constantly developing its technology and recording/production practice. This led to its early adaptation of the CD and continues to this day, as BIS shows integrity in continuing to release music on SACD, an audiophile medium abandoned by most record labels in the first decade of the 2000s. BIS recordings are also available on streaming platforms and have thus become highly mediatized in a global market for classical music (BIS www.bis.se). With its pragmatic approach to repertoire and musicians, BIS has fulfilled von Bahr's vision of putting Sweden on the musical world map. Overall, BIS has shown strong tendencies toward innovation on both the technological, aesthetic and musical levels – as well as commercially.

2.5 Antennae media's production of streaming albums during the Covid-19 pandemic: Lars Bröndum and the *Aleathoric Anthem Project's* lo-fi/hi-fi aleatoric network recordings

My third case study is a modern one. It involves the independent one-person record company Antennae Media and its managing director, producer, engineer and composer Lars Bröndum, and specifically, his *Aleathoric Anthem Project*. Bröndum (b. 1961), a Swede, started out as a performing musician (guitarist) in the 1970s and played in several rock bands before moving to the US to study classical guitar, completing a PhD in music theory and composition in 1992. After moving back to Sweden, he forged a career as a composer and performer. According to Bröndum, his music "often explores the interaction between acoustic and electronic instruments and integration of improvisation into through-composed music" (Burlin, 2022a). In 2014, he founded the record company Antennae Media, which publishes recordings (CD/streaming) and sheet music, among other composition-related services. The company has its own recording studio in Stockholm. Antennae Media has released several albums, for example, the award-winning *Fallout* (CD, 2015), *Phaeton* (CD, 2019) and *Aleatoric Anthems and Palindromes* (CD, 2021).

During the global Covid-19 pandemic, which began in early 2020, many musicians, composers and producers were forced to find safe ways to make music together in computer-based networks. This technical infrastructure had, of course, been established for at least a couple of decades (Théberge, 2004, 2012), but in Sweden, overall Internet standards had been gradually improving so that when the pandemic started, many activities could immediately go online. Among musicians, probably the most difficult challenge was how to overcome the lack of immediate interplay, both eye-to-eye and ear-to-ear.

It was in this context that the *Aleathoric Anthem Project* was performed. The project featured "aleatory orchestras" performing new ironic "national anthems", one for every country in the world, with each one, including Sweden and the other Nordic countries, treated equally. Individually invited musicians in locations around the world performed and recorded pre-written parts, which were then edited and aleatorically combined, mixed down and produced as electroacoustic compositions. In the case of several of the recordings, the musicians involved never even met. Such personal flexibility is not new *per se*, but the combination of advanced composing techniques, mobility, flexible networks and digital mediatization of the musical material is an innovative step forward. The project was conceived in response to the extreme nationalism that reared up worldwide during the pandemic, and represented the composer's protest against it. Bröndum embarked on the project because of the pandemic-enforced isolation when restrictions on gathering made rehearsals and concerts impossible. A long-distance recording project was a way to both keep creativity flowing and stay in touch with fellow musicians. The anthems were recorded by 19 musicians, who each interpreted a one-page graphical score. The radical idea was that the new national anthems thus created were immediately meaningless since all the anthems were variations on the same piece: as nationalism is an ideology that is replanted locally in each specific country but whose mindset remains the same, no matter where it is formulated (Burlin, 2022a).

The project ran for one year, from May 17, 2020, to May 16, 2021. The musicians used recording technology ranging from hi-fi quality digital DAW recording and field recorders (such as the Tascam DR-40) to lo-fi recordings on smartphones. They submitted their recordings via file transfer services. A large database was generated. The composer fragmented the recordings into phrases of 2–10 seconds and reshuffled them in a program he created and named the Anthem Generator. At the beginning of the project, Bröndum recorded the aleatoric performance directly inside the program as stereo files. Later in the project, he created an iteration of the program with which he "piped" the sounds from the Anthem Generator into Logic as multi-track recordings (Burlin, 2022a).

The vagaries of the Covid-19 restrictions in Sweden allowed for the live recording of some of the anthems. For the live recordings, a DAW, a laptop and a multichannel audio interface were used. The instruments were mostly acoustic: bass clarinet, saxophones, voice, theremin, guitar, bass, piano, carillon bells, percussion, flute, contrabass recorder, alto recorder, violin and double bass were all used. The electronic parts – recorded in the studio – made use of a variety of equipment, including modular analog synthesizers, computer-interfaced synthesizers, prepared guitars and percussion. Additionally, some "noise scapes" or soundscapes were made using sounds from cars, refrigerators, etc. ("Anthem for Hungary"). The sounds were sometimes digitally manipulated in the Anthem Generator program. The final mixing and mastering of the recordings was done with Logic DAW (Burlin, 2022a).

Let us, again, connect back to the purpose of *mobile recording and production practices in networks as a key to innovation in classical music production and mediatization of the* recordings. When it comes to mobility, these recordings nearly invalidate the need for it. They were made all over the world and merged together not only as compositions but as *works of phonography* – that is, final audio products that are both compositions and performances in one form (Brown, 2000).

The innovative aspects were several. One was the music-aesthetical idea and concept of using a short score that was open for interpretation, and the interpretative, improvisatory and aleatory freedom that gave both the composer and the musicians musical opportunities. That musicians recorded their own parts – regardless of technical proficiency – to create long-distance cooperation was also important for the end result. The project was innovative by combining the use of computer-generated algorithmic chance methods with human improvisation. When creating the database of recorded contributions, Bröndum retained the phrases from the musicians' contributions so that a musical result was achieved. For example, the piece *Three Variations on an Aleatoric Anthem* is a development of this idea, scored for a trio (Burlin, 2022b).

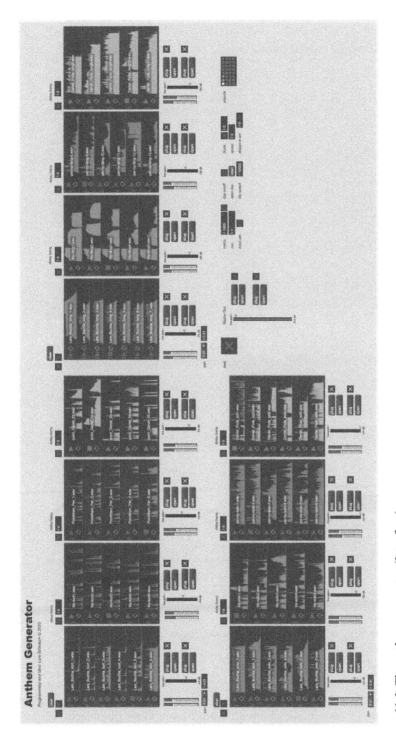

Figure 11.3 The anthem generator (Interface).

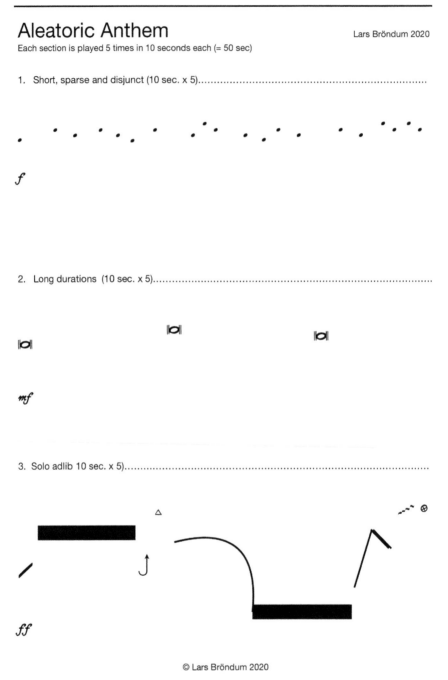

Aleatoric Anthem

Lars Bröndum 2020

Each section is played 5 times in 10 seconds each (= 50 sec)

1. Short, sparse and disjunct (10 sec. x 5)...

2. Long durations (10 sec. x 5)...

3. Solo adlib 10 sec. x 5)...

© Lars Bröndum 2020

Figure 11.4 The score.

   Bröndum's initial personal social network for this project consisted of a core group of four musicians with whom he worked frequently. He gradually expanded this network by doing "calls for participation" in social media and e-mailing musicians who might be interested. By the end of

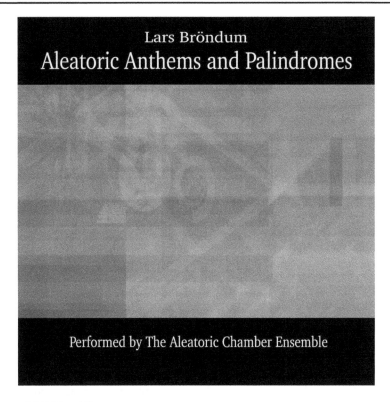

Figure 11.5 The Album.

Source: Photographs: Lars Bröndum

the project, the network had grown to include 19 participating musicians. The project was in its structure socially, aesthetically and technologically innovative.

As regards mediatization, the complexity of the recordings is clearly shaped by the technological conditions. The use of social media platforms such as Facebook and Bandcamp to promote the release of each new national anthem on that country's national day is also important. As mentioned, the 139 anthems were released on Bandcamp (Bröndum, Lars, *Aleatoric Anthems* vol. 1–6, Antennae Media 2021b), and selected anthems were released on the album *Aleatoric Anthems and Palindromes* (CD and Spotify) in 2021. The resulting recordings of anthems are not situated in one "place" – a studio, concert hall or even one country – but rather are free from "place", a non-place, played and recorded everywhere, pieced together and post-produced in Bröndum's studio: anti-nationalism canticles.

2.6 Summary

Lars Bröndum's Antennae Media has been producing both physical albums and streaming media for nearly a decade. It is a one-person company that has worked at a high level of innovation, both technologically and aesthetically, when it comes to releasing avant-garde classical music. At the same time, in the project described previously, Antennae Media has built a bridge between lo-fi and hi-fi technology in a way that is both possible and typical for this decade. The project's use of consumer technology to create long-distance cooperation sparked attention during the pandemic. Its use of computer-generated algorithmic chance methods in combination with human improvisation was also aesthetically innovative, bridging structure and chance, composition and improvisation. The network cooperation between the composer and participating musicians was a crucial element of the project and was socially innovative. The project was also highly mediatized with social media platforms used to promote the release of each national anthem on that country's national day.

3 CONCLUSIONS

3.1 Recording, innovation, mobility, networks and mediatization

In this article, this author has tried to develop and present some perspectives on recording, innovation, mobility, networks and mediatization in classical music production, using three case studies from Sweden that span a period of some 80 years. I will now summarize some points from these cases to suggest how changes in recording, mobility, networks and mediatization are linked to the evolution of innovation, both technologically as well as socially and aesthetically. The history of music recording and production and the music industry is a complex one. Here, I have sought to offer some "spots" or close-ups on historical classical music production, focusing on three Swedish one-person companies working between the 1940s and 2021. The first company, Discofil, was a pioneer in classical music production and saw a period of international success under the name Swedish Society Discofil. The second, BIS Records, worked on a local Swedish level before eventually becoming a major global classical music label – thus far, the only real Swedish success story in the classical music industry. The third, Antennae Media, works on a limited level but makes its advanced recordings within partly international networks (compare Van de Staey, 2013; Thulin, 2017; Théberge, 2012).

These three cases show some of the major changes that have occurred in recording technology and mediatization during the twentieth and twenty-first centuries (Tschmuck, 2012; Roy & Rodríguez, 2022). Mobile recording technologies – and associated practices – have moved from using reel-to-reel tape recorders performing recordings in local places to advanced digital recording and production connected to Internet-based personal networks, amplified by the pandemic of 2020–2021. There is a shift over time in "place" and "non-place": both SSD and BIS recorded in various locations such as concert halls, churches and castles. Most of Antennae Media's recordings – in the mentioned project – are made in many locations and thus lack a clear "place". When it comes to media formats, the history moves from directly engraved 78-rpm lacquer discs and 78-rpm records (Discofil) to groundbreaking, professionally produced LPs (Swedish Society Discofil and BIS) to CDs (BIS and Antennae Media) to streaming (BIS and Antennae Media). In subtle ways, the recording and distribution technologies in all three cases are linked to the companies' level of mobility and also to the strength of their networks (compare Tschmuck, 2012, p. 111). Together, these factors set the frame for the level of mediatization of the music. Besides the formal spreading of the music on phonograms, radio and streaming, the music was mediatized in subtle ways, for example, when it comes to duration, recording formats (mono, stereo), the sound and spatial perspectives and the visual and textual presentation on the sleeves.

What, then, is innovation in recording "classical" music? We know that new thinking, invention and innovation in the music industry often begin within small circles (Tschmuck, 2012). This is a common denominator in the examples of Discofil, BIS and Antennae Media. *Being innovative* or *making innovations happen* when recording classical music involves creatively and reflexively developing recorded instrumental performances and musicianship, recording techniques and tools for releasing music, which then becomes mediatized, spread across different media formats to reach a public that makes the music its own. In one way, this is probably easier to do within bounded social, technological and mobile contexts where decision paths are shorter. All three case studies are examples of this.

Finally, the three cases reflect changing attitudes to music and "nation" – of course, a special kind of "place". Discofil and Swedish Society Discofil had a national Swedish agenda – to introduce Swedish music to the world through recordings. "Sveriges flagga" was even an utterly nationalistic composition. BIS had a similar goal as SSD but focused less on Swedish compositions and more on a Swedish musical and industrial ability to record classical music and musicians from all over the world. Lastly, Antennae Media, with its anthem project, has offered an explicitly anti-nationalist musical commentary on the situation in the world today.

REFERENCES

BIS www.bis.se (website) [accessed October 2023].

Björnberg, A. (2020) *En trovärdig illusion av musik: den svenska hifi-kulturens uppgång och nedgång.* Lund: Mediehistoriskt arkiv 46.

Brooks, H. (1982) Social and Technological Innovation, in Lundstedt, S. B. & Colglazier, W. E. Jr. (Eds.) *Managing Innovation. The Social Dimension of Creativity, Invention and Technology.* New York: Pergamon Press.

Brown, L. B. (2000) Phonography, Rock Records, and the Ontology of Recorded Music. *The Journal of Aesthetics and Art Criticism*, Vol. 58. No. 4.

Burlin, T. (2008a) *Det imaginära rummet: Inspelningspraxis och produktion av konstmusikfonogram i Sverige 1925–1983.* Dissertation. Göteborg: Skrifter från musikvetenskap and Göteborgs universitet nr 92.

Burlin, T. (2008b, October 21) *Interview with Robert von Bahr* (b. 1943).

Burlin, T. (2008c, May 15). *Interview with Mark Blomberg* (b. 1929). Stockholm: Transcription and Translation Toivo Burlin.

Burlin, T. (2022a, October 12) *Interview with Mark Blomberg* (b. 1929), telephone.

Burlin, T. (2022b) *Interview, E-Mail Correspondence, Zoom-and Personal Meetings with Lars Bröndum* (b. 1961). 2020–2022.

Burlin, T. (2023, May 2) *Interview with Robert von Bahr* (b. 1943).

Bårdsen, T. (2019) *Sporfinnere: En undersøkelse av norsk musikkproduksjons teknologiske utvikling i et bevaringsperspektiv.* Doktorsavhandlinger ved Universitetet i Agder 243. Kristiansand: Universitetet i Agder. Fakultet for kunstfag.

Chanan, M. (1995) *Repeated Takes: A Short History of Recording and its Effects on Music.* London: Verso.

Dromey, C. & Haferkorn, J. (2018) *The Classical Music Industry.* New York and London: Routledge Taylor and Francis Group.

Gopinath, S. & Stanyek, J. (2014) Anytime, Anywhere? An Introduction to the Devices, Markets and Theories of Mobile Music, *The Oxford Handbook of Mobile Music Studies.* Oxford: Oxford handbooks and Oxford University Press.

Hedwall, L. (1979) Mera nordiskt på BIS. *Musikrevy* nr 1, pp. 48–49.

Kempe, H. P. (1952, October 8) *Letter to Hugo Alfvén.* Unpublished. Uppsala: Carolina Rediviva.

Nävermyr, S. (1993, April) *Interview with Hans Peter Kempe (1920–1994).* Transcription and translation: Toivo Burlin.

Nävermyr, S. (1994). Den första stereoinspelningen. *Booklet: Hugo Alfvén dirigerar Hovkapellet* CD 1994 SCD1003. Swedish Society Discofil.

Pleijel, B. (1953) Studiearbete per grammofoninspelning. *Musikrevy* nr 4, p. 120.

Ramsten, M. (1992) *Återklang: svensk folkmusik i förändring 1950–1980.* Göteborg: Skrifter från Musikvetenskapliga institutionen.

Roy, E. A. & Rodríguez, E. M. (2022) *Phonographic Encounters: Mapping Transnational Cultures of Sound, 1890–1945.* London & New York: Routledge Taylor and Francis Group.

Rumsey, F. & McCormick, T. (2014) *Sound and Recording: Applications and Theory.* Seventh Edition. New York and London: Focal Press.

Schumpeter, J. A. (2021). *The Theory of Economic Development.* Translated from the German by Redvers Opie with a new introduction by Richard Swedberg. Abingdon, Oxon: Routledge, 2021.

Théberge, P. (2004, October) The Network Studio: Historical and Technological Paths to a New Ideal in Music Making. *Social Studies of Science*, Vol. 34, No. 5, pp. 759–781, Special Issue on Sound Studies: New Technologies and Music. Sage Publications, Ltd.

Théberge, P. (2012) The End of the World as We Know It: The Changing Role of the Studio in the Age of the Internet, in Frith, S. & Zagorski-Thomas, S (Eds.) *The Art of Record Production: An Introductory Reader for a New Academic Field.* Farnham & Burlington: Ashgate.

Thomas, A. (2002) A Microphone to the People: The Recordings of the Mobile Unit of the New Zealand Broadcasting Service, 1946–1948. *The journal of New Zealand Studies*, No. 1, p. 77. ISSN: 1173–6348.

Thulin, S. (2017, April) Situated Composition in Emerging Mobile Sound Production Technologies and Practices. *Organised Sound: An International Journal of Music Technology. XXII/1*, Vol. 22, No. 1, p. 73. ISSN: 1355–7718. Context-based composition. Cambridge University Press.

Tschmuck, P. (2012) *Creativity and Innovation in the Music Industry*. Second Edition. Heidelberg New York Dordrecht London: Springer.

Van de Staey, Z. (2013) *Muziek voor mobiele media: Een overzicht binnen de hedendaagste kunstmuziek*. [Music for mobile media: An overview within contemporary art music] Dissertation Source: MA, from Katholieke Universiteit Leuven.

DISCOGRAPHY

Alfvén, Hugo/Kungliga hovkapellet (1994) [CD] *Hugo Alfvén dirigerar Hovkapellet: Midsommarvaka*. Sweden: Swedish Society Discofil.

Alfvén, Hugo/Kungliga hovkapellet (1957) [vinyl LP] *Dalarapsodi och Svit ur Den förlorade sonen*. Sweden: Swedish Society Discofil.

Bröndum, L. (2015) [CD] *Fallout*. Sweden: Antennae Media.

Bröndum, L. (2019) [CD] *Phaeton*. Sweden: Antennae Media.

Bröndum, L. (2021a) [CD] *Aleatoric Anthems and Palindromes*. Sweden: Antennae Media.

Bröndum, L. (2021b) [digital release] *Aleatoric Anthems* vol. 1–6, https://larsbrondum.bandcamp.com/Sweden: Antennae Media.

Joculatores Upsalienses (1974) [LP] *Antik musik på Wik*. Sweden: BIS Records.

Hans Peter Kempe (1952) [78 rpm record] Sweden: Discofil.

Kempekörerna under ledning av H. Alfvén (1952) [78 rpm record] *Sveriges Flagga: Olav Trygvason*. Sweden: Discofil.

12

"Culture produces an industry"

Production and promotion strategies of campus song records by Taiwanese Synco Corporation

Haoran Jiang

1 INTRODUCTION

Xiaoyuan gequ (campus song) or *Xiaoyuan minge* (campus folk song) is a genre of Taiwanese popular music that gained popularity from the mid-1970s to the early 1990s. The campus song began as a "folk song movement" by student songwriters. The record companies quickly noticed the potential this boom had for the record label market and launched the "campus song" genre. In the past decade, with a renewed interest in Taiwan's early phonograph records and inspired by British recorded music studies, many scholarly works on the history of Taiwan's recording industry have appeared (e.g., Huang, 2019; Shen, 2013; Shih, 2014; Wang, 2013). However, there has been no in-depth study on the recording industry of campus songs, with previous studies only focusing on the social history of the "folk song movement" and the lyrics of campus songs (e.g., Yang, 1994; Tzeng, 1998; Yeh, 1999; Chang, 2003; Ho, 2006; Moskowitz, 2010; Shih, 2014).

Utilizing Synco Corporation, the foremost record company for campus songs, as a case study, this study seeks to reconstruct the historical trajectory of campus songs within the recording industry, with a specific focus on the production and promotion strategies employed by Synco. Moreover, this study delves into the broader context, scrutinizing the ways in which the social, cultural, and political milieu of that era, along with considerations related to the target audience, influenced Synco's approach to producing and promoting this emerging popular music genre.

2 METHODS AND THEORIES

The methods of archival work, product analysis, and oral history interviews were adopted for this study. Based on archival work and oral history interviews, the recording industry history and production processes of Synco were reconstructed. Key sources were written records from newspapers, magazines, and insiders' narratives (e.g., interview transcriptions). An electronic database was used to retrieve the full texts of the *United Daily News* Group. The audiovisual records of secondary interviews with

DOI: 10.4324/9781003462101-14

musicians or industry practitioners were also important sources for this study. A series titled *Zishen yinyueren koushu yingyin jilu* (Oral History and Audiovisual Records of Senior Musicians) was consulted. This series was published by the Cultural Bureau of the Taipei Municipal Government and included interviews with a large number of artists and behind-the-scenes people from Taiwan's popular music scene.

Shelemay (2006) argues that ethnomusicologists are "able and empowered" (p. 33) to conduct historical research by studying memories elicited from ethnographic interviews. Two former Synco Corporation employees were interviewed for this study. One was a producer, Kuo-Chiang Lee; the other was a copywriter, Yu-Mei Tsao. It must be acknowledged that accessing artists and behind-the-scenes people of mainstream popular music has its challenges, which is why Pruett (2011) provides a few strategies to conduct fieldwork on mainstream popular music, especially through encouraging the building of a network among ethnomusicologists to obtain access to artists (p. 21). The interview with Kuo-Chiang Lee benefited from such a network among scholars.

Finally, the production strategies are evaluated by conducting a retrospective analysis of the final products – the LP records. The analysis involved examining melodies, lyrics, and instrumental arrangements. Album covers were taken into consideration, as this study sees popular music products as composed of musical sounds in conjunction with words, images, and movement (Shepherd, 1999, p. 33). This study accessed a few original campus song LP records from the author's collection, as well as collections at The Chinese University of Hong Kong and National Taiwan University. The sound files of campus songs from reissued CDs and online music streaming platforms were also accessed for this study. Moreover, this study referred to some album covers of LP records found through presswork and the Internet.

Regarding theoretical references, the presented study draws upon insights from popular music studies, particularly the perspectives on industry and genre. Negus (1999) maintains that "an industry produces culture, and culture produces an industry" (p. 14). From his point of view, cultural production is not only for profit but also a process by which production practitioners give various meanings to cultural products in a wider social and cultural context (p. 20). Negus, additionally, sheds light on the substantial influence of the target audience on musical production, underscoring that deeply ingrained beliefs tied to social divisions such as gender, class, and race, significantly shape practitioners' judgments and decisions (p. 21). His discourse extends to a reconsideration of genre, reframing it within a wider spectrum of social divisions (p. 25). This point echoes Frith's (1996, p. 76) opinion that genre combines an investigation of the music (what it sounds like) with the market (who will buy it).

Informed by these opinions and given that the campus song was a genre appearing in 1970s Taiwan and targeting university students, this study looks at how the social, cultural, and political environment in 1970s Taiwan, in conjunction with the university student audience, influenced the production and promotion strategies of Synco. In fact, such a theoretical perspective also affected the choice of research method. Looking upon the music industry itself as a culture, interviewing industry practitioners is like the job of most anthropologists and ethnomusicologists since it entails getting inside cultural communities and communicating with cultural insiders.

Finally, Actor-Network Theory (ANT) from sociology was consulted in this study. ANT suggests that "society, organizations, agents, and machines are all effects generated in patterned networks of diverse (not simply human) materials" (Law, 1992, p. 380). It also hypothesizes that the task of sociology is to describe these heterogeneous networks (p. 381). In a similar vein, within the field of popular music studies, Frith (1996, p. 88) notes that "the genre labeling process is better understood as something collusive than as something invented individually, as the result of a loose agreement among musicians and fans, writers and disc jockeys." Following ANT and Frith's views, this study describes how a diverse array of human actors, including the staff of Synco, the student singers and songwriters, publicists, and nonhuman actors such as musical texts and media technologies formed the network of campus songs. Although the audience is an important part of creating the network of campus songs, it is not discussed in this study.

3 SOCIAL AND CULTURAL CONTEXT

During the 1970s, Taiwan, officially known as the Republic of China, was still under martial law, which had been enacted by the Kuomintang-led government since 1949. Under martial law, the Kuomintang enforced military-style discipline on the people of Taiwan and imposed strict censorship on publication and speech, claiming that it was the inheritor of the true Chinese culture as well as being the legitimate Chinese government. Such claims were inculcated on the Taiwanese public through the continuous imposition of Chinese nationalism through education, media, and culture.

At the same time, Taiwan was about to undergo dramatic political and cultural changes, which were triggered by a series of diplomatic-political setbacks. In October 1971, the United Nations General Assembly expelled the Republic of China in favor of the People's Republic of China. The momentum of diplomatic shifts continued with President Richard Nixon's historic visit to the People's Republic of China in February 1972, followed by the May 1972 transfer of administrative control of the Ryukyu and Diaoyutai Islands to Japan, sparking the Diaoyutai Islands dispute. In September 1972, Japan no longer recognized the Republic of China as the sole official government of China. In January 1979, the United States broke diplomatic relations with the Republic of China. These events would cause Taiwan to gradually become marginalized and lose the international community's support.

On the other hand, these events also spurred a national crisis and the re-emergence of national consciousness, especially among young people, who began criticizing the cultural and economic neo-imperialism and neo-colonization by the United States and Japan. Unlike the previous generation, Taiwanese youth began to reject the Kuomintang's claim that Taiwan was merely a temporary base for "re-conquering the Mainland" and did not view themselves as exiles. This promoted a greater sense of duty to Taiwanese society and supported "return-to-reality" ideas as well as the restoration of Taiwan's local culture (Hsiau, 2021).

Politically, a student movement was launched in the name of Defend Diaoyutai Islands in 1971, and in 1972 and 1973, through a network of student clubs, movements appealing to caring for local society emerged by actively seeking social and political reforms. These movements also had a particular effect on culture with greater emphasis on native literature and fine arts, all of which aimed to reshape the local cultural identity and reaffirm the value of self-existence.

Although Taiwanese intellectuals in the 1970s began to pay attention to Taiwan's native culture, the generation who were immersed in the Kuomintang's nationalistic education were still inclined toward Chinese identity rather than Taiwanese, and their discussions about Taiwan's reality and future tended to be framed in the context of Chinese history (Hsiau, 2021, p. 52). And yet, this generation of Taiwanese young people had never been to the mainland. The land of Taiwan was the only "China" they knew.

The available music prevailing among Taiwan's young people during the 1970s was popular music from the US and the UK. Older Taiwanese people also listened to Mandarin Chinese and Hokkien (a dialect spoken among many Taiwanese natives) popular songs produced in Taiwan. The Kuomintang government often regarded these locally produced songs as "*mimi zhi yin* (decadent music)" and banned them under music censorship laws (see Scheihagen, 2015) because they were judged as being too sentimental.

Against this background, Taiwan's young people started a "folk song movement" with the slogan "sing our own song." On June 6, 1975, a young songwriter named Hsien Yang held a concert at the Taipei Zhongshan Hall and performed 8 original songs, which signaled the formal starting of Taiwan's "folk song movement." On December 3, 1976, another pioneering songwriter, Shuang-Ze Li, declared that "we should sing our own songs" at a Western popular music concert at Tamkang University in Taiwan, which became an important event in the folk song movement's early stage (see Chang, 2003). The word "own" here implies "our Chinese/ Taiwanese songs," distinguished from Western songs. It also meant "our young students' songs," distinguished from "decadent music." Inspired by Yang and Li, more and more students were now devoting themselves to composing original campus songs. With so many songs being written and performed, it was only a matter of time before Taiwan's local record companies would also see the potential commercial value, which eventually brought the "campus song" into the music marketplace.

4 CONSTRUCTING CHINESENESS

Influenced by the prevailing wave of nationalistic fervor in Taiwanese society and driven by the ethos of the folk song movement, especially the "sing our own songs" spirit, Synco adopted the mission of evoking a sense of national identity and cultural pride through their production of campus songs. This commitment is clearly articulated in the proposal presented by Harrison Yao, the Director of Synco's Production Department, for the creation of campus song records. Yao's proposal was a response to Taiwan's withdrawal from the United Nations during that specific period. In addition to commercial considerations, his primary objective in the proposal was to counter the allure of Western popular songs among Taiwan's youth and redirect their preferences toward locally produced popular music (see Tao and Yang, 2015, p. 71). Within this context, constructing Chineseness within campus song records became an integral and indispensable component of Synco's overarching production strategy.

In terms of repertoire, Synco selected a few songs that expressed patriotic feelings. The most representative work was the *"Long de chuanren* (Descendants of the Dragon)" (Lee, 1980), written by Te-Chien Hou in 1978 to respond to the breakup of the Taiwan-US diplomatic relationship. The lyrics describe China as a dragon and Chinese people as "descendants of the dragon." It traces the history of humiliation in modern China and articulates strong patriotic emotions. The initial four lines of the lyrics can be translated as follows:

> There is a dragon in the ancient East
> Its name is China
> There is a group of people in the ancient East
> They are all descendants of the dragon
> (Hou, 1978)

Many anti-imperialist and anti-colonial national references often align with a masculine ethos to emphasize the characteristics of power and strength of resistance (Shie, 2019, pp. 48–49). "Descendants of the Dragon" also expresses a masculine China. Synco assigned the song to a male singer, Chien-Fu Lee, who had a high, intense voice. Synco also added a powerful horn section and a heavenly chorus to the arrangement.

Aside from the works directly expressing patriotic emotions, there were many other ways for Synco to construct Chineseness. First, Synco chose some works depicting China's landscapes or appropriating Chinese literary classics. For instance, *"Gu guo jinxi* (Ancient Country, Present and Past)" (Wang, 1980) and *"Guiren sha cheng* (Return to the Sand City)" (Shih *et al.*, 1980) depicted an imaginary desert in the northern frontier of China. The lyrics of *"Yu Linling* (Bells Ringing in the Rain)" (Pao, 1978 [2007]) and *"Chaitou feng* (Phoenix Hairpin)" (Pao, 1978 [2007]) were both taken from ancient Chinese poems with the same names. *"Qiaoge* (Woodcutter Song)" (Pao, 1981) appropriated the image of the hermit from classical Chinese literature.

Synco also incorporated many Chinese traditional songs into the campus song records, such as Yunnan province's folk song *"Midu shange* (Song of Midu Mountain)" (Huang *et al.*, 1979), Qinghai province's folk song *"Siji huakai* (Flowers Bloom in All Seasons)" (Liu *et al.*, 1979), and the Xinjiang folk song *"Ni song wo yizhi meigui hua* (You Gave Me a Rose)" (Yang, 1979). In addition, Synco intentionally added traditional Chinese instruments to the campus song arrangements. Synco producer

Kuo-Chiang Lee (2019) told me that due to his extensive experience in studying and performing Chinese traditional music and collaborating with Chinese instrumentalists in Taiwan, the campus song records he produced often used Chinese instruments. For example, he invited *erhu* (Chinese two-stringed fiddle) player Yu-Ting Lin to perform in the recording of "Bells Ringing in the Rain," and the *sanxian* (Chinese three-stringed lute) appearing in "*Pin xiaoye* (Night Snack)" (Guitar Chorus, 1982) was played by Lee himself.

Synco sometimes even implemented Chineseness in the design of album covers to match the musical Chineseness. Taking *Descendants of the Dragon* as an example (refer to the album cover at: https://collections. nmth.gov.tw/CollectionContent.aspx?a=132&rno=2015.045.0150.0002), the album's front cover shows the singer Chien-Fu Lee wearing a traditional Tang suit and holding a traditional Chinese instrument. On the back cover, he is standing in front of a Chinese-style gate in one photo and standing beside a Chinese temple bell in another one. Another example is Siao-Rong Shih's *Knight* (1982). In order to match the Kungfu style of the album, Synco made a special design for the album cover, in which Shih wore a Kungfu costume and performed martial arts moves (see Liou, 1982; Tao and Yang, 2015, p. 90).

As mentioned previously, the youth in Taiwan during the 1970s were strongly influenced by Chinese nationalism. However, it's crucial to recognize that this generation also embraced a "return-to-reality" perspective, shifting their gaze toward promoting local Taiwanese culture. In fact, articulations of local Taiwanese elements can be found in some of the campus song records. For example, a few Hokkien songs were included in Synco's campus song records, such as "*Zhengyue diao* (New Year's Tune)" (Chien *et al.*, 1977) and "*Liuyue moli* (Jasmine in June)" (Chen, 1978). In another example, the singer Lai Su put unique touches on the Hengchun tune "*Sixiang qi*" sung by Taiwanese folk musician Da Chen, to the melody of the campus song "*Yueqin* (Moon Zither)" (Cheng, Wang and Ma, 1981). When Synco confronted the "raw material" of campus songs, which comprised works from songwriters, it chose not to "filter out" pieces with distinctive local characteristics of Taiwan, as discussed by Negus (1996, pp. 58–59) in the context of popular music production. This approach may indicate that Synco was also responding to the Taiwanese localism prevailing in Taiwan's cultural scenes at that time.

5 CREATING STUDENTS' INNOCENT IMAGE

Besides constructing Chineseness, Synco devoted itself to creating innocent images of students. This production strategy distinguished campus songs from other locally produced popular songs that often had negative and decadent stereotypes. Synco's campus songs did not heavily rely on the works of professional songwriters, and it did not invite famous Mandarin pop singers to sing them. Instead, Synco organized campus song competitions called "*Jinyun jiang* (Golden Melody Award)" to both recruit student singers and collect songs written by students. The Golden

Melody Award was held five times. The first four were held annually from 1977 to 1980, but the fifth was postponed until 1984 (United Daily News, 1984). The selection criteria for singers included being youthful and confident in appearance rather than flamboyant. Vocal interpretation needed to be clean and avoid the frivolous style of pop singers (United Daily News, 1979; Yao, 2012). In order to attract students to attend the competitions, Synco set high bonuses (Yao, 2012). After the competition, Synco would publish records for the winning singers, but the losing singers might still have the opportunity to record songs. Since many student singers' families objected to students becoming singers, Synco also needed to dedicate a significant amount of time negotiating with the students' families, who usually agreed to allow only a one-year singer contract (Tsao, 2019).

For the student songs collected through competitions, Synco generally maintained the original music and lyrics to uphold a straightforward and unadorned style. However, if necessary, the producers would also make some adjustments. For example, Lee once felt that the beat of a certain work was too flat-footed, so he suggested adding slow beats and off-beats to the original melody (Lee, 2019). In terms of content, love songs constituted the majority of campus songs. However, the expression of love in campus songs differed quite from other Mandarin popular songs in the same period. Mandarin popular songs usually used the words like "*ai* (love)," "*qing* (affection)," and "*lian* (longing for)" directly and extensively in the lyrics. By contrast, love songs in campus songs often used nature metaphors such as rain, flower, sea, and wind (Chang, 2003, p. 180). Such a textual characteristic was suitable to express the ignorant love of university students and made campus songs different from the "decadent" Mandarin popular songs.

To pursue a fresh and clean style, Synco's producers rarely used brasses in the arrangements of campus songs (Yu, 2012). Lee (2019) stated that he often asked the arrangers not to use drums or bass guitars. When recording the voice, the producers of Synco would intentionally retain the plain characteristics of student singers. Synco did not provide special singing training for its singers before recording, nor did it send demos for them to practice with in advance, but only invited them to practice in Synco's office during holidays or after-school hours.

In the recording process, producers generally did not give much specific guidance to the singers, which was different from the recording processes of Mandarin popular songs (Lee, 2019). Although Mandarin popular songs before the campus song era were often filled with strong reverbs and echoes, the producers and the recording engineers of campus song records intentionally reduced the reverbs and echoes to create more clean overall effects (Tao and Yang, 2015, p. 151). According to Doyle's (2005, p. 164) research, since the late 1950s, reverbs and echoes have been used to create a less natural and virtual space. From this perspective, Synco's deliberate reduction of reverbs and echoes helped to make campus songs sound more natural, sincere, and consistent with the student singers' expression.

The design of album covers also contributed to creating an innocent image. The album covers of campus songs were quite different from Mandarin popular songs in the 1970s and 1980s. At that time, the record covers of Mandarin popular songs often displayed photos of pop stars wearing heavy makeup on the cover, usually taken in photo studios. There was a title, the singer's name, and perhaps the titles of a few songs. By contrast, campus song record covers showed the student singers usually dressed casually and were photographed in natural environments. For example, Yu Chyi's (1979) album "*Ganlan shu*" (Olive Tree) showcased her casual image in a serene natural setting (refer to the album cover at www.books.com.tw/products/0020198300). In an interview, Chyi recalled, "At that time, no one helped us make up, and no one designed our hairstyles. We all bought clothes and skirts by ourselves" (Oriental Morning Post, 2007). Sometimes illustrations and statements were even used instead of the singers' photos. The statements were intended to deliver a youthful message, such as "*you zhe yi dai nianqing ren xinsheng suo pu cheng de* (composed by the aspirations of this generation of young people)" (see Huang, 2012).

6 TARGET AUDIENCE-DRIVEN PROMOTION

The target audience for campus song records was university students. Its promotion strategies were formulated driven by its target audience to deliver effective production information to university students. While TV and radio stations promoted Mandarin pop songs, they were not very interested in campus songs due to student singers' lack of wide popularity and attractiveness (Tsao, 2019). Kuo-Chiang Lee (2019) recalled that there were few radio programs that wanted to play Synco's campus songs. Among the limited examples were "*Pingan Ye* (Peaceful Night)," which was played by Police Radio Station, and "*Qili shijie* (Beautiful World)," played by Broadcasting Corporation of China. Chien-Fu Lee (2012) noted that only the radio programs hosted by Siao-Cing Tao, Di Fang, and Chen Ling were willing to regularly play songs by Synco's singers. Television programs were even worse. Yu Chyi remembers only appearing on TV twice when promoting the album *Olive Tree* (Huang, 1979).

Facing difficulties in promoting campus song records through radio and television, Synco decided to take a different strategy by using live performance as its main promotion channel. Promotion through live performance was very suitable for emergent or developing artists because it could build a base market and attract the attention of the mass media (Negus, 1992, p. 90). The vast majority of live performances organized by Synco were campus tours. Since campus tours could establish face-to-face contact with students, the tours ended up playing an important role in promoting Synco's campus song records through the entire era of campus songs. A news report in 1984 noted that when Synco promoted *Jinyun jiang chuangxin 3* (*Golden Melody Award Innovation Series 3*) published in that year, it held concerts in more than ten universities and colleges, including Fu Jen Catholic University, Tunghai University, and Tamkang University. This report also indicated that Synco would send letters to various universities and colleges to express the willingness to hold the concerts, which Synco funded and also exclusively controlled (Ming Sheng Daily, 1984).

In addition to the campus tours, Synco also held concerts for the public. These concerts were not too commercial but often combined with cultural and educational, charity, and patriotic (party) activities. For example, in May 1980, Synco held the "*Jinyun jiang zhi ye* (Golden Melody Award Night)" at the Sun Yat-Sen Memorial Hall in Taipei. The ticket revenue was donated to the National Salvation Corps, which was used as a part of the social relief fund (Tao, 1980). Such concerts contributed to the establishment of a healthy, positive brand image for Synco that was different from the Mandarin popular song market.

Another important channel to promote campus songs was the print media. Since university students were deemed a well-educated group by society and important readers of newspapers and magazines, the promotion strategy relied on the print media that was obviously tied to the target audience. Synco invested a lot of money to advertise campus song records in various Taiwanese newspapers, including *China Times*, *United Daily News*, *Taiwan Times*, *Taiwan Daily News*, *Youth Warrior Daily*, and *Taiwan Shin Sheng Daily News*. Unlike the previous practice of record companies only using small advertisements, Synco preferred to use half pages for advertising their records (Yao, 2012). Synco also advertised records through magazines. For example, the well-known Taiwanese music magazine *Gunshi* (which translates as *Rolling Stone* but is not related to the American music magazine) even published some advertisements for Synco's campus song records (see Tao and Yang, 2015, pp. 72, 87). The cost of Synco's investment in advertising design was quite high. Synco brought together a group of outstanding design talents. In addition to the copywriter Nian-Cih Wang and designer A-Ding of Growww Media Co., some photographers and artists were invited to participate in the design, such as Jhao-Tang Jhang, Ming-Sheng Ling, Jhih-Hong Yang, and Meng-Jia Yao (Yao, 2012).

Besides, Synco would provide singers' biographies and recent reports on singers to newspaper and magazine offices for publicity purposes (Lee, 2019). Like the gossip of popular stars, these reports discussed topics about the singers' love lives, blood types, and personal interests. What was special was that these reports also emphasized the singer's educational background and reported on the singer's academic life. For example, one piece identified that Yu Chyi was studying in the Department of Anthropology of National Taiwan University (Tu, 1979). Such a reporting strategy may have made student readers feel closer to these student singers.

7 CONCLUSION

This study attempts to illustrate that, against the background of martial law, diplomatic crises, nationalism, and localization, and under the practitioners' observation and imagination of the target audience, Synco's production of campus song records was around a clear "product image," a concept elucidated by Ryan and Peterson (1982) in the context of country music. This campus song image represented a new popular music genre with Chinese characteristics projecting on the innocent images of student cultures. Synco also established unique promotion strategies that prioritized campus tours and print media to deliver product information to its target audience. This study also shows how Taiwan's campus songs of the 1970s and 1980s were a network generated and maintained by an integration of musical texts, media, industry practitioners, and musicians. Following the success of Synco's campus song records, many other Taiwanese record companies also invested in producing this new music genre, including Haishan Records, Four Seas Records, and Kolin Records (Chang, 2003, p. 172). However, Synco was undoubtedly the most successful record company in the genre of campus songs, and its success is attributed to its effective production and promotion strategies.

Finally, it is worth noting the significant difference between the industry of campus song records and the industry of previous Mandarin popular song records. With the advent of campus song records, many young students became employed by the music industry, breaking the dominance of professional singers and songwriters. Although these young students still belonged to the "elites," at least in comparison to their lower-class peers, they were not the elites in the field of popular music. Therefore, the industry of campus song records implies a reversal of power within Taiwan's popular music industry. Given that, it is not difficult to understand why campus songs were also called "*xiaoyuan minge* (campus folk songs)" even if they were not authentic folk music. In the Chinese language, "*min* (folk)" means the common people, which is different from the meaning of the elite (Xu, 2006, p. 41). In this way, although the culture of campus songs constructed by record companies was commercial, it held a certain progressive significance.

REFERENCES

Chang, C.-W. (2003). *Shei zai nabian chang ziji de ge: Taiwan xiandai minge yundong shi* (*Who Were Singing Their Own Songs There: History of Taiwan's Modern Folk Song Movement*), Taipei, Rock Publications.

Doyle, P. (2005). *Echo and Reverb: Fabricating Space in Popular Music Recording, 1900–1960*, Middletown, Wesleyan University Press.

Frith, S. (1996). *Performing Rites: On the Value of Popular Music*, Cambridge, Harvard University Press.

Ho, W.-C. (2006). A historical review of popular music and social change in Taiwan, *Asian Journal of Social Science*, Vol 34, No 1, pp. 120–147.

Hou, T.-C. (1978). *Long de chuanren geci* (Lyrics of Descendants of the Dragon), *United Daily News*, 26 December, p. 12.

Hsiau, A.-C. (2021). *Politics and Cultural Nativism in 1970s Taiwan: Youth, Narrative, Nationalism*, New York, Columbia University Press.

Huang, B.-L. (1979). *Xuesheng gezhe guan changpian* (Student singers recorded records), *United Daily News*, 2 March, p. 7.

Huang, K.-C. (2019). The development of the indigenous "mountain music industry" and "mountain songs" (1960–1970s): Production and competition, in

Tsai, E., Ho, T.-H. & Jian, M. (eds.), *Made in Taiwan: Studies in Popular Music*, New York, Routledge, pp. 55–72.

Huang, Y.-Y. (2012). *Xinli gufen youxian gongsi faxing Synco pai changpian bianhao "VH-004" guoyu gequ zhuanji Jinyun jiang jinian zhuanji* (A cover for the mandarin song album Golden Melody Award Memorial Album published by Synco and Numbered "VH-004"), *Collections* (website), available online from https://collections.nmth.gov.tw/CollectionContent.aspx?a=132&rno=2003.001.1055.0001 [accessed July 2022]

Law, J. (1992). Notes on the theory of the Actor-Network: Ordering, strategy, and heterogeneity, *Systems Practice*, Vol 5, No 4, pp. 379–393.

Lee, C.-F. (2012). Interviewed by Cultural Bureau of the Taipei Municipal Government, *Zishen yinyueren koushu yingyin jilu* (*Oral History and Audiovisual Records of Senior Musicians*).

Lee, K.-C. (2019). Interviewed by Haoran Jiang [in person], 24 April.

Liou, J.-Y. (1982). Shih Hsiao-Jung wu qi lai le (Hsiao Jung Shih's martial arts are up), *Ming Sheng Daily*, 14 August, p. 9.

Ming Sheng Daily (1984). *Liang changpian gongsi chujiao shenxiang xiaoyuan* (Two record companies reached out to campus), *Min Sheng Daily*, 12 October, p. 11.

Moskowitz, M. L. (2010). *Cries of Joy, Songs of Sorrow: Chinese Pop Music and Its Cultural Connotations*, Honolulu, University of Hawai'i Press.

Negus, K. (1992). *Producing Pop: Culture and Conflict in the Popular Music Industry*, London, Arnold.

Negus, K. (1996). *Popular Music in Theory: An Introduction*, Middletown, Wesleyan University Press.

Negus, K. (1999). *Music Genres and Corporate Cultures*, London, Routledge.

Oriental Morning Post (2007). *Chyi Yu Pan Yue-Yun huanxing minge shidai jingdian yuanyin Shanghai chongxian* (Yu Chyi and Yue-Yun Pan awaken the era of folk song, the classic original sounds reappeared in Shanghai). *Sina* (website), available online from http://ent.sina.com.cn/y/2007-10-24/10341761563.shtml [accessed May 2019]

Pruett, D. B. (2011). When the tribe goes triple platinum: A case study toward an ethnomusicology of mainstream popular music in the U.S, *Ethnomusicology*, Vol 55, No 1, pp. 1–30.

Ryan, J. & Peterson, R. A. (1982). The product image: The fate of creativity in country music songwriting, in Ettema, J. S. & Whitney, D. C. (eds.) *Individuals in Mass Media Organizations: Creativity and Constraint*, Thousand Oaks, SAGE Publications, pp. 11–32.

Scheihagen, E. (2015). *Xishu jingge jinqu de gushou* (*A detailed story about the purifying songs and banned songs*), in Cheng A. *et al.* (eds.) *Zao yin fan tu: Zhanhou Taiwan shengxiang wenhua de tansuo* (*Altering Nativism – Sound Cultures in Post-War Taiwan*), Taipei, Cube, pp. 22–28.

Shelemay, K. K. (2006). Music, memory and history: In memory of Stuart Feder, *Ethnomusicology Forum*, Vol 15, No 1, pp. 17–37.

Shen, T. (ed.) (2013). Baodao huixiangqu: Zhou Lan-Ping yu sihai changpian (*Musical Recollection in Formosa: The Legend of Zhou Lan-Ping and Four Seas Records*), Taipei, National Taiwan University Press.

Shepherd, J. (1999). Text, in Swiss, T. & Horner, B. (eds.) *Key Terms in Popular Music and Culture*, Malden, Wiley-Blackwell, pp. 156–177.

Shie, S.-T. E. (2019). Jieji youguan: Guozu lunshu xingbie zhengzhi yu ziben zhuyi de wenxue zaixian (*Class That Matters: National Discourse, Gender Politics, and the Representation of Capitalism in Taiwan Literature*), Taipei, Socio Publishing.

Shih, C.-S. (2014). *Shidai shengxingqu: Chi Lu-Shyia yu Taiwan geyao niandai* (M*odern Song: Chi Lu-Shyia and Taiwanese Ballad's Era*), Taipei, Tangshan.

Tao, H.-C. (1980). *Remen yinyue ji jinyun jiang zhi ye* (Hit music, golden melody award night), *Min Sheng Daily*, 9 May, p. 5.

Tao, H.-C. & Yang, C. (eds.) (2015). *Minge 40: zaichang yiduan sixiang qi, 1975–2015 (Folk Song 40: Sing "Sixiang qi" Again, 1945–2015)*, Taipei, Locus.

Tsao, Y.-M. (2019). Interviewed by Haoran Jiang [in person], 22 March.

Tu, M.-H. (1979). *Ganlan shu tupo guonei dianying yinyue* ("Olive tree" breaks through domestic film music), *Ming Sheng Daily*, 2 September, p. 9.

Tzeng, H.-J. (1998). *Cong Liuxing gequ kan Taiwan shehui (Viewing Taiwan's Society from Popular Songs)*, Taipei, Laureate Book.

Wang, Y.-F. (2013). *Zuochu Taiwan wei: Riben xuyinqi shanghui Taiwan changpian chanzhi celue chutan* (Sounding Taiwanese: A preliminary study on the production strategy of Taiwanese records by Nippon Phonograph Company), *Journal of Chinese Ritual, Theatre and Folklore*, Vol 182, pp. 7–58.

United Daily News (1979). *Jinyun jiang geyao sai zuo juesai* (Yesterday was the final contest of golden melody award), *United Daily News*, 7 August, p. 9.

United Daily News (1984). *Wu jie jinyun jiang Pan Jhih-Cin duo guan* (Jhih-Cin Pan took the crown of the fifth Golden Melody Award). *United Daily News*, 7 July, p. 9.

Xu, J. (2006). *Minge yu guoxue: minguo zaoqi "geyao yundong" de huigui yu fansi (Folk Songs and Sinology: Review and Reflection on the "Song Movement" in the Early Republic of China)*, Chengdu, Bashu shushe.

Yang, F. C. (1994). The history of popular music in Taiwan. *Popular Music and Society*, Vol 18, No 3, pp. 53–66.

Yao, H.-S. (2012). Interviewed by Cultural Bureau of the Taipei Municipal Government, *Zishen yinyueren koushu yingyin jilu (Oral History and Audiovisual Records of Senior Musicians)*.

Yeh, Y.-Y. (1999). *Yingxiang wai de xushi celue: xiaoyuan minge yu zhengxuan dianying* (Beyond visual narration: College folk songs and policy films), *Mass Communication Research*, Vol 59, pp. 41–65.

Yu, J.-M. (2012). Interviewed by Cultural Bureau of the Taipei Municipal Government, *Zishen yinyueren koushu yingyin jilu (Oral History and Audiovisual Records of Senior Musicians)*.

DISCOGRAPHY

Chen, Ming-Shao (1978), [app] *Sanxia de shijie (World under Umbrella)*, Synco.

Cheng, I, Wang, Hsin-Lien and Ma, I-Chung (1981), [app] *Collection of I Cheng, Hsin-Lien Wang and I-Chung Ma*, Synco.

Chien, Shang-Jen *et al.* (1977), [app] *Jinyun jiang jinian zhuanji (Golden Award Melody Memorial Album)*, Synco.

Chyi, Yu (1979), [vinyl LP] *Ganlan shu (Olive Tree)*, Synco.

Guitar Chorus (1982), [app] *Album of Guitar Chorus*, Synco.

Huang, Ta-Cheng *et al.* (1979), [app] *Jinyun jiang 3* (*Golden Melody Awards 3*), Synco.

Lee, Chien-Fu (1980), [vinyl LP] *Long de chuanren* (*Descendants of the Dragon*), Synco.

Liu, Mei-Ling *et al.* (1979), [app] *Jinyun jiang 4* (*Golden Melody Awards 4*), Synco.

Pao, Mei-Sheng (1978 [2007]), [CD] *Ni zai riluo shenchu dengwo* (*You Are Waiting for Me in Deep of the Sunset*), Synco [Rock Records].

Pao, Mei-Sheng (1981), [app] *Qiaoge* (*Woodcutter Song*), Synco.

Shih, Hsiao-Jung *et al.* (1980), [app] *Jinyun jiang 5* (*Golden Melody Award 5*), Synco.

Wang, Meng-Lin (1980), [app] *Yi jia huanxi bai jia chou* (*A Happy Family and Hundreds of Sorrowful Families*), Synco.

Yang, Tsu-Chun (1979), [app] *Album of Tsu-Chun Yang*, Synco.

13

Business model innovation in the music industry

Liucija Fosseli

1 INTRODUCTION

The interest in Asian music markets has been increasing during the last decade, and especially recently, more focus has been dedicated to emerging markets such as China. China's music market went from 39th place in 2009 to 6th in 2021, according to IFPI global music markets reports (IFPI, 2009, IFPI, 2022). The enormous growth and changes within industry structures, in addition to experimentations of business models (Shen et al., 2019, Chen, 2021), make Mainland China an interesting case for music business scholars to examine. However, not only scholars see huge potential in China's music market, which is driven by the rising middle class and an increasing number of Internet users. Music creators are also looking into the Chinese market and trying to see if there are opportunities to either break into the market as an artist or produce and write songs for top artists in China.

However, although the amount of research within the field of music business in China has been increasing in the last couple of years, available sources in the English language are still scarce. In addition, the role of a songwriter is very often looked at through a singer-songwriter lens, leaving out topics of songwriting for other artists. This is especially common within the genres of K-pop in Asia, about which the research is also quite silent. Topics about collaborative songwriting are often focused on creative aspects of this type of interaction (Bennet, 2014, 2013, Gooderson and Henley, 2017, McIntyre, 2008), and just a few focus on the business side of songwriting (Blume, 2006, Pitt, 2015), especially when it comes to songwriting for other artists. Therefore, this paper aims to start a discussion about opportunities and barriers for European songwriters to write and produce songs for artists in China. I will draw on the concept of business model innovation to frame the discussion around change in the music industry and connect this concept to the existing collaboration and B2B (Business to Business) models that exist between the cooperation of European and Chinese music companies. The aim of this paper is to build a body of knowledge about European songwriters working towards China's market and identify influential factors for change through the concept of business model innovation.

DOI: 10.4324/9781003462101-15

This paper proceeds as follows: the background section will cover the notion of business model innovation and its application to the view of change within the music industry, providing an overview of relevant literature covering the music business in China. The paper ends with a discussion and conceptualization of the study's findings and suggestions for future research.

2 BACKGROUND

Business model innovation

The concept of the business model covers the way that the enterprise creates and delivers value to customers, entices customers to pay for value, and converts those payments into profit (Teece, 2010). In this context, innovation means change or improvement of the way the company is doing business. This might be driven by technological capabilities, internal motivations, competitive advantage, or other factors (Climent and Haftor, 2021). Although research on business models has spiked in the last two decades, moving from one publication in 1994 to 295 in 2017 alone, it is still 'considered to be in developing and consolidation phase regarding conceptualization, typologies, frameworks, applications, and the continuous theory development around the field' (Cuc, 2019). It was after the widespread use of the Internet, when technological inventions were becoming insufficient to create value for customers, that the focus on the 'business model' concept grew (Teece, 2010). Companies needed to rethink their strategies and their way of conducting business through the Internet, where users expected to get everything for free (Teece, 2010, Climent and Haftor, 2021). Analysis of business models, therefore, shifts the focus from the firm to 'value creation and appropriation' and multiple organizations rather than singular (Climent and Haftor, 2021).

The way business models or industries change is often related to technology, especially new technology or inventions that are becoming available to a wider population. Technological change has been widely discussed within the music business research field, putting weight on the development of technologies as the main threat and driver of change within the industry (Wikström, 2013, Hesmondhalgh, 2013, Frith and Marshall, 2004). Scholars often see inventions and development of, for example, MP3, CD-players, and P2P (Peer-to-Peer) file sharing as key drivers for change within the music industry. The discourse continues with discussions around potential developments within blockchain technology, AI, the Internet of Things, and Big Data, predicting changes it might bring to the music industry in the future (Owen and O'Dair, 2020; Torbensen and Ciriello, 2019; O'Dair and Owen, 2019).

And indeed, new technology does influence change within an industry as the technological shift also causes a dilemma for business models (Tongur and Engwall, 2014). However, framing changes within the technological realm through the concept of business model innovation might add another dimension to the discussion with a less optimistic role around technology and more weight on business decisions and organizational change. Chesbrough states that 'technology by itself has no single objective value' and that 'companies commercialize new ideas and technologies through their business models' (Chesbrough, 2010). There is a belief that the implementation of a technological innovation can have different outcomes depending on the business model that utilizes it (Chesbrough, 2010). Chesbrough (2010) draws from the research of Amit and Zott (2001) and Christensen (2003) when he explains:

> the root of tension in disruptive innovation as the conflict between the business model already established for the existing technology, and that which may be required to exploit in the emerging, disruptive technology.
>
> (Chesbrough, 2010)

He talks about barriers for experimenting on business models and that companies are not willing to change their models if it would jeopardize their current value creation. Indeed, this can be seen in a case study of the recorded music industry where Moreau (2013) argues that established players within the music industry have been reluctant to implement disruptive technologies that were not fitting or threatening to their business model. Moreover, the discussion around change and digital disruption was also addressed in a book by Nordgård (Nordgård, 2018), who concludes that changes in the music industry are more complex and go beyond the technological realm. Therefore, one could hypothesize that companies, especially in established music industries such as in the West, which hold market power, might not be willing to change their way of doing business if it would in any way threaten their current success.

China and the music business

While the core structure within music industries in the West has stayed somewhat the same for decades, in the last 20 years, China experienced enormous growth, changing core values and structures within their music industry (Shen et al., 2019, Chen, 2021). Therefore, it is not surprising that the interest in emerging markets like China is growing not only among scholars but also among businesses within the music industry. China is experimenting with their business models, and due to historical and structural differences from the Western market, China might provide a completely different outcome and structure of the industry in the future (Shen et al., 2019). However, there is still a need for more critical research in English around this topic in order to understand the dynamics and changes within the industry.

Shen et al. (2019) were the first to provide an in-depth, longitudinal study about the development of the music industry in China. The role of music has changed from an honored professional role within the government apparatus having nothing to do with commercial value to an extremely commercial industry led by tech and e-commerce companies (Shen et al.,

2019, Chen, 2021, Tang and Lyons, 2016). More recently, Zhen Troy Chen published the first book covering the contextualized development of the music business in China, dividing it into three models: the traditional proprietary model, the renegade model, and the platform ecosystem model (Chen, 2021).

The first one refers to the period from the 1980s to the 2000s after China had open-up reform, when the MCSC (Performance Rights Society in China) was established and physical consumption was still the norm. In the early 2000s, when the growth of Internet users and development in technology was increasing, consumers started to have different consumption patterns, and the market changed (Chen, 2021). The period from the late 1990s Chen (2021) is named 'The Renegade Model', which refers to unauthorized music file exchange via the Internet. China joined the WTO in 2001 and became part of the international music market, beginning to share in the development of technology that was to drive the digitalization of music (Chen, 2021). In the 'Renegade Model', music is seen as information in different digital formats and expected to be accessed for free. The last model described by Chen (2021) is the 'Ecosystem Model', which illustrates the time when major multi-platform mega apps appeared, containing both vertical and horizontal integration of services to create a fully integrated user experience.

Due to the rapid growth of platform economies as well as change within the popular music culture, demand for content surpassed supply (Zhang and Negus, 2020). According to Zhang and Negus (2020), K-pop and collaboration with Korean companies had a significant contribution to the growth of pop idol culture in the platformed industry. Cooperation with companies such as SM Entertainment (South Korean multinational entertainment agency) not only contributed to providing large amounts of content but also contributed in terms of knowledge exchange and expertise in the development of idol industries (Zhang and Negus, 2020, Ye and Kang, 2017).

The content creator's role in China's popular music industry is also viewed differently from the West's due to unique cultural differences and different developments in the industry. The music business in Mainland China first appeared through telecom companies and the growth of ringback tones (Shen et al., 2019, Chen, 2021, Zhang and Gao, 2011). Music streaming services arose from big search, e-commerce, and social messaging companies, which made it unsurprising that their view of music is different. BAT – Baidu (also a tech, search engine company), Alibaba (also a tech, e-commerce company), and Tencent (also a social messaging, tech company) are the biggest players in the music industry in China. It seems that these companies view music as content and part of the value chain that attracts customers to their services (Tang and Lyons, 2016, Shen et al., 2019). However, the core business of these companies is merely focused on the music itself, rather than on the additional services connected to the commodification of music (Montgomery, 2009, Shen et al., 2019).

The effect of these structures and focus on content providers has not been the focus of the research so far due to long-lasting piracy issues, which made it impossible to earn royalties from music. However, when it comes to B2B interactions between European creators and Chinese companies, a sustainable copyright environment is of extreme importance. Ironically, the notion of copyright took shape in China earlier than in many countries in the West (Morrow and Li, 2016). However, up until the government intervention in 2015 (Operation Sword Net), China was known for its well-established piracy environment (Shen et al., 2019, Montgomery, 2009). The Copyright Law of the People's Republic of China was first drawn in 1990, with smaller amendments in 2001 and 2010 (Chen, 2021). However, the biggest change in copyright law in China in the last 20 years came in 2020 and has been in effect since June 2021 (Zhang and Barata, 2021). This was the biggest revision of copyright law since its establishment and reinforced the protection 'in regard to the scope of copyrightable work, it also redefined fair use exceptions, authorization of technical protection measures, and heightened damage provisions' (Zhang and Barata, 2021). Although the effect of this change is yet to be seen, one can be hopeful that this might result in a better environment for creators and copyright owners in China.

3 METHODOLOGY

To investigate the current situation of European songwriters and producers working toward China's market, this study conducted qualitative semi-structured interviews within a chosen network of individuals who were pioneers in establishing contact with Chinese music companies. The interviewees included a European multi-platinum producer who lived and worked as a songwriter/producer in China for a period of time, a European music publisher who was one of the first ones to build and maintain a relationship with Chinese music companies, and two industry experts from two different music/content-related companies in China.

The identity of respondents is kept anonymous to get an honest account of existing business interactions. The data contains five hours of individual interview material with four respondents, which were collected digitally on Zoom and recorded on an audio recorder following the guidelines of the Norwegian Agency for Shared Services in Education and Research. The interview material was then transcribed and clustered. This study chose an inductive approach where the concepts and theories were conceptualized after the interview data was collected. Since the qualitative method is known to provide a rich account of a situation (Polit and Beck, 2010), the purpose of interview data was not to get generalizable results but to get in-depth, experience-based insight into the business practices and interactions between European songwriters and Chinese music companies.

Throughout the findings and discussion section, respondents will be referred to as 'Producer' and 'Publisher'. Since the identity of industry experts from China is held anonymous, they will be referred to as 'Industry Expert 1' and 'Industry Expert 2'. Findings are clustered into four categories: 'Background', 'Business Models', 'Platforms and Power Dynamics', and 'Challenges of working with Chinese Companies'.

4 FINDINGS

Background

During the interviews, respondents noted that for a long time, doing business within the music industry in China was challenging as music companies lacked an understanding of the European copyright system, including the meaning of publishing and copyright. They noted that the new generation in China is growing up listening more to world music, and the growing middle class have more disposable income now than they did before. In addition, due to the increasing numbers of Internet users, local music platforms are in constant need for new content (Publisher and Industry Expert 1). China's popular music is grounded in ballads and just in recent years, moved to world music and K-pop style music, which was a quick change for local writers to follow. Local songwriters were still more used to writing traditional songs, while the market needs shifted to solo pop artists and idol-culture music (Publisher and Industry Expert 1). As the interaction between Chinese and European companies increased, the skills of writing world music for songwriters, in addition to under-standing Western rules and norms for Chinese companies, increased as well (Publisher). European producers can produce quality music quickly, which is very appealing to Chinese companies (Industry Expert 1).

The need for local content has also increased after K-pop idols were unofficially banned in China and local music companies started produc-ing their own K-pop style music. Zhang and Negus noted that this might be a result of the 'deployment of Terminal High Altitude Area in Korea in 2016' (Zhang and Negus, 2020) and the increased tension because of that. This brought losses for Korean talent agencies (Kil, 2017). However, Publisher also notes that this created more opportunities for Chinese com-panies to develop their own talents and increase their market share, which also contributes to less income from entertainment industry leaving the country.

Business models

Although it seems that the copyright system is improving significantly, the respondents note that working as a songwriter or producer in China is still challenging as they do not have a good system for paying royalties to songwriters. 'While working with music companies in China, you always run into difficulties that you never even thought about' (Producer). As an example, Publisher mentioned that:

> Whenever we do a deal with a Chinese company, there is a govern-ment export tax agency that needs to approve everything; otherwise, the bank doesn't have permission to send the money out of the coun-try. There is a lot of paperwork, and they need to know exactly why the money is leaving the country . . . it has been especially strict dur-ing the Covid-19 pandemic.
>
> (Publisher)

Business models between songwriters and companies in China vary, but historically, the most popular model has been a buyout. However, the more used term in recent years has been a 'publishing advance', which in theory means that a songwriter does not sell rights to the copyright but is given an 'advance' until the day a copyright system is in place and working. According to these companies, you will then be able to collect royalties for your music. 'But it does not really work like that in China – if you don't ask, you don't pay and get paid' (Publisher and Producer). 'You usually read between the lines and take the money with no expectation to see any royalties in the future' (Producer). It seems that there are no standards while working with Chinese music companies, and European companies and songwriters need to improvise to create their own standards and norms.

> What you usually do is go for a buyout or publishing advance, 'first use' mechanical license, anything you can have some sort of mutual understanding about.
>
> (Publisher)

When it comes to the advances paid for content creators, it varies, but songwriters are usually able to get around $10,000 for a song, of which 50% is going to the publisher ('Which is smart since a publisher is often involved in the deal, so they just keep half of it' – Producer) and then the last $5,000 is split between the songwriters. If there are two, each ends up with $2,500. 'It's not something you can get rich off of and you can get more in Europe by just doing productions' (Producer). However, Publisher notes that it depends on how you look at it:

> It depends on how you look at it. If you make a song or two a day, making a couple thousand dollars might be okay. I mean, it's the same in Europe; if your song is not a huge hit, if it is not on the radio or at least in the top 50 on Spotify, then the songwriter maybe makes a thousand dollars or two. Also, all the songs we 'sell' in China are registered in the copyright societies (MCSC in China), and there is some small money coming from it.
>
> (Publisher)

The diversity of business models that companies use is widespread, and some companies even have songwriters as full-time employees who produce around two songs a day and do not own rights to the songs they make (Producer and Industry Expert 1). However, although the music business is very different from what European companies are used to, Publisher mentions the importance of mutual respect and understanding of the two systems to be able to work with Chinese companies.

Platforms and power dynamics

When it comes to platforms, business models differ as well. For example, although not a lot of companies admit it, Tencent almost exclusively works with buyouts, and it seems that the power is situated within platform companies. As Industry Expert 1 noted:

> content companies are not able to put a price on the song, it is the platform that comes up with the price, and we need to accept it or not. . . .
> Platforms have the power in China because they have the access to distribution. Some companies invest and produce 20,000 songs a month, so they have a lot of content to offer for companies, and the number of these companies is huge. Therefore, your number of published songs has to be the best. If you publish over 1,000 songs a year, you are the main vendor for the platform.
>
> (Industry Expert 1)

Companies working with content creators usually own the copyright from songwriters for a year, during which time they can sell their music to a platform.

> When we pitch a song, it goes very quick. The platform has staff, and they have listening sessions every week where they use both the feedback from the staff and AI to help choose the songs. Privacy laws are not the same in China as in Europe, so they have large numbers of Big Data of their users and capabilities of analyzing those. They know very clearly what their customers like and what kind of melody they prefer, so 60% of the decision goes to AI and 40% to the staff. It is kind of a fairer system since you avoid the under-the-table deals.
>
> (Industry Expert 1)

When it comes to economics within platform companies, Publisher noted that platforms take 50%, then, by law, 42% goes to the record label, and then 8% for the publisher to share with the songwriters. 'It is worse than in Europe but not that worse' (Publisher). It is, however, the label and the platform who are the ones that make money in these structures. Although the population size is much higher than in many other countries, and getting millions of streams on a platform is not that difficult, the amount of money users pay for platforms is also smaller. However, some areas in the industry are better than others:

> From the publishing side, sync works very well, and you can receive thousands of Euros every year (for example, televised music concerts and music galas). The big TV companies, which use music for live broadcast, know they need to pay for music.
>
> (Publisher)

Challenges of working with Chinese companies

Transparency is still a huge issue in China.

> Even if you get per-play money from a platform company in China, it is still not transparent, and you just get the money without the details why, so transparency is still a huge problem.
>
> (Industry Expert 1)

When asked about the challenges of working with European songwriters, Industry Expert 1 from China noted:

> Yes, some companies are also organizing writers from the States and Europe to write for the top artists. However, the numbers of these are not high. I do not have exact numbers, but it is in the hundreds compared to 20,000 songs per company that some companies produce. The problem usually is that Europeans do not know what the market in China needs and what songs we need. Therefore, we try to be very specific about the briefs of the songs, try to explain the background, the culture, so it is easier to understand. It works best for Europeans to write for artists that are not that famous; some independent artists who have their own style and are like the ones in Europe, they can write for them. If it's jazz or reggae, then writing for them suits best, but it is not a mass market.
>
> (Industry Expert 1)

There are private companies within the music industry in China that try to solve some of the problems with remunerations for content creators:

> There are companies in China that make audio fingerprints for every track needing monitoring and use AI-based technologies to acquire audio file samples and match the files (including original, cover, and UGC [user generated content] versions) in music platforms and video platforms. However, companies working with this service have three main issues. The first is that the client's music metadata is not complete, and they need to spend a lot of time to find the original audio file and the writer's information. And another problem is that the digitalization in the Chinese music industry is not high. Lots of data are kept in a traditional way. Lastly, music platforms and video platforms, short video platforms (like TikTok in China) do not provide usage data transparently, not like YouTube, Spotify, or TikTok outside China. Tencent and NetEase Cloud music take the monopoly position and do not want to share the data. But besides Tencent, NetEase, and TikTok, there are more and more medium and small apps appearing in China to do live-streaming, online Karaoke, or Chinese clubhouse.
>
> (Industry Expert 2)

It seems that there is a paradox in the music industry in China between the extreme technical capabilities of platforms (application of AI and analysis of Big Data) and on the other side the lack of digital capabilities (lack of transparency in usage data and digital database of writers' information). This example confirms that companies are reluctant to implement technologies that might harm their business model and, therefore, implement changes that fit their current way of doing business and their value creation model. However, this area and application of the concept of business model innovation is still in need of further research using a broader range of case studies and examples of business models within Chinese and Western music companies to confirm the hypothesis.

5 DISCUSSION

In the traditional comprehension of business model innovation, the value stems from both the supply and demand interactions. This study looked particularly at the supply dimension, analyzing business models between European songwriters and Chinese music companies and showing the nuances of these interactions. Interviews revealed that transparency is still one of the main issues when collecting remuneration for music. Music platforms use highly complex technology in analyzing user data and applying it to narrow down the potential content for the platform, while availability and transparency of this data are still not available for content providers' companies. Therefore, one could draw a conclusion that the situation is not merely grounded in technological challenges but rather highly dependent on the business model of the platform. This complements the theory that the technology implemented within a business model of a company reflects strategy, values, and economic models already existing within a company (Teece, 2010). Therefore, research predicting the future of the music industry should investigate both the R&D (Research and Development) strategies of dominant firms in addition to the ambitions of the newcomers. For example, some sources report that 66% of Tencent's' employees are in the R&D department (Zhang, 2020). Considering the power that the company has, there is a high probability that its R&D direction is an important factor for the innovation in the music business in China.

Also, from the literature and interviews, it seems that within platform companies in China, value is generated not only from the product itself (music) but also, probably even more significantly, from products and services around it (add-ons) (Tang and Lyons, 2016, Shen et al., 2019). Therefore, an additional dimension of 'value appropriation', in addition to 'value creation' (using add-ons), should be added to the concept of business model innovation. Value appropriation in music platforms is more complex than the traditional supply chain position and covers the acquisition of content through music content providers. This process is more complex than in a regular business, and from interview data, we see that the appropriation of the content contains a lot of different business models varying from songwriters getting a salary, using buyouts, publishing advances, and other models. There is a probability that changes within existing models might increase the price of the service in general and complexify the utilization of the add-on services. Therefore, it could be stated that the change in the model of appropriation of value would influence the value creation model.

After the termination of exclusive licensing deals in China (Shen et al., 2019), relying on the add-on services, in terms of competitiveness, even increased since it decreased heterogeneity between platform companies (Montgomery, 2009, Shen et al., 2019). Although Tencent and NetEase are adding value creation through the introduction of self-releasing functions for artists (Qu et al., 2021), royalty deals and possible remuneration for the music are still unclear. However, the situation is two-dimensional. On the one hand, the Chinese music platforms offer enormous commodification opportunities for artists to expand, communicate with, and grow their fan-base (Qu et al., 2021). On the other hand, it devalues creators, placing the music as merely a commodity and a product, and doesn't really benefit the songwriter's profession. However, for some writers, the current buy-out/publishing advance model might be acceptable when one takes into consideration the collection of royalties in Europe from songs that are not huge hits. Future research should exploit different business models look-ing into the contextualized probability of music platforms in China imple-menting an alternative model for the acquisition of content that would not jeopardize their current value creation.

The findings of the study also suggest that the B2B cooperation between European and Chinese music companies, in addition to the external (inter-national pressure and laws) and internal factors (motivation for international cooperation and knowledge growth, national laws, company's business models, and values in addition to local creators' capabilities), has an influ-ence on change within music business models in China. However, although platforms are dependent on content to attract customers, content creators do not have the negotiation power against platforms (as it was stated in the findings section). Taking into consideration the development of the music business in China, which is grounded in piracy issues (Shen et al., 2019, Montgomery, 2009), one could draw an assumption that 'something is better than nothing'. Historically, it has been difficult to get money from Chinese companies, and therefore, the deals that are being made also take into con-sideration the alternative – legal battles that would cost significant amounts of money. As the music businesses in China develops and the implementa-tion of copyright increases among music companies, the situation might be very different in the next five years from now.

As mentioned before, it seems that power over the price and distribution is situated within the platforms. However, if one of the big platform com-panies would implement a different strategy and business model, which would be more attractive for content providers, the company could get a competitive advantage in terms of access to a wider amount of con-tent. Therefore, it could be stated that business models within platform companies in the industry could have a significant effect on the formation of the industry. This would put the business model as a causation of the industry structure. In their research on the internationalization of Chinese enterprises, Alon et al. (2018) found that decisions and strategies for the internationalization of enterprises are often dependent on the company's capabilities and the government's ambitions in China. Therefore, by put-ting the emphasis on the company's strategies rather than the industry at large, scholars might be able to get a better understanding of the dynamics and influences within the music industry in China.

6 CONCLUSION

This study looked at business models between European producers and publishers who work toward the Chinese music industry. It provided an overview of the Chinese music industry in addition to business models and conditions for European songwriters to work within that market. Since the study is limited to a few interviews, it provides a unique opportunity for further research to expand, contextualize, and use the findings of this paper to continue building the body of knowledge in this area.

Although this paper analyzes the business model concept focusing on Mainland China, business models within the Western music industry have also been criticized and need further critical analysis (Pitt, 2015). The discussion around music businesses and platform economies is often based on the consensus that current models are not 'fair' for content creators (Nowak and Morgan, 2021). However, to find a 'fair' business model, I invite scholars to contextualize and expand the business model innovation concept, fitting in the complexities of the international music business, and discuss possible sustainable business models for the future.

REFERENCES

Alon, I., Anderson, J., Munim, Z.H. and Ho, A., 2018. A review of the internationalization of Chinese enterprises. *Asia Pacific Journal of Management, 35*(3), pp. 573–605.

Amit, R. and Zott, C., 2001. Value creation in e - business. *Strategic Management Journal, 22*(6–7), pp. 493–520.

Bennett, J., 2013. "You won't see me": In search of an epistemology of collaborative songwriting. *Journal on the Art of Record Production, 8.*

Bennet, J., 2014. *Constraint, creativity, copyright and collaboration in popular songwriting teams.* University of Surrey.

Blume, J., 2006. *This business of songwriting.* Random House Digital, Inc.

Chen, Z.T., 2021. *China's music industry unplugged: Business models, copyright and social entrepreneurship in the online platform economy.* Palgrave Macmillan.

Chesbrough, H., 2010. Business model innovation: Opportunities and barriers. *Long Range Planning, 43*(2–3), pp. 354–363.

Christensen, C.M., 2003. *The innovator's dilemma: The revolutionary book that will change the way you do business.* HarperCollins.

Climent, R.C. and Haftor, D.M., 2021. Value creation through the evolution of business model themes. *Journal of Business Research, 122*, pp. 353–361.

Cuc, J.E., 2019. Trends of business model research: A bibliometric analysis. *Journal of Business Models, 7*(5), pp. 1–24.

Frith, S. and Marshall, L. eds., 2004. *Music and copyright* (p. vi218). Edinburgh University Press.

Gooderson, M. and Henley, J., 2017. Professional songwriting: Creativity, the creative process and tensions between higher education songwriting and industry practice in the UK. In *The Routledge research companion to popular music education* (pp. 257–271). Routledge.

Hesmondhalgh, D. 2013. *The cultural industries.* Sage.

IFPI, 2009. *Digital music report 2009.* Available at: www.pro-musicabr.org.br/wp-content/uploads/2015/01/DMR2009.pdf (Accessed: 16 January 2023)

IFPI, 2022. *IFPI global music report.* Available at: www.ifpi.org/resources/ (Accessed: 16 January 2023)

KIL, S. 2017. China's blockade of cultural Korea marks troublesome anniversary. *Variety*, August 24.

McIntyre, P., 2008. Creativity and cultural production: A study of contemporary Western popular music songwriting. *Creativity Research Journal, 20*(1), pp. 40–52.

Montgomery, L., 2009. Space to grow: Copyright, cultural policy and commercially - focused music in China. *Chinese Journal of Communication, 2*(1), pp. 36–49.

Moreau, F., 2013. The disruptive nature of digitization: The case of the recorded music industry. *International Journal of Arts Management, 15*(2).

Morrow, G. and Li, F., 2016. The Chinese music industries: Top down in the bottom-up age. In *Business innovation and disruption in the music industry*. Edward Elgar Publishing.

Nordgård, D., 2018. *The music business and digital impacts: Innovations and disruptions in the music industries*. Springer.

Nowak, R. and Morgan, B.A., 2021. New model, same old stories? *Music and Democracy*, p. 61.

O'Dair, M. and Owen, R., 2019. Financing new creative enterprise through blockchain technology: Opportunities and policy implications. *Strategic Change, 28*(1), pp. 9–17.

Owen, R. and O'Dair, M., 2020. How blockchain technology can monetize new music ventures: An examination of new business models. *The Journal of Risk Finance, 21*(4), pp. 333–353.

Pitt, I.L., 2015. *Direct licensing and the music industry*. Springer International Publishing.

Polit, D.F. and Beck, C.T., 2010. Generalization in quantitative and qualitative research: Myths and strategies. *International Journal of Nursing Studies, 47*(11), pp. 1451–1458.

Qu, S., Hesmondhalgh, D. and Xiao, J., 2021. Music streaming platforms and self-releasing musicians: The case of China. *Information, Communication & Society*, pp. 1–17.

Shen, X., Zheng, S., Liu, Y., Williams, R., Li, Y. and Gerst, M., 2019. Online music in China. *Technol Forecast Soc Change, 139*, pp. 235–249.

Tang, D. and Lyons, R., 2016. An ecosystem lens: Putting China's digital music industry into focus. *Global Media and China, 1*(4), pp. 350–371.

Teece, D.J., 2010. Business models, business strategy and innovation. *Long Range Planning, 43*(2–3), pp. 172–194.

Tongur, S. and Engwall, M., 2014. The business model dilemma of technology shifts. *Technovation, 34*(9), pp. 525–535.

Torbensen, A. and Ciriello, R., 2019, June. Tuning into blockchain: Challenges and opportunities of blockchain-based music platforms. In *Twenty-Seventh European Conference on Information Systems (ECIS2019)*. Stockholm-Uppsala, Sweden.

Wikström, P. 2013. *The music industry: Music in the cloud*. Polity Press.

Ye, W. and Kang, S.H., 2017. The evolved survival of Sm Entertainment in the Chinese market: Legitimation strategies and organizational survival. *Kritika Kultura*, 29.

Zhang, B. and Barata, J. 2021. *Copyright law of the people's Republic of China (2020 Amendment). 3rd amendment to copyright law.* https://wilmap.stanford.edu/node/31101 (Accessed: 16 January 2023)

Zhang, M.Y. and Gao, J., 2011. The take-off of an interactive innovation: Evidence from China. *Technological Forecasting and Social Change*, 78(7), pp. 1115–1129.

Zhang, P. 2020. Tencent says 66% of its employees were in R&D in 2019. *Cntechpost.* https://cntechpost.com/2020/03/09/tencent-66-employees-in-rd/ (Accessed: 16 January 2023)

Zhang, Q. and Negus, K., 2020. East Asian pop music idol production and the emergence of data fandom in China. *International Journal of Cultural Studies*, 23(4), pp. 493–511.

14

Yellow music in diaspora

Re-inventing the sound of pre-1975 record production in Sài Gòn

Nguyễn Thanh Thủy, Stefan Östersjö, and Matt Wright

1 INTRODUCTION

This chapter outlines the history of record production in the south of Vietnam and its relation to *yellow music*, a form of popular music that thrived in the colonial urban metropolis of Sài Gòn until the fall of the city in 1975. This music became an important feature of diasporic Vietnamese culture and has retained its popularity until the present day. In later years, interest in the pre-1975 recordings from the scene in Sài Gòn has emerged among Western labels, as seen in the series of releases in the *Saigon Supersound* series (2017, 2018).

With this historical backdrop as a point of departure, the chapter seeks to unpack the artistic processes of creating experimental versions of pre-1975 *yellow music* songs while also approaching the sound of the original recordings in a project with the intercultural group The Six Tones and the turntable improviser and composer Matt Wright. The group has created several multimedia productions with Wright since the creation of the installation and performance work Inside/Outside in 2012 (Nguyễn, 2019). In the recording project with *yellow music*, the group engaged two Vietnamese singers living in diaspora, Lâm Mỹ Lệ in Denmark and Ngô Hồng Gấm in Australia. The Six Tones are Nguyễn Thanh Thủy (a *đàn tranh* player) and Ngô Trà My (a *đàn bầu* player), two Vietnamese performers, and the Swedish guitarist Stefan Östersjö. Since 2006, The Six Tones has been a platform for an encounter between traditional and experimental cultures in Asia and the West. Since the group was created, we have been collaborating with the composer and improviser Henrik Frisk, who has had an important role in the *yellow music* project, both as a saxophone player and in the design of electronic parts.

The artistic research, as well as the new album of *yellow music*, which the chapter discusses, has been documented and analysed as part of Nguyễn Thanh Thủy's postdoctoral artistic research project "Music and Identity in Diaspora: novel perspectives on female Vietnamese immigrants in Scandinavia". The project is funded by the Swedish Research Council.

DOI: 10.4324/9781003462101-16

2 BACKGROUND

2.1 *Yellow music*: a historical perspective

The development of popular music in Vietnam is immediately connected to the impact of colonisation, which entailed the context of the two Indochina Wars (1946–1954 and 1955–1975, the latter often referred to as the "Vietnam War" in the West). The origin of the First Indochina War was the political situation at the end of World War II. While France saw the opportunity to fully "return to Indochina, the Việt Minh's long-term strategic plan remained focused on ensuring the complete elimination of French colonialism in Indochina" (Moir, 2021, p. 141). The Second Indochina War followed the split of the country into the northern "Democratic Republic of Vietnam" and the southern "State of Vietnam" (in 1955, turned into the Republic of Vietnam), which was the outcome of the defeat of the French and the Geneva Accords in 1954.

After the Second World War, French popular and patriotic songs became popular with urban Vietnamese audiences and were first introduced as an element in the hybridised form of 'reformed' theatre called *Cải Lương* (Gibbs, 2003). Starting in 1930, the French established radio stations both in Sài Gòn and Hà Nội which became important exponents, both for Western music as well as for traditional and new forms of Vietnamese music coloured by Western influence (DeWald, 2012; Ó Briain, 2021). At around the same time, Western motion pictures began to appear, and Gibbs (2003) suggests that these were the reason for a second wave of interest in French songs, which led to performances of French songs in Vietnamese translation, often by the same actors as found in *Cải Lương* theatres. As a counterreaction to this, in the late 1930s, Vietnamese composers began creating original compositions in Western style, a musical form often referred to as *nhạc tiền chiến* (pre-war music). This became the beginning of *tân nhạc*, which could be translated as "new" or "modern" music, and which is a form of compositions that rest on tonal harmony but can often have pentatonic melodies, as is characteristic of traditional Vietnamese music.

During the first Indochina War (1946–1954), the nature of *tân nhạc* songs changed, and many composers wrote patriotic songs, or "resistance music" as termed by Henry (2005), rather than the love songs typical of the pre-war period. In this period, the most prolific and multifarious composer of *tân nhạc* became famous, as he produced resistance music in primitive *Việt Minh* camps near the military front (Henry, 2005).

Dale Olsen (2008) summarises the influence of Western music in Vietnamese urban music cultures in the early twentieth century by observing how "French colonial period dance bands were common in urban areas, as they provided entertainment for the French and Vietnamese elite, and American-style Vietnamese rock bands were popular during the American War as entertainment for American soldiers" (p. 95). Such bands contributed to developing the sound of *nhạc vàng* as the record industry in the south of Vietnam kept thriving in the colonial metropolis of Sài Gòn all the way up to the end of the Second Indochina War in 1975. Olsen (2008) further observes how many different terms have been applied to similar and related music, *nhạc trẻ* (youth music) being the most overarching term for popular music in Vietnam and is still today. The difficulties involved in defining the use of the many different terminologies are captured by Olsen in this definition of *nhạc trẻ*:

> Because the term means youth music, its usage expanded to include soft [or light] rock styles as well, and in 1981 *nhạc trẻ* was used for rock'n'roll which was also called *yellow music* (generally, however *yellow music* or *nhạc vàng* is the term ascribed to the southern Vietnamese sentimental songs from the period before the reunification of Vietnam in 1975).
>
> (Olsen, 2008, p. 6)

After the Fall of Saigon in 1975, which marked the end of the Vietnam War, many sentimental pop songs were banned by the Vietnamese communist party, who labelled them as *yellow music*. The use of the term *yellow music* may have had origins in China, where campaigns against bourgeois music cultures used the term in the early 1950s. The clash between the "revolutionary" culture of the north – between the anti-colonialist songs promoted as *red music* by the northern government on the one hand and what has come to be called *yellow music* of the south – was strong during the war. As part of the propaganda against the latter, a series of articles were published in the monthly magazine *Văn Hóa Nghệ Thuật* (Culture and Arts), which established an official definition of *yellow music*. In the very first of these, the composer/researcher Tô Vũ defined *yellow music* as a cultural expression, the overall effect of which was "to evoke in hapless listeners a gloomy, embittered, impotent and cynical mood towards life, an attitude negating youth's desire to be cheerful, a sensation of being drowned in loneliness in a withered and desolate world" (Tô Vũ cited in Taylor, 2001, p. 43).

However, since the music continued to be secretly performed and listened to within the country, the ban failed to achieve its aims. As mentioned previously, refugees from Vietnam brought this music with them and created a successful overseas Vietnamese music industry, first in France and the US, but later also reaching communities of Vietnamese immigrants all around the world. Hence, and with reference to the citation from Olsen (2008), we will in this chapter use the term *yellow music* for pre-1975 southern music, as well as for the diasporic music created by the Vietnamese after the Fall of Saigon.

2.2 A brief history of record production in the south of Vietnam

Already in the early twentieth century, the gramophone had become the major source for access to recorded music in Vietnam, and, as noted by Lonán Ó Briain (2021, p. 32), "newspaper advertisements for gramophones targeted both European settlers and indigenous consumers from around 1910 onwards". The earliest audio recordings in Vietnam were made by

Western labels, like the German Pathé and American Victor labels, making recordings of traditional music. The great pioneer of the record industry in the south of Vietnam was Ngô Văn Mạnh, a.k.a. Thầy Năm Mạnh (ca. 1908–1957). His brother-in-law, who had learnt the techniques for the entire production chain of vinyl records in France in the 1930s, passed this knowledge on to him. In 1936, Năm Mạnh purchased equipment for record production, mainly from the Pathé label, and built his own studio (Phạm, 2015). The first release on his label Asia was a recording of *Vọng Cổ*, released in 1936 or 1937 (Gibbs *et al.*, 2013). By producing more affordable records thanthe Western labels, the Asia label soon dominated the market in the south of Vietnam. The Asia catalogue consisted of music from traditional theatre, with a focus on theatre music of *Tuồng* and *Cải Lương* and its centrepiece, *Vọng Cổ* (Đông, 2021; Östersjö, 2022).

While traditional music remained as equally popular as Western music, for instance, in the broadcasts of Radio Saigon (DeWald, 2012), a new development was emerging on the music scene at the beginning of the 1950s. In his memoirs, the composer Phạm Duy – without doubt, the most influential composer of popular song in Vietnamese music history – notes how in 1951, the *Đĩa Hát Việt Nam* label, run by Lê Văn Tài, had become a reason for composers and performers to move south, since he had started recording not only traditional music but also Western-influenced popular song (*tân nhạc*) (Phạm, 1991). Lê Văn Tài's primary label was called *Đĩa Hát Việt Nam*, but they also had several sub-labels (Phạm, 2015, 2017).

Around the same time, Năm Mạnh's brother-in-law started *Sóng Nhạc*, a sub-label to Asia that would focus on Vietnamese popular music, and moved from the 78 rpm records, first to 45 rpm and eventually also 33 rpm records. Their recording studio was located at 37 Phạm Ngũ Lão Quận 1, where they also pressed the vinyl. By 1960, *Sóng Nhạc* had exclusive contracts with four

Figure 14.1 A release of *Tứ Quý* 2 in quadrophonic mix, recorded and mixed in Pat Lâm studio, released in 1971.

Source: Photo by Nguyễn Đức Dũng, printed with permission

leading singers of *yellow music* – Phương Dung, Thanh Thúy, Trúc Mai, and Minh Hiếu – and thereby strengthened their role in the emerging market for Vietnamese pop music in Sài Gòn: a position which it maintained until the early 1970s when vinyl records were replaced by more affordable compact cassettes, at which point the label closed down. Many of their recordings were, however, re-released by other labels, and therefore remained on the market. But the shift to tape also created novel possibilities that the record companies and artists were quick to exploit, and, in parallel with the releases of affordable compact cassettes, issues of reel-to-reel tape were also released commercially. In an interview with the collector Nguyễn Đức Dũng, we found that during a shorter period between 1970 and 1971, many of these releases were also made available in quadrophonic mixes, one of which can be seen in Figure 14.1.

2.3 The shotguns and the popular music scene up to the fall of saigon in 1975

A central figure in the development of the pop music industry in Sài Gòn was Nguyễn Ngọc Chánh. He was the founder of the Shotguns, a group that recorded many of the most famous *yellow music* songs with most of the most famous singers in the genre. The name of the group refers to the 1965 R&B hit by Jr. Walker released on Gordy's Soul Records, a subsidiary of Motown Records. This funky dance song (actually inspired by a dance called The Shotgun), with the prominence given to Jr. Walker's sax playing, suggests some of the influences on the sound of the Vietnamese group. But The Shotguns developed a sound that combined soul and R&B influences with sophisticated arrangements, weaving together elements from traditional Vietnamese music with a range of Western popular music genres from jazz to popular song.

In 1968, life in Sài Gòn changed radically, with the Tết Offensive starting on January 30. This series of surprise attacks in more than a hundred towns and cities was the largest military operation of the war thus far. Even if it was largely a failure for the northern side, it had many different consequences which are beyond the scope of this chapter, but for the fact that it caused a great crisis in the music business. All clubs were closed down, and the only remaining option for musicians to work was to play in the clubs of the American military. With the good contacts in the USO (United Services Organisation) provided by the singer Pat Lâm, Nguyễn Ngọc Chánh was invited to start a new group to play covers of American rock and soul music in several venues. This opportunity became the reason for the formation of the first edition of The Shotguns.

But, as observed by Phạm Duy (1991), it was the innovative use of audio recording technology that eventually created the fame of the group. Indeed, The Shotguns was not just a band but also a platform for audio production. In 1969, under the same name, Ngọc Chánh also started a label, joined by a sound engineer recruited from Radio Saigon. In The Shotguns, as a group and a record label, Ngọc Chánh played many roles as producer, keyboard player, arranger, and leader of the band.

In 1969, after the relatively unsuccessful release of the first volume with The Shotguns, Ngọc Chánh wanted to shift direction towards

Figure 14.2 A poster advertising a performance with Khánh Ly and The Shotguns (as well as advertising the extraordinary audio quality in the club) at Queen Bee.

Source: Trần (2017)

recording the pre-war songs that were popular with the upper-class Vietnamese audience in Sài Gòn, leaving the market as an American cover band. The Shotguns was one of the labels to introduce reel-to-reel tape in their studio, and therefore, also marked the transition to releasing compact cassettes rather than vinyl records. However, as discussed by Ngọc Chánh in an interview (Trịnh, 2017), it seemed that the choice of this new technology was out of sync with the intended audience. By shifting the repertoire to pre-war songs, the upper-class audience with access to technology could be reached. The success of this strategy became clear with the release of The Shotguns Vol 6 in July 1970, which marked the public breakthrough of the group. Around the same time, The Shotguns began to appear at the Queen Bee venue with Khánh Ly, one of the greatest stars of *yellow music*, and the transition was a fact (see Figure 14.2). In the following three years, the group played regularly at Queen Bee, inviting all of the leading singers of *yellow music*, including Thanh Thúy, Elvis Phương, and Dạ Hương. This club played a central role in the scene in Sài Gòn, advertising the high-end quality of their stereo sound system. In parallel with the live sessions every night at Queen Bee, Ngọc Chánh also produced an extensive series of over 30 releases with The Shotguns. Ngọc Chánh left Vietnam as a boat refugee in 1978 and arrived in the USA in 1979. By the end of this year, he reunited

The Shotguns, regularly playing at Maxim's discotheque in San Jose, California. In the next section, we will consider the history of *Yêu Một Mình*, one of the many songs recorded by The Shotguns, but now our focus turns to how The Six Tones have sought to experiment with the musical materials and the audio production of such original *yellow music* recorded before 1975.

2.4 *Yêu Một Mình*: a historical recording

Yêu Một Mình is a song composed by Trịnh Lâm Ngân, a collaborative songwriting group made up of Trần Trịnh and Nhật Ngân. The piece was first recorded by Chế Linh and released on *Đĩa Hát Việt Nam* in 1970 (Trịnh, 1970a). The piece was recorded by Trần Trịnh group and features a striking arrangement for a string orchestra. In particular, the ostinato in the instrumental introduction, which continues at the beginning of the first version, provides a surprising setting for the song. In 1972, a recording with the singer Dạ Hương was released in the Shotguns series. This recording constituted a public breakthrough for this young singer, although her career lasted only three years, until the Fall of Saigon in 1975. Dạ Hương's recording with The Shotguns was re-released in the US on the *Bốn Phương* label in 1986 (Trịnh, 1970b).

The Six Tones selected the recording with Dạ Hương and The Shotguns, much due to the striking instrumental parts and the sound production, which separates all instruments in a manner quite typical of early stereo production. In particular, we were attracted by the instrumental introduction and how it leads up to a beat which was sampled for further processing. But the rendering of the vocal part, including the choice of basic tempo, was also a reference in our work.

The use of sampling in this project reflects not so much the trans-Pacific communication between Vietnam and the Western US, but a parallel mid-twentieth century postcolonial exchange in the other direction, in this case between the Eastern US, the Caribbean, the UK, and the wider African diaspora, termed by Paul Gilroy as the Black Atlantic (Gilroy, 1993). Within this wider context, a vibrant musical network developed, and the techniques of Jamaican sound system culture, particularly the technique of *versioning* – whereby a popular song is remixed, manipulated, and reused by DJs in a form of sonic exchange – lay the ground for the use of sampling and remixing in hip hop from the early 1970s and drum n' bass from the early 1990s (Veal, 2007). Early forms of drum n' bass are almost entirely based upon samples of a six-second drum loop (known as the Amen break) to the point at which the concept of musical borrowing fails, and one might speak of a language of sampling, integral to the sonic identity of the music (Harrison, 2004). Many of the critical debates around sample culture are mirrored in early twentieth-century discussions of collage, the readymade and the assemblage being explored by the visual art avant garde, where the questioning of the authorship (a kind of ethical border crossing) becomes a fundamental tension within the experience of the artwork (Kelly, 2008).

Authorial rights in the pre-1975 popular music in the south of Vietnam is a complex matter. While the record industry was well organised, and musicians and composers indeed received royalties for their work, the legislation regarding intellectual property was not as strict as it is today (SoulGook, 2017). Further, since the industry was largely destroyed at the end of the war, with many producers and artists leaving the country for a life in diaspora, it is not trivial to obtain rights for using recorded materials, such as the sample of *Yêu Một Mình* discussed in this chapter. Ngọc Chánh, who was the copyright holder of the Shotguns label, has passed away, and although it is known that he generously shared pre-1975 materials and releases without restrictions (Nguyễn, 2023), at the time of writing, the process of obtaining rights to the recording is still in progress.

2.5 Negotiations of voice in studio production

The artistic interactions between musicians, producers, and engineers in the recording studio have still been relatively little researched, although the field has been developing quickly since the early 2000s (Frith & Zagorski-Thomas, 2012; Zagorski-Thomas *et al.*, 2020). In artistic research in music, Brooks et al. (2019) discuss the agencies of composer, performer, and sound engineer from a model of 'voice', drawing, first, on the concept of voice such as proposed by Cumming (2000), and second, on the development of a model of how a musician's voice is negotiated through artistic collaboration, as proposed by Gorton and Östersjö (2016, 2019). Their model builds on embodied music cognition but also regards the practices of composers, performers, and other music practitioners as socioculturally situated. Hence, in the art world (Becker, 1982) in which a particular practice is situated, "interactions between performers and their instruments are combined with other interactions in the formation of a performer's 'voice': with composers, with musical scores, and with the contextual practices within which the performer operates" (Gorton and Östersjö, 2019, p. 44). However, these individual voices are not only negotiated with other human and non-human agents but may also be negotiated between musicians to form shared voices, as can be seen in chamber music performance (Gorton and Östersjö, 2020), in composer-performer interaction (Gorton and Östersjö, 2016, 2019), and in intercultural collaboration (Nguyễn and Östersjö, 2019). What Brooks et al. (2019) bring to these perspectives is a further discussion of the many voices brought to play in studio work. The *Footnotes* project provides examples of how the voices of performer, composer, and audio engineer may also be brought together with many historical voices captured in reference recordings. In the next section, we will consider how *Yêu Một Mình* became the material for similar experimentation in the work of The Six Tones.

3 EXPERIMENTATION WITH *YELLOW MUSIC*

This section builds on data collected as part of Nguyễn Thanh Thủy's postdoctoral research project. Since the recording sessions were carried out during the COVID-19 pandemic, most sessions were either conversations between the participating musicians on Zoom, or documentation of recording sessions on video, which typically were carried out by one performer at a time, adding individual stems. Frequent references are made to video examples, which are all found in the same exposition published in VIS – Nordic Journal for Artistic Research (Nguyễn, 2022).

3.1 Approaches to the instrumental arrangements

A fundamental concept for how to create instrumental parts that do not follow the otherwise dominating tonal structures of *yellow music* was developed by Nguyễn Thanh Thủy, first in a solo version for *đàn tranh* of the song *Còn Thương Rau Đắng Mọc Sau Hè*. It entailed reducing the vocal part to a melodic framework, such as is typically the foundation of any traditional music performance in Vietnam, and applying a traditional mode to this melodic structure. This would also allow for a heterophonic approach to ensemble performance, again using performance practice of traditional Vietnamese music as a means for avoiding tonal harmony. In a video essay by Nguyễn Thanh Thủy titled *The Sorrow Turns Yellow* (2022), the process of creating this version is described in further detail. In *Yêu Một Mình*, three *đàn tranh* tracks were overdubbed, using a traditional approach to heterophonic organisation, but with an experimental feature in the bending of dyads, which further blurs the sense of tonality.

The guitar parts in the album use only acoustic and electric models of the Vietnamese guitar. This instrument, developed in the south of Vietnam in the late 1930s, has deeply scalloped frets and uses much lower tuning systems than on standard instruments in order to enable the same type of bending and ornamentation as on a đàn tranh (Östersjö, 2022). This instrument has not been commonly used in *yellow music*, most likely because it does not lend itself readily to chordal playing. Therefore, already by using this instrument, alternative approaches that avoid tonal harmony are invited, giving way to a more figurative, single-line approach with extensive bending and ornamentation, as in traditional music. As pointed out by Östersjö in an interview in the video essay *The (re)Turn*, the Vietnamese guitar:

> is an instrument that enables you to play the traditional music with the ornamentation correctly carried out, but at the same time, it is a really beautiful instrument to be experimenting with, so it allows you to do quite interesting things also harmonically and gesturally.

> (Nguyễn, 2022, 10:46–11:20)

Also, the tunings used are more designed for this modal style of playing (see further, Östersjö, 2022). Another feature of the electric guitar production in *Yêu Một Mình* is that the treble register and the bass are amped differently, treating the bass register as an electric bass and only the treble materials as a guitar, also adding different typical guitar effects.

A demonstration of the basic affordances of the instrument is given in the same video essay (Nguyễn, 2022, 7:26–9:40).

3.2 Audio production perspectives

In this section, the technologies used in performance and post-production are introduced, and we outline how these techniques enabled the group to experiment with connecting to the sound of the original pre-1975 sound of *nhạc vàng*. It may first be good to consider how the role of the audio engineer (very clearly embodied by Jez Wells in the *Footnotes* project mentionedpreviously) is divided between several individuals in the work of The Six Tones. In the making of the version of *Yêu Một Mình*, Östersjö and Wright take turns in audio engineering and producer-like practices. Hence, all instrumental recordings were engineered and edited by Östersjö, mostly in a studio at Inter Arts Center in Malmö, Sweden. Östersjö sometimes had a producer-like role, as can be seen in the video essay *The (re)Turn* (Nguyễn, 2022) in the following Zoom conversation between Nguyễn, Wright, and Östersjö:

Ö: I am quite impressed by this introduction; I think it is super cool, this opening.
N: I cannot, not smiling when I listen to it!
W: It's a beautiful production . . .
Ö: Yeah, it is. You know, it would be great to see what could be done by taking the recording I played first and just see in what ways we can use it to create both the opening and some kind of beat structure for the piece.

(Nguyễn, 2022, 3:00–3:41)

Although many attempts were made to cite the organ and guitar licks that open the piece, they seemed too particular to become material for a new opening, so the first idea suggested by Östersjö was eventually discarded. However, the second idea of creating a basic rhythmic structure for the entire piece based on the opening beat became a fundamental feature of the recording. We will now turn to some examples of how Wright would take on audio engineering and producer-like roles in the further development of the materials.

In Matt Wright's processing of the original sample, transposition was an important method, but so was also combining transposition and time compression. Through these combined methods, certain frequencies could be highlighted; for instance, in order to bring out the hi-hat, the stereo field was widened, but perhaps most importantly (and reflecting the influence of the Black Atlantic upon his work), a 'double speed' rhythmical counterpoint echoing drum n' bass could be created. Matt Wright demonstrates these different processes in the video essay titled *The (re)Turn* (Nguyễn, 2022, 3:40–6:34). Most characteristic of the version by The Six Tones is that the beat – which The Shotguns only employ in the opening, before the entry of the voice – here instead becomes the foundation for the entire piece, akin to the ubiquitous use of the Amen break in early forms of drum n' bass.

An example of post-production through which we sought to emulate the sound of the original pre-1975 recordings is vocal production. In the same video essay, Matt Wright shows examples of how he first brought out the higher partials in the voice by heightening the EQ at 1.3 kHz. All vocal production in Vietnamese studios was characterised by the generous use of reverb, but also commonly with bouncing delays, and Matt demonstrates how, in the recording by The Six Tones, a large reverb was sent through a bus with a delay to create such a characteristic bounce in the stereo field (Nguyễn, 2022, 17:10–18:28). In the final section of the piece, 'vocal chops' are used as 'instrumental' material, and woven into the basic beat-structure, as is typical in hip-hop production. This entailed some extreme transposition of individual samples (two octaves higher) but builds most of all on cutting up the original vocal part and creating new rhythmic figures (Nguyễn, 2022, 18:30–19:52).

4 DISCUSSION

In our explorations of pre-1975 *yellow music*, a consistent quality is the perception of the scene in Sài Gòn as a site in which musicians are engaged in intense and highly creative explorations of novel territory. It is surprising to note that this creativity also seems to be backed up with extensive resources, first by many highly skilled performers who join in large constellations, but second, also in terms of audio technology, wherein the cutting-edge releases of quadrophonic mixes of a number of albums is the most remarkable finding. Further research on this dynamic scene is needed, and it is our hope that the present chapter may spark interest and new research approaches.

Turning now to the accounts of the experimental work by The Six Tones and returning to the observation that the practices of audio engineer and producer were shared between Wright and Östersjö, such integrative collaboration (John-Steiner, 2000) evokes particular negotiations of voice. Since most of the work was carried out through remote interaction, this would entail a process of editing-processing-sharing and then responding through a similar process until a consensus is reached. Building on Lefford and Thomson's (2018) analysis of how a producer may use a reference recording in the negotiation of how to shape a new project, we believe that the process of creating a new version of *Yêu Một Mình* from the reference recording made by Dạ Hương and The Shotguns similarly was dependent, not so much on explicit analysis of the reference, but on a more spontaneous exploration of the source. Lefford and Thompson (2018, p. 546) conclude that "in such situations, metacognitive reflection is one way to explain this decision. Importantly, in both cases, the choice of template pre-supposes some form of meta-analysis". Perhaps one may see the example drawn from Nguyễn's video essay as one example of such meta-analysis when Östersjö suggests how the reference recording might be used in production with The Six Tones.

In their analysis of *Footnotes*, Brooks et al. (2019) not only refer to the negotiation of voices, represented both in reference recordings by the voice of the composer in the score, as well as the voices of the performer and audio engineer in the studio work, but also, these negotiations are analysed through the lens of authenticity, understood as a social construct with many different facets. To structure their discussion, Brooks et al. refer to Kivy's (1995) proposal of four different conceptions of authenticity as central to the discourse of Historically Informed Performance:

> What Kivy calls "authenticity as intention" refers to how a realisation of a composer's intentions for performance is imagined to define its authenticity. "Authenticity as sound" is instead related to the notion of recreating the original sonority of the music, first and foremost through the use of period instruments. "Authenticity as historic practice" is more widely related to the reconstruction and application of the original practice of performers in the context in which the score can be situated. The fourth category is of a different nature, and refers to the personal authenticity of the performer, a contrasting form which Kivy refers to as "the other authenticity." While Kivy aimed to create an opposition between the first three types and the "other" authenticity, we find all four to be relevant for a discussion of *Footnotes* and, in particular, of the process of post-producing the recording of the piece.
> (Brooks et al., 2019, p. 192)

Authenticity-as-intention is expressed in how The Shotguns relate the main part of the song to how the first recording in 1970, in the arrangement and performance recorded by (one of) its composers, also serves as a model for their performance in 1972, although they also clearly articulate difference and novelty in these parts (for instance, the lively bass playing, the higher tempo in the refrain, which reaches a more pop song-like character with the more prominent drums). In the recording by The Six Tones, authenticity-as-intention is mainly approached in the vocal part, which aligns with the mainstream tradition of this song and, hence, expresses a strife for authenticity situated between authenticity-as-intention and authenticity-as-practice. At the same time, when The Six Tones intentionally avoid tonal harmony and seek a heterophonic organisation of the instrumental, electronic, and vocal parts, authenticity-as-intention is countered by what Kivy calls The Other Authenticity, here expressed through a negotiated shared voice of the players in the group.

In a study of the diasporic Vietnamese music culture in California, Valverde (2003) observes that "what comforts the community in exile may be the very thing that keeps artists from creating new things" (p. 32). As mentioned briefly, *yellow music* and many of its composers and performers migrated to a great extent from Vietnam after the Fall of Saigon. Many gathered in Orange County, California, where not only karaoke bars would provide a site for nostalgic longing for a lost homeland (Wong & Elliot, 1994), but also, a new Vietnamese music industry emerged (the re-launch of The Shotguns being but one example out of many!). Valverde (2003) describes how the overseas Vietnamese – *Việt Kiều* – came to dominate the market and, although forbidden, it still remains possible to access within Vietnam. But she also seeks to explain what she describes as a decline and a shift of initiative from the exiled music industry back to the Vietnamese mainland. She continues to reference Thien Do, a musician in this scene who claimed that "Innovation is not considered a virtue in the creation process" (Valverde, 2003, p. 32). This statement, and the entire process that Valverde describes, is in stark contrast to the extraordinarily creative and explorative nature of the pre-1975 *yellow music* that was created in Sài Gòn. Valverde relates the stagnation of the diasporic music scene to a tendency to preservation, which she relates to the notion of "culture in a bubble" (p. 45). Looking at examples of transnational exchanges between Vietnam and overseas musicians, as well as more cross-cultural formations in California with younger musicians, she eventually suggests that such "cultural flows across national borders help to obliterate the distinction between Viet Kieu and Vietnamese music. The survival and development of music in both places requires continued collaboration and support to create a new kind of music blend" (Valverde, 2003, p. 46). The pre-1975 *yellow music* will never return, but its heritage can always be re-invented as a source for ever-new transformations.

REFERENCES

Becker, H. S. (1982) *Art Worlds*. Berkeley: University of California Press.

Brooks, W., Östersjö, S. and Wells, J. J. (2019) 'Footnotes', in C. Laws *et al.* (eds.) *Voices, Bodies, Practices: Performing Musical Subjectivities*. Orpheus Institute Series. Leuven: Leuven University Press, pp. 171–232.

Cumming, N. (2000) *The Sonic Self: Musical Subjectivity and Signification*. Bloomington, IN: Indiana UP.

DeWald, E. (2012) 'Taking to the waves: Vietnamese society around the radio in the 1930s', *Modern Asian Studies*, 46(1), pp. 143–165.

Đông, K. (2021) 'Đôi nét về hãng đĩa Asia Sóng Nhạc thập niên 1960 của ông Nguyễn Tất Oanh', *Nhạc Xưa*. Available at: https://nhacxua.vn/doi-net-ve-hang-dia-asia-song-nhac-thap-nien-1960-cua-ong-nguyen-tat-oanh/ [accessed 1 September 2022].

Frith, S. and Zagorski-Thomas, S. (2012) *The Art of Record Production: An Introductory Reader for a New Academic Field*. Surrey: Ashgate.

Gibbs, J. (2003) 'The west's songs, our songs: The introduction and adaptation of western popular song in Vietnam before 1940', *Asian Music*, 35(1), pp. 57–83.

Gibbs, T. *et al.* (2013) *Longing for the Past: The 78 rpm Era in Southeast Asia*. Atlanta: Dust to Digital.

Gilroy, Paul. (1993) *The Black Atlantic: Modernity and Double Consciousness*. Cambridge, MA: Harvard University Press.

Gorton, D. and Östersjö, S. (2016) 'Choose your own adventure music: On the emergence of voice in musical Collaboration', *Contemporary Music Review*, 35(6), pp. 579–598. Available at: 10.1080/07494467.2016.1282596 [accessed 1 September 2022].

Gorton, D. and Östersjö, S. (2019) 'Austerity measures I: Performing the discursive voice', in C. Laws, *et al.* (eds.) *Voices, Bodies, Practices*. Orpheus
Institute Series. Leuven: Leuven University Press, pp. 29–79.

Gorton, D. and Östersjö, S. (2020) 'Negotiating the discursive voice in chamber
music', in C. Laws (ed.) *Performance, Subjectivity, and Experimentation*.
Orpheus Institute Series. Leuven: Leuven University Press.

Harrison, N. (2004) Posted by Landon Proctor (2006) "Video explains the
world's most important 6-sec drum loop". Available at: www.youtube.com/
watch?v=5SaFTm2bcac&t=355s [accessed 13 Jan 2023]

Henry, E. (2005) 'Tân Nhạc: Notes toward a social history of Vietnamese music
in the twentieth century', *Michigan Quarterly Review*, 44(1), pp. 135–147.

John-Steiner, V. (2000) *Creative Collaboration*. New York: Oxford University Press.

Kelly, J. (2008) 'The anthropology of assemblage', *Art Journal*, 67(1), pp. 24–30.
Available at: www.jstor.org/stable/20068579 [accessed 13 January 2023]

Kivy, P. (1995) *Authenticities: Philosophical Reflections on Musical Performance*. Ithaca, NY: Cornell University Press.

Lefford, M. N. and Thompson, P. (2018) 'Naturalistic artistic decision-making
and metacognition', *Cognition, Technology and Work*, 20(4), pp. 543–554.

Moir, N. L. (2021) *Number One Realist: Bernard Fall and Vietnamese Revolutionary
Warfare*. Oxford University Press. Available at: doi:10.1093/oso/9780197629888.
001.0001 [accessed 1 September 2022]

Nguyễn, Đ. D. (2023) Interview by Nguyễn Thanh Thủy [Zoom], 5 Jan.

Nguyễn, T. (2019) *The Choreography of Gender in Traditional Vietnamese Music*.
PhD thesis, Lund University.

Nguyễn, T. (2022) 'Vietnamese diasporic voices: Exploring *yellow music* in a lim-
inal space', *VIS–Nordic Journal for Artistic Research*, 8. Available at: www.
researchcatalogue.net/view/1513023/1513024 [accessed 1 December 2022]

Nguyễn, T. and Östersjö, S. (2019) 'Arrival cities: Hanoi', in C. Laws, *et al.* (eds.)
Voices, Bodies, Practices. Leuven: Leuven University Press, pp. 235–295.

Ó Briain, L. (2021) *Voices of Vietnam: A Century of Radio, Red Music, and Revolution*. Oxford: Oxford University Press.

Olsen, D. A. (2008) *Popular Music of Vietnam: The Politics of Remembering, the Economics of Forgetting*. New York, NY: Routledge Studies in Ethnomusicology.

Östersjö, S. (2022) 'The Vietnamese guitar: Tradition and experiment', in M.
Dogantan-Dack (ed.) *Rethinking The Musical Instrument*. Newcastle: Cambridge Scholars Publishing, pp. 166–193.

Phạm, C. L. (2017) 'Hãng đĩa Lê Văn Tài: Dư Âm Còn Vọng', *Người Đô Thị*.
Available at: https://nguoidothi.net.vn/hang-dia-le-van-tai-du-am-con-
vong-8234.html [accessed 1 September 2022]

Phạm, C. L. (2015) 'Hãng đĩa hát xưa ở Sài Gòn', *2saigon*. Available at:
https://2saigon.vn/xa-hoi/net-xua-saigon/hang-dia-hat-xua-o-sai-gon.html
[accessed 1 September 2022]

Phạm, D. (1991) *Hồi Ký 3*. Available at: https://phamduy.com/en/ebook/
category/9-pham-duy [accessed 1 September 2022]

SoulGook. (2017) *Global Flows & Colliding Copyright Regimes, YouTube Dia-
ries 4 of 6*. Available at: https://soulgook.com/2017/05/29/global-flows-
colliding-copyright-regimes-youtube-diaries-4-of-6/?fbclid=IwAR3UX6

mw7X0QwfcKPAchYrF7J9rhalolMx8CykbnCAMxdGfgaLrc2xL5AGE [accessed Jan 15, 2023]

Taylor, P. (2001) *Fragments of the Present: Searching for Modernity in Vietnam's South*. Australia: ASAA Southeast Asia Publications Series.

Trần, Q. B. (2017) 'Nhạc sỹ Ngọc Chánh và ban nhạc Shotguns một trời huyền thoại', *Thế Giới Nghệ Sỹ* (109). Available at: www.tongphuochiep.com/index.php/bao-chi/tac-gi-tac-ph-m/23624-nh-c-si-ng-c-chanh-va-ban-nh-c-shotguns-ph-n-1-tr-n-qu-c-b-o [accessed 1 September 2022]

Trịnh, T. T. (2017) 'Sài Gòn và Nhạc Sĩ Ngọc Chánh, một thời vang bóng', *Việt Báo*. Available at: https://vietbao.com/p112a270891/sai-gon-vang-bong-ns-ngoc-chanh [accessed 1 September 2022]

Valverde, K. L. C. (2003) 'Making Vietnamese music transnational: Sounds of home, resistance and change', *Amerasia Journal*, 29(1), pp. 29–50. Available at doi: 10.17953/amer.29.1.1g7nm7m4715l40hv.

Veal, Michael E. (2007) *Dub: Soundscapes and Shattered Songs in Jamaican Reggae*. Middletown, CT: Wesleyan University Press.

Wong, D. and Elliot, M. (1994) '"I want the microphone": Mass mediation and agency in Asian-American popular music', *TDR (1988–)*, 38(3), pp. 152–167.

Zagorski-Thomas, S., Isakoff, K., Stévance, S. and Lacasse, S. (2020) *The Art of Record Production : Creative Practice in the Studio*. Ashgate Popular and Folk Music Series. Abingdon, OX; New York, NY: Routledge.

DISCOGRAPHY

Saigon Supersound (2017) [vinyl LP] *Saigon Supersound*, (1964–75), Vol. 1, Frankfurt Am Main, DE, Infracom.

Saigon Supersound (2018) [vinyl LP] *Saigon Supersound*, (1964–75), Vol. 2, Frankfurt Am Main, DE, Infracom.

Trịnh, L. N. (1970a) 'Yêu Một Mình', Chế Linh. *Hương Lan*. Sài Gòn: Đĩa Hát Việt Nam. Available at: Youtube [accessed: 30 August 2022]

Trịnh, L. N. (1970b) 'Yêu Một Mình', Dạ Hương. *Con Đường Mới 1*. Glendale: Băng Nhạc Bốn Phương. Available at: Spotify [accessed 30 August 2022].

15

Innovating music experiences

Creativity in pandemic times

Jenny Karlsson, Jessica Edlom,
and Linda Ryan Bengtsson

1 INTRODUCTION

The COVID-19 pandemic has had a significant impact on the music industry. Several studies and reports show that shutdowns in connection with the COVID-19 pandemic negatively affected creative industries, regardless of country or creative sector (Khlystova et al., 2022; see also OECD, 2020; Dümcke, 2021; Florida and Seman, 2020). The restrictions due to the pandemic forced the music industry to more or less cancel all live events from March 2020 through the spring of 2022. Artists and audiences could not meet and interact, which challenged industry participants in building relationships and staying socially connected to fans (Davies, 2020; Nguyen et al., 2020; Svensk Live, 2020; Tschmuck, 2020). Live events are key in the music industry, as they allow artists and their audiences to meet and form uniquely *cocreated experiences* (Bennett, 2015; Kronenburg, 2019), and they engage a wide range of actors, such as scene owners, organizers, sound and light technicians, and other subcontractors specializing in live music (Rendell, 2021). Consequently, an important part of *value creation* within the music industry is formed at live events.

To study the impact of COVID-19 on the music industry and the resulting innovation processes that took place during the pandemic, this chapter considers the music industry as a service ecosystem with multiple linked actors who integrate resources and cocreate value (Rundle-Thiele et al., 2019; Vargo and Lusch, 2008, 2016). The COVID-19 pandemic and its restrictions ruptured the existing ecosystem, shifting previous relations and value creation processes out of play and forcing actors to adapt, form new roles, and learn about new resources and how to integrate them in novel ways (Karlsson and Skålén, 2022). The study investigates how the music industry and music practitioners in Sweden responded to these new requirements and, more specifically, how the COVID-19 restrictions engaged actors in new creative innovation initiatives. To do so, this chapter presents an empirical case study of music actors in Sweden in general and in the region of Värmland in particular. Data were collected between March 2020 and May 2021 through the participation of musicians, music companies, light and sound technicians, suppliers, and other creative

DOI: 10.4324/9781003462101-17

actors in the music industry ecosystem. The data consist of a survey, inter-views, documents, and participant observations of innovation workshops and processes that focused on the cocreation of innovative ideas.

The empirical data show how actors within the music industry struggled due to the lack of knowledge and technological resources needed for a digital transformation. Specifically, actors needed knowledge and resources to produce and consume digital events, understand how to charge for these events, and determine how to reach and engage their audiences in novel ways. Simultaneously, an innovative drive to identify, pursue, and develop new ways to design and construct music experiences was detected. The pandemic thereby pushed actors and the industry as a whole to initiate service innovation processes and find new ways of creating value, not only monetarily but also in terms of social and societal impacts. Engaging in inno-vation processes through workshops that gathered a regional culture scene together came to be central to promoting cocreation, creativity, learning, and collaborations that led to new solutions and offerings.

2 BACKGROUND: SERVICE INNOVATION

When live venues were closed down due to pandemic restrictions, actors in the music industry started to engage in creative initiatives, seeking new ideas and generating new solutions to create value. These initiatives can be understood as service innovation through the cocreation of value, which is a process that can be described as 'collaborative re-combinations or com-binatorial evolutions of practices that provide novel solutions for new or existing problems,' leading to the development of new and useful knowl-edge (Vargo et al., 2015, pp. 63–64). Helkkula et al. (2018) identified four approaches/archetypes to service innovation in service ecosystems: 1) the output-based approach, referring to quantities and measurable results, such as the number of new offerings, 2) the process-based approach, com-prising innovation in the elements or phases of the offered service and how this process is changed, or to the service innovation process itself and how innovation is conducted, such as intentional, planned, struc-tured and sequential (Gallouj and Savona, 2009), or ad hoc (Gallouj and Weinstein, 1997) integrative and dynamic (Karlsson and Skålén, 2015; Toivonen, 2010), 3) the experiential approach, which relates to the indi-vidual experience and how the customer makes sense of it and creates value from it (Helkkula et al., 2018), both independently and in a social context (also see Rubalcaba et al., 2012), and 4) the systemic approach, which focuses on resource integration on the part of engaged actors that improves the viability of the service ecosystem (Helkkula et al., 2018), in which service innovation evolves from the actors' joint actions (Lusch and Nambisan, 2015).

Another important factor in innovation is to understand how the various actors use and integrate available resources, whether they are their own resources, those available from other actors in the market, or those publicly available in society (i.e., the social system). What this means is that the norms, values, ways of thinking, and power structures govern how people act (Edvardsson et al., 2011) within the framework of service ecosystems may be subject to change. Based on this reasoning, innovation can be seen as new ways of cocreating value and incorporating changes in existing structures and processes due to the new ways resources are integrated, which takes place in collaboration with other actors in service ecosystems (Skålén et al., 2015, Vargo et al., 2015). In the context of the pandemic, rapid external changes disrupted the entire music industry, and actors were forced to abandon previous working practices and engage in new innovative ways to integrate resources and enhance value cocreation in the service ecosystem in order to survive. Accordingly, this chapter investigates how actors in the Swedish music ecosystem responded to these changes and how they engaged actors in new creative innovation initiatives.

3 DESIGN OF THE STUDY

This study was initiated when the Swedish government introduced a ban on public gatherings in March 2020 (Regulation SFS, 2020: 114 with subsequent changes). The consequences of the restrictions in other European countries had already indicated that there would be ruptures within the music industry, which underpinned the importance of studying the Swedish music industry at this time. Therefore, an explorative study with the intention of following developments in real time was initiated. In addition to being unable to foresee how long the study would continue, the course of events could not be predicted. As a result, the study's focus and data collection methods were adapted to the course of events.

The respondents included individual, small, or medium-sized actors in the Swedish music industry, but also representatives from other creative industries, such as theaters. The respondents represented significant groups within the industry, including musicians, DJs, artists, songwriters, producers, managers, publishers, record companies, individual companies, event companies, interest organizations and non-profit associations, sound and lighting technicians, other technology companies, music journalists, and festival organizers, among others, which provided a wide range of data. The data collection was carried out as an iterative process (Alvesson and Sköldberg, 2009), continuously moving between the complex situations that industry actors found themselves in and emerging research on the phenomenon, as well as between different forms of data collection methods.

Qualitative data were collected through several sub-studies in which the main part consisted of observations conducted through participation in innovation workshops, complemented by a digital qualitative survey, interviews, and document studies. When the pandemic was a fact, a qualitative survey focusing on actors in the Swedish music industry was conducted between May and June 2020, with a total of 70 respondents. The survey aimed to generate an understanding of how actors had been affected by the situation and how they responded to it. To obtain a deeper knowledge of the pandemic's impact on the music industry, six individual interviews and one group interview were conducted, all between December 2020 and March 2021. The interviews were semi-structured, with a more in-depth and exploratory focus on experiences, creativity, and innovation. Respondents were allowed to describe, discuss, and elaborate on these topics in their own words, as well as give examples. The interviews lasted between 36 and 70 minutes and were transcribed verbatim. In addition, between March 2020 and August 2022, various types of documents were studied (e.g., industry-specific publications, popular science texts, and reports). Actors' communication and industry-specific content were also followed through social and traditional media.

Observations were carried out through participation (Spradley, 1979) in innovation workshops arranged by the research project Music Ecosystems Inner Scandinavia (MECO) in collaboration with Värmlandsteatern and Arvika Innovation Park. MECO was an EU-financed Sweden-Norway Interreg research project focused on education and industry to investigate, innovate, and optimize Inner Scandinavia's music service ecosystem, with the departure point of user experiences and digitization. The workshop series Arts & Music (February to June 2021) invited actors in the music, performing arts, and live industry to meet, cocreate, test, and drive ideas, as well as develop prototypes and facilitate the transformation of creative ideas into implemented innovations. The workshops were arranged as part of the Music Innovation Lab (MIL) concept that originated in the project. The MIL concept served as a platform for meetings among various actors (i.e., practitioners, researchers, and interest organizations) in the regional music service ecosystem. All activities within the MIL aimed to promote innovation, knowledge, and competence development, as well as value creation through cocreative activities involving music actors, industry representatives, and students in the music business and production.

Participants in the MIL were informed about the study and agreed that researchers could follow the innovation process, including the discussions, presentations, sharing, and development of ideas and prototypes. In order not to influence and direct the process, the participation was passive, with the only exception being if the researchers were directly asked to be involved in the discussion. Detailed notes were written down during and in direct connection with the implementation of the workshops. In addition, participants' digital bulletin boards could be saved for analysis. In total, 48 actors participated in the process of four organized workshops. Simultaneously, a digital research seminar series was arranged to invite actors to learn and cocreate with other actors, as well as with researchers in the project.

4 FINDINGS

4.1 From chaos to creativity

The devastating impact of the COVID-19 restrictions was prominent in our findings. Overnight, the music actors found themselves, as one of the interviewees expressed, in a 'free fall.' Almost all business disappeared. From one day to another, the industry went from fully booked calendars, sold-out venues, and planned incomes to a non-existent business. A whole life's work vanished in a short time: 'A decrease of 100%, all totally gone . . . it is a crisis. I don't know how I'm going to make it' (music technician). The cancellation of each event affected not only the artists but also the sound providers, stage builders, venue owners, and so on. The already difficult-to-navigate and fragile music and event industry was unprepared for such a crisis and lacked a financial safety net. The pandemic underlined the precarious situation and the low economic and social sustainability within the industry. In Sweden, subsidies were given to parts of the cultural industries during the pandemic, although many of the actors were not included among the recipients of such assistance. The lack of immediate solutions led many actors to seek ways in which to benefit from their knowledge and experiences in other organizations and industries, draining the music ecosystem of competencies and performances, as well as indicating long-term negative effects for the music industry.

Many of the respondents of the study expressed feelings of desperation in the beginning amid the inability to manage the consequences of COVID-19. In addition, the uncertainty of the new and consistently changing regulations (e.g., fluctuating numbers allowed at gatherings) and the lack of support systems targeted toward the cultural industry made the situation too complex to handle effectively. The situation demanded constant readjustments on the part of businesses and new ways of working, as actors had to focus on finding income-generating activities to 'keep the business going' (self-employed musician). Some actors found it more difficult than others. Specifically, actors with a variety of competencies and business pillars to stand on could more easily adjust to the situation. Nevertheless, many respondents pointed to their lack of crisis plans and the need to seek alternative solutions and adapt their work. Some respondents expressed feeling drained of energy and merely 'waiting for things to happen.' Others focused on creativity and did what was possible given the circumstances, like going into the studio to create new music and/or exploring new, and often digital, offerings for the audience. The potential of digital solutions was evident due to the fact that artists could reach far more people (e.g., the audience members did not have to go to Stockholm to see their favorite artist and could instead stream the performance in their own town), reduce requirements for security, and enact more control, the latter of which was much lower when the performance was not a physical activity:

> Live [music] has been an important source of income for the entire industry for a long time – small and large . . . It has therefore been an incentive for actors to find alternative, innovative solutions to recreate the live experience.
>
> (music artist)

Although respondents expressed difficulties in thinking in new ways and adapting to the circumstances, especially regarding technology and social/ digital platforms, others also expressed excitement. For instance, some thought that digital platforms and technological solutions were easy – and important – to make use of. The potential of technological solutions was given a central place in handling the pandemic's challenges early on (see, e.g., Hantrais et al., 2021; Keesara et al., 2020; Vargo et al., 2021), which demanded competencies and often also monetary funds create, for example, streamed concerts (Khlystova et al., 2022; Florida and Seman, 2020). A music band described how the conditions looked different for different types and levels of actors:

> If you were super famous and had a lot of money, you might have been able to solve a lot of things in a cool way (i.e., digitally), and so on. But it will be difficult for us. What should we come up with, and what is reasonable?
>
> (music band)

Many new solutions were initially simple, ad hoc, and experimental, but during the course of the pandemic months, knowledge and awareness grew regarding new and elaborate ways of working, both in relation to the audience and other actors in the music industry. There was an expressed need to create new forums to come together and cocreate: 'It will be a year that requires a lot of new contact making,' said a festival organizer, and another respondent reported the following:

> Live [music] is not only an opportunity for marketing and contact with fans, but also a forum for actors in the industry, such as organizers, bookers, and industry developers, to meet, interact, network, and cocreate.
>
> (music artist)

Thus, due to the absence of events, actors in the music industry identified the need to meet in new ways and learn to integrate resources through novel approaches to find solutions to the problems they faced, eventually finding a way to outlast the pandemic and enhance their creative possibilities even after.

4.2 Facilitating creativity and innovation

Based on the closures in society and as a result of the chaos experienced in the music industry, as reflected previously, the need for collaborations to increase (the regional) industry's capability and innovative power was evident primarily in the media but also in the survey and the more informal discussions with the actors. To respond to this demand, the MIL 'Arts & Music Innovation,' a digital meeting place, was staged in the region of Värmland, Sweden, to facilitate and explore cocreation based on actors' experiences and current circumstances. The starting point was to formulate new ideas together, develop and test them, and orchestrate and facilitate the transformation of creative ideas into innovations. Based on the notion that service innovation platforms form a common structure and are based on agreed-upon means of collaboration, both within the industry and with customers (Edvardsson and Tronvoll, 2019), the MIL platform was developed to allow people in the cultural industry (e.g., music, live performances, and theater) to explore, develop, and test new ideas together and to facilitate the transformation of creative ideas into innovations, primarily with each other, but in close relation to user's (e.g., audience, visitors, and customers) needs.

The development of innovation workshops departed from the service design perspective of the 'double diamond' (Design Council, 2005, 2018). The first part of Figure 15.1, Diamond 1, involves the exploration of problems and the need to identify them. This diamond illustrates the process of gathering problems, difficulties, ruptures, and complexities as a means of staying with the trouble (Haraway, 2016) and then narrowing the focus down to a more specific aspect or problem to further develop solutions in the next part of the process. The second part, Diamond 2, consists of idea generation and experimentation with different solutions to the problem. The diamond shape illustrates the wide range of ideas and solutions that emerge within the idea generation process, to be followed by testing, evaluating, and selecting one working solution for the problem.

In line with the first part of the double diamond approach, the first workshop focused on the worst way to work productively during a pandemic. Participants emphasized being too passive, ignoring problems, and doing things with no prospects of profit as the worst ways to work. This phase helped the participants to start thinking creatively and not only focus on solutions but also to see the bigger picture. Experienced problems often function as a basis for generating ideas and developing solutions, and this way of working allowed the participants to understand the possible negative experiences and how to deal with them (see, e.g., Helkkula et al., 2018). A major issue during the pandemic was to actually create new solutions for continuously changing problems due to the fact that the context and situation seemed to change from day to day, as discussed by several of the respondents. As one of the musicians explained, 'Generally, with the pandemic, there is this uncertainty. So, you don't know how it will turn out. . . . Should we plan for some gigs or not? Will it come off, or won't it? We don't know' (musician).

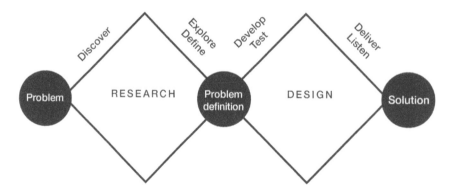

Figure 15.1 Double diamond model inspired by Design Council (2018).

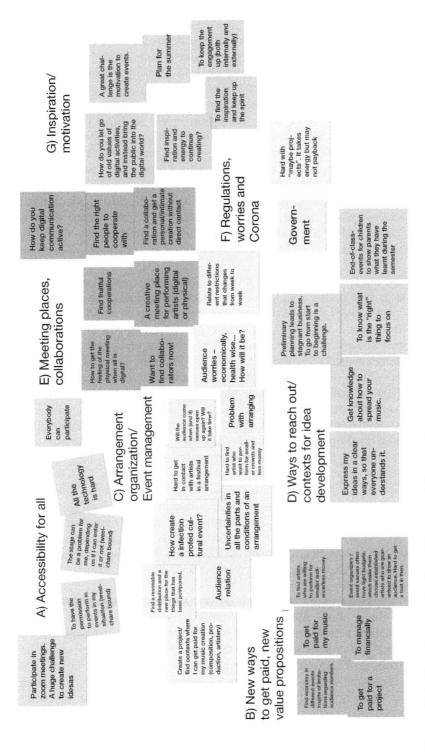

Figure 15.2 Clustering on a jamboard from workshop no. 2.

In the second workshop, the second phase of the double diamond was initiated as participants began to work creatively on turning problems around, taking advantage of the situation, and generating constructive ideas. In the first part of the workshop, the participants were encouraged to find positive aspects of the situation that were possible to turn into advantages and stepping stones into idea generation. Participants pressed on the need to look at what resources were at hand and use them in new ways – to think 'outside the box' to find new solutions and collaborative strategies, as expressed by one actor in the workshop: 'Dare to throw yourself into new collaborations where you don't know what they will lead to. Together is key' (quotation from jamboard). Creativity, positivity, and learning during the workshops were seen as central to keep trying new things and not be discouraged from continuing, as the objective was 'learning by doing instead of creating the perfect solution' (citation from Mentimeter by workshop participants). Thus, while the service innovation process was planned and intentional (Gallouj and Savona, 2009), the actors were encouraged to be iterative and learn along the way (Karlsson and Skålén, 2015; Toivonen, 2010).

During the second workshop, the participants also worked on so-called jamboards (see Figure 15.2), which allowed them to discuss and explore different aspects of the industry and start formulating more concrete ideas. After the second workshop, the participants were given homework to meet and discuss what was needed to realize the ideas and what additional actors could be involved. This was followed by the third and fourth sessions, which focused on actors/groups presenting and discussing ideas and developing prototypes (both physical and digital), which allowed them to identify the types of resources needed and how they could be integrated to realize the process of actually turning them into an innovation. The idea workshops followed a concept development model consisting of 1) describing target groups, 2) defining challenges, 3) describing the idea concretely, 4) describing success factors, 5) defining goals, 6) describing what needs to happen at the start, 7) discussing the time frame, 8) defining collaborators, and 9) involving the target group in development for quality assurance. Between the third and fourth sessions, the participants were asked to test the prototypes with potential stakeholders to gather feedback for further development and redesign. They were also asked to create prototype films that were presented and discussed among the participants during the fourth workshop.

The innovation workshops focused on involving actors from several parts of the creative and cultural (regional) service ecosystem. Actors worked locally and in close proximity and managed to utilize each other's knowledge and experiences across the industry. During the process, the participants reflected and acted on experienced situations, leading to innovative ideas and creative constellations and collaborations that evolved from the actors' joint actions (Lusch and Nambisan, 2015). It is important to note that the innovation process was heavily influenced by the ongoing pandemic, which led to ideas for several digital solutions; however, some of the realized innovations were based on physical activities. Cross-border collaborations with actors from different parts of the creative industry enhanced the sharing of knowledge, competence development, and sustainable relations:

> I have been able to have contact with and create, learn, and discuss with others in the industry . . . It has opened doors. It has also given me a sense of belonging with others in the industry.
> (citation from jam board by workshop participant)

An example of collaboration and output from MECO's innovation workshops is the innovative music puppet show 'The Big Little Circus,' a collaborative project between actors working in different art forms. A digital prototype was developed without the stage designers and the music producer meeting physically. The prototype later resulted in a physical theater performance, with a premiere in the winter of 2021. In addition to its innovative composition, the performance contains references to many social values and is about wanting to help others, daring to say what you want, and standing up for your values. Other examples consist of arrangements for safe events (regarding both COVID-19 and personal safety), cultural walks, alternative concerts, and festivals.

Several ideas were related to digital solutions, including how to produce and consume digital events and how to reach and engage audiences in novel ways. Nevertheless, the empirical data show that the actors reported a lack of knowledge and technological resources for a complete digital transformation. These shortcomings in competence imply problems in finding ways to perform and maintain relations with audiences and other actors in the ecosystem. In response to such problems, several solutions were generated and developed, such as the 'streaming box,' which was supposed to include equipment and instructions for how to conduct streaming practices (of concerts and activities) in a high-quality way to facilitate users' consumption processes and 'at-home-experiences.' Other solutions were related to concerns about charging for events and other activities. As one of the actors working with musicals and events described, 'You need to stop streaming for free. It kills the industry in the long run.' Based on this reasoning, actors initiated collaborations to build business models around, for example, live streams of concerts, but primarily focused on novel ways to cocreate within and across ecosystems (e.g., music, theater, etc.), with the objective of developing diverse sources of income that would secure actors' future survival. Despite the pandemic and the increased demand for digital solutions, a large number of identified problems, ideas, prototypes, and solutions also focused on physical and social needs to create social value.

Through the project, several music actors were supported with information and access to resources to start their own businesses, as well as to further develop their existing operations, products, and business models. Nevertheless, throughout the process, the need for ongoing meeting places (both physical and digital) for collaboration was discussed. For example, a joint Facebook group was started by the participants to be able to continue discussing ideas. However, other facilitating places and processes were requested. The need for additional support regarding finance and business establishments also grew during the pandemic.

5 CONCLUSION: LEARNING FROM INNOVATING MUSIC EXPERIENCES

This inductive study investigated the music industry through the lens of a service ecosystem and thus brought attention to the music industry's dependence on live performances, which can be understood as the cocreation of value with fans and with other actors in the ecosystem. The empirical findings illustrate the devastating effects that COVID-19 restrictions had on actors within the music industry. Many actors found themselves in a precarious position before the pandemic, with little means and abilities to act on the crisis. Specifically, this study identified an extensive struggle among music actors regarding both revenue streams and the creation of new music experiences that could be adjusted to the new situation. The pandemic also raised awareness of how sensitive the music industry is to ruptures within the music ecosystem, especially when live performances became close to impossible.

Within service-driven economies, the need to be adaptive and innovative is essential to survive and remain competitive (Edvardsson and Tronvoll, 2019). The music industry's ability to innovate and reinvent itself came to be essential in its handling of restrictions during the pandemic. Already at an early stage during the pandemic, innovative actions were identified whereby actors explored ways to engage with their audiences in novel ways. These were primarily experimental and ad hoc (Gallouj and Weinstein, 1997). Previously, the music industry played a central role in developing and exploring (digital) solutions, such as streaming platforms and social media for production, distribution, and building relations with audiences (e.g., Ali et al., 2021; Baym, 2018; Wikström, 2020). A major part of the experimentation during the pandemic also involved digital solutions. Turning to digital solutions was also suggested and sometimes economically supported by governmental initiatives, resulting in an acceleration of the digital transformation of cultural industries (Yue, 2022).

However, this study identified that the physical meeting places were perceived as specifically important by artists, not only as spaces for artists and fans to interact but also to cultivate musicians' well-being and sense of identity and to provide an arena for cocreative experimentation and learning. As argued by Edvardsson et al. (2011), social structures play a pivotal role in understanding how innovation takes place. To initiate and enhance innovation in the music industry, there is a need to understand the social context in which music is created, consumed, and experienced, as well as the resources needed to facilitate these processes. The empirical findings from this study showed that many of the actors lacked the tools and methods to make use of their own individual resources, as well as the ecosystem's common resources. In addition, many respondents lacked the knowledge and competencies to cocreate with others, and a major part lacked the ability to expand and explore innovation beyond their own network. Thus, the need for external facilitation to engage in structured innovation with other actors' resources was identified.

Despite the resignation and anxiety experienced during the pandemic, this study shows a creative and innovative industry with enthusiasm and a commitment to survival. Actors who had the opportunity to do so have invested in, for example, studio sessions or the creation of conditions for reaching out in new ways (e.g., through digital living-room gigs and cross-border collaborations, applying new genres, new platforms, and new geographical locations). The participants in the innovative workshops (Arts & Music Innovation) emphasized the importance of daring to charge for music, as well as the importance of gaining new knowledge and abilities for cocreation. However, they also brought attention to the benefits of acting within a specific local context, which was thought to enable networking and knowledge exchange. The importance of local anchoring as central to creating identity and belonging was also identified. Overall, in this study, creating a quality culture and, therefore, an improved quality of life for people in the region was at the core of the participating actors' motivation.

Travel restrictions in connection with the COVID-19 pandemic meant that large parts of the workshop activities took place in an online environment. This was thus an opportunity to digitally explore innovative ways of creating local anchoring and cocreating digitally. This approach brought access to participants in regions where it was otherwise difficult to attend such events due to geographical distances or functional disabilities. Thus, the active involvement of music industry actors in digital service innovation processes has been shown to be fruitful. The approach adopted here generated more inclusive conditions for a more inclusive music industry, strengthening the music industry's social sustainability, capability, and innovativeness.

This study also identified the importance of initiating cocreation and networking processes among actors. The collaborative method developed within the MIL has contributed to strengthening the actors' networks and shaping new collaborations. In addition, the actors have gained experience and competence in creative cocreation by being able to test and develop innovative ideas and through openness in the process, whereby actors could develop in different directions. During the workshops, the actors created a variety of digital live events and physical events, including boat concerts, culture walks, and the stage performance 'The Big Little Circus.' The Arts & Music Innovation workshops generated a number of process innovations that 1) enhanced customers' ways of consuming the service, 2) improved customers' value experiences, and 3) determined how to conduct value cocreation in a social context (Helkkula et al., 2018). Turning to technological innovations, this study suggests that processes of producing, delivering, and consuming a service (i.e., music experiences) can change.

The study also brings attention to what a well-functioning music ecosystem can contribute to regarding economic growth and occupation, as well as social and cultural value creation. Involving other parts of the culture industry in the workshops was an important success factor in prompting unexpected collaborations and innovations. The collaboration generated new constellations and attracted idea carriers from the regional culture industry at large. As one of the participants described, '[We have the] opportunity to meet other creative individuals and work together with them to develop an idea which we will implement . . .' Thus, the workshops helped to motivate the actors involved in the service innovation process (Helkkula et al., 2018) and strengthened the ties between them.

Previous research has shown that when actors in the music industry learn to integrate resources and cocreate value, they create the conditions needed to advance in their careers (Karlsson and Skålén, 2022). Informal learning through involvement in different communities has been proven to be more important than formal learning to succeed in the music industry. Also, as the influence of role models, networking, technology, and learning the industry's political game trigger advancements, the initiative of the workshops conducted in pandemic times has been shown here to facilitate service innovation by providing novel solutions for new or existing problems *and* for actors' knowledge and competence development, following Vargo et al. (2015). This chapter has thus illustrated how actors adapted to and took charge of their situations by generating ideas and elaborating and realizing new ways of integrating resources, resulting in innovative digital and physical solutions that have enhanced value cocreation in the music service ecosystem.

REFERENCES

Ali, M. M., Karlsson, J., and Skålén, P. (2021) 'How has digitalisation influenced value in the music market?', *International Journal of Music Business Research*, 10(2), pp. 53–63.

Alvesson, M. and Sköldberg, K. (2009) *Reflexive methodology: New vistas for qualitative research*. London: Sage.

Baym, N. K. (2018) *Playing to the crowd: Musicians, audiences, and the intimate work of connection*. New York: New York University Press.

Bennett, R. (2015) 'Live concerts and fan identity in the age of the Internet', in A. Jones, J. Bennett, and R. J. Bennett (eds.) *The digital evolution of live music*. Oxford, UK: Chandos, pp. 3–15.

Davies, K. (2020) 'Festivals post Covid-19', *Leisure Sciences*, 43(1–2), pp. 1–6.

Design Council (2005) 'The "double diamond" design process model', *Design Council*. Available at: www.designcouncil.org.uk

Design Council (2018) 'The design process: What is the double diamond?', *Design Council*. Available at: www.designcouncil.org.uk/news-opinion/design-process-what-double-diamond Retrieved: January 9, 2023.

Dümcke, C. (2021) 'Five months under COVID-19 in the cultural sector: A German perspective', *Cultural Trends*, 30(1), pp. 19–27.

Edvardsson, B. and Tronvoll, B. (2019) 'How platforms foster service innovation', *Organization Dynamics*, 49 (3), pp. 68–89.

Edvardsson, B., Tronvoll, B., and Gruber, T. (2011) 'Expanding understanding of service exchange and value co-creation: A social construction approach', *Journal of the Academy of Marketing Science*, 39(2), pp. 327–339.

Florida, R. and Seman, M. (2020) *Measuring COVID-19's devastating impact on America's creative economy*. Washington, DC: Brookings, Metropolitan Policy Program, p. 30.

Gallouj, F. and Savona, M. (2009) 'Innovation in services: A review of the debate and a research agenda', *Journal of Evolutionary Economics*, 19(2), pp. 149–172.

Gallouj, F. and Weinstein, O. (1997) 'Innovation in services', *Research Policy*, 26(4–5), pp. 537–556.

Hantrais, L. et al. (2021) 'Covid-19 and the digital revolution', *Contemporary Social Science*, 16(2), pp. 256–270.

Haraway, D. J. (2016) *Staying with the trouble: Making kin in the Chthulucene*. Durham: Duke University Press.

Helkkula, A., Kowalkowski, C., and Tronvoll, B. (2018) 'Archetypes of service innovation: Implications for value cocreation', *Journal of Service Research*, 21(3), pp. 284–301.

Karlsson, J. and Skålén, P. (2015) 'Exploring front-line employee contributions to service innovation', *European Journal of Marketing*, 49(9/10), pp. 1346–1365.

Karlsson, J. and Skålén, P. (2022) 'Learning resource integration by engaging in value cocreation practices: A study of music actors', *Journal of Service Theory and Practice*, 32(7), pp. 14–35.

Keesara, S., Jonas, A., and Schulman, K. (2020) 'Covid-19 and health care's digital revolution', *New England Journal of Medicine*, 382(23), p. e82.

Khlystova, O., Kalyuzhnova, Y., and Belitski, M. (2022) 'The impact of the COVID-19 pandemic on the creative industries: A literature review and future research agenda', *Journal of Business Research*, 139, pp. 1192–1210.

Kronenburg, R. (2019) *This must be the place: An architectural history of popular music performance venues*. London: Bloomsbury Publishing USA.

Lusch, R. F. and Nambisan, S. (2015) 'Service innovation: A service-dominant logic perspective', *MIS Quarterly*, 39(1), pp. 155–176.

Nguyen, M. H. et al. (2020) 'Changes in digital communication during the COVID-19 global pandemic: Implications for digital inequality and future research', *Social Media + Society*, 6(3), 2056305120948255.

OECD (2020) *Culture shock: COVID-19 and the cultural and creative sectors*. Available at: www.oecd.org/coronavirus/policy-responses/culture-shock-covid-19-and-the-cultural-and-creative-sectors-08da9e0e/ Retrieved: January 9, 2023.

Rendell, J. (2021) 'Staying in, rocking out: Online live music portal shows during the coronavirus pandemic', *Convergence*, 27(4), pp. 1092–1111.

Rubalcaba, L., Michel, S., Sundbo, J., Brown, S. W., and Reynoso, J. (2012) 'Shaping, organizing, and rethinking service innovation: A multidimensional framework', *Journal of Service Management*, 23(5), 696–715.

Rundle-Thiele, S. et al. (2019) 'Social marketing theory development goals: An agenda to drive change', *Journal of Marketing Management*, 35(1–2), pp. 160–181.

SFS 2020:114. Förbud mot att hålla allmänna sammankomster och offentliga tillställningar. Governmental regulation, March 11, 2020.

Skålén, P. et al. (2015) 'Exploring value propositions and service innovation: A service-dominant logic study', *Journal of the Academy of Marketing Science*, 43(2), pp. 137–158.

Spradley, J. P. (1979) *Participant observation*. Toronto: Wadsworth.

Svensk Live (2020) *Coronaviruset: Support your local scene!* Available at: www.svensklive.se/corona-support/

Toivonen, M. (2010) 'Different types of innovation processes in services and their organizational implications', in F. Gallouj and F. Djellal (eds.) *The handbook of innovation and services*. Cheltenham: Edward Elgar, pp. 221–249.

Tschmuck, P. (2020) 'The music industry in the Covid-19 pandemic – Live nation', *International Journal of Music Business Research*, 16.

Vargo, D. et al. (2021) 'Digital technology use during COVID-19 pandemic: A rapid review', *Human Behavior and Emerging Technologies*, 3(1), pp. 13–24.

Vargo, S. L. and Lusch, R. F. (2008) 'Service-dominant logic: Continuing the evolution', *Journal of the Academy of Marketing Science*, 36(1), pp. 1–10.

Vargo, S. L. and Lusch, R. F. (2016) 'Institutions and axioms: An extension and update of service-dominant logic', *Journal of the Academy of Marketing Science*, 44(1), pp. 5–23.

Vargo, S. L., Wieland, H., and Akaka, M. A. (2015) 'Innovation through institutionalization: A service ecosystems perspective', *Industrial Marketing Management*, 44, pp. 63–72.

Wikström, P. (2020) *The music industry: Music in the cloud*. Hoboken: John Wiley & Sons.

Yue, A. (2022) 'Conjunctions of resilience and the Covid-19 crisis of the creative cultural industries', *International Journal of Cultural Studies*, 25(3–4), pp. 349–368.

16

Connecting across borders

Communication tools and group practices of remote music collaborators

Martin K. Koszolko

1 INTRODUCTION

The contemporary remote music collaboration software (RMCS) is accessible via an increasingly complex set of specialised tools that facilitate various collaborative activities. This type of software has been steadily evolving over the years and can be traced to earlier developments, such as Res Rocket Network (Lefford, 2000; Koszolko, 2022) in the 1990s. The innovative functionality of RMCS manifested in its ability to transcend borders in music creation is significantly strengthened by its crowdsourcing and social networking potential.

In this chapter, I discuss selected approaches to communication within RMCS, which are at the heart of social actions that involve finding new creative partners, engaging them in the music creation process and leading projects to successful completion. This discussion stems from my decade-long, collaborative research practice involving various RMCS platforms (Koszolko, 2015, 2017, 2022; Koszolko and Montano, 2016). The experience I draw upon includes collaborative music-production projects with remotely located participants, live performances over the network and organising and coordinating the international Collaborative Music Contest. The latter is an initiative I founded in 2021, which brings together various stakeholders, including industry sponsors, established artists, and music industry practitioners in the jury panel, as well as contest participants who are musicians engaged in collaborative music-making online.

The first section of this chapter outlines available communication tools and their importance to group practices of music creators who engage and work with various platforms and services. What follows is a discussion on group practices and a classification of phases of communication as well as stages of collaborative project development. I argue that the full potential of RMCS is underutilised unless musicians using these platforms recognise the value of and fully engage with the available communication tools. This acknowledges the unprecedented potential of this software to facilitate creative crowdsourcing, which is enabled by interactions with a vast network of possible collaborators and by subsequent music-production activities.

DOI: 10.4324/9781003462101-18

Music production is often a complex process, and "given the array of aesthetic sensibilities engaged in the making of a single recording going well beyond a single individual's, the creative activity seen in the recording studio is very much a collective one" (McIntyre, 2012, p. 150). Related to this is Hansen's observation that "every complex enterprise requires collaboration" (2009, p. xi). While it is common to focus on the recording, editing and sound processing features when discussing music software – given the collaborative scope of the discussed platforms, their communication features are the enablers of collaborative music production and their most distinguishing factors. However, based on my experience, the importance of communication tools and strategies appears to be often overlooked even though they are critical to progressing projects to a successful conclusion and, importantly, finding new creative partners and crowdsourcing activities within RMCS. In this context, a successful campaign can be defined as one where we achieve our creative objectives. These can be predetermined or established during collective songwriting, performance and production sessions.

RMCS platforms cater to multiple approaches to cloud-based music creation, which include synchronous and asynchronous methods available through various types of collaborative software. The innovative design and disruptive potential of RMCS is evidenced in the availability of new forms of crowdsourcing of musical talent and access to advanced, cloud-based music-production technologies. Access is often provided on a free or freemium basis, which leads to a further increase in user engagement, resulting in millions of musicians using a broad range of collaborative software solutions.

2 TYPOLOGIES

Collaborative music in the cloud is a form of internet music, which is "music in which the internet is integral to its composition, or dissemination, or both" (Hugill, 2005, p. 431). In addition, as stated by Barbosa, "[t]he primary function that emerged from the use of internet technology in the musical context was to provide mechanisms that assist the composition of music pieces by means of network communication" (2006, p. 44). Collaborative communication tools used in computer-supported cooperative work can be categorised as groupware, defined as "software designed to run over a network in support of the activities of a group or organisation" (Olson and Olson, 2010).

Contemporary RMCS offers a virtual workspace where amateurs and professional music makers can connect, collaborate, communicate and learn from each other. However, musicians must effectively engage their collaborators via communication tools to achieve this. Innovations within RMCS led to creating and expanding various platforms that offer collaborative music-making solutions within the thriving and continuously growing online communities.

Considering online music collaboration activities focused on creative crowdsourcing, I distinguish between three main types of platforms and services:

A. Virtual Studio Platforms – collaborative DAWs and related software facilitating online recording, sequencing, and mixing. Examples include: Audiotool, BandLab, Endlesss, Soundtrap.
B. Telematic Platforms – facilitating networked live performance. Examples include: JamKazam, Jamulus, SonoBus, Soundjack.
C. Social Networking Platforms – facilitating social networking and crowdsourcing. Examples include: Kompoz, Metapop, Splice, Vampr.

RMCS platforms form a complex ecosystem and, depending on the manufacturer, are available as web-based and standalone software for Windows, MacOS, iOS and Android, as well as audio plugins and social networking websites. It is important to note that while the listed typology signals various ways of working with music collaboration platforms, some of the software allows working across groups A, B and C. For example, some virtual-studio platforms allow for synchronous work, which enables a form of a networked live performance. In addition, audio plugins such as LISTENTO and Source-Nexus and standalone applications such as Groovesetter allow to stream audio signals between remotely located DAWs and can be used for approaches that belong to groups A and B. While these audio signal streaming products are currently not designed to offer groupware functionality, some virtual studios (e.g., Audiotool, BandLab) come with user profile creation functionality as well as advanced built-in communication tools. There are also platforms (e.g., Endlesss, JamKazam, SonoBus) that currently offer only basic communication tools so, to network with others, their users implement third-party tools such as Discord and Facebook groups or dedicated social networking RMCS platforms that belong to group C. Consequently, this chapter focuses on implications stemming from the use of communication tools embedded directly in the music collaboration platforms or available as external, third-party tools.

Musicians engage in group practices within complex collaborative projects, taking advantage of the following built-in groupware (with availability depending on the platform):

- Discussion forums (examples of implementation can be found in Audiotool, Kompoz, Metapop)
- Direct messaging (e.g., BandLab, Kompoz, Soundtrap)
- Project text chat (e.g., Audiotool, SonoBus, Soundtrap)
- Project comments (e.g., Audiotool, BandLab, Metapop)
- Project video chat (e.g., Audiotool, Soundtrap)

When assessing communication tools built into RMCS, forums and direct messaging emerge as particularly effective for finding collaborators, inviting them to participate, and discussing the production processes. Successful implementation is strategically important for the facilitation and outcomes of crowdsourcing and music-production campaigns. Beyond the use of communication tools, user engagement and audience growth can be facilitated by actions such as user following (e.g., available on Audiotool and BandLab) and word tagging, aiding in content allocation (e.g., Audiotool, BandLab, Blend). Selected platforms (e.g., Audiotool, BandLab, Metapop) incorporate a personalised feed where activities of followed or trending users are displayed.

Many platforms allow users to create profile pages where they can provide detailed descriptions of their musical experiences and include links to past projects and other web pages. While not exclusively an RMCS feature, these pages constitute a significant collaborative aspect of the software. They feature virtual music players that visually represent audio tracks as waveforms. These music players enable quick previews of musical drafts or fully mixed, completed projects, and facilitate feedback from the user community in the form of comments. Remixes and collaborative projects created with RMCS, such as Endlesss, BandLab and Audiotool, can be showcased and promoted through various online outlets. This includes playback on users' social networking profiles, web page embeddable audio players, or blog pages. Project pages frequently offer URL sharing or embeddable player functionality, allowing creators to present their work to audiences beyond RMCS.

As indicated earlier, music makers often turn to non-RMCS groupware during their project work. Both built-in and non-RMCS communication tools are crucial elements in executing successful collaborative music creation campaigns (Koszolko and Montano, 2016). Supplementary communication tools that complement built-in groupware include:

- Email
- External private messaging and chat (e.g., Discord, Instagram, Messenger)
- External user groups (e.g., Discord, Facebook)
- Video chat (e.g., Jitsi, Messenger, Zoom)

While many RMCS technologies are not new, we have witnessed a consistent growth in their user base over the past decade, a trend that was significantly accelerated during the Covid-19 pandemic. For instance, the BandLab platform celebrated reaching 30 million users in 2021 and 50 million users in 2022 (Legrand, 2022). In the last two years, alongside the emergence of newer platforms like Endlesss and the demise of established ones such as Ohm Studio, we have seen various enhancements in available music production and communication tools. This process was accelerated during the Covid-19 pandemic. Improvements related to groupware across selected platforms include broader implementation of private messaging, text, and video chat, as well as forum functionality.

3 GROUP PRACTICES

RMCS platforms are collaborative environments that facilitate the formation of groups with a primary focus on various music-production activities. These activities encompass songwriting, instrumental performance, recording, as well as mixing and mastering. When examining the roles of 'users' and 'producers' within the collaborative-media infrastructure, Löwgren and Reimer (2013) observed that:

> the distinction between 'users' and 'producers' would be more or less eradicated, where any member could produce content, and where community mechanisms such as reputation points earned through voting would be used for validating contributions rather than structural mechanisms such as appointing some people to the role of 'producer'.
>
> (2013, p. 81)

To succeed in using RMCS for studio recording and live performance projects, one must demonstrate proficiency in tasks like recording, mixing, and understanding concepts such as signal flow and online latency. The latter issue is particularly critical in the context of synchronous project work. Therefore, possessing musical proficiency alone is insufficient for effectively utilising RMCS. This implies a specific target group of RMCS users and aligns with one of Burgess' functional typologies of music producers as artists who produce their own work (2013).

In the realm of RMCS-based group work, the spread of various music production and performance skills within a group is important; however, the possession of a broad spectrum of skills by an individual is also beneficial. Based on my experience, a blend of diverse technical and musical expertise is necessary to maintain efficiency and achieve swift results. Producers with a wider palette of musical skills can offer substantial input during the songwriting and arrangement phases. While there might be a potential risk of clashes in opinions among similarly skilled RMCS collaborators, given the relatively unstructured nature of RMCS group work, having multiple highly skilled individuals involved in a project serves as a safety net in situations where one of them is unable to contribute as required.

The provision of input is one of the challenges facing music production in the cloud, particularly in crowdsourced activities. Facilitating engagement in RMCS involves bridging the gap between users seeking contributions and those willing to provide them. My experience indicates that irrespective of RMCS, the number of users requesting collaboration exceeds the number of users willing to contribute to projects initiated by others. The most efficient way to bridge this gap is to engage users in conversations and conduct group and community-building activities.

Two important group-building actions involve what Jaques and Salmon (2010) describe as social and task dimensions. These actions play a significant role in building and maintaining RMCS communities and music-production projects. The social dimension provides emotional involvement, morale, interest, and loyalty. The task dimension offers stability, purpose, direction and a sense of accomplishment. Actively nurturing relationships within a group is an integral part of conducting projects in RMCS and seeing them to completion. Online producers frequently engage in actions such as initiating, coordinating, seeking and providing information, defining progress, and testing – all of which belong to the task dimension. Social and task dimensions were present in my project work and proved crucial to the success of the productions. Typically, the role of the project instigator, the executive producer or the leading artist is to ensure that social and task dimensions are established in group work. Additionally, members of well-functioning groups exhibit awareness of these dimensions when collaborating on a project. The effort and time invested in group-building and maintenance tasks within RMCS networks often result in successful music-production projects.

Building relationships and cohesiveness among group members is an element of group maintenance and an integral part of the social dimension that fosters a sense of loyalty within the group. Group cohesiveness is strengthened by non-musical conversations. In her ethnographic research on personal connections in the digital age, Baym (2010, p. 72) discussed a strong sense of online group membership serving as "bases for the creation of new relationships as people from multiple locations gather synchronously or asynchronously to discuss topics of shared interest, role play, or just hang out". The notion of 'just hanging out' is also a significant aspect of RMCS relationships. Many conversations I had, using tools such as private messaging and chat, were informal and often humorous discussions unrelated to any music-production projects. We frequently talked about our musical interests or personal lives, diverging from topics related to work on specific compositions. These conversations were instrumental in helping me to get to know collaborators whom I had never met face to face on a deeper level, fostering a stronger sense of connection with them. Building relationships within creative social settings generates "antecedent conditions" (McIntyre, 2008) that contribute to the formation of ideas and processes which enhance collaborative outcomes.

Groups formed within online communities and networks "develop a strong sense of group membership" (Baym, 2010, p. 72), and in my experience, the degree to which this sense of group membership can be developed is highly dependent on the communication tools available in a given platform, as well as various events that stimulate music creation. Some platforms (e.g., Audiotool, BandLab, Metapop, Splice) facilitate different forms of contests and creative challenges to foster creativity and increase community engagement and interactions between users. These events provide valuable stimuli to bring users of various experience levels together and create new musical works (Koszolko, 2017). As a result, platform-initiated events are important and frequently used strategies to stimulate engagement. However, events initiated externally can play a similar role. An example of an externally run contest boosting the engagement of RMCS communities is the Collaborative Music Contest (CMC), launched in 2021. This virtual event was organised by the School of Music Collaboration, of which I was the founder. To my knowledge, this was and still is the only international music contest with a significant focus on online music collaboration. In its inaugural edition, the event received submissions from over 100 participating musicians in multiple countries across Australasia, Europe and North America. Contestants used a range of RMCS, including platforms that do not have built-in community features. This suggests that RMCS musicians view public contests as opportunities to form partnerships and create new material.

Winners of CMC 2021 serve as a prime example of the global membership within RMCS groups. The first prize was awarded to three musicians who utilised Audiotool – Icebox, SIREN and dcln, based in Singapore and Malaysia. The second prize was awarded to a team of musicians from Norway, Germany and Australia, formed within Ohm Studio and was led by a French-based songwriter, Nikaule. Discussing the communication process within the first prize-winning group, Cialeo Matias, who releases music as Icebox, stated, "The three of us would get into a Discord voice call every night to work on the track simultaneously, with Audiotool providing the necessary needs for a live-action collaborative experience" (2021). Discord has also been used by the second prize-winning team and has proven to be a particularly useful communication tool for many members of the Ohm Studio community since its closure in 2021.

Groupware external to RMCS is commonly used as a starting point for discussions between users who know each other in advance and have a history of communicating with tools outside RMCS. While RMCS-based groupware is typically incorporated for crowdsourcing the input of new, previously unknown musicians, there are also situations where third-party user groups are utilised to commence discussions with previously unknown members of the communities of practice. This becomes a necessity for collaborative software with limited or no built-in groupware.

The ability to remain anonymous is sometimes a factor encouraging the use of RMCS. A large proportion of users I encountered employed pseudonyms and frequently did not disclose details such as location or age. In my experience, anonymity does not hinder the formation of closer creative bonds with users. I collaborated extensively with users without ever learning their real names or details about age or exact location. I also perceived the desire of some users to remain anonymous as a means of removing their ego from the collaborative process, as their musical contribution became their sole expression. On occasion, I worked with users who remained anonymous throughout the entire collaborative process, despite extensive discussions concerning the project, providing ample opportunities for them to share aspects of their identity, such as their name, place of residence, age or occupation.

RMCS is commonly utilised by skilled hobbyists seeking to expand their creative networks and engage in recording or live performance projects. The Covid-19 pandemic has brought much attention to online music collaboration and attracted new users, including those in educational settings. The use of RMCS in formal school settings, particularly at secondary and tertiary levels, has increased substantially during the Covid-19 pandemic. However, long before Covid-19, various online platforms provided an effective opportunity to learn the craft of music-making and technical aspects of software by participating in different communities of practice. Defining the meaning of communities of practice, Wenger-Trayner describes them as "groups of people who share a concern or a passion for something they do and learn how to do it better as they interact regularly" (2015). This definition can also be applied to RMCS communities.

As indicated previously, in RMCS communities, lesser importance is placed on a user's biography, age and social context. However, technical experience and musical and collaborative abilities take the highest priority. Based on their skills, users fulfill various roles, such as recording and mixing, in addition to playing musical instruments. It is much more likely that music producers working in the informal settings of RMCS will perform multiple roles simultaneously. Groups most effective at leading their projects to successful conclusions are often characterised by diversity and talent across multiple group members. In groups without the spread of abilities, projects often do not progress beyond the initial draft or early discussions. Informal groups created within online communities have limited potential to adjust when any gaps in the group makeup are recognised. Instead, it is often the case that a group dissolves, and a project remains unfinished.

3.1 Learning from the community

RMCS platforms can serve as valuable communal learning environments, including both virtual studio and live performance platforms. Interestingly, many companies offering virtual studio or live performance collaboration software do not emphasise the learning potential of their platforms as much as the music production or collaborative features. However, it can be argued that promoting this aspect of their products could attract new members interested in learning songwriting, music production or instrumental performance techniques in a practical manner from the members of RMCS communities.

Simon Little, who collaborated with me on the Blend platform, explains:

> To reiterate, what a great experience it has been working on so much different music and how much I have learned as a result. In the six months or so since signing up, I have improved my craft as a producer of electronic music at a much faster rate than in a whole year of tinkering on my own. It has provided me with great motivation to get involved and put in time and effort, which I would have struggled with on my own. The feeling of community and support is wonderful.
> (2017)

An additional aspect of learning from the members of RMCS communities is the opportunity to receive feedback on one's music and, therefore, learn how other music producers react to a particular piece: "A few key Blend members will usually have a listen to a track and give me their critique. It especially helps to have other people's take on a mix to gain some feedback as to what the music sounds like with: A) a different monitoring system and B) fresh ears" (Little, 2017). The prospect of receiving critique from other practitioners in the domain (Csikszentmihalyi, 1988) is highly valuable, particularly considering that this opportunity is more limited in the non-RMCS-based music-production landscape. One of the challenges faced by electronic music producers is that they often work independently. Consequently, it is more difficult for them to receive informed feedback about their work before publishing it. RMCS provides an environment where such feedback can be efficiently obtained, potentially from numerous other practitioners. This environment reflects Csikszentmihalyi's systems model of creativity (1988) and departs from the Ptolemaic view of creativity, favouring a more complex system of multiple influences.

A significant facet of learning from the community is how this translates into the feeling of being inspired by others. I frequently found inspiration in the actions of project participants, and their musical input influenced my responses. One of my collaborators, Connor O'Brien (2017), describes the compounding effect that hearing the input of collaborating musicians can have on the evolution of the song: "getting to hear the song from both viewpoints can evolve the sound into something neither of you could've made on your own, but it still retains the flair of both (or all, if more than two) original artists". In my experience, the inspiration can be uplifting when working with talented individuals. During collaborative projects, I felt motivated to match the musical standards of my collaborators. This concept aligns with the notion of being reciprocally influenced by the actions of other musicians (Weinberg, 2005) and symbolises the creative aspect of learning from others.

3.2 Following the flow of events versus forcing results

When I work on RMCS-based collaborative projects, I often strive to achieve musical outcomes within the broad parameters of a pre-defined musical style. In some projects, I also endeavour to find contributors able to provide a very specific sound; for example, searching for a male vocalist who can sing falsetto. In instances where I aim to achieve specific musical goals, two modes of attaining the outcome emerge. The first one involves pursuing the initial goal until the exact, initially desired effect is achieved. The second mode of work involves letting several members of the online community play to the best of their ability and later choosing takes from these recordings. Often, these takes have been far removed from my initial concept of what might be a suitable direction for a song. In the second mode, we are following the flow of events and letting the current of the collaboration carry us while still maintaining the power of veto. Going with the communal flow and permitting a more flexible approach can lead to interesting, unplanned, creative outcomes. Peter Goss, one of the musicians with whom I collaborated in Ohm Studio, has had a similar experience related to how the final creative output can vary from what was initially expected:

> Regarding your thoughts about Flow vs Planning. Yes, my observations have been the same. When I invited collaborators for the first project I created on Ohm, I asked for someone to play some fast guitar work, which I am not fast enough to play. The result was not what I

had in mind but still fitted the song. So, you have to make a compromise with what your head is hearing and what actually gets recorded. But the same is true when you play with a group of musicians in the same room. I have taken songs to band practice sessions with a particular riff or sound in my head, and when we start playing the song, it always transforms into something different. Sometimes you like the interpretation, sometimes you don't.

(2015)

The level of creative flexibility required from a project producer varies depending on the received input. As stated by another of my collaborators, "adapting to different ideas is elementary in the collaborative music process. If you cannot align your work to different inputs, you don't have to work together with other artists, in my opinion" (interview with Metin Filiz, 2017). While I often have stylistic considerations impacting my decisions on whether to go with the flow or reject it, for some of my collaborators, going with the flow is such an essential element of working in RMCS that they see it as a critical part of their work process. Simon Little (2017) asserts, "I go with the flow wherever possible. Otherwise, I might as well do it myself".

When the project creator has a firm idea of the required creative input and the community is steering the project in a new, unplanned and undesired direction, I sometimes had no other option but to deem the result unsuitable. Other factors that influence my decisions on whether to go with the flow of the communal input or reject it are related to the production and performance skills of the participants. When I deem the input of my collaborators to be of very high quality, I am more than happy to reconsider my initial plan for a given composition. When I perceive the input as low quality regarding production or performance, I feel that rejecting the flow is very important, even if it means not progressing with the composition and deeming it incomplete. Sometimes collaborators deliver a very acceptable performance, yet they steer the project in a stylistic direction far removed from my creative objectives as a producer. This signals another point where choosing between accepting or rejecting the flow is required.

4 PHASES OF COMMUNICATION AND PROJECT DEVELOPMENT

One way of testing the importance of groupware and its impact on creative crowdsourcing is by posting projects on RMCS platforms and passively waiting for a reaction. In my experience, this rarely results in forming fruitful collaborations. Yet, newcomers to RMCS often do not progress beyond this approach and quickly get disheartened by the lack of response from the platform's community. Communication strategies focused on attracting new collaborators tend to include the three phases outlined in Figure 16.1. Typically, a user would make a choice and incorporate either an active or passive way of communicating. In the active approach, potential or confirmed collaborators are addressed directly and engaged in a discussion. In contrast, the passive way resembles an announcement, a statement of facts rather than a conversation. Figure 16.1 illustrates which groupware is used during the stages of communication within RMCS.

In most cases, it is possible to draw a clear distinction between tools that enable active or passive communication. In my experience, only forums and external groups can be used in both capacities as they allow for both direct (active) and indirect (passive) communication. When communicating project-oriented ideas, these two tools are used passively only at an early stage of the project's life, which is when it is being advertised to a broader community of users. As work on a project evolves, a forum quickly becomes less relevant, whereas external groups such as Discord continue to be useful and lead to incorporating built-in private chat tools to address specific contributors. This switch from public to private discussions marks the transition from passive to active communication. Interestingly, in some situations, collaborators do not use any form of groupware, and their musical contribution becomes the sole means of communicating their ideas without targeting specific group members. This can take the form of replying with a recording to a demo of a composition where the initial creator solicits contributions from the community of users. An example of this approach was the lyrical and vocal contribution to my project, 'The Giver' (KOshowKO, 2016; Koszolko, 2017).

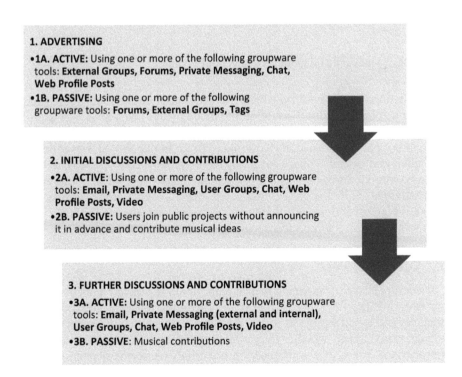

1. ADVERTISING

- **1A. ACTIVE:** Using one or more of the following groupware tools: **External Groups, Forums, Private Messaging, Chat, Web Profile Posts**
- **1B. PASSIVE:** Using one or more of the following groupware tools: **Forums, External Groups, Tags**

2. INITIAL DISCUSSIONS AND CONTRIBUTIONS

- **2A. ACTIVE:** Using one or more of the following groupware tools: **Email, Private Messaging, User Groups, Chat, Web Profile Posts, Video**
- **2B. PASSIVE:** Users join public projects without announcing it in advance and contribute musical ideas

3. FURTHER DISCUSSIONS AND CONTRIBUTIONS

- **3A. ACTIVE:** Using one or more of the following groupware tools: **Email, Private Messaging (external and internal), User Groups, Chat, Web Profile Posts, Video**
- **3B. PASSIVE:** Musical contributions

Figure 16.1 Phases and types of communication used in RMCS projects.

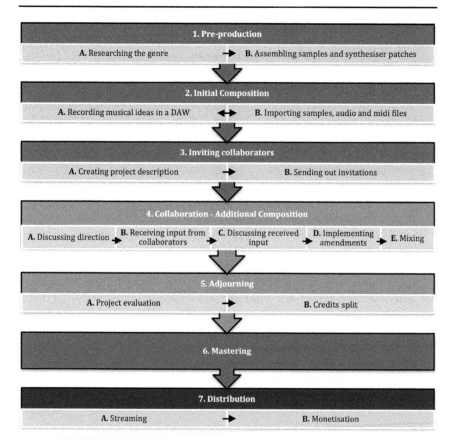

Figure 16.2 Phases of collaborative project development.

The collaborative process in which the previously mentioned phases of communication are utilised can be summarised by the seven phases of user-instigated collaborative project development (Figure 16.2), which I out-lined in my previous research (Koszolko, 2015). In this model, I expanded on Gellert and Nowak's phases of group development (2004, p. 183). In the process of collaborative project development, phases 1, 2, 3 and 6 are often solo activities led by the project instigator. Phases 4 and 5 are the main col-laborative group actions, while phase 7 is mainly automated and does not require input from the producer/creator past the initial set-up stage.

5 CONCLUSION

Considering Hansen's assertion that "collaboration is a means to an end, and that end is great performance" (2009, p. 16), I scrutinised various collaborative practices and groupware tools to ascertain their impact on music-production outcomes and assess whether they allow musicians to achieve the desired performance. Lines of communication in various platforms depend on the built-in groupware functionality. When native communication features are lacking, users take matters into their own hands, creating forums and groups, often turning to Discord or Facebook. The innovations afforded by collaborative music software are demonstrated in connecting music teams across borders but, importantly, are also manifested in the crowdsourcing potential of such software. Crowdsourcing opens creative networks to the global stage and expands music production opportunities.

The full potential of RMCS is not realised without the active implementation of groupware. If a platform lacks more sophisticated communication features, significant difficulties arise in engaging the community of users. This, in turn, neccessitates resorting to performing group-building actions via external groupware. While third-party tools can be efficient, not all RMCS members use them, which limits the social reach and means that collaboration is not as effective as when performing group-building tasks directly within RMCS.

This chapter has focused on the intersection of communal, collaborative work and communication tools that lead to forming new partnerships and taking advantage of the innovative music collaboration technologies available online. As asserted by Buckholtz:

> Online communities, social network sites, and virtual teams share common attributes. Two foundational commonalities are collaboration and information and communication technology (ICT). Collaboration occurs through the ICT medium. As technology became stable and more capable, the need to communicate advanced exponentially.
>
> (2013, p. 10)

The need to communicate is at the heart of RMCS. At this point, communication technology has been implemented in a range of advanced ways within multiple platforms that support collaborative activities through all stages of project development, as listed in Figure 16.2.

In relation to creative groups, Leonard and Swap (2005, p. 171) state that "interactive communication is the lifeblood of creativity", which, as my research shows, is also applicable to creating music in RMCS. Kibby (2000, p. 91) arrived at a similar conclusion while discussing virtual music communities and suggested that they "exist through dialogue; through an exchange of past social history and current social interaction".

Group behaviours across RMCS are varied and go beyond crowdsourcing; they present a strong potential for learning from the community and establishing music-production workflows defined by the nature of group dynamics. I suggest that successful RMCS groups are characterised by the spread of music-production abilities, while requiring each group member to possess a very good working knowledge of the chosen platform as well as a broad understanding of music composition and styles of music concerning the project.

One of the limitations of informal social groups formed within RMCS communities is their restricted potential to adjust when there is an imbalance, such as when a lack of a specific skill is identified. A factor impacting this limited potential is the unavailability of clearly defined structures and procedures, which are more often present in professional settings.

These structures can protect the group working towards a common goal by offering a set of defined expectations concerning collaborative teamwork.

In describing potential difficulties that might emerge in collaborative music work and referring to his pioneering online composition 'Cathedral' from 1997, Duckworth (2005) acknowledged that the complexity of creative options, along with changing group dynamics and new forms of expression, can lead group compositions in unpredictable directions. This discrepancy between the music producer's creative objectives and the creative direction enforced by the community of practice is a sign of challenges related to project management. When such challenges emerge, it is often necessary to reassess the initial objectives and decide whether to follow the flow of events within the community of practice and modify the project.

Assessing my collaborative work leads to the conclusion that there is a large element of unpredictability in the final creative output. While a user can choose to harness this unpredictability and follow the creative flow of the community, the musical results could be far removed from what was initially planned for the composition. When the production process is not firmly planned, the results can often bring elements of novelty, and it is up to the project's coordinator or group of coordinators to decide whether or how to incorporate the creative input received from the participants.

The social dimension of the group is a potent aspect influencing the group's adaptability and chances of survival in the face of adversity. All collaborative groups formed in my project work were informal, and many creative actions were spontaneous. I have observed members of RMCS communities generously offering their time and skills. Interestingly, most of my collaborators and interviewees did not pursue monetisation of their musical outputs. I also witnessed that RMCS is primarily utilised by amateurs rather than professional musicians, and a significant proportion of users are teenagers, although this tends to vary depending on the platform.

Digital group interactions are often affected by cultural (Markham, 2009) and social (McKenney and Zack, 2000) contexts within which group members operate, influencing how participants act within online networks. The perception of the distinction between digital and physical togetherness has changed in recent years, accelerated by remote working modes established during the Covid-19 pandemic. Working with RMCS confirms that synchronous and asynchronous connections within virtual relationships foster creative togetherness for group members who often have no face-to-face interaction. This togetherness and the resulting music-production outputs are largely facilitated by the groupware tools.

The aspect of synchrony, approached in various ways within RMCS platforms, is a significant consideration when selecting the appropriate RMCS. In the context of asynchronous virtual studio work, there can be a distinction between what Zagorski-Thomas describes as "playing music with other people" and "playing along to some music" (2014, p. 181). However, my creative work demonstrates the effectiveness of both synchronous and asynchronous approaches to RMCS-based collaboration and communal music production.

To fully benefit from the innovative technologies facilitating various music-production approaches in online collaborative creativity, musicians need to implement selected communication tools, particularly built-in forums, private messaging and chat rooms, as well as externally hosted groups and messaging groupware. These tools are critical to creative crowdsourcing. Understanding the dynamics of group work and creative processes in RMCS will help create groups with a stronger potential to complete their projects. These group processes do not run on autopilot; significant effort is needed to develop projects, particularly when working with collaborators who only meet online. This effort is not markedly different from traditional, face-to-face music-production activities, which include profile building, nurturing creative relationships, setting creative objectives, leading projects to conclusion, and disseminating their outcomes.

REFERENCES

Barbosa, A. M. (2006) *Computer-Supported Cooperative Work for Music Applications*. PhD thesis, Pompeu Fabra University, Barcelona.

Baym, N. K. (2010) *Personal Connections in the Digital Age*. Polity Press, Cambridge.

Buckholtz, D. R. (2013) *Classifying Virtual Collaboration Skills: A Case Study of Social Network Site Users' Skills and Transference To Virtual Teamwork*. ProQuest LLC, Ann Arbor.

Burgess, R. J. (2013) *The Art of Music Production: The Theory and Practice*. Oxford University Press, New York.

Csikszentmihalyi, M. (1988) 'Society, Culture, and Person: A Systems View of Creativity'. In R. J. Sternberg (ed.), *The Nature of Creativity: Contemporary Psychological Perspectives*. New York: Cambridge University Press, pp. 325–339.

Duckworth, W. (2005) *Virtual Music: How the Web Got Wired for Sound*. New York: Routledge.

Filiz, M. (2017) Author's interview with the user.

Gellert, M. and Nowak, C. (2004) *Teamwork, Team Building, Team Coaching: A Practical Guide to Working In and With Teams*. Limmer, Eutin.

Goss, P. (2015) Email communication with author.

Hansen, M. (2009) *Collaboration: How Leaders Avoid the Traps, Build Common Ground, and Reap Big Results*. Boston: Harvard Business Press.

Hugill, A. (2005) 'Internet Music: An Introduction'. *Contemporary Music Review* 24 (6): 429–437.

Jaques, D. and Salmon, G. (2010) 'Studies of Group Behaviour'. In H. Donelan, K. Kear and M. Ramage (eds.) *Online Communication and Collaboration: A Reader*. New York: Routledge, pp. 12–26.

Kibby, M. D. (2000) 'Home on the Page: A Virtual Place of Music Community'. *Popular Music* 19 (1): 91–100.

Koszolko, M. K. (2015) 'Crowdsourcing, Jamming and Remixing: A Qualitative Study of Contemporary Music Production Practices in the Cloud'. *Journal on the Art of Record Production* 10.

Koszolko, M. K. (2017) 'The Giver: A Case Study of The Impact of Remote Music Collaboration Software on Music Production Process'. *IASPM Journal* 7 (2).

Koszolko, M. K. (2022) 'The Virtual Studio'. In G. Stahl and J. M. Percival (eds.) *The Bloomsbury Handbook of Popular Music, Space and Place*. New York: Bloomsbury Academic, pp. 217–228.

Koszolko, M. K. and Montano, E. (2016) 'Cloud Connectivity and Contemporary Electronic Dance Music Production'. *Kinephanos, Journal of Media Studies and Popular Culture* 6 (1).

Lefford, M. N. (2000) *Recording Studios Without Walls: Geographically Unrestricted Music Collaboration*. Masters thesis, Massachusetts Institute of Technology, Cambridge.

Legrand, E. (2022) *BandLab Reaches 50m Users Milestone*, (website), available online at: https://creativeindustriesnews.com/2022/06/bandlab-reaches-50m-users-milestone/ [accessed August 2022].

Leonard, D. and Swap, W. (2005) *When Sparks Fly: Harnessing the Power of Group Creativity*. Boston: Harvard Business School Press.

Little, S. (2017) Author's interview with the user.

Löwgren, J. and Reimer, B. (2013) *Collaborative Media: Production, Consumption, and Design Interventions*. Cambridge, MA: MIT Press.

Markham, A. N. (2009) 'How Can Qualitative Researchers Produce Work That Is Meaningful Across Time, Space, and Culture?'. In A. N. Markham and N. K. Baym (eds.) *Internet Inquiry: Conversations about Method*. Los Angeles: Sage Publications, pp. 131–171.

Matias, C. (2021) Online communication with author.

McIntyre, P. (2008) 'The Systems Model of Creativity: Analyzing the Distribution of Power in the Studio'. *Journal on the Art of Record Production* 3.

McIntyre, P. (2012) 'Rethinking Creativity: Record Production and the Systems Model'. in S. Frith and S. Zargorski-Thomas (eds.) *The Art of Record Production: An Introductory Reader for a New Academic Field*. London: Ashgate, pp. 149–164.

McKenney, J. L. and Zack, M. H. (2000) 'Social Context and Interaction in Ongoing Computer-Supported Management Groups'. In David E. Smith. (eds.) *Knowledge, Groupware and the Internet*. Boston: Butterworth – Heinemann, pp. 171–218.

O'Brien, C. (2017) Author's interview with the user.

Olson, G. and Olson, J. (2010) 'Groupware and Computer – Supported Cooperative Work'. In Helen Donelan, Karen Kear and Magnus Ramage (eds.) *Online Communication and Collaboration: A Reader*. New York: Routledge, pp. 39–66.

Weinberg, G. (2005) 'Interconnected Musical Networks: Toward a Theoretical Framework'. *Computer Music Journal* 29 (2): 23–39.

Wenger-Trayner, E. and Wenger-Trayner, B. (2015) *Communities of Practice a Brief Introduction*, available at: http://wenger-trayner.com/introduction-to-communities-of-practice/ [accessed August 2022].

Zagorski-Thomas, S. (2014) *The Musicology of Record Production.* Cambridge: Cambridge University Press.

DISCOGRAPHY

KOshowKO. (2016) *The Giver (Download): Las Machinas 004*, available at: https://philosophyofsound.bandcamp.com/album/the-giver [accessed 5 August 2022].

17

From master pieces to masterpiece

Source selection and reformatting during the republishing process of legacy music productions

Thomas Bårdsen

1 INTRODUCTION

Music streaming services have made not only an increasingly broad palette of contemporary music available but also back catalogue productions. Legacy music productions, which are often referred to as catalogue music, have occupied an increasing share of total music revenue in recent years. According to the MRC Data report, the share of total album revenue from catalogue music increased to 70% in 2021 (MRC Data, 2022). In 2020, total album revenue from catalogue music reached 65%, which rose to 66% in the first half of 2021 (MRC Data, 2021). Thus, figures for 2021 reveal accelerating growth in the last six months of the year. Following this trend, the first half of 2022 showed continued growth, with catalogue music comprising 72.4% of total album revenue (Luminate, 2022). Catalogue music is in these reports defined as content released over 18 months ago. In Norway, increased attention to legacy productions can be seen in the music production archive that the music industry helped to establish as a part of the National Library of Norway. The library functions as the music industry's joint archive and contains assets from all major record companies, many recording studios, and artists. It offers transfer and pre-mastering services on demand from its audio laboratory. Internal documents reveal that, from 1998 to 2015, there was a steady demand for 100 to 200 recordings (tracks) per year for republishing purposes from the music industry. From 2016 onward, this increased to well over 3,000 recordings per year in 2020 and 2021 (Figure 17.1). The growth in demand from the music industry could be seen as a direct result of increased commercial attention to catalogue music, but there could also be other contributing factors. For the past decade, the National Library of Norway has increased its efforts to share metadata about the archive's content with the music industry and its capacity to handle requests in terms of both personnel and equipment. The audio laboratory currently employs 16 full-time audio engineers.

The republishing process encompasses several phases and aspects that are worth examining. Thus, the aim of this paper is to provide a better understanding of the initial steps of source selection and reformatting. It uses the

DOI: 10.4324/9781003462101-19

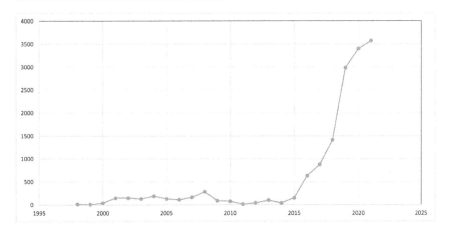

Figure 17.1 The National Library of Norway's provision of recordings to the music industry 1998–2021.

National Library of Norway's work with the music industry as a background and focuses on productions recorded on magnetic tape. In addition, the research aims to improve this area of practice. According to Gunnar Ternhag, one aim of academic research on music production is to provide audio engineers with the necessary knowledge in an increasingly complex profession (Ternhag, 2012). Source selection and initial transfer have been reported as consistent challenges in several publications on remastering (Bruel, 2019).

2 THE ILLUSION OF THE MASTER TAPE

The master is often a central element in discussions related to music production. One of these discussions concerns the ontological status of recorded music. Nelson Goodman originally placed music in the same ontological category as literature, describing them both as allographic art (Goodman, 1968). The term stood in contrast to autographic art, such as paintings and sculptures. To distinguish allographic and autographic art, he addressed their relation to their copies. Books and music can be reproduced without any copies being regarded as fake instances of the original. By contrast, a copy of a painting would be regarded as such, even if it was indistinguishable from the original. However, Theodore Gracyk (1996) used the example of the master tape to describe an ontological shift of recorded music to autographic art. Not using the master tape and re-recording a copy in its place would result in an artefact that could be described as a fake, even if the re-recorded production was indistinguishable from the original. Nevertheless, Simon Zagorski-Thomas maintained that recorded music could never be autographic. Unlike Gracyk, he asserted that the master recording is just something that may exist:

> A recording, even if it does constitute the musical work itself as opposed to a performance of a composition, is never an autographic

work. There may be an original master recording just as there may be an original manuscript of a novel but, in terms of someone engaging with the work of art, there should be no difference between that original and a reproduced instance.

(Zagorski-Thomas, 2014, p. 24)

Conflicting views of the master recordings can be found in other fields. For example, the reactions from a 2019 news article by Jody Rosen described a decade-old fire in one of Universal Studios' main master tape vaults (Rosen, 2019). Rosen compared master recordings to original paintings, such as the Mona Lisa. However, unlike original paintings, which can be visited and viewed by the public, the latter's view of master recordings is, in many ways, obstructed by technology. Through new technology, the public may have a better and fuller experience of the work in the future. If the master tape is lost in some way, then these possibilities are also lost (Rosen, 2019). Therefore, the news that Universal Studios had lost thousands of master tapes in a fire was devastating. Later, archivists at Universal Studios estimated that the original recordings lost in the fire accounted for only 0.1% of affected tapes (Aswad, 2020). The conflicting reports by Rosen and Universal Studios' archivists can be partly explained by conflicting definitions of "the master recording." Rosen's comparison of master tapes to the Mona Lisa is based on a view of master recordings as defined, singular, and unique. This view is often challenged when examining material in a music production archive. A possible explanation of this challenge in finding a defined master recording is a lack of labelling and archive routines in the music industry.

In 1986, the British Record Producers Guild and the Association of Professional Recording Services (APRS) introduced a tape labelling standard for master tapes in the United Kingdom. Later, the system was endorsed by the Society of Professional Audio Recording Services (SPARS) in the United States. In 1992, further efforts were made through the publication of The Master Tape Book (Parson, Foster and Hollebone, 1992) to address what was described as the greatest challenge facing the music industry at the time: tape labelling. The authors introduced the book by answering the following question:

Q: When is a master not a master? A: When it's a master. Confused? You're not alone. So are thousands of engineers, producers, and A&R people the world over every time they receive a tape labelled MASTER, COPY MASTER, PRODUCTION MASTER, or (and this is one of the best) a FINAL MASTER dated two months before yet another MASTER!

(Parson, Foster and Hollebone, 1992, p. 3)

In contrast to the view of a music production encompassing a single and unique master recording and its various copies, the book described several situations in which material could be labelled as a master. In audio engineering, the term master originated with direct-to-disc recording in the early twentieth century. At that time, the master disc was used directly to duplicate records. The master disc was defined by the physical shape of its grooves, which were transferred to available discs through casting. When professional tape machines emerged, they immediately began to use tape as an intermediate stage in the process. The goal was to edit the recording and make a better master disc. In many ways, tape technology was a medium for editing. It was possible to directly edit the production by cutting and splicing or manipulating the electronic signal from the tape recorder before cutting the master disc. The possibilities were endless, and the tape vault for a production could ultimately hold a variety of tapes for different stages in the process. The vault could also hold tapes that were put together for a specific use. Without proper labelling, the hunt for the best source for a new release was difficult. Along with the APRS and SPARS initiative, the Audio Engineering Society and The Recording Academy initiated a joint effort to label what they called recorded music projects (AES, 2014; The Recording Academy, 2018). The principle is process-oriented; the production material should be sourced from the end of each process and ready for the next stage. Thus, the tracking master should be ready for the mixing stage, the mixed master should be ready for the mastering stage, and the mastered master should be ready for duplication.

However, even with clear labelling, the selection of the original master was not given. There were different views about which stage of the production process the original master could be found. In the APRS and SPARS labelling system, there is an entity called the original master, which was described as "the earliest possible generation of the final stereo product" (Parson, Foster and Hollebone, 1992, p. 3). Furthermore, the description of the system explained that a tape labeled "original master" must be used with care and preferably cleared by the producer. Bob Katz (2002), on the other hand, considered the master to follow the mastering process and recommended avoiding the use of the word "master" to describe anything but the end product of the mastering process:

> The sources for an album are not the master; the album (production) master is the final, PQ'd, equalized, edited, assembled, and prepared tape or disc that needs no further audio work, and is ready for replication. Please label the source media: Submaster or Worktape, or Mix or Session Tape, or Edited-Mix or Compiled-mix or Equalized Mix, to name several possibilities.
>
> (Katz, 2002, p. 285)

Katz further explained that this naming strategy would prevent confusion in the future, as the one and only master would be found for republishing. If the republished edition wanted to redo the mastering using the original source rather than the production master, the diverse naming standard for source material suggested by Katz could be a problem.

3 TAPE LABELLING AND SOURCE SELECTION AT THE NATIONAL LIBRARY OF NORWAY

Research on historic tape labelling procedures in Norwegian recording studios found a clear trend of decreased information about the actual content from the 1950s to the 1980s (Bårdsen, 2019). In the 1950s, studios often used a dedicated master number from the very beginning of production. This number followed the content all the way to the disc and was etched into each copy as a matrix number. More complicated multitrack productions from the early 1960s involved the allocation of a master number to each recorded song on assets all the way from tracking through mixing and mastering. Towards the end of the 1960s, this practice was more or less lost, and the studios focused on increasingly detailed technical information. Even the names of artists and songs were sometimes left blank, let alone secure information about which version of the track would be used in the release (Bårdsen, 2019). Even the dating of tapes could be difficult. Not only were dates missing from approximately 17% of tapes, but the dates found could refer to everything from recording dates to copying dates for various rereleased versions. During the 1990s, tape labelling in the earliest stages of production deteriorated even further; in some collections, around half of all multitrack tapes appeared to completely lack any information. Further along the production process, towards duplication, labelling improved. In the 1990s, the old master number system was even reintroduced in the form of the International Standard Recording Code (IRSC). However, the main difference was that a number was not allocated at the beginning of production like in the 1950s and 1960s but only found on production masters for CDs. This left material from the earliest generations un-labelled.

During source selection at the National Library of Norway, all material related to the production is first sourced. The search is conducted among all in-house materials across the collections of various record labels and recording studios and the personal collections of producers, engineers, or artists. Internal documents from 2021 revealed that, during that year, the source was predominantly found in collections not associated with the record label that requested the master. Then, the library usually seeks the earliest generation of the completed mix. This often conflicts with original labelling procedures, which forces the selection of better-labeled production masters from later generations. When possible, the source selection is conducted in dialogue with the original producers or artists, who can guide the selection. However, the selection process is often left to the audio engineer, who combs through the available material and uses analytics and information to guide the choice. Ultimately, the final decision is often based on listening. Bruel described a similar challenge during the remastering of the band Sunnyboys (Bruel, 2019). The project began with five tapes, but further archival retrieval resulted in the identification of 30 tapes, which all needed assessment and close listening before the final sources could be selected. This challenge was also emphasized by Jim Sam of the Hoover Institute during a tutorial at the 131st AES Convention.

Shifting labelling procedures and the loose use of terminology can cause considerable uncertainty when selecting the best source for transfer (Rumsey, 2012).

Therefore, what should be a clear-cut hierarchy of master and copies often appears to be a chaotic collection of tapes, where many conclusions can be made about which tape constitutes the ideal master. The basis of this selection could change over time as more sources become available or more information about them is uncovered. This is further complicated by several factors, like tape degradation or developments in restoration techniques, that could affect the overall potential of a given tape over time.

4 THE ILLUSION OF THE CLEAN TRANSFER

Defining a master tape encompasses an evaluation of the best reproduction method. To understand the complexity of reproducing professionally recorded magnetic tapes, it is important to understand the weaknesses of magnetic tape compatibility (McKnight, 1967). Most people are familiar with consumer formats, in which reproduction is more standardized. However, professional formats tend to trade off compatibility with improvements in audio fidelity (Brixen, 1991), sometimes even deliberately to increase their own market standing (Burgess, 2014). Detailed information is needed to set up and choose the correct reproduction method. In a test sample of 150 tapes from the National Library of Norway, technical information needed for transfer settings was missing from all tapes (Bårdsen, 2019). In the 1950s and 1960s, technical information was especially scarce. From the 1970s onward, the amount of available information improved, but a level of uncertainty remains in most cases, which leaves the task of evaluating available information and choosing the correct playback up to the audio engineer. One uncertainty is the record head design. For common two-track magnetic tapes with a width of one-quarter inch, there are at least seven different head design formats (Bradley, 2004). In addition, tape manufacturers did not always follow these standards, often because they sought to improve the specifications of their own products (McKnight, 1978). Moreover, recording studios or broadcasters could specially order designs of their own liking (Brixen, 1991). Early on, track head design was discovered to be a cause of poor incompatibility between tape machines (Leslie and Snyder, 2010). Nevertheless, information about track head design is extremely rare in the National Library of Norway's collections. Using a magnetic visualizer like the Arnold B-1022, a granular assumption could be made by evaluating the replay head design (Casey, 2007). Another method is to use a special three track inspection machine and then compare the output level from the middle track with the two outer (Sjöberg, 2004). For a positive identification, listening is often needed (Casey, 2007).

Another factor in evaluation is reproduction equalization. In Norway, this is usually documented by simply stating whether the equalization follows European or American standards (Bårdsen, 2019). Granularity is often missing, as especially European standards could exist in both consumer or professional form, and in addition, change at certain years (Bradley, 2004). To add to this complexity, certain manufacturers tweaked their recording (and reproduction) curves to enhance their products (McKnight, 1978, 2006), again trading off compatibility.

The most important factor in ensuring compatibility is calibration to the chosen standard. The tape machine used in production should be routinely adjusted with a standardized calibration tape. The extent to which different studios calibrated their machines is another factor that creates uncertainty. However, even if the studios did everything correctly, differences in the production of the calibration tapes have been discovered, which prompts the question of which brand of calibration tape was used to calibrate the machine that recorded the tape (McKnight, Cortez and McKnight, 1998). Information about calibration routines is not commonly – if ever – found on tapes.

Along with the tape reproducer, there could also be different types of noise reduction systems in use. The most common is the Dolby A system used in the 1970s and 1980s. To avoid tape hiss, basically, a four-band compressor is introduced before the signal is recorded. Upon playback, the signal is then restored using a four-band expander. To ensure compatibility, the Dolby encoded tape should have a calibration tone recorded, which can be used to set up the Dolby A decoder. However, this tone only calibrates the level and does not compensate for deviations in the frequency characteristics of the playback system. Given the design of the system, Dolby A could triple any slight deviation between systems, even if it is calibrated perfectly (Brixen, 1991).

Often, final decisions are made by ear by trying different head designs, machines, and settings. The physical condition of the tape may also lead the engineer to choose a gentler tape machine that might deviate from some settings related to track head design or electronics. In the recording industry, both time and cost are also contributing factors. The availability of machines could vary, which affects final decisions about reproduction systems. When information is missing, the audio engineer must rely on their own assessment, which is often assisted by listening to different alternative setups or settings. This procedure was also described by Bruel (2019), Sjöberg (2004) and Casey (2007), whereby the selection of critical settings is based on listening.

Ultimately, both source selection and reformatting are dependent on several factors that contribute to overall project quality. The main factors are the competence and knowledge of the personnel involved and the information and resources available to them at the specific time of the project. Over time, the quality of several factors could increase or decrease. The condition of the original tapes and reproducers could also decline in the future, as could the availability of calibration tapes, spare parts, and skilled personnel. At the same time, there may be future innovations in reproduction techniques, treatments, or analytics to help overcome some of these challenges. Thus, conditions for transfer are constantly changing, which affects the overall quality (Hess, 2008). As a result, the reformatting process is greatly affected by evaluations and decisions made by personnel in the face of these changing conditions.

5 FROM DEFINITIVE TO CRITICAL EDITIONS

Problems associated with the contemporary dissemination of legacy works are not limited to music productions. Similar challenges have been addressed with older forms of art. Perhaps the closest analogues are score-based music and literature. The critical editing process involves critically examining every available source, and then presenting an edition of the work best suited to the project's goals through a transparent and documented process. By studying digitization projects in libraries, Dahlström (2010) observed conflicts and tensions between ideals and strategies, which are in many ways similar to patterns in scholarly editing. In general, two positions can be described. The first category is the critical or scholarly editing process:

> It examines a bulk of documents, compares their texts, normally clusters these around the abstract notion of a work, arranges them in a web of relations, and attempts to embody this web in the scholarly edition. The edition, then, becomes a surrogate purporting to represent, tag and comment upon the edited work. In a sense, the editor reproduces existing documents by making a new document that also embodies a documentation of the textual history and the editorial process.
>
> (Dahlström, 2010, p. 79)

By contrast, the non-critical process is centered around transparently disseminating a source document, seemingly without alterations. For example, identifying the oldest version of a document and presenting a digitized photo of it, along with notes about its provenance. In this way, the information in the source document is presented as transparently as possible, leaving all judgement up to the recipient. However, a possible disadvantage of this method is that it could mispresent content. Without proper knowledge about the artist's intent, production methods, and other factors, a sketch or unfinished version of the work could be misinterpreted. Dahlström (2010) questioned whether a truly transparent copy can exist. Even for paper documents, there is a process in which the producer of the edition influences the results. Some information and aspects are always prioritized at the expense of others (Dahlström, 2019). Thus, a documented critical examination of the source, the techniques used, and the end format could prevent misunderstandings and clarify the circumstances of the edition. A distinction between the two approaches, therefore, exists between the acknowledged presence and the presumed absence of the editor (Dahlström, 2010).

Luca Cossettini emphasized the need to understand audio documents as information carriers in need of critical review (Cossettini, 2009). Cossettini described an attitude in the archive world in which digital copies are treated like definite clones. A closer examination reveals that, through digitization, documents undergo a process of recontextualization that can radically transform their understanding and interpretation. Cossettini argued that the transition from an analog to a digital medium is not a simple process of duplication but a real mutation. Although digital backups may appear neutral and resemble clones of the original document, it is important to understand that any form of repositioning carries an element of change that requires critical reflection and assessment (Cossettini, 2009). In collaboration with Angello Orcalli, they described the preservation of audio documents using a diasystem adapted from Cesare Segre (Cossettini and Orcalli, 2017). The copyist has an internal language system that comes into contact with the original text during transcription. The copyist cannot completely suppress this, which contributes to a certain degree of subjective influence. Therefore, Cossettini and Orcalli claimed that this subjectivity must be considered in relation to the restoration work. Rather than refer to a one-directional digital preservation, Cossettini and Orcalli argued for selection, playback, and production to be part of the scientific editing process. The result from this process is not final or set but in constant contact with the time in which the preservation work is produced. This results in critical editions of the work, not exact digital preservation files. Such productions of critical editions are not final, complete clones of the source material but part of an ongoing process in which all sources, including previously produced editions, are evaluated and re-evaluated.

The task of critical editing is described by Orcalli with a strong link to further complement the artistic project rather than to preserve information in single documents: "The task of the critical editing of recorded music is to bring musical works back to life for publishing and performance, re-coded and re-presented according to the present media environment" (Orcalli, 2017, p. 27). Thus, the character of the process changes from a one-directional project that aims to produce the ultimate edition to a complementary process that aims to contribute to an ongoing artistic project.

6 REPUBLISHED MUSIC AND TRACEABILITY

One key effect of a critical stance towards digital transfer is a deeper focus on documentation and metadata (Dahlström, 2019). This could potentially address some of the concerns facing the music industry. Several authors have discussed the continued re-issue of legacy recordings in relation to authenticity (Alleyne, 2020; Bruel, 2019; Lawson, 2008; O'Malley, 2015; Winters, 2016). Both O'Malley and Winters used a definition of authenticity with a focus on the accurate reproduction of an original. Winters partly attributed the surge of vinyl records to authenticity and the fact that the public came closer to the original master tape through physical vinyl records – not necessarily closer to the sonic content but closer through a more traceable copy history or provenance. A digital file on a streaming platform contains few or no details on its copy history. Digital files are easy to manipulate. Although the source and reformatting process is often quite blurred, even in the rerelease of vinyl records, the grooves themselves are difficult to alter once cut, and the relationship to a master disc is present through the master disc number (Winters, 2016). At the very least, the disc is a clear copy of the authorized master disc. Lawson made a similar point, explaining that Universal Music Group used pictures of master tapes on republished editions of ABBA albums to enhance and signal the product's authenticity (Lawson, 2008). Providing listeners with similar verification in the digital domain is one of the novelties of the Master Quality Authenticated (MQA) format. Bob Stuart claims that building provenance in the distribution chain would improve the experience of listeners (Stuart, 2022). Based on this logic, the potential for improvement should be even greater at the other end of the production chain by ensuring transparent traceability all the way from the original source. In the early days of music production, this was not much of an issue, as distributed content could be more easily trusted. However, as dozens of versions of the same recording were issued and re-issued on multiple formats over the decades, the question of what exactly one is listening to began to grow in importance. Bruel found that the creativity and potential for alterations in remastering could possibly falsify the meaning of original productions (Bruel, 2019). O'Malley (2015) also indicated that previous editions are suppressed when new ones are released. The new editions are not necessarily the most preferred editions. Mike Alleyne even saw this as the potential cause of a rupture in the historical narrative of popular music:

> As expanded reissues assumes a greater role in sustaining the commercial viability of catalogue material, the circumstances under which works are sonically repackaged with supplementary production represents a potential rupture in popular music's historical narrative. It suggests that ultimately there might not be a definitive version of a recording around which authenticity debates can actually occur, thus undermining aspects of critical authenticity.
>
> (Alleyne, 2020, pp. 25–26)

There is great potential to improve legacy music production by connecting the listener more closely to the original content in archives and the processes used in production – not by simply stating "master tape quality" on the recording but by providing listeners with detailed and transparent information about the production process and assessments. Creativity in the republishing process could, at the same time, be of value, for instance, by attracting new listeners to the work. In a critical process, creative input from contemporary agents should not be hindered; instead, documentation should be demanded to clarify what is presented and, thus, prevent misunderstandings and illuminate the circumstances of the edition.

7 TOWARD A MORE CRITICAL DOCUMENTATION OF SOURCE SELECTION AND TRANSFER

Based on an examination of the developments and challenges that face the music industry in Norway with regard to republishing legacy productions, it is clear that a recognition of the critical and subjective factors that influence this work is needed. More critical documentation could bring listeners closer to the production and compensate for the deterioration in traceability that has occurred through the loss of physical media and extensive re-issuing. Critical reflections could enable alternative conclusions and additional work in the future, engaging both listeners and scholars in the field. At the same time, the rapid evolution and size of the music industry make in-depth work on every republished recording unrealistic. In my view, the first step would be to emphasize descriptions of the most important evaluations and re-use production metadata that could be automatically sourced to build a final report suited to future critical, in-depth investigations. Such reports could be submitted to the record label with the final media files, linked to related materials in the archive's database, and potentially be made available to the public. Cossettini and Orcalli (2017) identified four tools that the critical editing of recorded music must include:

> a spectromorphological analysis supported by time/frequency and time/amplitude representations, a survey of the physical editing cues on the original carriers, a historical reconstruction of the laboratorial practices of the time, research on the phenomenology of circulation of the documents, the interpretation of intentional and unintentional alteration to the signal.
>
> (p. 414)

Building on this description, I propose a framework for more critical documentation of source selection and transfer adapted to the National Library of Norway's work with the music industry. In addition, the project's background and goal should be described, as these can be quite diverse. Some projects have simpler aims (e.g., making the content available in a new format), while others are more ambitious (e.g., correcting errors in previous editions, improving fidelity, or adapting the sonic content to attract new listeners). Thus, the first part of the framework focuses on the background of the project – both the goal of the current edition, a description of known previous editions, and self-descriptions of the parties involved.

The next part focuses on descriptions of available resources or assets. For each resource, four main pieces of information should be included. First, the history of ownership or provenance should be described. Hopefully, most of this information can be drawn from acquisition metadata related to the asset's deposit. Second, the asset's physical history and status should be documented, including the tape's condition, what is known about its storage condition and handling, any previous restoration work, and whether the asset requires any treatment. Both conditions and treatments should be described using standard terminology as used by the International Association of Sound and Audiovisual Archives (Bradley, 2004). Third, the asset's integrity should be documented, including any alterations, annotation of editing cues and other causes for concern, and whether the content aligns with written information. Finally, the asset's

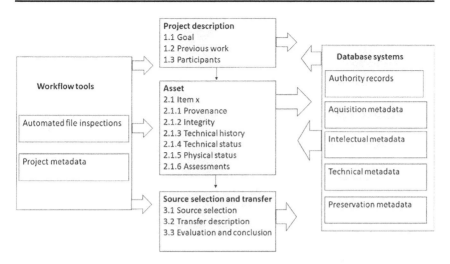

Figure 17.2 Framework for documentation of source selection and transfer.

technical history and status should be described, such as how and for what purpose it was produced. The description of the asset's written information should also mention the recording studio, dates, which production process the asset results from (e.g., tracking, mixing, or mastering), known information about its replay characteristics, whether machines that match these characteristics are available, and whether the tape has been used in productions in the past (e.g., as a production master for a specific edition).

The third and final part of the report describes the selected sources and the transfer process, with a focus on the end result. For example, on what basis were the sources selected, and what arguments contributed to the choice of replay system and settings? Did everything go as planned? Several analysis methods could be used to compare resources for selection and underpin the final result. By using existing library database systems and workflow tools to automate tasks and re-use as much existing documentation as possible, the effort required from project staff could be minimized (Figure 17.2).

8 CONCLUSION

The first century of recorded music elapsed nearly a generation ago. Nevertheless, interest in and continued appreciation of music productions from this period only appear to be growing. Revenue from older music productions has surpassed contemporary productions for some time and continues to grow. Based on statistics from Norway, the number of new editions of legacy productions derived from the master tape vault at the National Library of Norway has exponentially increased. An examination of the initial steps of source selection and reformatting for republished music productions shows that both these processes are dependent on various shifting factors, which influence the final results. Furthermore, both processes depend on assessments and decisions made by personnel who must contend with these factors. A lack of detailed information is the factor that contributes the most to uncertainty in identifying the best source and selecting the procedure for playback and transfer. These findings align with arguments from recent research, which have called for a shift to a more critical view of digitization and archiving. Building on this work, more critical documentation of source selection and transfer is proposed to improve the republishing process in the music industry. Both current and future editions would benefit from a better understanding of circumstances and decisions related to this process. In addition, documentation could provide insight and details that are important to in-depth critical work on the production in the future.

REFERENCES

AES. (2014). *Recommendation for delivery of recorded music projects (AES TD1002.215–2)*. New York: Audio Engineering Society.

Alleyne, M. (2020). Authenticity in music production, in Bourbon, A., and Zagorski-Thomas, S. (Ed.), *The Bloomsbury handbook of music production*. New York: Bloomsbury Academic.

Aswad, J. (2020). Read Universal Music Group chief archivist's update on damage from 2008 fire, *Variety*, March 5, available online from https://variety.com/2020/music/news/universal-music-fire-archive-damage-update-2008-1203525454/ [accessed August 2022].

Bårdsen, T. (2019). *Sporfinnere: en undersøkelse av norsk musikkproduksjons teknologiske utvikling i et bevaringsperspektiv*. Ph. D. thesis. Universitetet i Agder.

Bradley, K. (Ed.). (2004). *Guidelines on the production and preservation of digital audio objects: IASA TC-04*. Auckland Park: International Association of Sound and Audiovisual Archives.

Brixen, E. B. (1991). *Lyd på bånd: om båndoptagerteknik*. Copenhagen: Teknisk Forlag.

Bruel, S. (2019). *Nostalgia, authenticity and the culture and practice of remastering music*. Ph. D. thesis. Queensland University of Technology.

Burgess, R. J. (2014). *The history of music production*. Oxford: University Press.

Casey, M. (2007). *The field audio collection assessment tool: Format characteristics and preservation problems*. IN: Indiana University, available online from www.dlib.indiana.edu/projects/sounddirections/facet/facet_formats.pdf [accessed August 2022].

Cossettini, L. (2009). Le registrazioni audio dell'archivio Luigi Nono di Venezia, *Musica e Technologia*, Vol. 3, No. 3, pp. 99–112.

Cossettini, L., and Orcalli, A. (2017). Towards a systemic approach to the critical editing of music at MIRAGE, in Cossettini, L., and Orcalli, A. (Ed.) *Sounds, voices and codes from the twentieth century: The critical editing of music at Mirage*. Udine: Cossettini, L. and Orcalli, A., pp. 401–418.

Dahlström, M. (2010). Critical editing and critical digitisation, in van Peursen, W. T., Thoutenhoofd, E., and van der Weel, A. (Ed.), *Text comparison and digital creativity: The production of presence and meaning in digital text scholarship*. Leiden: Brill Academic Pub, pp. 79–97.

Dahlström, M. (2019). Copies and facsimiles, *International Journal of Digital Humanities*, Vol. 1, No. 2, pp. 195–208.

Goodman, N. (1968). *Languages of art: An approach to a theory of symbols*. Indianapolis: Bobbs-Merrill.

Gracyk, T. (1996). *Rhythm and noise: An aesthetics of rock*. Durham: Duke University Press.

Hess, R. (2008). Tape degradation factors and challenges in predicting tape life. *ARSC Journal*, Vol. 39, No. 2, pp. 240–274.

Katz, R. A. (2002). *Mastering audio: The art and the science*. Oxford: Focal Press.

Lawson, J. (2008). *The compression and expansion of musical experience in the digital age*. M. Sc. thesis, University of Vermont.

Leslie, J., and Snyder, R. (2010). History of the early days of Ampex Corporation, *Audio Engineering Society* (website), available online from www.aes.org/aeshc/docs/company.histories/ampex/leslie_snyder_early-days-of-ampex.pdf [accessed August 2022].

Luminate. (2022). *Midyear report: U.S. 2022*. Los Angeles: Luminate.

McKnights, J. G. (1967). Tape reproducer response measurements with a reproducer test tape, *Journal of the Audio Engineering Society*, Vol. 15, No. 2, pp. 152–156.

McKnight, J. G. (1978). Low-frequency response calibration of a multitrack magnetic tape recording and reproducing system, *Journal of the Audio Engineering Society*, Vol. 26, No. 4, pp. 202–208.

McKnight, J. G. (2006). Tape recording equalization fundamentals and 15 in/s equalizations, *Magnetic Reference Lab* (website), available online from www.mrltapes.com/equaliz.html [accessed August 2022].

McKnight, J. G., Cortez, B. E., and McKnight, J. A. (1998). Tape flux measurement revisited, *Journal of the Audio Engineering Society*, Vol. 46, No. 10, pp. 845–857.

MRC Data. (2021). *Midyear report: U.S. 2021*. Los Angeles: MRC Data.

MRC Data. (2022). *Year-end report: U.S. 2021*. Los Angeles: MRC Data.

O'Malley, M. (2015). The definitive edition: Digitally remastered, *Journal of the Art of Record Production*, No. 10, available online from www.arpjournal.com/asarpwp/the-definitive-edition-digitally-remastered/ [accessed August 2022].

Orcalli, A. (2017). Recorded music: From the ethics of preservation to the critical editing. In Cossettini, L., and Orcalli, A. (Ed.) *Sounds, voices and codes from the twentieth century: The critical editing of music at Mirage*. Udine: Cossettini, L. and Orcalli, A., pp. 3–81.

Parsons, A., Foster, B., and Hollebone, C. (1992). *The master tape book*. Reading: APRS and the British Record Producers Guild.

The Recording Academy. (2018). *Recommendation for delivery of recorded music projects including stems and mix naming conventions*. Nashville: The Recording Academy.

Rosen, J. (2019). The day the music burned, *New York Times Magazine*, 11 June, available online from www.nytimes.com/2019/06/11/magazine/universal-fire-master-recordings.html

Rumsey, F. (2012). Pound of cure or ounce of prevention? Archiving and preservation in action. *Journal of the Audio Engineering Society*, Vol. 60, No. 1/2, pp. 79–82.

Sjöberg, T. (2004). Inspecting tapes: A box experiment, *International Association of Sound and Audiovisual Archives* (website), available online from www.iasa-web.org/information-bulletin-no-51-december-2004 [accessed August 2022].

Stuart, B. (2022). Provenance and containers, *Bob Talks* (website), available online from https://bobtalks.co.uk/blog/provenance/provenance-and-containers/ [accessed August 2022].

Ternhag, G. (2012). Musikproduktion-ett nytt ämne i högre utbildning. In Ternhag, G., and Wingstadt, J. (Ed.) *På tal om musikproduktion: Elva bidrag till ett nytt kunskapsområde*. Gothenburg: Bo Ejeby Förlag.

Winters, P. E. (2016). *Vinyl records and analog culture in the digital age: Pressing matters*. Maryland: Lexington Books.

Zagorski-Thomas, S. (2014). *The musicology of record production*. Cambridge: Cambridge University Press.

Index

Note: Numbers in **bold** indicate a table. Numbers in *italics* indicate a figure on the corresponding page.

1XTRA 84
3D: Atmos audio HN-FS 55; audio on stage 33; immersive music 35; stereo record production and 3–17
5Alarm Music 156
6-second drum loop 223
"19" (Paul Harding [song]) 106
31 Records 81

Aareskjold-Drecker, Jon Marius viii, 104–113
Ableton/Ableton Live 37, *128*; pitch tool 110, 112; Simpler 109, 112
acid house 76
acousmatic 108; intimacy 5; scenography 7; sounds 112
acoustic: conditions 175; constraints 109; equipment 169; instrumentation 94; laws 108; locations 148; non-coherent (N-C) design 44; problems 45, 48; treatment 44
Acoustical Engineering 49
acoustics 36; psychoacoustics 37–39, 43; room 37, 42; of Samlingslokalen 175; small control room 43–47; small space 35
actor-network theory (ANT) 192
ADA *see* analogue-digital-analogue
Adams, Kyle 62
"A.D.H.D." (Kendrick Lamar; song) 71
ad-libs: in rap 68–69; vocal 95, 101
ADM *see* Audio Definition Model
AES *see* Audio Engineering Society
affiliating identifications 156
AirPods 38
Akai S1000 84
Akai S900 106
Akai S950 84

Akil 66–67
aleatorics 171
Aleathoric Anthem Project (Lars Bröndum) 181–185
Alfvén, Hugo 175–176
algorithmic chance methods 182, 186
Allen, Ioan 48
Alleyne, Mike 273
Alton Everest, F. 36
amateurs 70, 154, 172–174, 248
Amen break 223
American Horror Story television show 157
amped: bass 225; wah-wah 96
analogue-digital-analogue (ADA) 52
analogue equipment 77–78, 80, 82–83, 92, 96, 98, 101, 143; digital versus 86
Angas, Dominic *see* Dom & Roland
ANT *see* actor-network theory
Antenna Media 170–171, 181–187
Anubis 40, 42, 52
Aphex Twin: "Windowlicker" (song) 106
API Vision channel strip 96
APL *see* Applied Psychoacoustics Lab (APL), University of Huddersfield, UK
Apocalypse Now (film) 38
Apple Music 6, 19, 38, 40
Apple Spatial Audio 26, 39
Apple Logic Pro 26
Apple TV 40
Applied Psychoacoustics Lab (APL), University of Huddersfield, UK 38
arpeggiation 98
artificial intelligence (AI) 161
"As I Am" (Todd Edwards [song; remix]) 106
Association of Professional Recording Services (APRS) 266–267

asynchronous: collaboration 117; discussion sessions 131; mixing **126**; operational mode 128; platforms 118
asynchronous/synchronous hybrid approach 119, 248, 252, 260
Atarodiyan, David 110–111
ATC-SCM20-ASL PRO MKII reference monitor 50
Athauda, Rukshan viii, 117–133
Atmos *see* Dolby Atmos
audience interaction 18, 115
audience: acoustics and 175; immersive experiences intended for 25–27; interaction with 21; music technology experts as 29–31; songwriters and 19; target audience-driven promotion 197–198
audio: 3D 7, 33; 3D Atmos 55; Apple Spatial Audio 26; binaural 41; Dolby Audio Bridge 27; Dolby Audio Room Design Tool (DARDT) 36; immersion and spatial audio 24–25; immersive 31–33; Pro Audio 55
Audio Blueprint 81
Audio Definition Model (ADM) 27
audio education 131
audio engineering and engineers ii, x, 37, 119, 125, **126**
Audio Engineering Society (AES) 267; Convention 268
audio examples: Dolby Atmos man 13; drums 12; guitar 11; lead vocals 10; premix 12; stereo master 13
audio files 158, 161, 211
audio fingerprints 211
audio history 38–39
audio interface 182
audio mix, audio mixing: Hyper Near-Field Tiny Studio (HN-FTS) built for 35; immersive 29; remote multiparty in-the-box 117–133; spatial 23–30
Audiomovers Listento 118
Audio Network and Epidemic Sound 156
Audio Over Internet Protocol (AOIP) 51
audiophile medium 178, 180
audio plugins 249
audio production perspectives 226–227
audio recording: Vietnam 219, 221
audio staging 16
Audiotool 250
audio track 69, 159, 250
Audio Unit plug-in MackEQ 85

auditory: human auditory biology 50; human auditory system 40; information viii; science 37
Auditory Scene Analysis (Albert S. Bregman) 61
auditory streams, composite 60–72
Australasia 252
authenticity-as-historic-practice 228
authenticity-as-intention 228
authenticity-as-practice 228
authenticity(ies) 70; defining 272; folk music 199; Kivy's four conceptions of 228; legacy recording in relationship to 272–273; period 157; Master Quality Authenticated (MQA) format 273; special 175
autoethnography 90, 137–138; music production as 142–145
autotune 104, 113
Avid 117
Avid Cloud Collaboration 118
Avid Pro Tools 117–118

B2B (Business to Business) models 203, 207, 213
backtracks, in rap 68–69
Bahr, Robert von 171, 178–180
Bandcamp platform 185
Barbosa, A. 248
Bårdsen, Thomas x, 264–276
Bartleet, Brydie-Leigh 137–138
Barton, Paul 48–50
Baym, N. 252
BBC Radio 1 (one) 81, 84
beat: Schloss's definition of 91
Beatles: *Abbey Road* (album) 117
Beatles Recording Session, The (Mark Lewinsohn) 140
Behr, A. 152
Belle-Fortune, B. 81
bells: carillon 182; Chinese temple 195
"Bells Ringing in the Rain" [*Yu Linlin*] (Pao [song]) 194–195
Ben E. King 158–159
Bengtsson, Linda Ryan ix, 232–244
Berg, Alban 179
Berg, Espen 109–110
Berklee Online 131
Beyoncé: "Run the World (Girls)" (song) 107
Bieber, Justin 105, 107, 109–110; "Peaches" 113; "Sorry" 107, 109

Billboard Hot 100 (one hundred) 104, 107
binary data 121
binary DAW functions 130
binaural stereo sound 38–39
BIS records 170–171, 178–180, 186–187
Black art, hip-hop as 62
Black Atlantic diaspora 223, 226
Black Box: "Ride on Time" (song) 107
Black Cat super fuzz pedeals 92
Black culture 75–76
"Blinding Lights" (The Weeknd [song]) 112
Blistein, J. 152
Blomberg, Mark 173–175, 177, *177*
Blumlein, Alan 38–39
Bond, James (fictional character), theme
    song 154
Bốn Phương label 223
Boon, Hussein ix, 151–162
Botos, Robi 35
Bourbon, Andrew vii, 19–33, 77
Boymerang 78
Bregman, Albert S. 61–66, 71; *Auditory
    Scene Analysis* 61; *see also* chimericity;
    stream segregation
Bresler, Zack 7–8, 16
Bridgerton television series 157
Bristol, England 81, 85
British Record Producers Guild 266
Bröndum, Lars 171, 181–186; *Aleathoric
    Anthem Project* 181–185; *Fallout* 181
Brooks, H. 170
Brooks, W. 224, 228
bro-step 78
Brøvig-Hanssen, Ragnhild viii, 65, 70–71,
    104–113
BT: "Somnambulist" (song) 106
Buckholtz, D. 259
Bukem, L. T. J. 79–80
Burgess, R. 251
Burlin, Toivo ix, 169–187
Bush, Kate 106
Butler, Judith 153–154
"Bye" (J Dilla [song]) 106

Cage, John: "Fontana Mix with Aria" 105
Cải Lương music 218, 220
call-and-response: cartoon 95; effect,
    between normal and processed vocals
    113
Camilleri, Lelio 5
campus song records in Taiwan, promotion
    of ix, 190–199

cannabis 71
canons 140–142
Caruso, Enrico 169
Cash, Johnny 157
CBS 156
Cederberg, Christer-André 3, 9, 12–13, 15
chains: A, B, and QC 39–40
Chainsmokers, The: "Roses" (feat. Rozes
    [song]) 107
"Chainsmokers, The" (Kanye West, feat.
    sirenXX [song]) 107
Chaka Khan 106
Chali 2na 66
Chanan, Michael 140
Chika 69
chimericity viii, 60–72; Bregman's concept
    of 61, 64–66
China 170; Broadcasting Corporation
    197; copyright and Copyright Law
    207; European songwriters in 203;
    "*Long de chuanren* (Descendants of
    the Dragon)" (song) 194–195; music
    business in 204, 205–207, 212, 214;
    music market of 203; music platforms
    in 210–211, 213; open up reform in 206;
    People's Republic of China 192; piracy
    environment in 207; popular music
    in 208–211; 'renegade model" in 206;
    Republic of China 192; WTO joined by
    206; yellow music in 219
China Times 198
"chipmunk soul" sound 106
chopping 92, 98; Schloss's definition
    of 104
Christodoulou, C. 80
Cialeo Matias 253
Clarke, Eric 107
Clarke, Myles 20, 23–24, 28–30, 32
Clark, Jacob 183
CMC *see* collaborative music contest
cocreated experience 232
cocreation 233–235, 237, 241–244
codeine 71
Coessens, Kathleen 137
"Cold Water" (Major Lazer, feat. Justin
    Bieber and Mø [song]) 107
collaboration and performance 248, 258
collaborative music contest (CMC)
    252–253
compositional design 6–7
compositional intention vii, 3–17; aesthetic
    intentions and 9; case and method

8–9; background and theory 4–8; compositional design and 6–7; Dolby Atmos format and 6; ideal sonicprint and 5; notion of 4; notions of space and 5–6; recording and mixing 'Ventetid' (song) 8–13; realizing in 3D of 15–16; as reference point 14

composers and songwriters 31; buyouts 153; creative pedagogy for teaching 142; electro-acoustic experimental 105; intent 4; Nordic classical and modern 179; self-producers and 137–140; *see also* Alfvén; Bröndum; Peel

content-based transformations 159

Cook, Nicholas 154

Cousins, M. 93

COVID-19 *see* pandemic

"Cowgirl" (Underworld [song]) 106

creative cultural work 151

creative industries 241, 243; impact of COVID-19 on 232

creative methodology for self-production 137–162

creative production practices vii, 1–166

creative research group 20

creative vision 153; re-cover approaches and 157–159

'crew' (rap) 65; 'ad-libs' 69; doubling rhymes by 70

crossfeed 37, 41, 55

Csikszentmihalyi, Mihaly 19–22, 254–255

Cubase Pro 120–121, *122–123*, 125; DAW platform 128–129

Cubase VST 78, 117

Cue Tube, The 155

Cumming, N. 224

Cure, The 157

Dahlen, Erland 9, 11

Dahlström, M. 271

Dạ Hương 221–223, 227

Danger Mouse: "Dirt Off Your Shoulder" (song) 106

Dangerous 2-Bus+ mixer 92

Davidovic, Zorica 44

Davinci Resolve 37

DAW *see* digital audio workstation

dcln 253

Dear VR plugin 96

Death in Vegas (band) 20, 22

Deep Listening 145

de-monetization 156

demos 161, 196

"Descendants of the Dragon" [*Long de chuanren*] (Te-Chein Hou [song]) 194–195

Dewey, Chris viii, 75–87

De Wolfe 145

Đĩa Hát Việt Nam 220

Dice Game (Mozart) 161

digital: analogue-digital-analogue (ADA) 52; disruption 205; distortion 84; events 241; experimentation ix; formats 206; home recording studio 70; mixer 86; music production 78; networks 170; plug-in 87; recording technologies 20, 186; solutions 242, 244; "space" 171; streaming 35; tapes 85; technology 171

digital audio workstation (DAW) viii, 60, 94, 162, 169, 182; 1990s increase in popularity of 78; control data resolution 130; DAW Collaboration Framework viii, 119–128; Cubase Pro 133; DAW mixing functionality, extending 129; DAW/sequencer platforms 117; DAW-specific and DAW-agnostic music production 118; introduction of Atmos into 19, 26–27, 37, 39; recording 182; TRXD's use of 111–112; virtual studio platforms using 249

digital streaming providers (DSPs) 35

Dilla, J *see* J Dilla

Diplo: "Where Are Ü Now" (with Skrillex, feat. Justin Bieber [song]) 105

"Dirt Off Your Shoulder" (Danger Mouse [song]) 106

Discord messaging platform 249–250, 253, 257

disco 106

Discofil *see* Swedish Society Discofil (SSD)

disco sound 113

distortion: history of, in drum and bass viii, 75–87; electric guitar 76; harmonic 77; heavy 77; introduction of, to drum and bass 79–86; minimal phase 43; as production tool 77–78

distortion effects 78

DJ Fresh 75

DJ Only Records 81

DJs 223, 234

DJ Snake: "Lean On" (with Major Lazer, feat. Mø [song]) 107, 109; "Let Me Love You" (feat. Justin Bieber [song]) 107

DJ TC 81

DJ Trace 79–80, 82–83
Dodge, C. 159–161
Dolby A system 270
Dolby Atmost 43; exploring past, present,
    and future of 19–33; Hyper Near-Field
    Dolby Atmos Tiny Studio viii, 35–56;
    realising compositional intention in 3D
    and stereo record production through
    vii, 3–17
Dolby Room Curve 48
Dom & Roland 80–84, 86
"Don't Start Now" (Dua Lipa [song]) 113
"Doo Wop (That Thing)" (Lauryn Hill
    [song]) 67–68
Doyle, Peter 64, 196
Dramastik Audio Obsidian VCA-style
    stereo analogue compressor 92
drum and bass, history of distortion in viii,
    75–87
Dua Lipa: "Don't Start Now" (song) 113;
    "Scared to Be Lonely" (with Martin
    Garrix [song]) 107, 109, 111–112
dub (or dubbing) 67, 68; overdubbing 64,
    68, 93, 225
dub music 145
dubstep 78, 107
Dub, Steve 28
Duinker, Ben 62
Dupé, Tony x, 137–149; Everything's a
    Love Letter 142, 144; Sound of a Room,
    Memory and the Auditory Presence of
    Place (Street) and 144–145
duplication 267–268, 272
Dupont, Fab 38
dynamic meta-spatialization 90–101
dynamic range 39, 50, 52; compression 179
Dynascore 161
Dyrstad, Truls 110–111

"ear candy" 105, 159
Early Reflections Delay Encryption
    (ERDE) 44
ecological affordance theory 104
ecological listening 64
ecological perception, theory of 107
Edlom, Jessica ix, 232–244
EDM (Electronic Dance Music) see
    Electronic Dance Music
Edvardsson, B. 242
Edwards, Todd: "Guide My Soul" (song)
    106; "Saved My Life" (song) 106; "As I
    Am" (song; remix) 106

eigenfrequencies/eigenmodes/eigentones
    43, 48
electro-acoustic: experimentation 105;
    mass 105
electroacoustic music: composition 19;
    playback 26
Electronic Dance Music (EDM) 105–107
electronic instruments 182
electronic music and electronic music
    community 75, 79, 83, 111, 254–255
electronic system polarization 43
electronic tuning 55
Ellis, Carolyn 137–138
Emagic Logic 117
embodied: activity, listening as 145–146;
    activity, music production as 139;
    approach, to music production 137;
    creative practice 140; dimensions, of
    song narrative 5; elements, of self-
    production 142; emotional spaces 141;
    music cognition 224; music practice
    143; understanding, of a song 4
Emotif records 84
English language, Asian sources in 203
ensemble playing and performance 174,
    225
Epidemic Sound 153
ERDE see Early Reflections Delay
    Encryption
erhu 195
entrainment: Carlson's three concepts for
    evaluating a performance including
    20; EDM 30–32; entrainment errors in
    EDM 33; lack of 26
ethnomusicology 191–192
"Etude for Pianoforte" (Nam Jun Paik) 105
"Etude Pathétique" (Schaeffer, Pierre) 105
Everything's a Love Letter (Dupé, Tony)
    142, 144
Exarchos, Michail viii, 90–101

Facebook 185, 241, 249–250, 259; Atmos
    Music Mixing Professionals group 36;
    Atmos Post-Mix Professional group 36, 40
Fairlight CMI 106
Fallout (Bröndum, Lars) 181
Fabb, Nigel 62–63
Ferguson, P. 118
Ferrigno, E. 76
film genres, association of music with
    153–154; sci-fi 77
'flipped' stereo remix 97–99

'fluxed' respatialized mix 99–101
Focusrite Green EQ 85
Following, The (television show) 158
"Fontana Mix with Aria" (John Cage) 105
Fosseli, Liucija ix, 203–214
Foster, B. 266
Foster, David 106
freedom: of performance 148; of self-production 146
free-jazz improvisation 92
freemium access 248
Frith, S. 152, 191–192

Garrix, Martin: "The Only Way Is Up" (with Tiësto [song]) 107; "Scared to Be Lonely" (with Dua Lipa [song]) 107, 109, 111–112
gatekeepers 151
Gellert, M. 258
Genewick, Steve 38–39
"Gesang der Junglige" (Karlheinz Stockhausen) 105
Gibson, James 107–108
Gilroy, Paul 223
global hi-fi record company, BIS records as 178–180
global Tiny Home movement 36, 40
"Gold" (Kiiara [song]) 107
Gomez, Selena: "It Ain't Me" (and Kygo [song]) 107
Gorton, D. 224
Goss, Peter 255
Grande, Ariana: *thank u, next* (album) 157
Greene, Maxine 142
Grey's Anatomy (TV show) 152
Grieg, Edvard 179
Grimshaw-Aagaard, Mark 138
groupware 248–250, 253, 256–261
"Gucci Gang" (Lil Pump [song]) 69
"Guide My Soul" (Todd Edwards [song]) 106

Hansen, M. 248, 258
Hapi MKII 40, 52
Hardcastle, Paul: "19" (song) 106
Harper *see* TRXD featuring Harper
Harris, Calvin: "This Is What You Came For" (feat. Rihanna [song]) 105, 107
Hawkins, Stan 7–8
Head Related Transfer Function (HRTF) 38, 95, 101

Heap, Imogen: "Hide and Seek" (song) 156
Helkkula, A. 233
Henry, E. 218
Hepworth-Sawyer, R. 93
Herbst, J. 76–77
"Hide and Seek" (Imogen Heap [song]) 156
Hill, Lauryn: "Doo Wop (That Thing)" (song) 67–68
hip-hop 60–72, 227; 'flipping' in 98; sample-based 91, 104; turntables used in 105; underground 106
Hockman, J. 79–80
Hokkien 193, 195
Hollebone, C. 266
Holloway, Loleatta: "Love Sensation" (song) 106
Holst, G. 154
Hook, D. 118
Houben, Eva-Maria 143
Hou, Te-Chien: "Descendants of the Dragon" [*Long de chuanren*] (song) 194–195
"House Is a Feeling" (Todd Terry [song]) 106
Howlett, Mike 4, 6
Husum 175, 177
hybrid: approach, to parallel processing 96; approach, to spatialization 99; approach, using spatial/non-spatial staging 97; channel-based/object-based 27; headphone/speaker system 38; human/machine 104–113; mixing/routing 122; surface 44, *45*
hyperbolizing 108
hypernatural sound 110
Hyper Near-Field Tiny Studio (HN-FTS) 35–36, 40–41, *46*, 52, 55

Icebox 253
ILD *see* interaural level difference
IMDB 155
Indochina Wars 218
infrastructure: collaborative-media 251; computer-based musical 181; DCF text-chat facility 121–122; Dolby Atmos viii; networking 119
innovating music experiences, COVID-19 pandemic and ix, 232–244
intellectuals, Taiwanese 193
intelligent drum and bass 76, 79, 83
intellectual property 224

intention, as a concept 4; *see also* compositional intention
interactive: analysis 20; communication 259; quizzes 131; spreadsheet tool 40
interaction: B2B 207; between auditory stream separation as a cognitive listening phenomenon and as a music production technique 61; call-and-response 95; collaborative musical 117, 230; composer-performer 224; creation emerging from interaction, Csikszentmihalyi's tripartite system regarding 21–23; between humans and environment 137; mixing and in-studio 127; real-time 128; between performers and instruments 224; supply and demand 212; synchronous 132
interactivity of domain and field 22, 23, 30
interaural level difference (ILD) 38
interaural time difference (ITD) 38
interplay 23; DCF-DAW and WebRTC data channels *121*
invisible artefact 145
iterative: approach 125; mix-file 128; practice-based framework 90; process 234
ITD *see* interaural time difference
"It Ain't Me" (Kygo and Selena Gomez [song]) 107
"I Took a Pill in Ibiza (Seeb Remix)" (Mike Posner and Seeb [song]) 107, 109–110

JACK 118
JackTrip 118
Jack Ü: "Scary Monsters and Nice Sprites" (by Skrillex with Diplo and Justin Bieber [song]) 107
Jadakiss 67–68
JamKazam 249
Jamulus 248
Jaques, D. 251
Jarman-Ives 64, 67
JavaScript/JSON 129
jazz 79; free-jazz improvisation 92; *Mutant Jazz* (T Power) 82–83; Western 221
J Dilla: "Bye" (song) 106; "One for Ghost" (song) 106
"Jealous" (TRXD feat. Harper [song]) 107
Jiang, Haoran ix, 190–198
"Jinyun jiang (Golden Melody Award)" 195

Jinyun jiang chuangxin 3 (*Golden Melody Award Innovation Series* 3) 197
"*Jinyun jiang zhi ye* (Golden Melody Award Night)" 198
Joculatores Upsalienses: *Antik musik på Wik* 180
Johnson, C. 85
Jones, Grace 20, 22
JSON Web Token (JWT) 122
jungle drum 75–76, 79, 86
jungle records/labels 83–84
Jurassic 5 (five) 65, *66*, 68
JWT *see* JSON Web Token

Karlsson, Jenny ix, 232–244
Kassabian, A. 156
Katz, Bob 267
Katz, Jonah 62
Katz, Mark 65
Kautny, Oliver 62
Kaye, P. 152
Kempe, Carl 175
Kempe, Hans Peter 172–178, 180
Kempekören 172, 175
Keyes, Cheryl 62
Kiiara: "Gold" (song) 107
Kibby, M. 259
King, Ben E. 158–159
Ki:Theory: *Stand By Me* (song) 158–159
Kivy, P. 228
Koksvik, Ingvild vii, 3–17; *Mørketidssanger* ("Dark Season Songs" [album]) 8; *see also* "Ventetid" (song)
Komaniecki, Robert 62
Koszolko, Martin x, 247–261
Kraugerud, Emil 64
Krims, Adam 62
Kuomintang 192–193
Kygo: "It Ain't Me" (and Selena Gomez [song]) 107

Lacasse, Serge 7, 64
Lamar, Kendrick: *Section.80* (album) 70; "A.D.H.D." (song) 71
landscape, Chinese 194
laptops 27, 38; speaker systems 80
latency 27; online 251
layering, in rap 62–64, 66, 68
"Lean On" (Major Lazer, with DJ Snake, feat. Mø [song]) 107, 109
Lee, Chien-Fu 194–195, 197
Lee, H. 24

Lee Kuo-Chiang 191, 195, 197
Lefford, Mara Nyssim 227
legacy music production: authenticity in relationship to 272–273; republishing and x, 264–276
"Let Me Love You" (DJ Snake feat. Justin Bieber [song]) 107
Lê Văn Tài 220
Li, Shuang-Ze 193
Lil Pump: "Gucci Gang" (song) 69
Lin, Yu-Ting 195
Little, Simon 254, 256
LiveSwitch Cloud Client 122, 129
London: Dolby headquarters 24, 29; University of London 49
London, Justin 61
"*Long de chuanren* (Descendants of the Dragon)" (Te-Chien Hou [song]) 194–195
loops 159–160; drum (Amen break) 223; rhythmic 143; short 105
Lord, Jo viii, 90–101
"Love Sensation" (Loleatta Holloway [song]) 106
Lucasfilm 36
Lucid Air 35

machines 27; drum 84, 92; engraving 173; human/machine hybrid, vocal chops and 104–109; tape 83, 143, 267; *see also* MIDI Machine Control (MMC)
Major Lazer: "Cold Water" (feat. Justin Bieber and Mø [song]) 107; "Lean On" (with DJ Snake, feat. Mø [song]) 107, 109; "Pon De Floor" (feat. Vibz Kartel [song]) 107
Malaysia 253
Mandarin-language pop songs 197
Marc7 66
Marshall amplifiers 77
Massey, H. 140
Master Quality Authenticated (MQA) format 273
Mattessich, John J. 62
McIntyre, P. 20
Mcleod 76
MCs 105
MCSC (Performance Rights Society in China) 206, 209
MC Solaar 79
MCU *see* multipoint connection unit

MECO *see* Music Ecosystems Inner Scandinavia
Messiaen, Olivier 179
Metalheadz 79, 83
metal music 76–79
meta-music 91
Metapop 252
Miami Vice television show 152
MIDI *see* musical instrument digital interface
MIDI Timecode (MTC) 121, *123*
MIDI Machine Control (MMC) 121, 122, *123*
Minchella, Damon 141, 145
Ming Sheng, Ling 198
Minh Hiếu 221
Miyakawa, Felicia 62
MMC *see* MIDI Machine Control (MMC)
Mø: "Lean On" (by DJ Snake and Major Lazer [song]) 107, 109
Mo & Domsjö 172, 175
Moog 77, 98
Moore, A. 93
Moore, Allan 7–8, 14
Moore, Austin viii, 75–87
Moorefield, Virgil 140
Moreau, F. 205
Mørketidssanger ("Dark Season Songs" [album]) (Ingvild Koksvik) 8
Morrison, Dave 50
motifs 60, 159; lyrical 99; musical 95; vocal 97–99
Mozart: Dice Game 161
Moylan, William 6–7
MP3 204
MPC 92, 96–101
MPC60 106
MQA *see* Master Quality Authenticated (MQA) format
MTC *see* MIDI Timecode
multimedia production 217
multipoint connection unit (MCU) 122
Murch, Walter 38
musical instrument digital interface (MIDI) viii, 10, 82; continuous controller (CC) 120, 130, 132; DAW mixing functionality and 129; file sharing 117; MIDI 1.0 130; MIDI 2.0 130; Web MIDI APIs 121–125
music: 3D immersive 35; association with film genres 77, 153–154; in China 203, 204, 205–214, 219; collaborators

(*see* remote music collaborators and remote music collaboration software (RMCS)); digital production 78; dub 145; electroacoustic composition 19; electroacoustic playback 26; electronic 75, 79, 83, 111, 254–255; embodied approach to production of 137; embodied, cognition 224; experiences, innovating during COVID-19 pandemic ix, 232–244; folk 199; industry, business model innovation in ix, 203–214; meta-91; metal 76–79; motifs 95; *nhạc trẻ* (youth music) 219; production of, as autoethnography 142–145; production of, as embodied activity 139; Renaissance 179–180; resistance 218; synchronicity or sync ix, 151–162; *Tuồng* 220; virtual communities 259; *see also* digital audio workstation (DAW); Electronic Dance Music (EDM); interaction; legacy music production; pandemic (COVID-19); remote music collaborators and remote music collaboration software (RMCS); rock bands, rock music; Sweden; *yellow music*

Music Ecosystems Inner Scandinavia (MECO) 235, 241

musicking: music production and 139; sample-based viii, 90

musicology and musicologists 62, 172; ethnomusicology 191–192

Musicology of Record Production (Zagorski-Thomas) 78

Mussorgsky, Modest 179

Mutant Jazz (T Power) 82

"My Red Hot Car" (Squarepusher [song]) 106

MyRoom (also "My Room") principle 43–47

Nam Jun Paik: "Etude for Pianoforte" 105

Năm Mạnh, Thầy 220

Nävermyr, S. 172

Near-Field 32X32 i/o 52

Negus, Keith 4, 191, 195, 206, 208

Neon Aeon spatial mix 94–97

NetEase 211–212

Neumann U 47 microphone 173, *177*

Neumann U 49 microphone 173

neurofunk viii, 76, 81, 87

Newell, Phillip 36–37, 44, 50

Ngô Văn Mạnh, a.k.a. Thầy Năm Mạnh 220

Nguyễn Đức Dũn 221

Nguyễn Ngọc Chánh 221

Nguyễn Thanh Thủy ix, 217–226

nhạc trẻ (youth music) 219

Nhật Ngân 223

Nico 79–80

Nielsen, Carl August 179

NodeJS 122

noise criterion 35–36, 47

"noise scapes" 182

non-exclusive rights 156

non-linear distortion 77

non-proprietary formats 90, 97

non-sample-based elements in production 91

non-spatialized signals 96

Nordgård, D. 205

nostalgia 228

No U Turn Records 79–80, 83

Novotny, Paul viii, 15, 35–56; *Summertime in Leith* (album) 35

Nowak, C. 258

Nuendo 37

object of belief 153–154

Ó Briain, Lonán 219

Oddekalv, Kjell Andreas viii, 60–72

Odesza: "Say My Name" (song) 107

O'Grady, Pat 139

ogre voice 69

Ohm Studio 253

Ohriner, M. 62

Oliveros, Pauline 145

Olive Tree ("*Ganlan shu*") (Yu Chyi [album]) 197

Olsen, Dale 218–219

"One for Ghost" (J Dilla [song]) 106

"The Only Way Is Up" (Martin Garrex and Tiësto [song]) 107

Optical (producer and artist) 81, 83, 85

Östersjö, Stefan ix, 217–226

OutKast 69

OWSLA 81

P2P (peer-to- peer) connections 121–121, 132; file-sharing 204

Paik, Nam Jun 105

pandemic (COVID-19) ix; Antennae Media's streaming albums during 181–182; China cash-flow paperwork during 208; groupware and 250;

"guerrilla Atmos music installation"
(Genewick) 39; impact on music industry
of 232, 235–236, 241–243; innovating
music experiences and creativity during
ix, 232–244; internet-facilitated music
interactions and collaborations during
117, 169, 253; post-COVID-19 job
precarity for creatives 151; RMCS
technologies and 250; safety and safe
events during 241; Swedish restrictions
during 182; *Yellow Music* recording
experimentation during 224
Pao, Mei-Sheng: "Bells Ringing in the
Rain" [*Yu Linlin*] (song) 194–195;
"Phoenix Hairpin" [*Chaitou feng*]
(song) 194; "Woodcutter Song"
[*Qiaoge*] (song) 194
Pathé 220
"Peaches" (Bieber, Justin [song]) 113
Peel, Hannah 157
Pennington, Bryan 45, 47, 49–50
Penny, Greg 38
performativity, theory of 153–154
Petrovic, Bogic 44
Phạm Duy 220–221
"Phoenix Hairpin" [*Chaitou feng*] (Pao
[song]) 194
phonograms 171, 173, 179, 187
phonographic ephemera 90–91, 94
phonographs 190; effects 65
phonography 170, 182
Pickering, Michael 4, 92
pirate radio 76
Pixar 39
plausibility, concept of 24, 32
Pleijel, Bengt 174
polyphony 7
"Pon De Floor" (Major Lazer, feat. Vibz
Kartel [song]) 107
Posner, Mike: "I Took a Pill in Ibiza
(Seeb Remix)" (with Seeb [song]) 107,
109–110
Pratt, Dan vii, 19–33, 77
procedural videos 131
procedurals, police 153, 156
provenance 271–274
Pruett, D. 191
PSB CS 500 W Architectural Subwoofer
Amplifier 49
psychoacoustics 31, 39, 43, 55; Applied
Psychoacoustics Lab (APL), University
of Huddersfield, UK

Public Enemy 62
Pyramix 37

Quinn, Matt ('Optical') 85
Quinn, S. 75–76

Radiohead 157
radio market 155
Radiotjänst 173, 177
Radio Science Orchestra 22, 28
RAM records 81
rap: backtracks in 68–69; as composite
auditory streams viii, 60–72; cultural
politics and 70; Lamar 71–72;
musicological interest in 62; speech-
likeness of 67
rappers' lines 62
'rap stream, the' 63
Rathbone, S. 75–76
real-time analysis (RTA) 43
Reaper *128*
Red Panda Tensor 92–93, 95
Reece, Alex 79
remote music collaboration software
(RMCS) x, 247–261; collaborative
music contest (CMC) and 252–253
Renaissance music 179–180
Republic of China 192; *see also* China
Republic of Vietnam 218; *see also*
Vietnam
republishing process, of legacy music
productions x, 264–276; ABBA 273;
critical documentation of source
selection and transfer in 273–275;
critical editing of recorded music,
four criteria for 274; digitalization
and archiving 276; MQA format 273;
traceability and 272–273
resistance music 218
Res Rocket Network 247
retrospective analysis, sensemaking
properties of 24
Reuter, A. 78
REW Room EQ Wizard 51, *51*
Reynolds, S. 75
Rhythm Control 106
"rhythmic speech" 62
riddim 78
"Ride on Time" (Black Box [song]) 107
Rihanna: "This Is What You Came For"
(by Calvin Harris [song]) 105, 107
Rinse Out Records 84

RMCS *see* remote music collaboration software
Robots on Mars 19, 22, 25, 28–30, 32
Rocket Network 118; RocketControl middleware 117
rock 66, 76–78, 181; electronica/rock crossover 93; mobile equipment used to produce LPs by 169
rockwool 52
Rodrigo, Olivia 112
Rogue Agent (film) 157
Rohrer, Tim 139
ROLI 98
Rose, Tricia 62
"Roses" (The Chainsmokers, feat. Rozes [song]) 107
royalties 155, 206, 208, 209
royalty-free 152
Royal College of Music (KMH) Sound Dome, Stockholm 26, 29
Royal, Marc 84; *see also* T Power
Rozes 107
Rudjord, Lars Jakob 9
"Run the World (Girls)" (Beyonce [song]) 107
Rush, Ed 85
Ryan, J. 198

SaaS *see* Software-as-a-Service
Saddleback: *Everything's a Love Letter* 142, 144; *see also* Dupé
Saigon: fall of 219, 221–223, 228; Radio Saigon 220
Saigon Supersound 217
Salmon, G. 251
Sappleton, Andrew 84
Sappo 84
"Saved My Life" (Edwards, Todd [song]) 106
"Say My Name" (Odesza [song]) 107
"Scared to Be Lonely" (Martin Garrex and Dua Lipa [song]) 107, 109, 111–112
"Scary Monsters and Nice Sprites" (Skrillex with Jack Ü, Diplo, and Justin Bieber [song]) 107
Schaeffer, Pierre: "Etude Pathétique" 105
Scheps, Andrew 38
Schiøtt, Katrine 9, 12
Schloss, Joseph 91, 104
Schroeder frequency 42, 52
Schumpeter, J.-A. 170
Scott, Nathan viii, 117–133

Section.80 (Kendrick Lamar [album]) 70
Seeb 107, 109–112
Segre, Cesare 272
self-production, creative methodology for 137–162
sequencer platforms 117
sequencer programs, development of 106
service ecosystems 233
service innovation 244
Sessionwire Communications Sessionwire Studio 118
Shields, Leigh viii, 75–87
Shih, Siao-Rong 195
Shotguns, The 221–223
Shure 520DX 93, 95
Shy FX 83
Sibelius, Jean 173, 179
Silvola, Juhani 9, 11
Simpler sampler 109, 112
Singapore 253
SIREN 253
sirenXX (singer) 107
"Sixiang qi" (Da Chen) 195
Six Tones, The ix, 217, 223, 224, 226–228
Sjöberg, T. 270
Skrillex: "Scary Monsters and Nice Sprites" (with Jack Ü, Diplo, and Justin Bieber [song]) 107; "Sorry" (with Justin Bieber [song]) 107, 109, 110, 112; "Where Are Ü Now" (with Diplo, feat. Justin Bieber [song]) 105
Skynet 79, 81, 87
Skywalker Sound 36
Small, Christopher 139
Smalley, Dennis 94, 107
smartphone, recording with 182
Society of Professional Audio Recording Services (SPARS) 266–267
Software-as-a-Service (SaaS) 130
"Somnambulist" (BT [song]) 106
Sóng Nhạc 220
sonic(s) 87, 93; aesthetics, of hip hop 91; artefacts 82; boundaries 27; cartoons 78, 95; characteristics, of distortion 76; content and context, consideration of 94, 97; environment 90; fingerprint 9; narratives 99, 100; objects 91, 98; outputs 84; possibilities, in home recording 70; relationships 37; space 5, 95; world 6
sonicprint 5, 8, 113, 16
SonoBus 249

sonority 175, 228
"Sorry" (Skrillex, feat. Justin Bieber [song]) 107, 109, 110, 112
sound(s): acousmatic 112; aesthetics 88; binaural stereo 38–39; "chipmunk soul" 106; disco 113; experimentation 105; field 95–96, 99, 100, 101; hypernatural 110; object ix; as spectra 94; stage, as term 7; staging 90, 94; studies 137–138, 148; *see also* vinyl records
soundbox 7
Soundfield Calrec microphone 51
Sound of a Room, Memory and the Auditory Presence of Place (Street) 144–145
Sound of One 106
Sound On Sound magazine 36
Sound Reproduction (Toole) 37
soundscape 60, 78, 145, 182
soundsphere 12
soundtrack 152–153; commissioning of 156
Soundtrap (Spotify) 118, 249
soundwaves 42
Soundwhale 118
Source Elements Source Connect 118
SOUR Records 81, 83
space, staging notions of 3–17
SPARS *see* Society of Professional Audio Recording Services
spatial: colorations 94; complexity 147; formats 94; hearing 38; identity 6; immersiveness 29; panning 99, 100; parallel processing 96; placement 95; relationships 7; signifiers 93; sonic objects 91
spatial audio 20, 30; Apple Spatial Audio 26, 39; emerging domain of 23–27; hardware translation and 27; immersion and 24–25; object-based 40; playback systems definitions and boundaries 25–26; software 2 (two) 26–27
spatialisation 8, 20, 38; dynamic meta-spatialization 90–101
spatial stage stacking viii, 90–101; five creative phases in 90; phase 1 (one) 91–92; phase 2 (two) 92–94; phase 3 (three) 94–97; phase 4 (four) 97–98; phase 5 (five) 99–100; *see also* staging
Spector, Phil 140
spectral: coloration 41; height 47; response 51
spectra, sound as 94

spectromorphology 94, 95, 100, 274
speculative entrepreneurship ix, 151; ideas underpinning 154–155
Splice platform 252
Splice sample library 111, 152, 249
Splice Studio 118
Spotify 112, 185, 209; Soundtrap 118
spring reverb 92–93
Squarepusher: "My Red Hot Car" (song) 106
SSD *see* Swedish Society Discofil
staging: as analytical concept 7; audio 16; compositional designs 14; concept of 90; definitions of 7; notions of space 3–17; as a practice 8; spatial 90, 94–95, 97, 101; theoretical concepts of vii; timbral 98; vocal 64, 102
Stagle, David 40
Stand By Me (Ki:Theory [song; cover] 158
Stargate SG-1 (television series) 154
"Stay Fly" (Three 6 Mafia [song]) 106
staying with the trouble 238
Stravinsky, Igor 179
Steinberg 84; Cubase Pro 120, 129; Cubase VST 117; VST 3 (three) 130; VST Connect 118
Stengers, I. 146
Stenhammar, Wilhelm 179
Sterne, Jonathan 64
Sterne, Jonathan 138
Stevens, Cris 81–84, 86
Stickland, Scott viii, 117–133
Stockhausen, Karlheinz: "Gesang der Junglige" 105
Stranger Things television show 152
streaming: albums, by Antennae Media 181–185, 187; audio 117–118; audio signal 249; audio-visual channel connections 121; live-streaming, in China 211; platforms 6, 180, 191, 242; playback 39; services 36, 206
'streaming box' 241
stream segregation 62–63, 71
street culture 62
Street, S. 144–145
Stuart, Bob 273
Supremes, The 157
Swap, W. 259
Sweden: Antennae Music 181–186; BIS records 178–180; mobile classical music, three case studies from ix, 169–187; music industry 176; music scene 1950s 175; Recorda/Discofil 172–177

Swedish Broadcasting Corporation 173
Swedish Society Discofil (SSD) 171, 179,
    186–187; 1940s and 1950s 172–177
Sweeney, The (British police procedural)
    156
synchronicity 145
synchronization ix; DAW Collaboration
    Framework for viii, 118, 121, 125;
    music 151–162
synchronous or asynchronous
    collaboration 117–119
synchrony 260
Synco Corporation ix, 190–198; innocent
    images of children created by 195–197;
    target audience for campus songs of
    197–198
synth 9, 10, 82, 99–101; bass 11; line 28;
    -pop 106
synthesizer 110–112, 182

Taiwan 192; *Gunshi* magazine 198;
    Kuomintang in 192–193; native culture
    of 193; localism in 195; recording
    industry ix, 190–197
Taiwan Daily News 198
Taiwan Shin Sheng Daily News 198
Taiwan Times 198
Tangcay, J. 151
tân nhạc 218, 220
Tao, Siao-Cing 197
Techstep 87
temporal: distance 92; duration 106;
    organization 61
Tencent 206, 209, 211–211
Terrorist (producer) 83
Terry, Todd: "House Is a Feeling"
    (song) 106
Théberge, Paul 20, 171
Thien Do 229
"This Is What You Came For" (Calvin
    Harris feat. Rihanna [song]) 105, 107
Thompson, P. 21–22, 28, 227
Thompson, R. 152
Three 6 Mafia: "Stay Fly" (song) 106
"Through the Wire" (West, Kanye [song]) 106
Tiësto 107
TikTok 155–156, 159, 211; Sound 153
Tobin, Margaret (Maggie) 38
Toole, Floyd E. 36–37, 43–44, 49–50
Tô Vũ 219
T Power 81–84
transducers 147

Trần Trịnh 223
Trịnh Lâm Ngân 223
TRXD 112
TRXD featuring Harper: "Jealous" (song)
    107, 109–111
Tschmuck, Peter 170
Tuồng music 220
tweeter-on-top 47
tweeters 48
Twitter 110
two-bar piano figure 159
two-channel i/o bank 40
two-stringed fiddle, Chinese 195
two-track magnetic tapes 269

Underworld: "Cowgirl" (song) 106

'value appropriation' 212
value chain 206
value cocreation 234, 242–244
value creation 204, 211–213, 232–235
Valverde, K. 228–229
Văn Hóa Nghệ Thuật (Culture and Arts)
    magazine 219
Vanilla Fudge (singing group) 157
Vargo, D. 244
Värmlandsteatern and Arvika Innovation
    Park 235
"Ventetid" (song): mixing 12; realizing
    compositional intent in 3D of 15–16,
    17; recording additional vocals (other
    than lead) 10; recording lead vocals 10;
    recording and mixing "Ventetid" (song)
    8–9; rough demo recording of 14
versioning 223
Việt Kiều 229
Việt Minh 218
Vietnam, record industry in, pre-1975 ix,
    217–229; see also Saigon; *yellow music*
Vinell, Nathan 79, 87; *see also* Skynet
vinyl records 105; authenticity associated
    with 272; bass sound associated with
    50; production chain in France 220;
    replacement by cassettes of 221, 222
virtual learning environments (VLEs) 131
virtual music communities 259
Virus Records 81
Visser, Andy vii, 19–33, 77
vocal chops viii, 99, 104–113, 227;
    ambiguity of 108; defining 104;
    evolution of 112–113; "Jealous" (TRXD
    featuring Harper) 110–111; pop hooks

using 105; rise of 105–107; "Scared to be Lonely" (Martin Garrix and Dua Lipa) 111–112; "Sorry" (Skrillex, featuring Bieber) 110; various takes on 109–110
vocal(s): delivery 97; distortion 100; gloss 64, 67; manipulation 105–107; 'top' 100; whispering 99
vocoder 104, 113
V Records 84
Vũ *see* Tô Vũ

Walker, Jr. 221
Walker, R. 44
Walking Dead television series: *Fear the Walking Dead* 158
Walser, Robert 62
Warner Brothers 152
waveform 250
Way, Dave 38
Web MIDI API 121–125
WebRTC 121–125, 133
Weeknd, The: "Blinding Lights" (song) 112
Weick, K. 24, 32
West, Kanye 106–107; "The Chainsmokers" (feat. sirenXX [song]) 107; "Through the Wire" (song) 106
Westworld (television show) 157
"Where Are Ü Now" (Skrillex and Diplo, feat. Justin Bieber [song]) 105
white-label release 152
white noise 105
Wiks Slott castle 180
Williams, Alan 140–141

Williams, J. A. 91
"Windowlicker" (Aphex Twin [song]) 106
Windows (Microsoft) 249
Winters, P. 272
wizard: REW Room EQ Wizard 51, *51*
Wolfe, Paula 138, 141
"Woodcutter Song" [*Qiaoge*] (Pao, Mei-Sheng [song]) 194
Wright, Matt ix, 217–226

Xhail 161
Xiaoyuan gequ (campus song) 190
Xiaoyuan minge (campus folk song) 190, 199
XML 120

Yang, Hsien 193
Yang, Jhih-Hong 198
Yao, Harrison 194
Yao, Meng-Jia 198
yellow music ix, 217–229; experimentation with 224–227; historical perspective on 218–219; leading singers of 221; pre-1975 227, 229; stars of 222
Yêu Một Mình 223–227
YouTube 153, 155–156; China and 211; No U Turn 80
Yu Chyi 197–198; *Ganlan shu* ("Olive Tree" [album]) 197

Zaakir 66
Zagorski-Thomas, Simon 265
Zhang, B. 206, 208